The First Anglo-Afghan Wars

The First Anglo-Afghan Wars

A READER

Antoinette Burton, *editor*

With a Foreword by Andrew J. Bacevich

Duke University Press *Durham and London* 2014

Printed in the United States of America on acid-free paper ∞
Typeset in Minion Pro by Westchester Publishing Services

On page viii: Rajkamal Kahlon, *Shadow of the Future*, provided courtesy of the artist.

Library of Congress Cataloging-in-Publication Data
The First Anglo-Afghan Wars : a reader / Antoinette Burton, editor ; with a foreword by Andrew J. Bacevich.
pages cm
Includes bibliographical references and index.
ISBN 978-0-8223-5650-9 (cloth : alk. paper)
ISBN 978-0-8223-5662-2 (pbk. : alk. paper)
1. Afghan Wars.   2. Afghanistan—History—British Intervention, 1838–1842.   3. Afghanistan—History,
Military—19th century.   4. Great Britain—History, Military—19th century.   I. Burton, Antoinette M., 1961–
II. Bacevich, Andrew J.
DS363.F57 2014
958.1´03—dc23   2013044873

To all those who have died or lost loved ones

in "just and necessary" wars

this book is humbly dedicated

CONTENTS

FOREWORD

ANDREW J. BACEVICH

"History," Mark Twain reputedly remarked, "does not repeat itself, but it does rhyme." For a student of twenty-first-century American wars in the so-called Greater Middle East, this immensely instructive collection of documents relating to British wars in nineteenth-century Afghanistan serves to affirm Twain's famous dictum. Here was a usable past, ready to offer instruction. Here was an alarm, loud, insistent, unmistakable.

Why did the architects of U.S. policy after 9/11 show so little interest in examining that past? Why were they deaf to history's warnings? Policymakers in the age of George W. Bush ignored the British experience in Afghanistan for precisely the same reason that policymakers in the age of John F. Kennedy and Lyndon Johnson ignored the French experience in Vietnam: persuaded that America's motives are inherently different—more enlightened, benign—U.S. policymakers believed that the experience of others had nothing to teach. After all, unlike the European imperial powers, the U.S. Army fights not to dominate or exploit, and certainly not to colonize, but to liberate and uplift.

Imbued with this conviction of American singularity, those wielding power in Washington reject out of hand the possibility that others might construe U.S. policy as a variant of imperialism. Yet it is imperialism, however much U.S. officials and ordinary Americans insist otherwise. The "global leadership" that the United States purports to exercise is little more than a euphemism for *empire*. As with most euphemisms, its purpose is to conceal. Alas, by employing it, we succeed chiefly in confusing ourselves.

In her insightful introduction to this volume, Antoinette Burton notes that British critics of the Anglo-Afghan Wars tended to be "antiwar even as they were proempire." These critics could not see that the wars they opposed were an inevitable outgrowth of imperial ambitions to which they gave tacit approval.

Much the same can be said about critics of U.S. policy in our own day. The wars that have extended across the past decade command little popularity. Even on the political right, enthusiasm for invading and occupying countries has faded. On the left, it has vanished altogether. Yet the political mainstream, Republican and Democratic alike, remains committed to the proposition that providence has summoned the United States to lead the world, presumably until the end of time.

It's time to call a spade a spade: If empire, however styled, is necessary to sustain the well-being of the American people, then something similar to perpetual war will form part of the ensuing cost. If Americans are unwilling to pay that cost, then they will need to forgo their imperial ambitions. For those with guts enough to reflect on that choice, *The First Anglo-Afghan Wars* contains abundant food for thought.

ACKNOWLEDGMENTS

I've incurred a number of debts in the course of this project that I will likely be unable to repay, given the generosity of time and expertise they represent. John Randolph led me to the Gorchakov Circular and Jeff Sahadeo also pointed me in the right direction early on. Jeff's willingness to read a draft of the introduction and offer detailed feedback is utterly characteristic and most appreciated as well. Thanks to Bonnie Smith for helping me learn some important lessons. Samia Khatun is an invaluable interlocutor: she asked me hard questions and pushed me to see both the limits and possibilities of my arguments and interpretations, for which I am exceedingly grateful. Martin Smith also read the introduction, offering helpful comments and real solidarity. Tom Bedwell handled all the money and extended himself, as ever, way above and beyond. Meanwhile, Roberta Engleman's index is a thing of beauty for which readers will long be grateful. Paul Arroyo saved the day with technical assistance in the eleventh hour and, as usual, he never broke a sweat.

Versions of the introduction were given as talks at St. Joseph's University; the Center for South Asia and Middle East Studies at the University of Illinois, Urbana; and the annual meeting of the Pacific Coast Conference of British Studies. I am grateful to Jay Carter, Valerie Hoffman, Randy McGowen, and the energetic audiences of students and faculty in those venues. Throughout my struggles to come to grips with the material at hand, Zarena Aslami's work has been an inspiration. It's been a real privilege to think through the question of representing Victorian Afghanistan with her. As ever, Miriam Angress has been not just a fabulous editor but a sage and calming influence as well: I feel so lucky to have her in my life. Gerri Burton's interest has never flagged, and as for my father, well, I am sure he never imagined I'd be doing military history. His World War II stories poignantly and grippingly unfolded in long drives to and from Mater Misericordia many years ago. They left an indelible imprint whose echoes are to be found here. Thanks and more love than I am capable of expressing to Paul, Nick, Olivia, and the irrepressible Murphy for always being there.

INTRODUCTION

The Anglo-Afghan
Wars in Historical Perspective

Most university-age students know that the United States, the United Kingdom, and their allies have fought a war in Afghanistan with huge stakes for national sovereignty and global security in the post-9/11 era. These students have less understanding, perhaps, of how U.S. and European involvement in Afghanistan is an indirect consequence of two centuries of modern warfare in the region. Simply put, the series of Afghan wars fought between the British and the native leaders of the Afghan region in the nineteenth and early twentieth centuries was the result of both imperial ambition and a desire to forestall Russian expansion into the North-West Frontier, which was considered the gateway to India, the notorious jewel in the crown of the early Victorian British Empire. Though neither the British nor the Russian state would have used the American phrase *Manifest Destiny*, each one believed that it had a, if not *the*, providential right to central Asia. Yet while the British oversaw the installation of successive emirs, from Shah Shujah in 1839 to Abdur Rahman Khan in 1880 to Habibullah Khan in 1901, typically going to war to do so, the hold on the region by the British was always tenuous: Afghanistan was never settled, either literally or figuratively The documents in this collection train our eye on how and why a determination to hold central Asia posed significant challenges to European powers from the early Victorian period until the aftermath of

World War I. Taken together, these sources allow us to put twenty-first-century struggles over Afghanistan in historical perspective and remind us of how fragile and precarious imperial power has been on the ground for would-be conquerors in Afghanistan during modern times. As Robert Kaplan wrote presciently in 1989, "Afghanistan may evoke the military past, but its importance is as a preview of the battleground of the future."[1]

THE GEOPOLITICS OF THE GREAT GAME

One of the most arresting British images of the First Anglo-Afghan War is Lady Elizabeth Butler's painting *Remnants of an Army* (1874). It shows William Brydon, an assistant surgeon in the East India Company, astride a bedraggled horse, limping across an otherwise deserted plain. Brydon was one of the sole survivors of a force of 4,500 strong that was routed from Kabul in 1842 after the city's three-year occupation by the British. Though the British eventually returned to retake the city and burn the bazaar, that rout was an inglorious end point in a war that would entangle the British Raj in the region for the next eight decades. Having been promised safe passage out of the city by the tribal leaders of an antioccupation insurrection—rebel leaders to whom guns and treasure had been handed over—British military personnel and some twelve thousand camp followers were ambushed and massacred on their way to Jalalabad in January of 1842.[2] Another major defeat for the British Army took place at Gandamak a week later, when officers and soldiers of the 44th Regiment of Foot were effectively decimated by Afghan tribesmen who, using the advantages of local knowledge about the terrain as they had throughout the war, roundly defeated what remained of that portion of the Army of the Indus (as the British Indian army was called) charged with the defense of Kabul. Though the First (1839–42) and Second (1878–80) Anglo-Afghan Wars ended in diplomatic settlements that secured some balance of power in the region, they were effectively defensive campaigns. This was true not only because tribal leaders and their allies played the Russians and the British off each other but because the tribal leaders had a home-court advantage: they knew the lay of the land. Afghan leaders and their allies used the environment accordingly, outmaneuvering the British in the infamous passes, keeping them perennially at bay, and—in the case of the rout of 1842—subjecting the Army of the Indus to a humiliating defeat.

The legend that Butler's painting helped to promote notwithstanding, Brydon was not the sole British survivor of the Kabul rout. Several dozen others were captured, among them Lady Florentia Sale, wife of Major General Sir Robert Sale, who commanded the garrison at Jalalabad. Florentia Sale survived her nine months of captivity and wrote an account of her experiences, *A Journal of the Disasters in Afghanistan, 1841–42*, and was widely admired for her acts of bravery during her imprisonment.[3] But despite individual acts of resilience, the British retreat from Kabul and the subsequent massacre came to be symbols not just of a single military disaster but also of a precarious imperial strategy that formalized the interregional conflict and far-reaching geopolitical crisis known as the Great Game. Attributed to Arthur Conolly (an East India Company captain and intelligence officer), the Great Game refers to the contest between Britain and Russia over which aspiring imperial hegemon would dominate central Asia in the nineteenth century. In fact, British and Russian designs in the late 1830s were part of a multisited struggle between would-be global powers on the one hand and local forces on the other—including the once formidable Sikh Empire and a complex of regional tribesmen seeking dominion, if not sovereignty, in this "graveyard of empires."

The British feared Russia's ambition along the North-West Frontier, which was viewed by both parties as the access point to the British Raj and, thereby, to the center of British imperial power, profit, and security. But the British were also wary of the Persians, who in 1834 had their eye on Herat—one of a number of strongholds they had lost in the wake of the collapse of the Safavid dynasty in the second half of the eighteenth century and had been striving to recover ever since.[4] In that sense, the Great Game involved more than two players. In fact, it had many dimensions, only some of which depended on the mutual suspicions of the European powers. Though later historians have famously viewed the war as a "tournament of shadows" between the major Western states with locals as proxies, Victorians exhibited more respect, albeit often grudging, for the power, impact, and historical significance of indigenous dynastic regimes, even as Victorians often relished seeing these regimes caught in the crosshairs of a wider global-imperial struggle for hegemony.[5]

The key to British stability on this fraught frontier was thought to be the emir of Afghanistan, Dost Mohammad Khan, scion of the Barakzai tribe and a man at the intersection of several imperial gambles.[6] Though he was courted by the British and sought alliance with the Russians, he was preoccupied with the empire of the Sikhs and more particularly its seasoned leader, Ranjit Singh, who was his longstanding nemesis. Singh, the first Sikh maharaja, was at the end of his life when these tensions flared, but he was a formidable warrior almost until the end (a series of strokes beset him in 1837 from which he was unable to recover). Singh had been engaged in conflict with the Afghans for the better part of twenty years and specifically with the Barakzais, whom he defeated in 1834. His forces fought Dost Mohammad again in 1837, and that victory allowed him to retake Peshawar, thereby consolidating the Sikh Raj and capping his career as the so-called lion of the Punjab.

So while the British sought in Dost Mohammad a bulwark against Russian imperial ambition, the Great Game was arguably a sideshow to local imperial-dynastic contests in which he and his family had been entrenched for decades. Though he had pledged fealty to the British, his relationship with the Russians was a cause for concern; once he was perceived as a double-crosser, his reputation in British imperial history as a duplicitous warlord was sealed, only negligibly revised by the fact that he was again an ally after the end of the war. This is not to say that the British did not try to play him against Singh or against the Russians. The British were attuned to the regional stakes of their diplomatic mission and divided on the prospect of an alliance with Dost Mohammad: George Eden (Lord Auckland), the governor-general, was less well disposed toward Dost Mohammad than Eden's political agent on the ground, Sir Alexander Burnes. Eden and Burnes were not capable of fully appreciating the fact that their quest to bind Dost Mohammad fully to them was not to be. For Dost Mohammad's main concern was the East India Company's support against the Sikhs in the recapture of Peshawar, which the British were unprepared to offer.[7] Eden's Simla Manifesto of 1838—which stated that the British needed a reliable ally on the North-West Frontier in order to secure India— was not exactly a declaration of war against Barakzai rule, though it was a pretext for intervention in Afghanistan. Failing to garner Dost Mohammad's cooperation, in March of 1839 Sir Willoughby Cotton advanced through the Bolan Pass, installed Shuja as the new emir, and occupied Kabul. Mohammad obtained a fatwa and declared jihad, but

the local histories of Barakzai aggression meant that his natural base in southern Afghanistan was loath to support him. He fled, later giving himself up after attempting a failed insurrection, and he ended up in exile in India.[8]

Shah Shuja had long been tethered to the British, not as ally so much as supplicant; he was the former emir, and he had been overthrown by a rival in 1809 and had been living in exile in India ever since. The singular advantage he had over Dost Mohammad was that Shah Shuja was an ally of both the British and the Sikhs, with whom he had actually brokered a treaty in 1833. The British determined, in other words, that embracing Dost Mohammad—an enemy of the Sikhs—was worse for the security of British rule in India than supporting Shuja—their nominal ally.[9] Though the march to Kabul was by no means easy, though the countryside was not subdued until well into 1841 (if ever), and though local tribesmen and peasants continued to attack supplies and convoys on a regular basis, the fortress of Ghazni fell relatively quickly in the summer of 1839. And though today's historians may assess that particular conquest as self-evident, eyewitness accounts testify to the stop-and-start character of the struggle on the ground and the lack of finality, if not of victory, that characterized the whole campaign for Afghanistan in this period. Meanwhile, the occupation of Kabul—undertaken to stabilize Shuja's early reign—dragged on for three years and looked increasingly permanent to a variety of observers, Afghan residents prime among them.

In part to palliate British officers and soldiers, military officials encouraged families to join the occupying army in the city. Life under the occupation was routinized and pleasant, at least for some: Florentia Sale had an elaborate kitchen garden attached to their house where she grew sweet peas, geraniums, potatoes, cauliflowers, radishes, turnips, artichokes, and lettuce. Though she professed the Kabul variety of the lettuce "hairy and inferior to those cultivated by us," she found the

Kabul cabbages "superior, being milder," and remarked on how well the red cabbage grown from English seed did even in the bracing climate of Afghanistan.[10] Others were more restless: and surely for many Afghan women, the British occupation overlaid yet another matrix of patriarchal rule that brought its own attendant gendered violences. What we do know is that Afghans were particularly discomfited by the traffic in local women that moved in and out of the cantonments. As one historian notes, "The proverb 'necessity is the mother of invention and the father of the Eurasian' was manifest."[11] In fact, contemporaries both British and Indian suggested that improper conduct of British officers who took up with Afghan women caused scandal, "open, undisguised and notorious," and prompted some Afghan men, like Mir Ahmad, to join the insurrection "in retaliation later on."[12]

The cost of maintaining such a large military and civilian contingent was a drain on the Indian treasury; the danger to supplies and to the occupiers themselves at all ranks was considerable and, in some cases, fatal. Burnes was assassinated in 1841 in the context of a local uprising directed at least in part against the British occupation forces: he was hacked to death by a mob despite trying to reason with them, it is said, in his best Persian.[13] The revolt spread; the Afghans were bombarding the cantonment, and it was clear that the security of Kabul was in peril. Sir William Macnaghten, advisor to Eden, was forced to negotiate with the new Afghan leader, Akbar Khan, son of Dost Mohammad. The terms were humiliating—total withdrawal of the British in exchange for safe passage out of Kabul—but Macnaghten was confident that the safety of all Britons was guaranteed. Instead, Akbar ambushed Macnaghten and his three assistants. Macnaghten's body was dragged through the streets of Kabul and his head paraded as Akbar's prize: symbols of British defeat and humiliation and a harbinger of worse to come.

The retreat of the British Army from Afghanistan and the massacre that followed were among the bloodiest episodes in British imperial history. One witness estimated that three thousand men and women died on January 7, 1842. As they died they could look back and see "the glow of the fire that now consumed their cantonment."[14] Sir William Elphinstone and several other officers were taken prisoner by Akbar, which added to the demoralization and sheer despair. Any resistance that British troops were inclined to put up, either as a fighting force or as a human collectivity, was significantly hampered by the notorious mountain gorges and by the bitter cold and snow, which survivors described in vivid terms as red with the blood of men, women, and children, not to mention camels and horses. The destruction of the retreating army—what one historian in the nineteenth century called "the shock of the catastrophe in the passes"—galvanized Eden, who authorized the field marshall Sir George Pollock to organize an "army of retribution, even though this had not been part of the original plan."[15] Kabul was retaken by the fall of 1842, and its central bazaar was destroyed by British forces in retaliation. The British hostages were released via negotiations that granted their guardian, Sahel Muhammed, a pension for life. Akbar was finally defeated, though his father—whose political activities had not been diminished by exile—quickly reestablished his authority in Afghanistan, where he continued to shape the fortunes of central Asia, mostly in alliance with the British, until his death in 1863.

Despite his "relative powerlessness" during the early years of his reign, Dost Mohammad shaped Victorian Afghanistan as much if not more than the British. He may be seen as part of a long line of patrimonial dynastic state builders: a prime example of the "empire of tribes" at the heart of Afghan state formation and one of the region's three "giant players" in the Victorian period—of whom his son (Akbar) and grandson (Abdur Rahman) were the other two.[16] Just as significant for the region's history was the death of Ranjit Singh in 1839, which left his kingdom vulnerable and drew his successors into several wars with the East India Company in the late 1840s. The annexation of the Punjab to British-controlled territory was the result. Following so closely on the heels of the debacle in Afghanistan, these postwar events demonstrate how inextricably linked the empires of tribes were with each other, with the fate of the Great Game, and, of course, with the conflagration yet to come: the Indian Mutiny of 1857. Significantly, Dost Mohammad kept his alliance with the British in that fight, even though his aid to the rebels might have made a difference in the short- if not the long-term.

JUST AND NECESSARY WAR?

If these imperial histories—Afghan and European— are tightly woven, it is easy enough to miss them in the binocular vision entailed by the Great Game theory of modern central Asian history. Indeed, only very recently have Western scholars tried to conceive of this region, punctuated by multiple spheres of influence and ambition, as having its own autonomous histories of "frontier governmentality," however fragmented it was.[17] The years between the recapture of Kabul by the British (1842) and the outbreak of the Second Anglo-Afghan War (1878) saw the British and the Russians dancing anxiously around each other via competitive policies of "forward movement" that were effectively mirror images of one another. The Russians, for their part, saw an opening in the aftermath of the mutiny in 1857, sensing opportunities and possibilities in pockets of "latent hostility" to British rule both in and out of India.[18] If Benjamin Disraeli, the Tory prime minister, were inclined to be skeptical of Prince Alexander Mikhailovich Gorchakov's 1864 circular, which professed Russia's "unwillingness" to extend its frontiers—or even less likely, were Disraeli willing to countenance the professed neutral-

ity of the reigning emir—he could not ignore Russian advances into Turkestan by the mid-1870s. His viceroy of India, Lord Edward Bulwer Lytton, was blunt on the question of where the allegiance of Sher Ali Khan, son of Dost Mohammad, should lie: "Afghanistan is a state far too weak and barbarous to remain isolated and wholly uninfluenced between two great military empires. . . . We cannot allow [Sher Ali] to fall under the influence of any powers whose interests are antagonistic to our own."[19] The British invasion of 1878 was prompted by a familiar game of diplomatic missions first offered and then refused: Russia and Britain each sent envoys to pursue their interests while the emir tried to hold his ground.

Facing invasion by the British in 1878, Sher Ali fled and died on the run, leaving pamphlet material calling for jihad in his wake: "Wage a holy war on behalf of God and his prophet, with your property and your lives. . . . Let the rich equip the poor. Let all die for the holy cause. A foreign nation, without cause or the slightest provocation, has made up its mind to invade our country and conquer it."[20] Once the British forces invaded, Pierre Cavagnari, the British envoy, negotiated the Treaty of Gandamak with one of the emir's sons, Mohammed Yaqub Khan. Shortly thereafter Cavagnari was murdered along with other members of the British mission, throwing the whole conflict open anew. Contemporary observers found it hard not to superimpose the events of 1839–42 onto those of 1878–80: as Lieutenant Colonel R. D. Osborn observed, Lytton "deliberately aimed to reproduce, for the edification of Asia, the tragedy of Shah Shujah and Sir William Mcnaghten, the only difference being that on this occasion the principle parts were played by Yakoub Khan and Major Cavagnari."[21]

Abdur Rahman Khan, the grandson of Dost Mohammad, whom the British put into place via a durbar in 1880, played the "masterful double game" his predecessors had engaged in, albeit more successfully. By the mid-1880s Abdur Rahman had made it clear that he was his own man, in part because he was successful not just in individuating from the superpowers but in pacifying rival tribes and indigenous threats to his sovereignty.[22] Though he deemed Abdur Rahman's tenure "extremely precarious" at first, Archibald Forbes, a war journalist turned historian, had to concede that within a year of Abdur Rahman's accession, the new emir was in control of the country—which was more than the British had ever managed to accomplish fully. Forbes concludes his narrative of the second Afghan war by observing that "Candahar and Herat had both come to [Abdur Rahman], and . . . without serious exertion. He continues to reign quietly, steadfastly and firmly; and there never has been any serious friction between him and the Government of India, whose wise policy is a studied abstinence from interference in the internal affairs of the Afghan kingdom."[23] The cost of the 1878 war to Britain? "The lives of many gallant men[,] . . . the expenditure of about twenty millions sterling," and precious little in the way of frontier territory, stability, or security.[24] By 1897, one year after the publication of the third edition of Forbes's popular history, *The Afghan Wars*, Winston Churchill was in the Swat Valley and the North-West Frontier was ablaze again.

Forbes's account of how the two wars unfolded reads as much as a brief for the demonstrable limits of British military leadership on the ground as it does for the ungovernability of the region. Afghanistan was never settled, and holding it remained as critical to imperial security as it was challenging militarily. Britons, meanwhile, debated the very legitimacy of the second Afghan campaign. Handel Cossham's 1878 speech to the members of the Bath Liberal Association questioned the justness of the cause against Tory hawks who "explain and defend" this campaign as a "just and necessary war"—a phrase that leaps out for its contemporary resonance. Cossham recounted how his local alderman made a case for Afghanistan

on the grounds that it is a "defensive" strategy: "May I ask the worthy Alderman to tell me[,] if this is a 'defensive' war[,] whoever engaged in an aggressive war? We go into a neighbour's territory who has not attacked us, who has done us no wrong, we seize his strongholds, desolate his country, murder his subjects, and seek to take his capital, and then roll our pious eyes up and thank God we are only engaged in a 'defensive war.'" It is tempting to superimpose this rhetoric onto the kinds of antiwar talk that erupted in the United States and Britain in the context of the 2001 war in Afghanistan. More provocative still is the echo of Sher Ali's arguments about jihad—in which he too called for objections and resistance to unwanted aggression by an alien invader—articulated at almost exactly the same historical moment when Cossham addressed his countrymen at Bath.

ENDURING IMAGES: REPRESENTING AFGHANISTAN

Then as now, party politics helped to shape how ordinary people understood the stakes of war in Afghanistan in ways that could help to determine electoral outcomes. William Gladstone stumped successfully against Disraeli, his rival for the office of prime minister, on just such a critique of the Tories' Afghan policy in his Midlothian campaign speech of 1879.[25] Popular histories also played their part in shaping Victorian memories of the war and its costs and follies. From the nineteenth century onward historians have more typically than not linked the first war with the second, chiefly wrestling with the question of blame for the former. Forbes took issue with official views that the British had done all they could in the face of Dost Mohammad's betrayal and that this was a justifiable rationale for installing Shah Shuja. Forbes was also highly critical of Eden, as numerous historians had been before and have been since. Indeed, it is not uncommon for Afghan war narratives to make reference to that common Victorian sobriquet for the war, "Auckland's folly." Afzal Iqbal, writing under the imprimatur of the Research Society of Pakistan in the 1970s, concurred with these indictments and even sought to rehabilitate the ill-fated Burnes in the process.[26] Punjabi scholars, for their part, have had a lot to say about the role of Mohan Lal, who was engaged by Burnes as a commercial agent because of the Persian language skills Lal had acquired in Delhi. Lal's writings remain a major source for how events unfolded, especially during the insurrection in Kabul in 1841; he was also at least indirectly involved in the assassination of Mir Masjidi, an Afghan chief who was a sworn enemy of the British.[27]

Afghanistan was and is notorious for its punishing terrain, harsh climate, and impassable gorges and defiles. But British memoirs of all three Afghan wars are filled with descriptions of both the rough landscape *and* its lush fruits and captivating vistas. Officers such as Henry Havelock and James Atkinson, both of whom chronicled the first war only up to 1840, were repeatedly taken by sights such as the "picturesque ravine, fringed with high reeds and groves of the jujube and the neem tree," and the "sweet silver line of river" that might erupt in the most unexpected places.[28] At times their narratives read like naturalists' accounts, if not also environmental histories. In that sense, those who chronicled the first Afghan war fell in behind a long tradition of ethnographic writing about the region: from Elphinstone's 1815 two-volume *An Account of the History of Cabul* onward, the British viewed knowledge about local flora and fauna as military intelligence despite the fact that it appeared to do them little good in the actual field. And because the Afghan wars were only intermittently "battle-centric," the British were perpetually bracing against the possibility of sudden skirmishes and sniping.[29] These were the kinds of guerrilla tactics that would keep them on the defensive along the North-West Frontier at least until the end of the century, when Winston Churchill wrote about the Malakand field forces

as a war correspondent and recorded similarly failed and fitful British military responses to well-practiced anticolonial tribal warfare.[30] The role of the sepoys, Indian soldiers who fought in the British Army (from the Persian *sipahi*), has also been extensively noted by both witnesses to and historians of the campaign. The sepoys' bravery and their capability come across vividly in a variety of accounts, and in some of the paintings of the war as well. James Atkinson, superintending surgeon to the Army of the Indus, not only wrote of his experiences but produced images of Indian soldiers as well, including a watercolor titled *Sepoys Attacking Baluchi Snipers in the Siri-Kajur Pass* (1839).[31] Though sepoys may not have had as intimate a knowledge of the local terrain as Khyberees and Baluchis sniping at them, by all accounts the sepoys were more adept at maneuvering in the rough terrain than the average British soldier. Without them, British losses would have been far higher and the tenuous victories that the British Army managed to achieve would possibly have been unattainable.

Significantly, while narratives of the First Anglo-Afghan War have their share of orientalist tropes, representing Afghans and tribesmen as savage, deceitful, and terrifying opponents, such rhetoric was arguably more common in and around the second war, as was the British preoccupation with jihad and other forms of frontier fanaticism. This was true despite the fact that jihad and jihadists had been critical to Afghan power politics in the region well before that campaign.[32] The "mad mullah"—Saidullah, also known as the "mad fakir of Swat"—was one face of anticolonial response to alien occupation in the last quarter of the nineteenth century. A messianic figure who articulated a popular critique of British imperialism, Saidullah raised thousands of tribesmen against the British according to contemporary observers. Although he was defeated, he nonetheless "provided some of the sternest and hardest fighting we have known on the North-west Frontier."[33] And he was by no means the only one who prodded the regional tribes to the brink of insurgency via far-flung, though well-established, networks of communication across the landscapes of the nineteenth-century Raj. Though historians writing in English have mainly drawn on the imperial archive for their understandings of jihadists such as Saidullah and his contemporary Mulla Hadda, what is clear is that a major obstacle to the success of these clerics was Abdur Rahman himself, despite the fact that the British thought the emir was aiding the jihadists.[34] David Edwards observes, "The matter of who had the right to declare jihad was tremendously important to [the emir]." This was in part because Abdur Rahman was suspicious of the tribal resistance that had kept the British at bay, and he moved quickly to suppress any insurgent challenges to his own political and military authority.[35] Even allowing for the fact that the emir was an especially prickly and "ambiguous" ally, British imperial policymakers and military men alike either typically failed to grasp the realities of Afghanistan on the ground or did so belatedly, in terms of the unfolding of events and fields of power in what we might today call "real time."[36]

Victorian representations of Afghanistan and environs—such as the one from an 1897 issue of The Graphic with the "mad mullah"—conveyed a sense of the ongoing challenges to imperial security and stability that Afghans and their allies routinely posed, both in and out of battle. Even those who admired the strongman capacities of Abdur Rahman were uneasy about his power, as is evident in Rudyard Kipling's short story "The Amir's Homily," about Abdur Rahman's role as arbiter of justice and dispenser of law. Whether they were enemies or allies, Afghans were unsettling precisely because Afghanistan itself was only ever a nominal possession despite successive wars aimed at subduing it for good. As Zarena Aslami has so aptly written, "Afghanistan was conceived in the Victorian imaginary as a raw, inhospitable space

that could be made into a protective zone against Russian attempts to invade India. At the same time, it provided the setting for the destabilization and reformulation of British national identity during the years when the circulation of state fantasy generated conflicting feelings of hope and anxiety."[37]

Perhaps because it inaugurated almost a century of hope and anxiety about the region, the First Anglo-Afghan War has had an especially long life in the British imperial imagination. Even as the Second Anglo-Afghan War was breaking out, historians were busy producing histories of its predecessor and predicting future failures.[38] In his novel To Herat and Cabul (1902), G. A. Henty prefaced his fictional account of the first Afghan campaign with the observation that "in the military history of this country there is no darker page than the destruction of a considerable British force in the terrible defiles between Cabul and Jellalabad in January, 1842."[39] Fiction writers have been consistently fascinated by the spectacular failure of this first campaign. Treatments include Maud Diver's 1913 Judgment of the Sword, which focuses on Herat, and George Macdonald Fraser's best-selling 1969 Flashman novel (the first of a series). The latter has been the most popular vehicle for bringing the First Anglo-Afghan War to twentieth-century readers. Larger than life, Harry Paget Flashman is the protagonist in Gandamak, Jalalabad, and Kabul, imprinting generations of imperial adventure fans with images of British derring-do.[40] Meanwhile, Patrick Hennessey's 2009 The Junior Officers' Reading Club, subtitled Killing Time and Fighting Wars and dedicated to memorializing his own Afghan tour (among others), is the most recent echo of the bravado and nervy self-confidence of English men "growing up in today's messy small wars," as the back-cover blurb enthusiastically—and all too blithely—proclaims.[41]

In these narratives, as in the great majority of representations of the Victorian wars, Afghanistan was a white man's world. Characters such as Lady Sale, an officer's wife caught up in occupation and the madness of battle, offer a window into what the campaigns were like for the British women who found themselves there as spouses or camp followers. Perhaps unsurprisingly, not all were as self-reliant and brave as she. In his *Memorials of Afghanistan* (1843), J. C. Stocqueler records English ladies mute with grief at the sight of the bloodstained uniforms of the British dead. He also notes that those who, felled by illness in the wake of the rout, were "in a state that rendered their removal impracticable"—a condition that Akbar Khan was said to express sympathy for.[42] As for Afghan women, Stocqueler described them as "fair and handsome," noting that "those of the upper classes are kept within the purdah; but the lower, who perform the menial offices of the household, are exposed," according to religious custom.[43] Even though eyewitness narratives in English give only the occasional glimpse of local women at the very margins of battle or encampment, chroniclers of the Great Game might vividly evoke these women, as Kipling did in a stanza of his poem "The Young British Soldier" (1895):

When you're wounded and left,
On Afghanistan's plains,
And the women come out,
To cut up your remains,
Just roll on your rifle,
And blow out your brains,
And go to your Gawd,
Like a soldier.

If this poem was intended to be a harrowing spectacle, it served Kipling's view of empire as a terrible burden to be borne by white men for the good of the race. As was common in other parts of empire, the system of gender relations that imperial observers recorded fulfilled stereotypes, especially of non-Christian populations. The folk heroine Malalai, a young girl thought to have encouraged Afghan fighters in their ultimate victory in the Battle of Maiwand in 1880, is an interesting if elusive figure; though little nineteenth-century documen-

tation in English exists on her, she recurs in Afghan storytelling and national imagery.[44]

Even when observations of Afghan women were cast in the most sympathetic of terms—as with the newspaper account of the "Cabulese lady" in the *Hampshire Telegraph and Sussex Chronicle* of 1880 (see chapter 14)—Afghan women appear mainly as backdrop or ornament, signaling the ways that orientalist images emerged in the very heat of imperial battle while competing powers, indeed competing masculinities, fought for control and possession of the region. Unsurprisingly, British representations of Afghanistan as an imperial frontier made their way into literary and cultural forms at home. They have exercised enduring power in shaping "the Afghan woman" as a pretext for intervention in the region in various forms of Western media to the present. Indeed, the First Anglo-Afghan War arguably gave rise to the very idea of "the fair maid of Cabul" in the Western imagination.[45]

AFGHANISTAN THEN AND NOW

Kipling's poem has enjoyed new life on the Internet in the first decade of the twenty-first century as Westerners sought links to soldiers' experiences of Afghanistan in earlier wars. In keeping with this curiosity about past campaigns, a robust combination of histories and soldiers' memoirs of the war in Afghanistan have been flying off the shelves since the invasion in 2001. While some of these works give a detailed account of the British campaigns, most refer to the earlier conflicts only in passing. And even critics of the way the wars were fought do not rail against imperialism per se: like many of his compatriots in the nineteenth century, Forbes was antiwar even as he was pro-empire. Meanwhile, there is a remarkable continuity between the accounts of nineteenth-century historians and those who have written subsequent histories of these conflicts in English. Indeed, accounts of the wars that center Afghan's history independent of Western projects for control, if not sovereignty, are comparatively rare, especially among the popular histories. Those that do tend to establish the pre-1839 story instrumentally, as a backdrop for the wars to come. We await, in other words, a truly, robustly postimperial history of the Anglo-Afghan Wars: one that reorients the narrative from a Great Game–centric focus toward the considerable power of, say, the dynastic base whence Dost Mohammad and his successors came, or one that writes the story of the wars as the long-range fallout of Persians and Sikhs struggling to maintain their own power—and fighting with one eye on "local" contenders as much as on "global" power struggles.[46] Surely such a history would also emphasize the role of Indian troops in the various campaigns, and the links between sepoy experiences on the North-West Frontier, from the Anglo-Sikh wars of the 1840s to the end of century when, at the Battle of Saragarhi in 1897, a Sikh regiment fought valiantly and fatally in a contest that has been compared with Thermopylae.[47] Such a history may only be possible once Western empires are well and truly withdrawn from the region, which returns us to the endlessly deferred horizon of postcolonial history itself.

And yet, there are traces of this counternarrative to be found even in the most Eurocentric and imperial of documents from the Anglo-imperial archive of Victorian Afghanistan. Beyond the glimpses we get of sepoy capacity or Afghan agency, many of these texts show the repeated failure of Western, and especially British, imperial power in the face of insurgency and instability. They are a testament to the kind of permanent insecurity produced by the resistance of the so-called enemy tribesmen and their allies. Whether the archives record military struggles or ethnographic snapshots, they capture the defensiveness of Western imperial power in the face of indigenous landscapes and peoples. If this is true in texts that are written in the firestorm of war, it is even more evident in those that exhibit what we might

call proconsular distance. Writers such as Lord George Curzon and Churchill could only note the precarious hold both British and Russian "civilizations" had on native peoples in central Asia, whether it was with respect to territorial hegemony or religious custom. That these writers did so with an equal measure of acumen and sympathy for the Russian "Bear" tells us a lot about how much these professed enemies had in common in their quest to subdue the North-West Frontier throughout the long nineteenth century and beyond. On the threshold of World War I, the Russians were "well aware of the difficulty Britain was facing in taming its so-called dependent"; and they had a global view of that difficulty as they monitored Britain's "growing embroilment" in and around the outer edges of central Asia (i.e., Tibet).[48] The Bolshevik Revolution of 1917, erupting as it did in the middle of the global conflagration that was the Great War, raised the stakes of the contest for Afghanistan's future and threw the outdatedness of a century of British strategy into bold relief—as did the centrality of Kabul in the plots of Indian revolutionaries to seize power from imperial officials and overthrow the British government in 1915.[49]

Lieutenant General G. N. Molesworth recalled half a century later: "War was forced on us by Afghanistan" in 1919.[50] The seizure of power by the son of Abdur Rahman's successor, Habibullah, resulted in Afghanistan's independence from Britain, though Afghanistan's history in the next century was tumultuous, to say the least. That son, Amanullah Khan, lasted only ten years. Driven out of power by an upstart Tajik, Amanullah died in exile in 1960, two decades before a new version of Great Game geopolitics seized central Asia in the form of the 1979 Soviet invasion—a last gasp of cold war proxy wars that played out with long-term ramifications for the global order, and its multinational engineers and its untold casualties as well.

Martin Ewans, formerly of the British Diplomatic Service and a keen historian of conflict in

Afghanistan, writes: "The Third Anglo-Afghan War differed from its two predecessors in several ways. It was instigated by the Afghans, not by the British; there were no diplomatic overtures; and it lasted no more than a month. But there was one similarity: when it ended, the advantage lay squarely with the Afghans."[51] Given eighty years and more of British determination to quell frontier unrest and stabilize Afghanistan, this is quite an indictment of the empire's "forward policy" in the region. Students can and will draw their own conclusions about how best to assess the connections or disruptions between the histories of these wars and their twenty-first-century counterparts. There is undoubtedly a familiarity, born of structural continuities from the Victorian imperial world, that must strike even the readers of today's imperial wars and will propel them, one hopes, toward a deeper knowledge and understanding of the patterns made by what has come before. This requires a longer history of the puzzle of Afghanistan than most accounts of the twenty-first-century wars are prepared to engage with.[52] How future historians and fiction writers will take up the First Afghan War as they seek to make connections and disconnections with contemporary events remains an open question, though the chain of narrative has already begun. In 2010 the Tricycle Theatre in London ran a series of plays about the first two wars that created fictional scenes drawn from many of the nineteenth-century texts collected there.[53] The plays dramatize the sharp and poignant encounters between Britons and Afghanis then and now. The combination of native resistance and imperial failure that the plays capture is striking for its echo of campaigns in both the nineteenth and the twenty-first centuries. If Afghanistan tells us anything about modern empire, it is that histories that represent modern empire only as extension and hegemony rather than as a series of fitful, harrowing, and partial victories are not as true to what happened on the ground as they might—or should—be. In the case

of the Victorians, the perpetual instability of the frontier region represented by Afghanistan reminds us that the Pax Britannica the British sought was elusive at best.

The real challenge for those seeking genuinely anti-imperial histories of the first Afghan wars is to break free of the dichotomous Great Game story and rematerialize Afghan tribes, anticolonial mullahs, and other local actors as agents, rightsizing their roles in shaping the character of these earlier wars and their outcomes. This will recapture the histories of Afghanistan and its first modern wars from multiple perspectives. Perhaps then we can begin to understand with more precision how, why, and under what circumstances all empires since the time of Alexander the Great have left, or been driven from, Afghanistan.

NOTES

1. Cited in Martin Ewans, *Conflict in Afghanistan: Studies in Asymmetric Warfare* (New York: Routledge, 2005), frontispiece. The original is from Robert Kaplan, "Afghanistan Postmortem," *The Atlantic Monthly*, April 1989, accessed June 2013, http://www.theatlantic.com/past/docs/issues/89apr/kaplanpostmortem.htm.

2. J. A. Norris, *The First Afghan War, 1838–1842* (Cambridge: Cambridge University Press, 1967), 378. For a detailed account of the insurrection, see M. E. Yapp, "The Revolution of 1841–42 in Afghanistan," *Bulletin of the School of Oriental and African Studies* 27, no. 2 (1964): 333–81. Some elements of my introductory essay can be found in Antoinette Burton, "On the First Anglo-Afghan War, 1839–42: Spectacle of Disaster," BRANCH: *Britain, Representation and Nineteenth-Century History,* accessed June 2013, http://www.branchcollective.org/?ps_articles=antoinette-burton-on-the-first-anglo-afghan-war-1839-42-spectacle-of-disaster. See also Zarena Aslami, "The Second Anglo-Afghan War, or The Return of the Uninvited," BRANCH: *Britain, Representation and Nineteenth-Century History,* accessed June 2013, http://www.branchcollective.org/?ps_articles=zarena-aslami-the-second-anglo-afghan-war-or-the-return-of-the-uninvited.

3. Patrick Macrory, ed., *Lady Sale: The First Afghan War* (Hamden, CT: Archon Books, 1969).

4. Ewans, *Conflict in Afghanistan*, 21.

5. See, for example, Patrick Macrory, *Signal Catastrophe: The Story of the Disastrous Retreat from Kabul, 1842* (London: Hodder and Stoughton, 1966), 19.

6. According to the historian Edward Ingram, "On his travels two things impressed [Alexander] Burnes, the river at Oxus

and the emir of Kabul, Dost Mahomet Khan; the first might be an opportunity or a danger, the second British India's best defence." See Edward Ingram, *The Beginning of the Great Game in Asia, 1828–1834* (Oxford: Clarendon Press, 1979), 120.

7. Victoria Schofield, *Afghan Frontier: Feuding and Fighting in Central Asia* (London: I.B. Tauris, 2003), 65.

8. Arley Loewen and Josette McMichael, eds., *Images of Afghanistan: Exploring Afghan Culture through Art and Literature* (Oxford: Oxford University Press, 2010), 19.

9. Fakir Azizuddin reassured Eden when he was about to meet Ranjit Singh in 1838: "The lustre of one sun [Ranjit] has long shone with splendor over our horizon; but when two suns come together, the refulgence will be overpowering." See Khuswant Singh, *Ranjit Singh: Maharajah of the Punjab, 1780–1839* (London: George Allen Unwin, 1962), 209.

10. Florentia Sale, *Journal of the Disasters in Affghanistan, 1841–42* (London: John Murray, Ablemarle Street, 1843), 29.

11. Schofield, *Afghan Frontier*, 71.

12. See Hari Ram Gupta, *Panjab, Central Asia and the First Afghan War* (Chandigarh, India: Panjab University, 1940), 160–62.

13. Schofield, *Afghan Frontier*, 72.

14. Norris, *The First Afghan War*, 379.

15. Archibald Forbes, *The Afghan Wars, 1839–1882 and 1878–80* (London: Seeley and Co., 1896), 135; Frank A. Clements, *Conflict in Afghanistan: A Historical Encyclopedia* (Santa Barbara, CA: ABC-CLIO, 2003), 204.

16. Christine Noelle, *State and Tribe in Early Afghanistan: The Reign of Amir Dost Muhammad Khan (1826–1863)* (Surrey, UK: Curzon, 1997), 36; Nabi Misdaq, *Afghanistan: Political Frailty and Foreign Interference* (London: Routledge, 2006), 48–49; M. Hassan Kakar, *A Political and Diplomatic History of Afghanistan, 1863–1901* (Leiden, Netherlands: Brill, 2006), 1.

17. Benjamin D. Hopkins and Magnus Marsden, *Fragments of the Afghan Frontier* (New York: Columbia University Press, 2011).

18. For one example of this, see "Nikolai Ignatiev: Russia's Agenda in Central Asia," in *Islamic Central Asia: An Anthology of Historical Sources*, edited by Scott C. Levi and Ron Sela (Bloomington: Indiana University Press, 2010), 295–99.

19. Quoted in Asta Oleson, *Islam and Politics in Afghanistan* (Surrey, UK: Curzon Press, 1995), 25.

20. Quoted in Gregory Fremont-Barnes, *The Anglo-Afghan Wars, 1839–1919* (Oxford: Osprey Publishing, 2009), 58.

21. R. D. Osborn, "India and Afghanistan," *Contemporary Review* 36 (1879): 206.

22. Alex Marshall, *The Russian General Staff and Asia, 1800–1917* (New York: Routledge, 2006), 139. Even before British troops withdrew from Kandahar in 1881, Abdur Rahman was looking to establish his authority beyond the territorial limits (Pishin) that London envisioned for him. See D. P. Singhal, *India and Afghanistan: A Study in Diplomatic Relations* (Brisbane: University of Queensland Press, 1963), 87.

23. Forbes, *The Afghan Wars*, 327. In fact, between 1880 and 1896, the new emir faced no fewer than forty uprisings, which he quelled by a combination of "peaceful penetration" and military suppression. See Kakar, *A Political and Diplomatic History of Afghanistan*, chapters 4 and 5.

24. Forbes, *The Afghan Wars*, 324.

25. Zarena Aslami, *The Dream Life of Citizens: Late Victorian Novels and the Fantasy of the State* (New York: Fordham University Press, 2012), 71.

26. Forbes, *The Afghan Wars*, 32; Afzal Iqbal, *Circumstances Leading to the First Afghan War* (Lahore: Research Society of Pakistan, 1975).

27. Gupta, *Panjab, Central Asia and the First Afghan War*, 245–46. This edition has an introduction by Jawaharlal Nehru, who calls Lal a "fascinating person" who "in a free India . . . would have risen to the topmost rungs of the political ladder" (iv and iii).

28. Henry Havelock, *Narrative of the War in Affghanistan in 1838–39*, vol. 1 (London: Henry Colburn Publishers, 1840), 202; James Atkinson, *The Expedition into Affghanistan: Notes and Sketches Descriptive of the Country, Contained in a Personal Narrative during the Campaign of 1839 and 1840* (London: William Allen, 1842), 184.

29. See Montstuart Elphinstone, *An Account of the Kingdom of Cabul and Its Dependencies in Persia, Tartary and India* (London: Longman, Hurst, Rees, Orme, and Brown, 1815); Kaushik Roy, "Introduction: Armies, Warfare and Society in Colonial India," in *War and Society in Colonial India*, edited by Kaushik Roy (Oxford: Oxford University Press, 2006), 6.

30. Winston Churchill, *The Story of the Malakand Field Force* (London: Leo Cooper, 1989).

31. Atkinson, *The Expedition into Affghanistan*. For the watercolor, see the Europeana website, http://www.europeana.eu/portal/record/92037/D1CD9875D70D9C904A2079F2D43FAFF6FD828BB3.html (accessed June 2013).

32. Ayesha Jalal, *Partisans of Allah: Jihad in South Asia* (Cambridge, MA: Harvard University Press, 2008), 84–105.

33. A. H. Mahon and A. D. G. Ramsay, *Report on the Tribes of Dir, Swat and Bajour* (Peshawar, Pakistan: Saeed Book Bank, 1981), 28.

34. David B. Edwards, *Heroes of the Age: Moral Fault Lines on the Afghan Frontier* (Berkeley: University of California Press, 1996), 172–201. For official details on Saidullah's origins and movements, see *Military Operations on the North-West Frontiers of India: Papers Regarding the British Relations with the Neighboring Tribes of the North-West Frontier of India* (London: India Office Publications, 1898), 85–86; and Mahon and Ramsay, *Report on the Tribes of Dir, Swat and Bajour*, 27.

35. Mahon and Ramsay, *Report on the Tribes of Dir, Swat and Bajour*, 199. "Hadda Sahib . . . was one of the few, perhaps the only, religious leader who consistently stymied the Amir, staying just beyond his grasp and out of his control. Consequently, it was important for the Amir to preserve what advantages he had, and one of those advantages was certainly the doctrine that only an Islamic ruler could declare a jihad." See also Thomas Barfield, *Afghanistan: A Cultural and Political History* (Princeton, NJ: Princeton University Press, 2010), 147–49.

36. Keith Surridge, "The Ambiguous Amir: Britain, Afghanistan and the 1897 North-West Frontier Uprising," *Jour-*

nal of Imperial and Commonwealth History 36, no. 3 (2008): 417–34. This would seem to be true not only in the context of settling wars but drawing boundary lines, as in the case of the 1893 treaty that Abdur Rahman signed with Sir Mortimer Durand to set what was to become known as the Durand Line. See Bijan Omrani, "The Durand Line: History and Problems of the Afghan-Pakistan Border," *Asian Affairs* 40, no. 2 (2009): 177–95.

37. Aslami, *The Dream Life of Citizens*, 69.

38. Henry Marion Durand, *The First Afghan War and Its Causes* (London: Longman's Green, 1879).

39. G. A. Henty, *To Herat and Cabul: A Story of the First Afghan War* (London: Blackie and Sons, 1902), v.

40. George Macdonald Fraser, *Flashman: From the Flashman Papers 1839–1842* (New York: World Publishers, 1969).

41. Patrick Hennessey, *The Junior Officers' Reading Club: Killing Time and Fighting Wars* (London: Penguin, 2009).

42. J. C. Stocqueler, *Memorials of Afghanistan* (Calcutta: Ostell and Lepage, 1843), 279.

43. Stocqueler, *Memorials of Afghanistan*, 11.

44. There is some evidence that her name has left an inspirational trace in the titles of girls' schools; see Valentine Moghadam, *Modernizing Women: Gender and Social Change in the Middle East* (Boulder, CO: Lynne Rienner Publishers, 2003), 235–36, 240. Moghadam also tracks how and why, as was the case in Egypt and Turkey in the early twentieth century, women were key to the modernization schemes that Abdur Rahman's successors carried out in the legislative realm, chiefly under the rubric *himayat-i niswan* (the protection of women) (237).

45. See Charles Finch Mackenzie's extensive poem, *Zeila, the Fare Maid of Cabul: A Tale of the Afghan Insurrection and the Massacre of the British Troops in the Khoord-Cabul Passes* (London: Palmer and Clayton, 1850). For a sense of how Afghan women today represent themselves in response to occu-pation and fundamentalism, see the homepage of Revolutionary Association of the Women of Afghanistan, http://www.rawa .org/index.php (accessed June 2013).

46. For a few key examples of conventional histories, see G. B. Malleson, *A History of Afghanistan, from the Earliest Period to the Outbreak of the War of 1878* (Peshawar, Pakistan: Saeed Book Bank, 1984 [1878]); and Victoria Schofield, *Every Rock, Every Hill: The Plain Tale of the North-West Frontier and Afghanistan* (London: Buchan and Enright, 1984). For an Afghan-centric account, see Noelle, *State and Tribe in Early Afghanistan*.

47. Michael Barthorp, *The North-West Frontier: British India and Afghanistan; A Pictorial History, 1839–1947* (Dorset, UK: Blandford Press, 1982), 128.

48. Jennifer Siegel, *Endgame: Britain, Russia, and the Final Struggle* (London: I.B. Tauris, 2002), 172, 173.

49. A. C. Bose, *Indian Revolutionaries Abroad, 1905–1922: In the Background of International Developments* (Patna, India: Bharati Bhawan, 1971), 106; and Maia Ramnath, *Haj to Utopia: How the Ghadar Movement Charted Global Radicalism and Attempted to Overthrow the British Empire* (Berkeley: University of California Press, 2011), 124.

50. G. N. Molesworth, *Afghanistan 1919: An Account of Operations in the Third Afghan War* (Bombay: Asia Publishing House, 1962), 87.

51. Ewans, *Conflict in Afghanistan*, 89.

52. Toby Dodge is keen to make such connections in his *Inventing Iraq: The Failure of Nation Building and History Denied* (New York: Columbia University Press, 2003), xxi–xxxvi. For an example of a short view of Afghanistan in historical context, see Tim Bird and Alex Marshall, *Afghanistan: How the West Lost Its Way* (New Haven, CT: Yale University Press, 2011).

53. See Richard Bean et al., *The Great Game: Afghanistan* (London: Oberon Books, 2010).

PART I

Strategic Interests
on the Road to Kabul

The road to Kabul—which is to say, the path to the occupation of the city by the Army of the Indus in late 1839—was paved by several imperial interests. For the British, the security of India depended on control over the North-West Frontier against the Russians, whose designs on the Raj were a motivating factor for Britain's colonial policy throughout the nineteenth century. Both countries mapped the region, fully aware that the remnants of the Persian Empire and its enemies, the Afghans, patrolled the very peripheries that both the British and the Russians coveted. Britain was particularly anxious about the threat that Russian power posed to its own global ambitions. As important, given the necessity of local alliance making, was the power of the Sikh kingdom, its historic rivalry with its Afghan neighbors, and the challenges to imperial hegemony all kinds of native interests Afghanistan posed, at least until the death of its powerful leader, Ranjit Singh, the lion of the Punjab, in 1839.

A Sketch of the Military and Political Power of Russia (1817)

ROBERT WILSON

Sir Robert Wilson's survey of Russian territorial ambition and "frontier creep" grew out of his career interest in the health and security of the British Empire. Though his highest post was the governorship of Gibraltar (1842–49), he served in several theaters of war as a young man, mainly in connection with the Napoleonic Wars and most notably the British expedition to Egypt, about which he wrote a best-selling history in 1802.

These experiences gave Wilson (1777–1849) a unique perspective on Britain's global fortune and a correlative suspicion of all possible threats to it. In this selection his cartographic precision is punctuated by his palpable alarm at the prospect of what an ambitious Russia means for global security, from Eastern Europe to Persia and beyond. Lest there be any doubt, his chief concern is India, that focal point of British diplomacy and military strategy since the Battle of Plassey (1757). Here Wilson calculates that by virtue of its capacity to mobilize its forces from the Baltic Sea to the Caspian Sea and the Persian Gulf, Russia was in easy striking distance of both Bombay and Madras (Chennai).

Anticipating critics who doubted Russia's determination to attack, Wilson was unequivocal: "The answer is, She can." In his view it was a matter of urgency for all governments, not least because Alexander I had ambitions for a maritime as well as a land empire: a global imperium, in short, that would know no earthly bounds. Wilson asks, "Must the fiat of Alexander be the law of the universe?" And, as if to set the Great Game afoot, he asks, "is Russia, like Rome under the image of Milo the wrestler, to be looking round in vain for an antagonist"?

In the year 1800, Russia rested her right flank on the North Sea; her frontier line traversing Russian Lapland, ran fifty miles in advance of the White Sea: then covering the province of Olonetz, approached the Lake Ladoga within twenty miles, and fell upon the Gulf of Finland, at the distance of only one hundred and fifteen miles in a direct line from Petersburgh; so that Sweden not only commanded near two thirds of the northern coast of the Gulf of Finland, but ranged herself in view of, and at the distance of not more than thirty miles from, the port of Revel, situated in the province of Livonia, wrested from her by Peter the Great, and which she might always hope to reoccupy, so long as she preserved such contiguity.

The frontier of Russia opposed to the frontier line of Prussia, commenced near Memel; and reaching the Niemen, between Tilsitz and Kovno, continued along that river as far as Grodno, when it ran in a southern direction upon the Bug river between Drogutchin and Brestlitov; then descending to Wlodowa, on the frontier of Austrian Gallicia, continued along that province until it reached the Dniester, near Chotev when it followed the course of that river into the Black Sea.

On the side of Asia, the frontier was separated from the Turkish possessions by the Cuban, a small river, which flows at a little distance from the very narrow strait which divides the Crimea from the continent of Asia, and connects the Sea of Azov with the Black Sea. It then continued along that river to its source, and passing in front of Georgiesk, and behind or to the northward of the mountains of Caucasus, joined the river Terek, and followed its course into the Caspian.

In the year 1817, the right of the frontier still rests on the Northern Ocean, but, advancing a hundred and sixty miles, touches the frontier of Norway, and bends round it for a hundred and ninety miles, until it reaches a line drawn due north from the Torneo, when it descends on that river, and continues running parallel until it falls into the Gulf of Bothnia, intersecting a country through which the Swedish troops always passed into Finland, but where, from the severity of the climate and the poverty of the soil, none can move without previous arrangements.

The difficulty, indeed, of the communication contributed to the loss of the Swedish provinces; since Sweden could not sustain with a population of little more than two millions of people, and a revenue of not much more than one million, the heavy expenditure of men and money. These difficulties, however, will be less felt by Russia, since the command of the Gulfs of Finland and of Bothnia would facilitate the operations.

A line is then drawn through the Gulf of Bothnia, which sweeping round Aland, regains the continent in the province of Livonia, thus giving to Russia the ports of Abo and of Sweaborg, which was the great naval establishment of the Swedes on the coast of Finland, and all the numerous islands which cluster between Aland and the main land, and which are inhabited by a rich and happy population. But the island of Aland is distant from the shore of Sweden only twenty-four miles, from the Archipelago of islands in advance of Stockholm not above thirty, and not above seventy from Stockholm itself; while the intervening sea is frequently frozen, so that carriages may pass.

Thus Russia has completely changed her relative position with Sweden. Instead of her former vulnerable and humiliating defensive attitude, she not only menaces but awes; and not only awes; but, from a variety of contingent circumstances, all favourable to her authority, she commands.

On the Niemen, the frontier remains in statu quo for about one hundred miles; when it traverses the Memel or Niemen river, and running along East Prussia, strikes the Vistula near Thorn, from whence Dantzic is distant about seventy miles, and Berlin only one hundred and seventy.

The line then crosses the Vistula, and advances to Kalish, a point nearly equidistant from Dresden and Berlin; thence taking a southern direction and passing within thirty miles of the Oder, it bends in an eastern course along the district of Cracow, which it respects; but at this point its distance from a third capital, Vienna, is again only one hundred and seventy miles; the Gallician frontier is then rounded, when the line traverses the Dniester, allongates the Bukovine frontier, until it reaches the river *Pruth;* thus circumventing all that part of Poland, except the

Duchy of Posen, which belonged to Prussia by the partition-treaties.

In this position, which may be called the very heart of Europe, she rides alongside the Brandenburgh possessions with the lofty and fearful superiority of one of her hundred and twenty gun ships over a Prussian galliot, when there is no escape from pressure, and when the weaker must be crushed or overwhelmed.

Notwithstanding the possession of the forever of Dantzic, Giandents and Goibengt Prussia can never attempt to defend any territory north of the Oder, and her line of fortresses on that river is now the only rampart of Germany, a rampart too of no value, if there are not supporting armies in the field equal or nearly so to the attacking force, and especially in the arm of cavalry; which is almost impossible; since Russia, without any extraordinary exertion, could bring one hundred and twenty thousand (regular and irregular) cavalry into action on the Prussian frontier.

It is no wonder, then, that Prussia interweaves the myrtle with the olive, that she may preserve the ground for the laurels she has won! Had she a hundred daughters and Russia as many sons, she would willingly unite them all.

On the side of the frontier, from Cracow to the Pruth, the kingdom of Poland reposes on a friendly population, and not merely friendly, but one in which the white eagle is building, as it were, a native aerie: a territory which, in time of peace, occasions jealousy to the present possessor, and which, if the disaffection of the people were less unequivocal, could not be defended in time of war; notwithstanding political considerations render Sclavonian contact with the Carpathian mountains perilous to the Austrian monarchy.

The Russian frontier having reached the Pruth, continues along that river (so disastrous in her history) to its confluence with the Danube; when this great artery of Austria, and main support to the Turkish frontier, rolls its streams, now also tributary to the flag of Russia, into the waters of the Black Sea.

In this position Russia is distant only one hundred miles from Transylvania; about two hundred and fifty from Constantinople by water, and three hundred by land, in a direct line: whilst the two interjacent provinces of Moldavia and Wallachia are in fact regulated by her policy, though the Ottoman Porte retains the nominal sovereignty.

Russia had endeavoured to obtain the line of the Sereth, when she found that Austria was not willing that she should occupy the whole of the provinces of Moldavia and Wallachia, and throw her frontier upon Illyria and the higher Danube; a boundary-line which, in fact, would have uncovered not only Illyria, but the Banat, Transylvania, and Hungary; and brought her within a little more than two hundred miles of Constantinople.

The preparations of Napoleon had induced Russia to accelerate the signature of peace; Andréossy's arrival to counteract the negotiations had been fortunately protracted, and the Turkish ministers signed the conditions of a treaty, for which they afterwards lost their heads, on the charge of having received the bribes of Russia.

It is probable that Russia, under the circumstances of the subsequent invasion, might have been persuaded to return to the Dniester.

The recovery of Besserabia was a great object to the Porte, on account of the Danube line, and it was also desirable for humanity; since Moldavia, like Saxony, cut in twain seen her population divided; and under governments with adverse interests, feels all the sufferings which such policy is calculated to inflict; and which the King of Saxony so well described in his protest, when he observed, "that it had no principle for basis but the convenience of the partitioning powers, and no regard for the welfare and internal relations of the people."

These considerations, added to the importance of pacific relations with Turkey (in virtue of which the Moldavian army was rendered disposable for the very service which it afterwards executed), might perhaps have obtained a voluntary restitution of the Moldavian acquisition, if the future safety of Turkey had then engaged sufficiently the attention of her allies, or if they had exercised the forethought of Alexander at Abo; but the occasion was lost, and fortune, like other females, generally resents the slight of proffered favours.

Here then Russia stands: no longer menaces in flank or on her communications by the Uhlans of Poland, but supporting her attitude with the soldiers, the population, and resources of that rich and warlike country!—no longer fearful of a diversion from a Swedish army, where kindred ties might still have favoured the operations of the invader. While Turkey, deprived of these auxiliaries, abandoned to her daily impoverishing means of defence, sees a danger still more formidable approach on a frontier which heretofore had been inaccessible to any enemy.

After the acquisition of the Crimea in 1791, the Cuban river, as before observed, separated the Turkish and Russian frontier. The river itself is of no importance; but from thence a very narrow isthmus formed by a small gulf (through which the waters of the Cuban flow), and the Black Sea, runs for about twenty miles to the point of Anapa, where the mountains of Caucasus approach close to the shore, and contract the line of defence to a point.

Now, instead of the Crescent waving on the batteries of the Cuban, the Mahometan banner, replaced by the Russian eagles, has been driven across and beyond the navigable Phasis, and is not to be found until the river Bathus in Armenia presents a feeble barrier, while the Russian advanced frontier, supported by the mountain line, which connects Georgia with her new position, secures an indisputable sovereignty over the acquired country, and bids defiance to attack.

Thus here, as on the Swedish, Polish, and Moldavian frontier, invulnerable herself, she stands ready to strike and to wound; to hurl her thunder over Asia whenever her policy deems the moment expedient: for her routes of march to all the points which attract her, are now but marches of a few days.

The distance is to Trebisond, but eighty miles; to the western bank of the Euphrates, not above ninety; to Arzroum, one hundred; to Sinope, two hundred and seventy; to Scutari, opposite Constantinople, a little more than five hundred; across the Isthmus of Asia Minor to Alexandretta (a seaport town opposite Cyprus in the Mediterranean), and only sixty miles from Aleppo, little more than four hundred; and to the Red Sea from thence not five hundred.

Here then she is moreover posted with perfect communications, with a sea road for the transport of her stores and magazines, awaiting but a signal to advance, and make herself *mistress of those communications along which the Turks in Europe must receive their Asiatic reinforcements.* Here she is posted to lance the Greek fire from the shore of the Bosphorus on the towers of the Seraglio, if the Sultan does not obey the Russian Ukase!

The guns of Napoleon at Acre shook the Ottoman empire to its foundations. If the French armies had been lodged as the Russians now are, on the Danube, and in Armenia, with the Black Sea under their dominion; or if but one army could have reached Asia Minor, isolated as that army would have been, and deprived of the advantages which Russia possesses by her religious connexion with the Greeks, there is little doubt but that Armenia a second time would have seen a handful of soldiers regarded "as too many for an embassy, and too few for a fight," make before the setting sun her multitudes the chase of their discipline; and that the tricoloured flag would have waved on the walls of Byzantium.

It may be said, however, that Persia would march to the aid of the Mussulmans, although the religious quarrel between these nations renders them deadly enemies, when Christians do not menace the overthrow of both; but Persia by the late treaty, made under the auspices of England, is herself prostrate at the feet of Russia.

Russia has descended from the mountains! She is no longer struggling against the hostility of nature and barbarians in the regions of the Caucasus; she has advanced into the plain, and sweeping with her frontier round Georgia, absorbing the Persian provinces of Daughistan and Shirvan, so as to consolidate and cement all her possessions, she has raised a pillar of her empire at the mouth of the river Kur; and to complete her triumph, to remove all rivals, and monopolize commerce, she has stipulated that her flag, and her flag alone, shall sweep the Caspian.

Thus Persia is humbled to the dust, and her court to eastern dependence and bondage. It is true, that Persia, unfettered by Turkish prejudices, has long solicited, and has at length obtained, the instruction of Europeans, of French officers, officers of the army of Napoleon proscribed by Louis; and it is not probable that they have carried with them feelings of ill will to Russia so strong as those towards England; that they would rather storm the frozen Caucasus than join in an expedition to share the spoil of Asia, and avenge in the East, their humiliations in Europe.

To reach Tehran, the capital of the Shah, the columns have to march only three hundred miles; and by the navigation of the Caspian they can be disembarked within one hundred! Thus an army might sail from the Baltic through an internal navigation from Petersburgh to Astracan, and landing on the southern shore of the Caspian, pitch their tents within four hundred miles of the Persian Gulf; from whence the voyage to Bombay is only from twenty-four to thirty days, in both Monsoons; and to Madras, but eight or ten days longer in the S. W. Monsoon.

This, then, is the territorial attitude of Russia. But can any power sustain a force sufficient to garrison a frontier, whose *points d'appui* are the Northern Ocean and the Caspian, as well as the frontiers of China and Armenia; on whose line Swedes, Austrians, Turks, and Persians, are arrayed with feelings and interests at war with the power that would enslave them?

Can Russia, who in the year 1799 had a disposable army of only fifty thousand men; in the year 1807, not more than eighty thousand to defend both capitals; and in the year 1813, only three hundred thousand on her whole territory, after several years preparation; can she, notwithstanding a destructive invasion and wars of such great waste and expenditure, have collected and re-equipped armies sufficient to defend her acquisitions and improve her advantages? The answer is, She can; and Europe and Asia must acknowledge the truth of that assertion: for, both quarters of the globe are overshadowed by the mass of six hundred and forty thousand men, which an establishment of one million two hundred thousand ranges in order of battle, exclusive of militia, Tartar cavalry, &c.

The fact is, that Russia, after posting thirty thousand men of appropriate force, with artillery, &c. in Finland, eighty thousand on the frontier of Gallicia, sixty thousand in Moldavia, thirty thousand on the frontier of Armenia, as many in Persia, and leaving a reserve of one hundred thousand men to sustain these armies, possesses still a disposable force of above two hundred thousand infantry, eighty thousand cavalry, and one thousand two hundred guns better horsed for service than any artillery or cavalry in the world—an army, than which, there is none more brave, and with which no other can march, starve, or suffer physical privations and natural inclemencies. She has moreover a population equal to the needed supply, and to a great portion of whom the habits and sufferings of war are familiar; while no power in Europe can raise, equip or maintain their forces, with such disdain of the price of blood.

Such is Russia—such has been her gigantic growth within a short century! The elements of her greatness, no doubt, previously existed, but, like the treasures in the bowels of the earth, they were undiscovered, and, when produced, were still too full of dross for use, without skilful separation.

Alexander now wields the huge sceptre of Russia, and displays an ability equal to the task. His philosophical views have indeed been enfeebled by pernicious advisers; but those who have known him in other days, still cling to the hope that he will not substitute an unfeeling policy, of which the pillars are tyranny, ignorance, and fanaticism, for the sentiments of that genuine philanthropy, which must still have possession of his heart, though they do not animate his councils.

If, indeed, Alexander had resisted the enemies of liberty and human happiness—if he had persevered in the wish he once professed, to see governments and nations so constituted, that sovereigns should be only the executive representatives of represented states, whose action depended not on the character of the individual chief, but on general, fixed, and self-operating principles; he would have added to his glory, the more illustrious and imperishable title of the "Benefactor to Mankind."

Now he appears only in the character (and his enemies triumph in the result) of a conqueror, who engages the consideration of the universe by the immensity of his power to do real mischief and problematical good.

How he will employ the vast force at his disposition, is certainly a most interesting question. Whether he will take the line of the Vistula or even Oder for himself; push Prussia into Holland; instigate France to imitate England, and complete and terminate her revolution by the election of a sovereign from the family of Nassau; or whether he will enter into negotiations with Austria for a new arrangement of Europe, which may restore the balance; are speculations, which have excited the hopes and fears of many. Whether he will profit by the positions and present superiority of Russia, to accomplish other projects long assigned to her system of policy, must interest all governments, not excepting the government of the East Indies; whose attention may also be more excited by the information, that General Yermoloff, the governor of the Caucasus line, who probably at this very moment has reached the capital of Persia on an embassy, is an officer of the highest merit and capacity as an administrator as well as a soldier; and that he has gone assisted not only by the French officers employed by Napoleon, under Gardanne, in Persia, and whom Alexander, with the exception of three, engaged in the Russian service, but with the reports and maps sent by that mission to Napoleon, and which being carried into Russia at the time of the invasion, were found during the retreat, in two abandoned tumbrils.

These reports and plans had convinced Napoleon, that the expedition to India was practicable; and it is a positive fact, that he had resolved on sending an united Russian and French force on that expedition, in case Russia had been compelled to make peace on his terms.

Alexander has already a much larger army than his defensive line requires, or his finances can justify; and yet he continues to increase his force.

Russia, with a line of coast upon two seas, on which there is not navigation above half the year, and in one of them, the Baltic, no competitor, not content with an establishment of above *eighty* sail of the line in the ports of Archangel, Cronstadt, Revel, Sevastopol, Cherson; notwithstanding the pressure of the French war, has been incessantly building, and is building with increasing activity, the heaviest line of battle ships.

Alexander knows as well as any British admiral, that ships of any force or of any amount are of no value without seamen to navigate them; and that seamen cannot be formed on inland seas alone. He also knows and feels as well as any economist in Europe, that ships are costly vanities, if built only for ostentation. There is no sovereign who would have been less inclined to divert his treasure from state necessities, for the indulgence of this unprofitable pursuit, than Alexander.

There is, therefore, evidence amounting to conviction, that he has always proposed to accomplish the instructions of Peter the Great, and extend his empire until he can establish that real maritime power which himself and people have coveted more since they have seen so much commercial wealth, or, as they term it, colonial gold, flow into their country. *Putani enim, qui mari potitur, eum rerum patiri.*

It is not likely that he will be satisfied with a Dutch permit; but whether he will seek to establish himself in the ports of Norway, in Zealand, in the Archipelago, in the Mediterranean; or whether, like the son of Jupiter Ammon on the banks of the Hyphasis, he will say, "Our empire shall have no other bounds than those which God has set to the earth"—time will show.

Are then Europe, and Asia, and America (of which hemisphere nothing has been said, for the hour is not yet ripe, though it teems with matter of the highest moment to the world); to make no effort for the preservation of their independence?

Must the fiat of Alexander be the law of the universe? Is Russia, like Rome under the image of Milo the wrestler, to be looking round in vain for an antagonist?

Painful as it is to reflect, that a war for the restoration of the balance of power should have ended in the overthrow of all balance; in the substitution of solid dominion, for a momentary authority; in a national supremacy, instead of the supremacy of one extraordinary man, subject to all the vicissitudes of fortune and the infirmities of humanity: it is nevertheless true; and *so long as France is not reunited to Europe*, so long as she cannot be rendered contributive to the general system of defence, every monarch and nation on the continent must owe their existence to the forbearance of Alexander.

2 / Journey to the North of India (1838)

ARTHUR CONOLLY

This travelogue by Arthur Conolly (1807–42) is a colorful guide to the interdependency of Russian, Persian, and Afghanistan, as well as the North India territories, enabling readers then and now to appreciate the intrigues and dangers of the central Asian landscape on the verge of the First Anglo-Afghan War. Conolly was a captain in the East India Company who is credited with coining the phrase *the great game* to describe British and Russian competition for central Asia. He undertook a number of reconnaissance missions over the course of his career, often in disguise and using the persona Khan Ali, a pun on his own name. His *Journey to the North of India* offers a local history as well as a contemporary account of petty rivalries, prejudices, and "rascality." His narrative evokes the lawless and colorful spaces between the major cities of the region.

In one particularly vivid scene in the excerpt, Conolly thwarts a robbery by throwing the would-be thief down the stairs. This is followed in short order by a midnight visitation from armed men in search of valuables. Conolly's protestations that he is an English officer have no effect; what matters more in this demimonde are his local associations and patrons, who have power if not to protect him, then at least to help escort him across the wild frontier world of the northwest. Conolly was not so lucky as the contest for Afghanistan developed into war. On a mission to free a fellow British officer held captive in Bukhara in 1841, Conolly too was captured and executed as a British spy.

Quitting London on the 10th of August, 1829, I travelled through France and the North of Germany to Hamburg, and, embarking on board a steam-vessel at Travemunde on the 1st of September, sailed up the Baltic and the Gulf of Finland in four days to St. Petersburg.

In this capital I was joined by two friends and fellow-travellers to Persia, Captain Strong, of the Bombay military service, and Captain Willock, R.N., who had come from Hamburg viá Denmark and Sweden. We spent a pleasant month here, being enabled, through the kindness of the premier, Count Nesselrode, and other gentlemen to whom we brought letters of introduction, to see much of what is interesting in this wonderful and ever new-looking city of palaces; then, as winter was fast approaching, and as our journey was to be a long one, we prepared to journey on to Persia. My friend S. and I purchased, for 900 roubles, a light britchka on four springs, which we provisioned, and fitted up for day and night travelling; and for 550 roubles we bought a smaller carriage to contain our baggage, of which we gave charge to our French valet. Captain W. bought a good English-built carriage for himself; and, at the cost of 1000 roubles, we jointly engaged the services of an Englishman many years resident in Russia, who, as servant and interpreter, accompanied us to Tiflis.

The last things that we provided for our journey were sable caps, and soft leather jack-boots lined with wool, to keep our extremities warm, and racoon skin *shoobes*, huge cloaks, worn with the fur inside, which are a defence against old Hyems himself. Our money we carried in bills upon Moscow, and, provided with necessary letters of introduction as far as Tiflis, we drove out of St. Petersburg on the noon of the 8th of October, and travelled, in five days and nights, 727 verstes to the city of Moscow.

On our route we passed through the once great city of Novgorod, which is now only remarkable for the decayed vestiges of its former magnificence, and for being the head-quarters of the first military colony, established by the therefore famed Count Arrachief. There was little in the general appearance of the country to interest the eye: we saw parts of a very fine macadamised highway, which it was said would be thrown open the next year; but our road was a very bad one, sandy, muddy, or over the trunks of trees which had been laid across it, and we experienced so much weariness from the jolting, that we were very glad to see the spires of the ancient capital of the Muscovites.

At Moscow we remained only four days, for the first snow of the season falling on the second day after our arrival, we became anxious to be across the Caucasus: we made the most of our time however,—ascended heights to survey the city in its different aspects, and wandered, with intelligent guides, through its quarters, which are fast rising, phœnix-like, from their ashes, though they still bear many traces of the conflagration which was so heroically fanned. We saw the Kremlin, and the curiosities that its walls contain—were shown splendid modern buildings, with churches and convents of most ancient, strange, and varied architecture, and had reason to be delighted with all that we witnessed among the semi-Asiatic people of this extraordinary city, except a gross and idolatrous superstition, which can scarcely be imagined by a Protestant, and which cannot be too deeply lamented by any Christian.

Here we cashed our bills for Russian ducats, which I believe are a good remittance to most parts of the world, and on the 17th of October resumed our route. From the last of a succession of hills, which rise gradually above each other in a distance of four verstes, we looked back upon the painted and gilded roofs and cupolas of "the city of forty times forty churches," which lay en masse on either side of the river Moskva, backed by a deep blue sky that told of snow: while we looked the flakes began to fall thick about us; so, wrapping ourselves in our fur cloaks, we set our faces resolutely towards Asia, and bade the Isvoschtshicks give the rein and whip to their horses.

The thermometer this afternoon stood at 34° F; a week later, when, after travelling day and night, via Toula and Eletz, we reached the town of Veronetz, at nine in the morning it was 6° below zero. As we ran south, we seemed just to keep ahead of the snow; whenever we halted it overtook us, and we hurried on day and night with as little intermission as possible.

On the night of the 24th we crossed the Don into the Cossack country; halted the 26th and 27th at Tcherkask, the recent capital of the Don Cossacks, on the 28th again crossed this noble river into Asia, and continued our rapid journey over the steppes to the Caucasus.

We chose our own road upon the turf of these vast plains, and galloped across them with six sturdy ones attached to each vehicle, halting only an hour, morning or evening, to refresh ourselves with ablutions and food, or occasionally for a few minutes during the day, to get a shot at bustard, florican, or wild fowl. There was nothing else on the face of the country to invite our stay, and the less we entered houses, the less we suffered from the attacks of the vermin which have taken a lease of Russia; the road was as safe as easy, and after rolling smoothly along all day, we used to put a board between the seats of our carriage, and, buried in our furs, sleep soundly, if not very comfortably, through the bright cold nights.

During this part of our journey, we saw no people except those inhabiting the small villages at the government posts, and the few Cossack guards connecting them, links in the chain of communication thrown over this vast empire, through which the mandates of the Czar are conducted to their point as by electricity, and to which *kootoo* is performed as reverentially as to the indisputable decrees of the Emperor of China.

Our onward route lay through the towns of Stavrapol, Alexandrof, and Georgevsk, to Ekaterinegrade, where we arrived on the 3rd of November, and were detained until the 8th, when, a sufficient party of travellers having assembled, we were allowed to proceed slowly under escort of some Terek Cossacks, a party of infantry, and a twelve-pounder, to defend us against attack from any of the yet unsubdued Circassian tribes. In this manner, we travelled to Vladi Caucase, which we reached in three days: this is the last station on the northern side of the Caucasus, and, as the key to the pass into Georgia, a military post of importance. On the 12th of November we set out again, still escorted by soldiers, and marching under their protection through and over these stupendous mountains in five days, in the course of two more we drove to Tiflis.

We had two rather laborious days' journey over the snow in the Caucasus; our carriages however were not much injured. On our route we met a troop of horse artillery coming from the war, the soldiers attached to which seemed to make light of every difficulty, assisting the horses where the road was heavy, and occasionally unharnessing them, while with ropes they drew or lowered the guns up and down the slippery steeps. As a specimen of Russian soldiership, I may mention that, early one morning, we came upon a regiment of infantry bivouacked in regular order upon the snow.

The Russians do not yet command free passage through the Caucasus; for they are obliged to be very vigilant against surprise by the Circassian sons of the mist, who still cherish the bitterest hatred against them. In some instances, the Russian posts on the right of the defile were opposed to little stone eyries perched upon the opposite heights; and when any number of the Caucasians were observed descending the goat-paths on the mountain's side, the Russian guards would turn out and be on the alert. We learned that not very long before our arrival a party of Circassians had, in the sheer spirit of hatred, lain in ambush for a return guard of some sixteen Cossacks, and killed every man.

Such facts seem to argue much weakness on the part of the Russians; but great have been the difficulties they have contended with in keeping the upper hand over enemies whose haunts are almost inaccessible to any but themselves. Several colonies of these ferocious mountaineers have been captured and transplanted to villages of their own in the plains, where they are guarded, and live as sulkily as wild beasts; and a general crusade, if I may be allowed the expression, has been talked of for some years past, to sweep such untameable enemies from the mountains, and settle them on the plains in the interior of Russia. Whatever policy is now adopted towards this people, the Russians will find it an easy task, comparatively with former times, to reduce them to obedience, since they have obtained possession of

Anapa and Poti, on the east shore of the Black Sea, where the Turks used to furnish their friends with supplies which enabled them to sustain the war.

On the morning of the 22nd we rode into Heraut: villages, and well-watered fields and gardens, crowded upon each other as we advanced into the valley, and our road lay through them to the very walls of the city. Long before we reached the town, we were met by parties of the inhabitants, who came out to welcome friends; but most of these were disappointed, the astrologers having determined that an auspicious hour for entering the city would not occur for four days. We met in the crowd a merchant, with whom we had made acquaintance at Tehran, and under his guidance proceeded to a caravansera in the city, where, as we would not engage a cell for six months, they put us into a dark and filthy hole off the range of chambers, which smelt so abominably that it was distressing to be in it. The Syud, "accoutred as he was," went out at once to search for better lodging, but was met by a servant of Abbas Khan's, whom that nobleman had kindly sent to tell us that he had ordered a small house to be cleared for our reception.

24th.—Finding it impossible to sleep in our cell, I spread my bed in the gallery which ran round the chambers, and slept comfortably till, aroused by a kick in the back, I looked up and saw an old Affghaun Moollâ standing over me. "Have you no shame," he asked, "to be sleeping an hour after prayer-time?—get up." I assured him that I was very unwell, and needed rest; but he authoritatively insisted upon my removing myself and my bed out of sight, and I had nothing for it but to obey him. I was alone in our cell later in the morning, when two men entered, one in the dress of a Syud, and seating themselves without ceremony, addressed several impertinent questions to me. The Syud was the one who chiefly spoke; he addressed me in the Hindoostânee language, desiring to know why, having set out for Bokhara, I had come down to Heraut. I declined giving an account of myself to strangers, upon which he said that I must recollect having seen him at Astrabad, when Gholam Ali Shah (an Indian derveish) and he had visited us, to make arrangements for travelling to Khiva together. I did recollect the circumstance of two Indians having called on us the day that we quitted Astrabad, but this man's face was not familiar to me; however I did not deny that I might have seen him, and thereupon he proceeded to tell me what had happened subsequent to our departure.

"When you went," he said, "and it was known that you were a Russian, there was a hue-and cry after those who had been seen to communicate with you; the Shahzadeh killed Gholam Ali Shah, and beating me within a little of my life, took to the value of one hundred tomauns from me, after which he turned me out of the town, as this man who was with me can testify; was it not so?"—"Bulli," answered his colleague, "Yes, it was just so."

Had this attack been more covert, I should have been alarmed at it; but I felt so secure, as to be amused at their rascality, seeing that they had fairly outwitted themselves, and therefore replied ironically, that I felt pleasure at being able to inform him that his friend Gholam Ali Shah was alive and well, we having dined with that person on our return from the desert; that with regard to his own particular loss, I could only regret that he had come (as in the present instance) uninvited to visit a suspicious person, and strongly recommended his taking himself off quickly, lest a similar disaster should again befall him.

This fellow had left Astrabad at the same time that we did, and therefore knew not of our having returned; but seeing that he had overshot his mark, he assumed a bullying tone, said he knew who I was, and what my object was in travelling; that I was in a country where life was held cheap, and that as a few words from him would have the effect of endangering mine, I had better not provoke him, but at once pay the money that he claimed. I now felt the want of assistance against this villain; the Syud and his protegé were away with our servant, arranging the house which Abbas Khan had lent us, and the odds would have been against me in a quarrel (an infidel against a Syud), therefore I assured him that we really had very little money, but that of what little there was the Syud kept the keys, and that if he would favour us with a visit on the morrow, we would talk the matter over; with this he was obliged to be contented, and so took his leave.

25th.—This morning we removed into Abbas Khan's house, the upper part of which, consisting of two rooms separated by a small open passage, we occupied, picketing our horses in the court below. About noon came the strange Syud, according to my invitation: I had prepared my companion to receive him, and accordingly, the moment that the man reached the head of the stair, Karaumut Ali went forward to meet him, led him to the highest seat, and quite oppressed him with asking after the state of his health. No sooner did the stranger open his mouth, than my friend addressed a florid compliment to him, "How strange and delightful it was that they should have met in Heraut again!—How little a man knew what fortune had in store for him!" &c.

I saw by the flush on the stranger's countenance that this could not last long, and presently, as if determined not to be worried out of his self-possession, he assumed a determined countenance, and asked the Syud if he knew the reason of his visit. "Something I have heard," answered the Syud, "but kindly indulge us with a full detail of your wishes."—"Then I wish to know, shortly, if you intend to restore what you caused to be extorted from me." "As shortly, then," said the Syud, altering at once his tone and manner, "we do not; and for several good reasons, Agha, the best of which is, that if we had one hundred thousand tomauns, you should not touch the value of a copper coin of them. Brother! we are no fish for your net; so be satisfied with the assurance, and do not waste time and roguery which you may employ to better purpose elsewhere." The man's face actually became

livid with rage, and when he could find utterance, he said in a choked voice, "You do not know me that you contemn me; perhaps when you have been dragged before the Shah, and skinned with whips, your tone will be different; we will have you to the ordeal of the oven,* and then it will be seen what sort of a Syud you are, leading about a professed infidel to spy all countries." "Not know you!" retorted my friend, now fairly roused, "not know you! are you not that beggar to whom I gave half a real in charity at Astrabad? Dog of a bad breed, who have now turned to bite the hand that fed you! Go! man without honesty! go thief! go rascal! go! I spit upon you." The dialogue now became shorter, both being enraged to such a degree, that they abused each other in the most unmeasured terms. "Pay me two thousand tomauns," screamed the impostor, "help against robbers!"—"Seize him!" returned the Syud; "I recognise a man who murdered my father, and stole ten thousand tomauns." Our Persian friend and our servant came in at the noise, when seeing that it would bring a crowd in upon us; we all set upon the fellow, and thrust him down the narrow staircase, he, as he was borne down backwards, a step at a time, venting the grossest abuse upon us and our ancestors, and swearing to return presently to play the very deuce with us. Some hours elapsing, without our hearing more of him, the Syud went out, and calling upon Hyder Kouli Khan (Shumloo), a Persian nobleman in Kamraun's service to whom we had an introductory letter, he mentioned the circumstance. The Khan kindly sent a man to remain at our house, but we dismissed him late in the evening, feeling satisfied that our enemy had thought better of his attempt.

We had made a party to go the next morning to visit the shrine of a famed saint, buried four miles

---

*A hot experiment upon a person's virtue, answering to our ancient test of walking upon hot irons. If Monsieur Chabert should fancy travelling in these countries, he might pass for a Syud of the first order.

from the city, therefore being awakened from sleep, and seeing a person standing in the passage in which I lay, I thought it was the Yezd merchant, and spoke to tell him that he had come too soon. Receiving no answer, I raised my head, when I saw a small party of men at the foot of my bed, and was aware that they had come from the roof, by a small flight of steps down which others were still descending. Had my sword been near me, it would have been a mere bravado to draw it against such numbers, and as they were now round the bed, I sat up, and asked the reason of my being thus broken in upon, at which one having an air of authority, called me rascal, and giving me a poke in the stomach with a long stick, bade me rise and see. "It is the kotwâl," said the man, seizing my wrist at the same time, and a second one placing himself on my other hand, they led me into the room in which slept the Syud, whom I found standing on his bed, held by the wrists by two or three armed persons, and threatening all the intruders with the vengeance of Shah Kamrann, for whom we had letters.

There had been talk about the felek* and sticks to beat us, but at the Syud's words our hands were loosed, and the armed men stood across the door, while the kotwâl seated himself and ordered lights. Our terrified servant ventured up from the court in which he had been sleeping, and lighted a lamp at a lantern which they had brought with them; I then observed our visitor of the morning, who, leaning forward, said in a low sarcastic tone to the Syud,—*"Have you seen? can I make good my words?"* He, and three or four others who were respectable looking men, sat down near the kotwâl; we also seated ourselves, and the magistrate proceeded to examine us à la Dogberry.

Keraumut Ali, who had recovered his temper, was not to be daunted by the kotwâl's high tone, and answered with an air of great nonchalance to the queries put, that I was an English officer trav-

---

*A bar of wood to which a culprit's feet are fastened, so as to expose the sole when he is laid on his back to be bastinadoed.

elling to India, no Russian, and no thief to be broken in upon at midnight, against all law and decency; that he was a Syud of Hindoostan, and my fellow traveller: as for that *goorumsauk* (scoundrel), said he, "who has come to forswear himself, let him look to his own skin."

"Now for *your* story," said the kotwâl to the Indian. "Bulli!" answered this villain, "by your excellent leave I beg to state that I knew these men six months ago. (Would to God I had never met them, I should not then be as I am.) I was at Damghaun, I beg to state, about to set off with a kafilah, when these men, and another who is not with them now, came up to me and asked what I was cooking; I replied kitcherree (a dish of rice and peas), upon which they invited me to eat with them, saying that they would treat me to better fare. I at first declined, but they pressed me much, so I went, I beg to state, and they gave me sweetmeats, which as soon as I had eaten I felt my head go round, and my eyes grow larger and larger, and I became without sense. My companion also partook, as he will tell you," looking round for his ally, who apparently not well pleased with the part he had been brought to play, had taken place among the men at arms, and whom we now noticed for the first time. "A whole day and night," continued the Indian, "we lay stupified, and when we came to ourselves, the kafilah was not; our horses were picketed near, but the prisoners were gone, having taken with them a carpet bag, in which were eight hundred tomauns, two muslin caps, and a piece of kimcob. I saw no more of them till the day before yesterday, when I recognised them as they rode into the town, and having ascertained their residence, for I beg to state that they have changed their lodgings more than once, I laid my request before your consideration! Further, what shall I petition? my case is in your hands, to recover pe-money, or to deal with these men as seems most fit to your excellent judgment."

"Ullah!" said the kotwâl, at the end of this wild story, "is it thus that a traveller and a Syud is robbed? Bring forward their effects, mayhap some of the stolen property may be forthcoming."

"What is the Darogha's name?" asked the Syud, with perfect self-possession, of one who sat near. "Meerza Agha," was the answer. "Then, Meerza Agha," said my friend, coolly, "you have no law for what you are going to do, that is, if the men of Heraut are Mooselmauns: we are no *shraubee kabaubees* (revellers on wine and kabaubs), that you should take us by storm, and do offence to your dignity by clambering in by the roof of our house. That man has told nothing but lies; we never were at Damghaun, for we came by the direct road through Mazenderaun to Astrabad, where he saw us; if you suspect us, bring us and our accuser before the Cazee in open day, but do not forget that we are guests of Abbas Khan, and that violence to us is offence to him: further, before you treat this man with indignity, know who he is, and see a letter which we have for the Shah."

This letter, which had been given me by Sir John Macdonald, was directed to Shahzadeh Kamraun, news of Mahmoud's death not having reached Tabreez when I started: the kotwâl, looking at the superscription, pronounced it a forgery, and throwing it from him, proceeded to the examination of our effects, causing search to be made even into the pockets of our dresses, and under the corners of the carpets. Had we been thieves, there was nothing in our baggage to prove us such; we were not possessed of a sous, scarcely of any thing worth one, and except, in his estimation, a rather superfluous quantity of shirts, the kotwâl found nothing to call forth an exclamation. Two or three books which lay on a shelf, were handed down to Meerza Agha by one of his obsequious myrmidons as they hunted about the room, and one of them chanced to be a receipt-book for Indian cookery. "Ah!" exclaimed the kotwâl, when he had looked into it, "hence the receipt for that intoxicating food which took away the senses of this unfortunate person; say, O man! what are these?" But the Syud, seeing the silliness of our inquisitor,

and observing that his own address had produced a favourable effect upon those who attended, took the book, and adroitly quizzed the magistrate, reading out receipts for well-known good dishes, and hinting that if they had been at all injurious in their effects, Meerza Agha would not have been in such good case: a servant of Abbas Khan's too now coming in, and, I imagine, warning him confidentially who I was, the kotwâl said, with an affectation of dignity, that he would have the matter sifted on the morrow, and that we were not to consider ourselves at liberty to leave the house until he authorized us to do so. We had an opportunity of showing our civility by letting the party out at the door, but we had reason to regret that they did not retire as they came, by the house-top, as some of them cut the blankets from our horses' backs and carried them off.

This outrage having been committed in the house of a nobleman high in favour with Shah Kamraun, we guessed who had ordered it, and the next day recognising as men of rank, two of those who had accompanied the kotwâl, we had no doubt upon the subject, and resolved to sit down quietly under the affront; indeed, we were congratulated upon it by our friends, who assured us that we might now travel where we would, since no one could possibly suppose us possessed of any thing valuable, if the kotwâl had not found it. I need scarcely say that we did not consider ourselves bound by that worthy's arrest, and that we were no more troubled either by him or by the Indian. The latter, we learned shortly after, having made the place too hot to hold him, had taken himself quietly away, and gone, it was supposed, to Candahar; intelligence which only interested us so far as to make us resolve to be on the look-out for a rascal whose villainy we might not be able to defeat where we had no patrons.

The Syud had in the city of Heraut a long intimate, and very excellent friend, Hadjee Moollâ Ramazaun, a Sheah divine, who, for his great age and his good character, was looked up to by every body in the place. We called upon the old gentleman, and he carried his kindness so far as to promise to introduce me properly to the Sirdar after his entry, so as to ensure me good treatment, and the means of intercourse with the Shah if I desired it. "It is perhaps the part of Abbas Khan," said the old Hadjee, "seeing that you are his guests; but he was my pupil, and dare not be offended with me; moreover, as I am an old man, and probably, save the mark! as much in the esteem of the Sirdar as any one, my introduction may serve you most. Have you any present to offer the Sirdar? any thing uncommon? 'Yaik cheesee, Yaik taroofee,' a something or other; a compliment, just to mark your respect: all men like to be approached with an offering, let it be ever so trifling, and, between ourselves, the direction of most affairs here rests with Yar Mohummud Khan." The only things that we possessed, capable of being offered to so great a personage, were a few penknives, and some cases of fine gunpowder. These the Hadjee said would be sufficient to show our wish to be attentive, and he undertook the delivery of them.

27th.—Early this morning a great Peshwaz went out to meet the army and welcome it to the city. The Sirdar hit the exact minute for entering the gate, and proceeded at once with the chiefs of the army to audience of the Shah, making their salutes to him as he sat in open durbar. Moollâ Mohummud was in high spirits, for he and his father-in-law had been the astrologers called upon to determine the fortunate hour, and the generalissimo had been so favourably *accueillé* on his return, that he had promised to give our friend a fine colt. "I thought you took an oath against ever wearing boots again," said the Syud jocularly to him. "I did, and I will be true to my word."— "Then what good will the colt do you?"—"Oh! I will give it to one of the khans here, who will return me something more in my way."

About sunrise on the morning of the twenty-eighth, we went with Hadjee Moollâ Ramazaun to see the Sirdar. At the outer portal of the minister's quarters we met three servants, one of whom carried on his back an elderly and respectable-looking man, who had been beaten on the soles of his feet until he could not stand upon them. In great pain as he evidently was, he did not forget the respect due to our old friend, ordering his bearer to stand on the side of the path to let the Hadjee pass: the latter shook his head, and on our inquiring what fault the man had committed, we were told that he had been in the habit of beating an obstreperous wife, as he considered her, who petitioned the king, and obtained a royal mandate for her better treatment; but the husband, like a good Mohummudan, choosing rather to be guided by the law which authorizes the faithful to beat their wives *à discrétion*, corrected his lady for her next fault, upon which she sought the refuge of the Shah's harem, and his majesty ordered her spouse to be beaten as we saw, for disregarding his injunctions. The woman, once within the walls of the Shah's harem, could never pass it again, and if the man cared in the least for her (as it is to be presumed he did, by his taking such trouble to correct her), he was thereby punished, not to say that he was more than sufficiently so, by the scandal of his wife's *bona gratia* divorce, and doubtless the Hadjee shook his head because Kamraun had exercised his power at the expense of the law; but it was amusing to an European to hear what, according to our civil code, would be considered a commonly just interposition of authority, stigmatized as an act of unwarranted interference, an impeachment of the rights of man.—"Agha Jan," said an acquaintance to whom we related what we had seen, "*Een zoolm ust!*" "This is oppression!"

The Hadjee led us through several enclosed courts into a small one, at a door leading from which were seated a couple of withered eunuchs, who, after a little demur, allowed us to pass into a paved square, in which were the quarters of the Sirdar's brother, a singularly manly and handsome nobleman, whom we found superbly dressed in shawl cloth, seated at the head of a select company, entertaining them with an account of the events of the late campaign, romancing considerably, as was to be expected from a man so connected, and who had not taken part in the expedition, telling how "the troops of the Shah had gone to the assistance of the troops of the Shah of Persia," and how, Inshallah, they had gotten themselves a name all over Iran, &c. We sat here long, in expectation of the Sirdar's coming out, and then our old friend, leading us down into the court below, bade us stay there while he went to speak privately with the minister. During the half-hour that we were kept here, the court was gradually filled by those who had influence enough to obtain the entrée, and some feroshes, bringing in bundles of long willows, cut them into proper lengths, and threw them into a basin that occupied the centre of the court, to keep fresh till any one should be ordered to receive the bastinado.

At last Sirdar Yar Mohummud Khan came out, attended by a few particular friends, the chief of whom was Hadjee Moollâ Ramazaun, who, beckoning us to keep near him, desired a ferosh to look to us; a necessary precaution, for the great man was presently lost in the crowd who hurried round him to offer their compliments: he took some to his bosom, and gave his joined hands to the less distinguished, moving across the court the while, as well as he could, to a flight of steps which led to a large upper room: the crowd pressed after him with little regard to order, and but for the assistance of the ferosh, we might not have obtained place in the apartment. When we were all seated on our heels, nearly as many as the room would contain, Hadjee Moollâ Ramazaun, who was on the right of the Sirdar, sat up, and with a manner which was rendered peculiarly impressive by his venerable appearance, gave thanks for the Sirdar's happy return, and prayed for a blessing upon him, the company joining in the wish, passing their hands down their beards at the conclusion, and repeating severally, "Ulláho Ukbur." Then the Sirdar was particularly

greeted by friends among the company: "Shé raughlé Sirdar! Sirdar, shé raughlé." "You are welcome, Sirdar." He answered them nearly in the same words, and looked round the apartment, nodding kindly to those who met his eye.

When we saw Yar Mohummud Khan in camp, he struck me as rather a course, vulgar-looking man; looking at him now, as he sat, handsomely dressed, in the seat of honour, he appeared to be a person of considerable dignity: his thick black beard had been combed out to its length, and a pair of large dark eyes animated with the pleasure that he felt at the attentions lavished upon him, gave an intelligent expression to what otherwise would have been a heavy countenance. He was now at the pinnacle of court favour; premier, and commander-in-chief; and his brothers held all the good appointments that Kamraun had in his gift. When we inquired if the Shah was going to march upon Candahar, we were answered, "That depends upon the Sirdar; we shall see what he will advise." Our audience did not last long; the Hadjee's rising to take leave was a signal for the rest of the company to retire, and we dispersed to our homes. Our friend told us on the way that the Sirdar was well disposed towards us, and that he would take an early opportunity of explaining to the Shah who I was.

In the evening we went to see Abbas Khan, whom we found engaged in the ceremonious task of receiving a crowd of visitors of different ranks, "deed wo bâz deed," as they term it, or the interchange of visits; a person of any consideration, returning home from travel, being formally waited upon by all the respectable men of the place, whose visits to a certain extent he is obliged to return.

Among the men of degree seated with him, Abbas Khan introduced us to the Attar Bâshee, or apothecary-general, a man so entirely in the confidence of the Shah, that he was scarcely ever out of the private apartments in the palace, honour which, to look at his wasted figure and sunken eye, he had earned at some cost. He must have been a man of merit, for he contrived to enjoy the favour of the Shah, keep on good terms with the minister at war, and please all classes of the people. His original rank was that of a druggist in the city, in which capacity he enjoyed a consideration which eventually led in a singular manner to his rise. When Prince Hadjee Ferooz Oodeen, after a long rule at Heraut, was seized and plundered by Futteh Khan, his chief officers, fearing lest their effects should be confiscated, privately confided their valuables to the care of the druggist, who, it was thought, would not be suspected; but Shahzadeh Kamraun coming to Heraut shortly after, received intimation of the circumstance, and set about possessing himself of the wealth. The Attar was asleep in the interior of his house one night, when he was broken in upon by a party of thieves: he awoke at the noise of their entrance, and would have given the alarm, but glancing at the intruders, he saw that Kamraun was one of them; so covering his head with the bedclothes, he lay quiet, and suffered them to break boxes and carry off what they sought. From that time he had gradually risen to dignity, and a short time before, having watched Kamraun through a dangerous illness, he had quite won the favour of the monarch, who, it was said, trusted him with all his secrets.

It so happened that our Persian companion, Agha Hossein, was related to the Attâr Bâshee, and as he had told our history, the minister bowed graciously when Abbas Khan introduced us, and took charge of the letter for Kamraun which had been rejected by the kotwâl. The latter worthy was seated among the visitors when we entered, and appeared ill at his ease when Abbas Khan introduced me as an Elchee from the great Elchee at Tehraun, a gentleman of distinction, his friend and guest, and the Syud, as a man of the highest acquirements, and a person in every way to be esteemed. My friend's eye sparkled at the opportunity, and in the most cutting manner, yet with an air of studied politeness, he told our host that we

were already so fortunate as to know the kotwâl, he having conferred upon us the honour of a visit only the second night of our arrival; and he quizzed the magistrate with so much address, that though the man could have stabbed him for his sarcasms, he could not well openly take exception at the words. A young Affghaun nobleman named Shumshoodden Khan, a favourite of the Shah's, who had married his said beautiful sister, occupied the seat next to the Attâr Bashee: he appeared to enjoy the joke much, and doubtless so did our host, though he was too well bred, on such an occasion, to show resentment for the indignity put upon his guests.

My coming caused the conversation to turn upon Frang, which they understood to be a different country from that inhabited by the Oroos. In comparison with the Russian, I found that neither my countrymen, nor the people of any other European nation, were considered of consequence: indeed some conceived from his title, Imperatoore-Azum, "The Supreme Emperor," that the Russian Autocrat gave the law to the kings of Europe. Wonderful things were asserted of the Oroos, particularly about their military deeds. Shumshooddeen Khan, who engrossed much of the conversation, among other things, told the company that no fort could hold out against this people, for that they never stopped at a ditch, marching soldiers into it until it was filled, and so on over their heads to the storm; and our host, whom I had credited for better sense, said he understood that on a certain occasion provisions falling short in his army, the General-e Oroos gave orders that fifty thousand men should be killed and served out as rations. "*Ullah ho Rubbee!*" ejaculated an old Affghaun gentleman, "God is my protector! Is it possible? why they are cannibals, and must have a larger army than Timour had."

I could scarcely believe Abbas Khan was not speaking in jest, but he seemed quite serious, and I really believe mentioned the anecdote to illustrate the discipline of the Russian army: certainly his company credited the story; but what bounds can be set to the credulity of men who believe that the Chinese are such skilful mechanics, that they can make horses which will go for two or three days, and sell them as real animals? Abbas Khan made us return to dinner, and was as good as his promise at Meshed, establishing us in the house which had been emptied for our accommodation, frequently seeking our society, and endeavouring to make our time pass agreeably.

3 / The Court and Camp of Runjeet Sing (1840)

W. G. OSBORNE

The Sikh Raj, led by the formidable Ranjit Singh, was more than a backdrop to British struggles for Afghanistan: it was part of an old, even ancient, rivalry between native kingdoms in the region, in which Sikh-Afghan conflicts played a major role. Singh (1780–1839) spent his life consolidating an empire based in the Punjab at the expense of a number of local power brokers, the Barakzai tribe of Dost Mohammad, emir of Afghanistan, among them. In this selection, W. G. Osborne, military secretary to George Eden (Lord Auckland), the governor-general of India, records his mission to the maharaja, where they exchange views on troop strength and other matters. Though Singh died in 1839, the same year that Kabul fell to the British, his dynastic legacy—chiefly through his pacification of the Punjab—was critical to Anglo-Afghan relations well into the 1840s, if not beyond.

Cross-legged in a golden chair, dressed in simple white, wearing no ornaments but a single string of enormous pearls round the waist, and the celebrated Koh-y-nur, or mountain of light, on his arm,—(the jewel rivalled, if not surpassed, in brilliancy by the glance of fire which every now and then shot from his single eye as it wandered restlessly round the circle,)—sat the lion of Lahore.

On Runjeet's seating himself, his chiefs all squatted on the floor round his chair, with the exception of Dheean Sing, who remained standing behind his master.

After dinner, we repaired to a terrace on the banks of the canal, where we found eight young ladies assembled, and a display of fire-works prepared for our amusement on the opposite bank.

The four Cachemirian girls were very pretty; and one of them, Sabhoo by name, would have been thought beautiful anywhere. They were richly and gracefully dressed in scarlet and gold embroidered shawl dresses, with large and enormously loose petticoats of handsomely worked silk. Their head ornaments were singular and very becoming; their glossy black hair hanging down the back in a number of long plaits, with gold coins and small bunches of pearls suspended to the ends, enormous strings of pearl for earrings, and large gold rings, with several pearls and emeralds attached to them, passed through their noses. They are very fair, with expressive countenances, and large and lovely eyes, but their beauty is much disfigured by the custom which prevails amongst all the Mogul women of covering the lower eyelid with gold leaf, which gives them a ghastly appearance.

One of these girls, called the Lotus, is rather a celebrated character at the court of Lahore. Ranjeet Singh received her with the tribute of Cachemire about two years ago, when she was said to have been very beautiful. He fell violently in love with her, and fancied that his affection was as violently returned. One evening in the course of conversation with Monsieur Ventura, an Italian officer in his service, when the girl was dancing before them, he made some remark upon her attachment to him, which he declared was purely disinterested, and too strong to be shaken by any offers of advantage or affection she might receive from other quarters. Ventura was incredulous; and Ranjeet Singh, highly indignant at this doubt of his powers of attraction, defied him to seduce her, and promised to put no obstacles in his way, further than stipulating that she should be placed in the customary seclusion of his zenana. After several polite speeches on the part of Ventura upon the impropriety of his attempting to rival his sovereign, the challenge was accepted, and the young lady immediately transferred to the royal seraglio, with every precaution to ensure her safety . . .

Scarce had eight-and-forty hours elapsed ere the hoary old lion of Lahore was aroused from his happy dreams of love and affection by the intelligence that his guards were faithless, his harem violated, and himself deserted, and that the lovely Lotus had, nothing loth, been transplanted from her royal lover's garden to the Italian's, where she was then blooming in all her native beauty.

Ranjeet Singh bore her desertion with great equanimity, and in a short time she returned to her allegiance, and is now enrolled in his corps of Amazons. She has lately been very ill, and is said to be much altered in appearance, but is still a very lovely girl.

31st May.—Faqueer Uzeez-oodeen called to say that the Maharajah would receive the mission this morning, for the purpose of hearing Lord Auckland's letter read; and at 9 o'clock we accordingly proceeded to the palace, where we found Runjeet seated as on the former occasion. After a few inquiries and compliments, he proceeded to his private apartments, and in the course of a few minutes we were requested to follow him. He was sitting cross-legged in a large silver chair, very much resembling in shape what is called a *hip bath*, with Heera Sing seated at his side, and Dheean Sing standing behind his chair. Rajah Govind Juss, (his *vakeel** to our resident at Loodhiana,) the old Faqueer, and Sirdar Liana Sing, were sitting at his feet.

The Governor General's letter was then read to him by Mr. Mc Naghten, and the part he was expected to take in concert with the British Government, for the restoration of Shah Sooja-ool-mulk to the throne of Cabul explained to him, giving him to understand, at the same time, that if he preferred taking his own course, and relying solely upon his own military force, he was at perfect liberty to do so; but that if he should choose the other line, a British force would be ready to march, and cooperate with his own. Dheean Sing here shewed manifest tokens of disapprobation; and though not daring to make any remark, could not refrain from expressing, both by his countenance and sundry ominous shakes of the head, his dissatisfaction at the idea of any alliance with us.

Runjeet Sing, on the contrary, agreed to the arrangement with the greatest apparent cordiality and eagerness; and after an audience of two hours, we took our leave of him, it having been settled that all minor arrangements should be made hereafter.

We have broken the ice, and so far proceeded with flying colours, and may venture to hope

*Vakeel, agent or envoy.

that our visit will not be prolonged many more days; but Runjeet is, I fear, far too selfish not to endeavour to obtain an equivalent, in some shape or other, for his promised assistance, and the permission to march an army through his country. His hatred of Dost Mahommed, and the hope of seeing him driven from his kingdom, may do much, but I have little doubt that, cordial and willing as he now appears, he will yet find some difficulty to throw in the way of any final arrangement. After our departure, all his chiefs endeavoured to persuade him to reject all cooperation with or assistance from us, and to take his own independent course; to which he replied, that having made up his mind, he wished to hear nothing more said on the subject. In the course of the evening, we had the usual music and fireworks.

1st June.—Agreeably to invitation, we repaired this morning to meet the Maharajah, and see some of his regular infantry upon their parade. We found about two thousand men under arms, and some foot artillery. They are a fine-looking body of men, dressed in white jackets and trowsers, with black belts and pouches, and wear the yellow Sihk turban. They submit willingly to the same discipline and regulations as our own Sipahis, but have a prejudice against wearing a cap or shako, and previous to their enlistment make an agreement that they shall not be required to do so, or to shave.

They work in three ranks, and do everything by beat of drum, according to the French fashion; are not what is called well set up, but beautifully steady on parade, and fire with greater precision and regularity, both volleys and file firing, than any other troops I ever saw. They are paid the same as the Company's Sipahis, or rather are promised that such will be the case, though they are frequently upwards of a year, and seldom less than ten months, in arrears. When they are half-starved, and growing desperate, and Runjeet thinks they will bear no more, he makes a compromise with them, and giving half or one-third of what is due to them,

half frightens and half cheats them into giving up all further claims. They are finer men, I think, than the Company's Sipahis, have fewer prejudices than most natives, and are more easily managed; and though, as a nation, the Sihks are generally supposed to be wanting in courage, it is impossible to deny that Runjeet's troops have occasionally fought well. They are tall, rather slight, but very manly-looking men, with great length of limb, and broad, open chests; are excellent marchers, both as regards speed and bottom, for they are capable of making very long marches, not only on emergencies, but have done so with cheerfulness and alacrity for days together. They are hardy far beyond the generality of natives, and seem a merry, light-hearted race of people. All their movements on parade are very steady, but much too slow; they have but one pace for everything, and the double step is unknown to them.

The Sihk army possesses one great advantage over our own—the ease with which it can be moved. No wheel carriage is allowed on a march, their own bazars carry all they require; and thirty thousand of their troops could be moved with more facility, and less expense and loss of time, than three Company's regiments on this side the Sutlege.

At the conclusion of the field day, I accompanied Runjeet for some distance on his usual morning's excursion. He asked me if I had ever seen any Burmese troops; on my replying in the negative, he said, I have heard that they fight well, and beat your Sipahis. I told him that they fought well behind their stockades, but could not face us on a fair field; and that the Goorkhas were, I thought, a braver race and better soldiers. "True," he remarked; "they are fine fellows. I have got a regiment of them at Lahore which I will shew you." "How many troops have you got in this country altogether?" "About two hundred thousand." "So I have been told; but you could not bring that number into the field at once, or at any one place?" "Certainly not; it is unnecessary. Twenty, or at the most, thirty thousand British troops could march from one end of India to the other, and no power in the country could stop them." "You are fine fellows; how many Frenchmen can an Englishman beat?" "At school, in England, the boys are always taught to consider themselves equal to three Frenchmen." "And how many Russians?" "The French beat the Russians, and we beat the French." "If the Russians cross the Indus, what force could you bring against them?" "Quite enough to drive them back, with your Highness for our ally." "Wah! wah! so we will." I asked him some particulars about his Goorkha regiments, and how he managed to recruit for them, as we found the greatest difficulty in keeping our own two regiments complete, from the jealousy of the Nepaulese. He replied, that he found difficulty himself; but that by paying them much higher than any other troops, he managed to keep his regiment in very serviceable order. The truth I afterwards ascertained to be, that not above one man in twenty is a real Goorkha, but they come principally from Cachemire; and as they are small and active men, they answer very well for the purpose of hill warfare.

At the conclusion of our interview, Runjeet asked me to come and see his artillery practice on the following morning, which I promised to do; and making my salaam, galloped off to my tent to breakfast. It is quite impossible to recollect the number of his questions with sufficient accuracy to write them down; but those I do remember I have written in his own words.

4 / A Narrative of the Russian Military Expedition to Khiva, under General Perofski (1839)

This excerpt details why Czar Nicholas I determined to mount a campaign to take Khiva (Uzbekistan) in 1839, ostensibly to protect Russian trading interests there, but ultimately to secure greater Russian influence in the region. This occurred almost simultaneously with the British launch of the First Anglo-Afghan War. General Vasily Alekseevich Perovsky (1794–1857), governor of Orenburg, led the unsuccessful invasion. Though not the same kind of debacle as the British retreat from Kabul in 1842, Perovsky's defeat suggests how defensively the Russians played the Great Game as well. Brought back to the region in the 1850s, he did eventually subdue Khiva and thus helped to strengthen the Russian empire's hand in central Asia in midcentury.

No one can seriously affirm that the English are not anxious for the welfare of other nations, but each, we trust, will agree with us when we say that, nevertheless, the interests of England are held by them as paramount to everything. It is also generally known that the English have from remote times diligently watched the progress of events in the whole world (in the interest of Great Britain be it observed), and that they are always troubled and dissatisfied if fate allows any other nation to have influence over the progress of mankind; this is the policy of the ancient Phoenicians and Carthaginians, and of the more modern Venetians, Genoese, Spaniards, and Dutch; in one word, this is the policy of maritime and commercial powers.

It is not astonishing, therefore, that the English, not being thoroughly acquainted with the existing state of affairs in Central Asia, should have been considerably alarmed at the Russian proceedings in the Kirghiz Steppe, and have attributed the measures adopted by the Russian Government for securing the boundaries and trade of the Empire to aggressive projects, and even to the old project of penetrating into India, the possibility of which was again recalled to their recollection by the first Napoleon's well-known scheme of an overland expedition to India. Hence arose a natural desire on the part of the English to ascertain the real importance in political respects of the possession of the Central Asiatic Steppes by Russia, and the possibility of penetrating from this side into India.

From 1824, therefore, a succession of English Agents, regardless of all obstacles, penetrate into Central Asia, and even some of them return to their native country through Russia.

At first (in the year 1830), many Englishmen, under motives ostensibly evangelical, settled themselves in the town of Orenburg; but when it was perceived that these Missionaries turned their attention to other matters, they were requested to leave. Losing all hope of extending their influence in Central Asia from the side of Russia, the English commenced penetrating thither principally from India and through Persia. Thus from 1824 Central Asia had been visited by Moorcroft, Connoly, Wolf, Burns, and Strange, and later by Stoddard, Abbot, Shakespere, and again by Burns near the time of the Russian Khiva Expedition, or during the very period.

All the persons here enumerated, with the exception of Wolf, were in the employ of the enterprizing East India Company, and, of course, it was not curiosity alone and their own affairs that allured them into Central Asia. While these English agents were collecting every possible information on the spot, the Russians had no means of following this example, and were even unacquainted with their movements; the visits of these English agents to the various Khanats and the details of their journeys became only known to Russia incidentally through their published works, which, of course, did not contain all the results of their investigations. All the information that the Russians procured was meagre and obscure, and was supplied to them by Asiatics, who either through ignorance or timidity were not always able to furnish really important and useful accounts: owing to a want of officials well acquainted with the Oriental languages, it was found necessary to confide in uneducated Asiatics, or to employ agents who, being ignorant of the Oriental languages, were obliged to have interpreters attached to them. The principal purveyors of intelligence to the Russians were consequently almost always Mahomedans, who being involuntarily under the influence of the Rulers of Central Asia, in whom under the régime of Mahomedanism was also centred the highest ecclesiastical power, did not discharge their duties very willingly, nor in a reliable manner they were not always able to disclose all they knew, and were altogether very uncertain media of communication, notwithstanding that, as Mahomedans, they had in every respect much greater facilities than Christians for gaining access to the different countries of Central Asia.

Already in 1828 Alexander Burns commenced his survey of the River Indus, and having become convinced in 1830 of the navigability of the Indus over its whole course of about 700 miles, he represented to the English Government all the importance of this river, both in political and commercial respects. At the same time some Russian goods which had by accident found their way to the banks of the Indus, led him to the conclusion that rivalry between the Russian and English manufactures had already commenced at this point, and he not only succeeded in convincing his Government of this false supposition, but also induced it to believe in the possibility of the appearance of Russian political agents on the River Indus, and even of a Russian force.

Here then we have an explanation of the repeated attempts made by English agents to penetrate from India through the whole of Central Asia as far as the Russian boundaries, in order to assure themselves of the justness or otherwise of these apprehensions, and these movements on the part of the English were at the same time a source of serious alarm to the Russian Government.

The Russians had reliable information that the agents of the East India Company were continually appearing either at Khiva or Bukhara; they were also aware that this enterprizing Company having enormous means at its command was endeavouring not only to establish its commercial influence throughout the whole of Asia, but was also desirous of extending the limits of its Asiatic possessions. The law of England, the industry and wealth of the people, the tendency of the English to act in unison in commercial associations, and lastly the cupidity of the Asiatic Rulers,—all this supplied the English with great facilities for strengthening their influence in Central Asia, the principal market for Russian manufactured goods, and for doing her serious damage by establishing regular commercial relations with Central Asia; it was only necessary to allow the possibility of the English supplying the Khivans and Turkmen the nearest and most hostile neighbours of Russia, and likewise the Kirghizes, with arms and ammunition in order to become convinced of the necessity of counteracting the schemes of England, whose agents did not even try to conceal their hopes, in their published accounts, of becoming masters not only of the whole trade between the River Indus and the Hindoo Kush, but likewise of the market of Bukhara, the most important in Central Asia.

It was accordingly decided in 1835, in order to watch the English agents and counteract their efforts, to send Russian agents into Central Asia, and to establish a Russian Company so as to enable Russia to compete then with the English trade. Although a small trading Company was formed after the Khiva expedition, when the Steppes were rendered comparatively safe, the Company soon suspended operations. At the same time, in order to watch the march of events in Central Asia, Sub-Lieutenant Vitkevitch was despatched thither in the capacity of agent: in the winter of 1835 he accidentally got to Bukhara accompanied by some Kirghizes, and without concealing the fact of his being a Russian Officer, spent several months at Bukhara, and returned safely to Orenburg, proving his aptitude for such a mission. This Officer travelled several years in Persia and Caboul during the most interesting period of the English expedition to Afghanistan, contrived to acquire the friendship of Dost Mahomed of Caboul, whom he succeeded in disposing favorably towards Russia,

and returned to Petersburg in 1839. Unfortunately, in the same year, he committed suicide, destroying before his death all the materials he had collected.

Meanwhile the intelligence which reached the Russians from Central Asia in 1839 gave rise to further apprehensions. Tulia-Bergan, a caravan leader, on his return from Bukhara in the same year, reported "that 25 English had arrived at Khiva from Caboul with offers to the Khan of troops and money against the Russians." The reports of the appearance of English agents and of their persistent interference in the relations between Khiva and Russia received still greater confirmation at later periods, and as at this time the English forces had penetrated into Caboul, whence they had expelled Dost-Mahomed, who was favorable to Russia, and were only divided from the territory of Bukhara by the Hindoo Kush; it was to these circumstances that the vacillation of the Khan of Khiva in the matter of the surrender of the Russian prisoners was attributed at Orenburg. It was, therefore, of the greatest importance to hasten the expedition for the punishment of Khiva, so as to prevent the English from supporting the resistance of this Khanat against Russia, and to anticipate the possibility of any other Central Asiatic Rulers being induced to join Khiva by means of any threats and promises of reward that might be employed by the English agents.

The English agents who were in Central Asia during the years 1839 and 1840 were Abbot and Shakspeare. In May 1840 Captain Abbot, of the East India Company's service, reached Novo-Alexandrofsk Fortress from Khiva, and proceeded thence to Orenburg. Whether Abbot had the intention to return home through Russia, or whether, like Burns, he selected this route for the purpose of making a survey of the Caspian and of the Russian fortresses on it, is subject to much doubt; in his communications, however, he styled himself English Chargé d'Affaires to the Russian

Court, by the order of the Khan he was robbed and wounded on his route to the Caspian by a gang of Turkomans (who had even been instructed by the Khivans to kill him), and from Orenburg he was sent in a suitable manner to Petersburg, whilst the Afghans that had accompanied him were sent back to their native country. Shakspeare, the other English officer, reached Orenburg via Novo-Alexandrofsk with the Russian prisoners who had been released from Khiva; he was likewise immediately sent on to Petersburg. Both these agents strove to take an active part in the Russian affairs with Khiva, especially Shakspeare, who wished to take credit for the release of the Russian prisoners; these, however, prior to his arrival at Khiva, had been collected and registered by the Russian Cornet Aïtof, which circumstance will be more fully dwelt on in the following chapters. Shakspeare even quarrelled on the road with the Khiva Envoy Ataniaz, in charge of the Russian prisoners, about the gifts sent to the Russian Court, alleging that their delivery had been entrusted to him, and during his stay at Orenburg, he likewise attempted to interfere in local political matters, but was told that everything of a political nature was decided at Petersburg, whither he was despatched.

From all this, it will appear that the main objects in view in a war with Khiva were—

a. —To secure permanently the south-eastern boundaries of the empire by the subjugation of the Kirghiz Horde, which could not be effected without the punishment of Khiva, the chief author of all disturbances in the Khirghiz Steppes.

b. —To secure the Russian trade with Central Asia by putting a stop to the plundering of caravans, and this also could not be carried out without the punishment of Khiva.

c. —To release several thousands of Russians from cruel bondage.

d. —To establish not the dominion, but the strong influence of Russia in the neighbouring Khanats for the reciprocal advantages of trade, and to prevent the influence of the East India Company in Central Asia, so dangerous to Russia, from taking root in Central Asia, and lastly

e. —To take advantage of this favorable opportunity for the scientific exploration of Central Asia, by making a survey of the shores of the Sea of Aral and of the mouth of the River Amu, and settling the long disputed question of the original course of this river to the Caspian.

PART II

The First Anglo-Afghan War, 1839–1842: Occupation, Rout, Defeat, Captivity

In order to secure India against what they believed to be plans for a Russian invasion, the British sought an alliance with the emir of Afghanistan, Dost Mohammad Khan. Though he initially seemed favorably disposed—he welcomed the British envoy Alexander Burnes to his court—the British did not trust him to rebuff Russian overtures, and in March 1839 the British dispatched troops through the Bolan Pass. Kandahar was taken; Shah Shujah—the deposed Durrani ruler—was installed as the fifth emir of Afghanistan; and Kabul was occupied. Dost Mohammad fled but was captured in 1840 and exiled to India. But anti-occupation forces were never totally quelled. Burnes was murdered in November 1841 in the context of an insurrection; the assassination of another British envoy, Sir William Macnaghten, at the hands of Dost Mohammad's son, Akbar Khan, followed in December. The British were forced to retreat from Kabul, with the infamous massacre and rout of Major General William Elphinstone's army ensuing in January 1842. British officers, soldiers, and camp followers were taken into captivity. Kabul was retaken by the fall of 1842 and the British withdrew via the Khyber Pass. By 1846 Dost Mohammad was back in Afghanistan, where he continued to be a significant player until his death in 1863.

5 / *Narrative of the War in Affghanistan* (1840)

HENRY HAVELOCK

Though better known for his role in the Indian Mutiny of 1857, when he died of dysentery after helping to lift the siege of Cawnpore, Henry Havelock (1795–1857) served under Major General Sir Robert Sale in Afghanistan and left one of the liveliest chronicles of the war up to 1840. In this excerpt from the second volume of his *Narrative of the War in Affghanistan in 1838–39*, Havelock records the British approach to the city of Candahar in rich detail. We can appreciate what British officers and soldiers would have seen through this comprehensive urban tour, which highlights the fortifications, the bazaar, the mansions, and the sepulchers of past and future rulers. Though he did not himself witness it, Havelock reconstructs the ceremony of Shah Shujah's installment as emir of Afghanistan following Britain's support of him against Dost Mohammad. It was a spectacle the city's residents took little joy in—a sign of their discontent with their new "puppet" ruler and British occupation more generally.

Though we had yet found no enemy capable of opposing our progress, it was not without some feeling of exultation that we moved across the plains towards the walls of Candahar. The length of the route since we had left our own provinces, the noble river, and lofty mountain ranges which we had crossed, the desert tracts and arid plains which we had traversed, the privations which our troops had endured, and the harassing and vexatious, though paltry attacks to which they had been subjected, all forced themselves upon our recollection as we gazed upon the city, the possession of which was the present recompence of our exertions.

Candahar is situated on an extensive level, which is bounded on the north and west by picturesque mountains of primitive rock. The city is quadrangular, and its defences uniform. They consist of a wall of mud hardened by exposure to the sun, thirty-three feet in height, without *revetement* of stone or brick. The *enciente* is divided into curtains and semi-circular towers, is strengthened by a low *fausse braye*, and defended by a ditch ten feet in depth and twenty-four in width, at present only imperfectly filled with water, but which could in a few hours be well supplied from the canals of the Urghundab that intersect the city. The southern side of this vast area is thirteen hundred, the northern, eleven hundred, the eastern, sixteen hundred, and the western (which is, in fact, two sides meeting in a large angle,) nineteen hundred feet in length. There are four great gates in this extensive *shuhur-punah*.* The northern is entitled the Eedgah; the southern, the Shikarpore; the eastern, the Cabool; and the western, the Herat. Besides these, there are two less considerable portals in the eastern and western fronts of fortification, denominated the Berdooranee and the Topkhanu, or Artillery. The parapet is battlemented and loop-holed, and pierced, as is the custom in Asiatic fortresses, with apertures for the purpose of throwing vertical missiles into the ditch. The towers, including those over the gates and at the four grand angles of the place, are sixty-two in number, and on these guns might have been mounted, as the rampart is wide, and there are good embrasures in the parapet; but such had been the neglect of the Barukzyes, that we found their artillery, consisting of some twenty indifferent pieces, parked in the open space in front of their citadel. That defence consists of an inner quadrangle of two hundred yards retrenched in the centre of the northern face. Within its inclosure are the several courts and apartments of the royal palace, lately usurped, together with the rule of their master, by the brothers of Futih Khan. Its wall is protected on three sides by a good *fosse;* there is a large bastion in its southern face, and four small towers flank its eastern, and four more its western front. The principal angles of the outer wall of the city are covered with circular counterguards. Such, as a place of strength, is Candahar. Even if treachery and pusillanimity had not opened its gates to us, it is not probable that it could long have resisted the fire of our batteries and the onset of our troops. The Sirdars might, if they had acted with ordinary resolution, have got together a garrison of three or four thousand troops, for which force they had ample supplies for a full month at least; but there

*City wall.

was nothing in the nature of the bulwarks of this capital, or in the character of its constituted defenders, to have saved it from the rapid fall by which two of the strong holds of Central Asia have since been prostrated. Its gates were as vulnerable as those of Ghuznee or Kelat; and in any event, an extensive wall flanked only by very paltry towers could not have offered a protracted resistance to its assailants, if they had proceeded by the slower method of a regular siege.

But no such efforts had been demanded from us. A portion of the troops of Shah Shooja already held possession of the ramparts, gates, and citadel of Candahar, when on the morning of the 27th of April we arrived in front of it; and the population, if not in ecstasies of enthusiasm on occasion of the revolution which they had witnessed, were at least tranquil, and disposed to be outwardly civil to the army of *Feringees* which had effected this great change. As we moved down towards the city, across plains much intersected by watercourses, but already covered with waving crops of barley and wheat, and verdant and luxuriant lucerne, the picture before us was fine. Above the line of the extensive battlements of Candahar were seen the domes of its great central mart, or Charsoo, of the monument of Ahmed Shah, the founder of the Dooranee dynasty, and of several mosques; and behind these the eye embraced a romantic range of hills. Amongst these was particularly distinguished the mount inclining over its base, which had attracted our attention at Khooshab by its singular conformation. Sir John Keane had pitched his tents in a very extensive garden, or orchard ground, of peach, plum, and apricot trees, belonging to Kohun Dil Khan, and situated near the south-western angle of the place. The cavalry, and the armament of the Shah, were encamped on the western side of the town, opposite the Heratee and Topkhanu gates; whilst the Bengal infantry and artillery were aligned, as their successive portions came up, in the plains to the southward. Our divisional headquarters took up the ground which we occupied during the whole of our long halt at Candahar. It was about a hundred yards from the Shikarpore gate, from which it was separated by some fields of barley and lucerne, fenced in with low mud walls. Our pavilions were fixed on a narrow strip of pasture ground of the most brilliant green; its herbage had been closely cropped by sheep, and its closely woven and elastic turf, so different from the covering of the naked and withered grass lands of Hindoostan, reminded us of English downs under their most verdant aspect. We were delighted at first with this little *chummun,* as Persians and Affghans denominate their flowery meads and inclosures of pasturage; but soon discovered its disadvantages. In the level around Candahar, water is found at the distance of from three to six feet from the surface, as we discovered by boring beneath the green carpet of our encampment. The consequence is a damp most prejudicial to health, and especially productive of low fever, dysentery, and jaundice, which last is the most prevalent disorder of Western Afghanistan. The Bengal departments and the general of cavalry found space for themselves in the same succession of grazing fields, at no great distance from us. Shah Shooja at first occupied his tents under the walls, but on the evening of the 27th April took possession of the palace of his ancestors in the citadel. The Envoy and Minister, and his assistants, and Sir Alexander Burnes, also occupied apartments within its walls.

Access to the city was at first, as a precautionary measure, denied to our soldiers and followers; but officers speedily made their way into it, curious to traverse the streets of the western capital of Afghanistan. During the period of exclusion, marts were established beyond the walls, to which the inhabitants freely brought their wares for sale. The temporary bazar near the Shikarpore gate was quickly crowded with vendors of rose-water in large green and blue bottles, of sherbet, and *shikunju-been*—the former, simple water, vinegar, and sugar; the latter, a mixture of the same ingredients, with the juice of fruits. There, too, were seen traffickers in asses' loads of lucerne grass, of wheat, barley, wood, and chopped straw; whilst other small merchants claimed attention to their *poshteens* (sheep-skin pelisses), flowered linen *alkhaliks,* and carpets from Yuzd. The horse-dealers of Herat were not long in finding out that a glorious opportunity presented itself of getting good prices for their steeds, which they were seen hourly shewing off to the best advantage in front of our camps, and our followers found no small attraction in places of resort, where they could procure, at any cost whatever, fowls, *doomba* sheep, onions, milk, tobacco, and spices.

From each principal gate of the fortification runs a street of houses of sun-dried brick. These four grand avenues meet in the centre of the city under the vast dome of a circular bazar denominated the Chuhar-soo, or "Four-ways." These lines of access, as well as the great building to which they lead, are filled with shops, and crowded from daylight to dark with horsemen and foot passengers, as well as asses and camels, laden with commodities. To the northward of the great *goombuz* is a covered bazar, over which is a gallery, containing the *noubut-khanu,* or *nakara-khanu* of the city. From this is heard at sunrise, mid-day, and sun-set, the dissonant clangour and din of trumpets, tabrets, pipes, and drums, with which strangers are always stunned at stated hours in Asiatic cities. In the shops is exposed for sale wheaten bread made up in cakes of an irregularly oval shape. It is soft, and a little acid, but not decidedly unpalateable or unwholesome. The smell of the *kubabs,** which are to be seen in the stalls on every side, certainly does not belie the character for savoriness which the Affghans give them. Near them were seen on shambles the carcasses of doomba sheep, ready slaughtered, skinned, and cut in pieces.

The fruit season of Candahar had not yet fairly commenced, but red and white mulberries were, on our arrival, plentiful, and another fortnight

*Messes of meat, cut into small pieces, and fried or roasted.

brought us a profusion of plums and apricots. In the shops of other dealers are to be found horse furniture, looking-glasses, and ornaments of lacquered ware; blue writing paper of Russian manufacture; loaf-sugar, prepared in the same country; and tolerably good, but highly-priced tea, both black and green. The costumes of the people who crowd the various places of resort differ much. Some wear long cloaks or *chogas* of chintz, or of the woollen cloth, or *pushmeena* of the country, with turbans of very ample fold, their whiskers, moostaches, and beards being allowed to grow long and bushy, and the latter being often dyed red with the juice of the *hinna* (*lawsonia inermis*); others are closely shaven, and habited in jackets and trowsers of blue linen, or tunics of drab cloth with long pendent sleeves, their heads being protected by cotton skull-caps of various colours.

The streets are filthy to an excess not to be conceived by one who has not travelled in Asia, and mendicity is to be seen in them in its most loathsome and repulsive forms. Blind, maimed, deformed, ragged, and unspeakably squalid men, women, and children (the last in the greatest numbers), not only stand and sit, but lie grovelling in the dust and mire, and under the very horses' feet, perpetually exclaiming, *"Buraee khooda, buraee khooda!"* "For the sake of God." In the *chuharsoo*, and in other parts of the city, are public *humams*, or warm baths, where visitors, for the small sum of a rupee, are passed through a course of Asiatic ablution, and peeled, kneaded, and dried, after the Affghan fashion, which differs little from that of Hindoostan. The principal streets have been described as consisting of shops. The citadel contains the palace, and its various courts and gardens. In front of it is an open space, on which are parked the abandoned guns of the Sirdars. A battalion of the Shah's infantry are now also quartered on this Champ-de-Mars of Candahar, which is connected by a narrow street with the *Dunwazu-i-topkhanu*. The mosques are neither numerous nor splendid, and worship appeared to me to be much neglected, though the sonorous voices of the Moowuzzins were heard with great regularity at the stated periods of prayer. There is, to the westward of the Shikarpore gate, a large *suraee* for merchants and travellers, but it was, during our stay, empty, or nearly so.

The rest of the buildings which fill the extensive area of this city are the houses of *Moollas*, doctors of the Mahomedan law, *Akhoonds*, teachers of youth, and *Tubeebs*, physicians. In retired quarters of the town are also the residences of the sirdars, who were accounted influential under the Barukzye régime. That of Meer Ufzul Khan was one of the handsomest; the house was not large, but its outer walls were tastefully painted in fresco, and it looked down upon a pleasing garden of vines, cypresses, poplars, sycamores, and mulberry trees, in the centre of which was a piece of water. It was surrounded by a battlemented wall, also painted within in fresco. To all the better dwellings are attached *tuhkhanus*, or subterranean chambers, to which the inmates retire in the heat of the day, taking good care to avoid them at night, when the damp produces fevers. The retreat of Meer Ufzul, who will be remembered as the chief who so cautiously reconnoitred the Kozuk, suffered much in the late change of masters. It was despoiled of the wood-work of its doors and lattices in that season of confusion, and would probably have been subjected to further devastation, had not the edifice and its surrounding courts been taken under the protection of Lieutenant Simpson, one of our Commissariat officers, who established in its outhouses the central depôt and magazine of the force.

I saw more of the dwelling of another refugee of the period, Moohummud Sudeeq Khan, son of the elder Barukzye, Kohun Dil. Sir Willoughby Cotton, and his personal staff, occupied it during the greater part of the months of May and June. A description of it may serve to give a general notion of the mansions of the wealthier Affghans. It consisted of two courts. In the outer area the retainers of the lord of the mansion had been quartered in a series of small apartments, connected by narrow staircases and passages. Below, the horses of the establishment had been stabled. A strong gate, and long dark passage, gave access to the inner quadrangle. In the centre of this was an oblong piece of water in a stone reservoir. On either side of this tank, in the wings of the building, were two small sleeping chambers, and attached to these, to the westward, were a gallery and some apartments, which seemed to have been set aside for the women of the *zenana*. The central pavilion looked towards the north, and the slanting rays of the rising and setting sun never touched it. It consisted of an ample chamber below the level of the court, which, from its situation, was tolerably cool even at mid-day in the month of July. Two flights of stairs conducted to the principal suite of rooms. The central chamber had an arched roof, and its doors and windows, and numerous *taqs*, or niches, were of a species of Moresco architecture. Above was a flat roof, or *Balakhanu*, which commanded a view of the city. All the walls of the several rooms were plastered with a glittering species of stucco, or *chunam*, as it is called in Hindoostan. It is said to be composed of pounded and calcined *mica*, and has a smooth, but glittering surface. The Affghan builders divide this inner coating of their walls into compartments, and stamp it, whilst yet wet, with tasteful devices.

The finest monument in the city is the mausoleum of Ahmud Shah Abdallee, the founder of that dynasty which we are labouring to restore. It is an octagonal building, raised on a stone platform, and surmounted by a dome, which is a conspicuous object in every direction from the plains beyond the walls. The materials are partly stone, partly sun-dried brick, coated on the outside with stucco. This covering is painted red and blue in the Persian and Affghan manner, with devices of chaplets of flowers in compartments. The pavement within is covered with a carpet, and a shawl is respectfully thrown over the *toorbut,* or sarcophagus of the monarch. The sepulchre itself is composed of a not very fine stone found in the mountains near Candahar, but is inlaid with wreaths of flowers of coloured marble. Twelve lesser tombs, which are those of the children of the Abdallee, are ranged near the receptacle of the ashes of the father. The interior walls are painted in devices similar to those which adorn the exterior, but the execution is more regular, and the colours, having been less exposed, are fresher and more brilliant. The lofty dome above the centre imparts an air of grandeur to the little temple, and its windows of trellis-work in stone admit a solemn and pleasing light. On the eight cornices under the niches of the building is the following inscription in the Nuskh Taleek character:—

شاه والا جاه احمد شاه دورانی که بود
در خوانین آمور سلطنت کسرا منش
از نهیب قهرمان سطوتش در عهد او
شیر اهو را شیر خویش دادی پرورش
میرسید از هر طرف در گوش بد خواهان او
از زبان خنجرش هردم هزاران سر زنش
روان شد جانب دارالبقا تاریخ بود
سال هجری یک هزار یکصد و هشتاد و شش

The following is a nearly literal translation in prose of this poetic memorial:—

"The king of high rank, Ahmed Shah the Dooranee,
Was equal to Kisra* in managing the affairs of his
    government.
In his time, from the awe of his glory and great-
    ness,
The lioness nourished the stag with her milk.
From all sides in the ear of his enemies there ar-
    rived
A thousand reproofs from the tongue of his
    dagger.
The date of his departure for the house of mor-
    tality
Was the year of the Hijra 1186."

*Cyrus, Choeroes.

The tomb which covers the remains of the sovereign is sculptured over with passages of the Koran, and a copy of the sacred volume is kept in the sanctuary, out of which a succession of moollas belonging to the establishment of the place are wont to read aloud. Sir Willoughby Cotton made me the bearer of a handsome gratuity on the part of government to the *mootuwullee,* or superintendent of the mausoleum, and the Envoy and Minister was in like manner munificent. Ahmed Shah possessed many of the highest qualifications of a prince and a warrior, and it may be regarded as an act of piety to be generous to those who are charged with the care and reparation of his sepulchre, whilst the army of the Indus is contributing to perpetuate his renown by consolidating the empire which he erected, that nobler monument of his energy and genius.

In the meantime, what has become of the late rulers of Candahar? They have been permitted, without interruption, to fly towards the Helmund, accompanied by a cumbrous train of camels loaded with *kujawus,** containing their women and treasure. Their troops have diminished by degrees, until at length their handful of horse barely suffices to guard their baggage animals. It is scarcely possible to conceive a less enviable position than that of these men. Antecedently to the occupation of Candahar, they might, by timely submission, have received at the hands of the British government a comfortable provision, and an honourable asylum in Hindoostan. They have now no resource but flight into Persia. It is known that Moohummud Shah bribed them, with the promise of uniting to their rule the conquered state of Herat, to join in an alliance for its destruction. It remains to be seen what treatment they will receive at his hands now that they are overwhelmed with calamity, the result of adherence to his pernicious

policy. But to reach Persia is for them no easy matter. The direct route through Herat they dare not take. Shah Kamran, against whom they have plotted, and who barbarously murdered their ambitious brother, the Wuzeer Futtih Khan, would shew them little mercy; and if they attempt a *détour* through Seistan, the predatory Beloochees of the desert of that country, who seldom allow a kafila to pass unmolested, will hardly suffer these sirdars to escape them, since they are reported to have yet a lack and a half of rupees on their camels. I must add, that I am wholly at a loss how to vindicate satisfactorily our own measures with respect to these fugitives. They abandoned the capital on the 24th; on the 25th Shah Shooja entered, and claimed it as his own. Why was not a prompt pursuit commenced in the direction of the Helmund? There seems to be little reason to doubt that this branch of the Barukzyes was utterly contemptible in the eyes of those over whom they ruled, but the possession of their persons would secure the important advantage of preventing their becoming tools in the hands of the Persians and Russians, and the means of disturbing the peace of the restored empire. The most sagacious of the counsellors who have accompanied their flight is said to be one Moollah Rusheed, the owner of two mansions in Candahar, and a master in intrigue, as well as a graduate in Moohummedan theology.

The 8th of May was fixed for the ceremony of the solemn recognition of Shah Shooja in the plains to the northward of the city, not far distant from the fatal field on which he lost all present hope of empire in 1834. But this spectacle I was not permitted to witness. As the Commander-in-Chief was required on this occasion to be in close attendance on the monarch, the command of the troops would have devolved on Sir Willoughby Cotton. But low fever had been creeping round the frame of the General since the day of our encampment on the Dooree. He had at first disregarded its symptoms, but on the 5th of May, became so ill as

---

*Panniers of wood or wicker work, which are slung over camels. In these, men and women ride, balanced on either side, and goods are conveniently carried.

to render medical advice indispensable. On the 6th, with the view of avoiding the excessive heat of the camp, he removed to the vacant mansion of Moohummud Sudeeq Khan, in a street in the western quarter of Candahar. He did not begin to recover until some days after, and on the 8th could not have sat upon his horse. General Willshire therefore commanded the troops, and I give from the report of actual spectators all that I have to record of the ceremonial. The monarch, attended by the Commander-in-Chief, the Envoy and Minister, and the *corps diplomatique*, accompanied by Syuds and Moollahs, and escorted by his own troops, issued from the Eedgah gate. A throne and splendid canopy had been prepared for him in the centre of the plain. Seated on this, in front of the deployed forces of the British army, Shah Shooja was honoured with every mark of gratulation and homage which the customs of Europe and Asia recognise and enjoin. Royal salutes were fired as he passed beyond and returned within the walls of the capital; the troops received him with presented arms, and defiled past him; *nuzzurs* were presented by the Envoy on the part of the British government, and by a certain number of distinguished Affghans in his suite, and one hundred discharges of ordnance shook the ground when he had taken his seat in the *musnud*. But unless I have been deceived, all the national enthusiasm of the scene was entirely confined to his Majesty's immediate retainers. The people of Candahar are said to have viewed the whole affair with the most mortifying indifference. Few of them quitted the city to be present in the plains, and it was remarked with justice that the passage in the diplomatic *programme* which prescribed a place behind the throne for "the populace restrained by the Shah's troops" became rather a bitter satire on the display of the morning.

No charge of precipitation can be brought against our measures in pursuit of the ex-sirdars. On the 25th of April, Shah Shooja took possession of his capital; and now at length, on the 12th of May, a force consisting of three thousand of the Shah's horse, and a squadron picked from the Bengal 2nd and 3rd Light Cavalry, one hundred men of the 13th Light Infantry, the 16th Native Infantry, reinforced by disciplined foot of the Shah Shooja's army, to the strength of one thousand native soldiers, the camel battery, two eighteen pounders, and two five-and-a-half inch mortars, manned by European artillery men, has marched under Brigadier Sale for the Helmund. It seems not to be doubtful that the Barukzyes will fly before him, and that he will meet with no difficulty but the passage of a broad and rapid stream. It is stated that these fugitives remained, after the abandonment of the capital, eight days on the left bank of the Helmund without the means of crossing it, in trembling expectation of pursuit, and no doubt as much surprised at, as delighted with, the forbearance, or unaccountable apathy, of their opponents. They have since so far taken heart as to send their families into the fort of Girishk, and to strive artificially to deepen the water of the Helmund at a point near it. Brigadier Sale, in his first march from Candahar, was impeded by several smaller streams besides the Urghundab, which, after flowing to the northward of the western capital, fertilizing the valleys near it, and supplying it with water, crosses the route to Herat a few miles from our encampments.

Shah Shooja, as if feeling that he now grasped firmly the sceptre of one portion of Afghanistan, appointed the 27th May for the public reception of the officers of the British army at his court. The slightest acquaintance with Asiatic rulers and their durbars suffices to convince that it is vain ever to expect punctuality in the atmosphere of oriental rule. The British officers were not therefore on this occasion much surprised at having to wait a full hour in one of the courts of the palace which constituted the residency of the Envoy. They felt that it was better that their time should be sacrificed than the dignity of a newly restored monarch compromised by departure from an usage which European precision might deem reprehensible, and even a mark of bad taste, but which Asiatic stateliness regards as inseparable from true dignity. At length, a summons reached them to repair to the apartments of the King.

The Commander-in-Chief and the Envoy led the way, followed by about two hundred and fifty officers of all ranks and arms in full dress, to a garden in front of the royal dwelling. It was planted with cypresses and other trees, the inclosure walls, like those at the domicile of Meer Ufzul Khan, being painted in fresco. The monarch was seated in the Asiatic manner with crossed legs, upon a low *musnud*, or carpeted throne, erected under a crimson canopy on the edge of a piece of water, clear, and cooling to the air around. Before him was a table covered with brocade. He was fanned with the *chuonree* of the tail of the Tibet cow, and on either side of him, over and above a double row of menials in scarlet turbans, and *ulkhaliks*, were seen the commandant and his staff, and the other officers of his disciplined troops. The Shah, richly habited, looked kingly and well. His manner was, as it always had been towards the British, benign and affable; and he found something courteous and apposite to say to each as the Commander-in-Chief and the Generals and Brigadiers were successively presented to him. He spoke in Persian, which Mr. Macnaghten and Major Todd interpreted. The ceremony of offering *nuzzurs* followed. His Excellency first laid at the feet of the Shah one hundred *ushrufees* in a red silk bag. Then each officer in succession made his offering by spreading or depositing the glittering ore on the steps of the *musnud*. Every general thus presented twenty-one gold mohurs, every field-officer five, and every captain and subaltern one. These sums had been previously disbursed out of the treasury of the Envoy. According to the custom of Oriental durbars, the British were covered in the royal presence, but each respectfully saluted the Shah as he passed the throne, and having presented his *nuzzur*, retired to the lower end of the garden. The monarch is not yet ashamed of a public profession of his gratitude to the army which has brought him to Candahar. Looking with an air of benignity on this occasion at the circle of officers around him, he said with apparent emotion, "I now feel myself to be a king indeed."

We have had a dreadful exemplification of the lawless state of the country, and the sanguinary character of the people, in the barbarous murder of one of our officers in the immediate vicinity of our camps. The Urghundab flows a few miles to the northward of Candahar. Its stream is clear and rapid, and branches of irrigation from it carry fertility all over the surrounding country. In describing the environs of the city, mention has more than once been made of a remarkable mount, which seems to incline over its base; this eminence forms one side of a mountain pass. By skirting it, access is gained into a valley near the hamlet of Bala Wulee, picturesque, and planted with fine trees, and watered by the Urghundab. Attracted by the beauty of the spot, many of our officers have formed parties of pleasure to visit it during our prolonged stay at Candahar, and after amusing themselves with angling in the stream, have been accustomed to pitch their tents on its margin for their evening repast.

A fish closely resembling the trout is caught here, and in other parts of the empire.* It was remarked by our sportsmen, that the finny species of the Urghundab would rise to a bait, but never to an artificial fly. On the 28th of May one or two little groups, social and piscatory, had been formed in the valley. All the parties but one, however, broke up in good time, and the individuals composing them returned in safety to Candahar. Two young gentlemen only, Lieutenants Inverarity and Wilmer, of the 16th Lancers, lingered on the river bank till after sunset. The hazard of this was the greater, as armed men, whose appearance stamped

---

*The real English trout (salmo trutta) has since been found in the streams near Bamian.

them as belonging to some of the predatory gangs of this ill-governed country, had been seen in the morning lurking near the gorge of the neighbouring pass. With fatal imprudence these officers sent off to the camp their tents and servants, and prepared to return towards the capital wholly unarmed. As if to render escape impossible, they even parted with their horses, which their *syces* led in advance. The moon shone brightly, and, unconscious of the impending danger, the young men strolled leisurely up the *durru*. Lieutenant Wilmer remained considerably behind his companion. It would appear that the latter had not proceeded far alone, when he was assailed by armed men, who cut down, and savagely mutilated him. Lieutenant Wilmer, on reaching the scene of this atrocity, was himself attacked by from twelve to fifteen assassins. He parried their cuts for some time with his walking stick, and then taking to flight, reached, with a single scratch in the face, the camp of a detachment of the Shah's infantry, not many hundred yards distant from the defile. The *syces* also saved themselves by a rapid retreat, abandoning both horses to the robbers.

Instant aid was afforded to Lieutenant Wilmer, when he arrived breathless at the tents of the contingent. An armed party returned with him to the fatal spot, and there his unfortunate companion was found, yet alive. He had received several mangling wounds across the shoulders, back, and loins, the direction of which fully proved that the assailants had rushed upon him from behind. One of his hands was nearly cut through, doubtless in the efforts which he had made to defend his head. The sufferer recognised his friend, faintly asked for water, cooled his parched lips, and soon after expired. Shah Shooja, when this outrage was reported to him, blamed indeed the imprudence of these young officers in remaining to so late an hour in so retired a spot, but expressed the utmost abhorrence of the crime which had been perpetrated, and declared his resolution to inflict condign punishment on the murderers, if they could

be detected. He repeated often, with apparent emotion, during his conversation on the subject, "Oh! gentlemen, you must be more cautious here; remember you are not now in Hindoostan."

Brigadier Sale's force returned from the Helmund on the 28th May. The ex-sirdars abandoned Girishk on his approach, and fled into Seistan, where they are believed to have obtained refuge for the moment in the territories of the petty chief of Bukwa. The Brigadier had ferried across his force, and guns, on rafts of timber buoyed up on empty rum casks, having previously fixed a rope to the right bank by attaching it to a shell, which was then projected from the mouth of a howitzer. Girishk is a miserable mud fort, on the ramparts of which one gun only was mounted. It is now garrisoned by the troops of the Shah. Lieutenant Edward Connolly, Assistant to the Envoy, has also taken up his residence there, with the intention, since fulfilled, not only of watching the movements of the Barukzyes, but of exploring Seistan. The Helmund is a grand barrier; but the country between it and Candahar, the first march down to the Urghundab excepted, is little better than a desert. The frontier river is in some places eight hundred yards in width, but in one point narrows to ninety yards, and is there of unfathomable depth, and tremendously rapid. Here the opposite bank could of course be swept with artillery, and a passage forced. It is remarkable that on the Helmund the thermometer did not rise higher under canvass than 75°.

As the harvest ripened around Candahar, in the beginning of June, large quantities of grain were collected by the Commissariat, and every preparation made for an advance towards Cabool. The carriage cattle had been recruited in strength by repose, and had fattened on the *juwasa*, or camel thorn, which was found in abundance near Dihi-nou, and other places, to which they had been sent in a body to graze, under escorts of irregular horse. An *elches* (ambassador) arrived from Herat, whilst the affairs of that state were under discussion at the court of the Shah. Finally, Major Todd was directed to repair to the rescued city, accompanied by Captain Sanders of the engineers, and Lieutenant Abbott of the artillery. They were charged to negotiate a treaty, offensive and defensive, with Shah Kamran, and to proffer assistance in repairing and improving the fortications of Herat, so as to render them secure against any new attempt of the Persians.

His Majesty the Shah has experienced much mortification in all his attempts to bind to his allegiance the warlike and predatory tribes of the Ghiljees. Their forts and cattle are thickly spread along both banks of the Turnuk, and up to the walls of Ghuznee, whilst detached *kheils* are found beyond Cabool, and even at the base of the Teera mountains. The seat of the rule of Abdooruhman, their principal leader, is Kelati Ghiljee. The refractory chiefs of this wild people, one of the most influential of whom is Gool Moohummud, more commonly known by the title of Gooroo, have received the gratuities scattered amongst them by the Shah's agents, and then sent back indignant and contumacious replies to his overtures, whilst their armed parties have been employed in the most audacious *chupaos* against our carriage cattle, even to the very walls of Candahar. In one of these, a very salutary lesson was read to the marauders by a party of sipahees of the 16th Native Infantry; and, in another, the Ghiljees surprised, shot, and cut down several unarmed soldiers of Her Majesty's 13th, who, at an unjustifiable distance from their protecting guard, were driving their camels to water. Their barbarity was likewise evidenced by their having decoyed into one of their forts, plundered, and savagely murdered, a portion of a party of about three hundred profligate, dishonest, and home-sick followers of our army, who had deserted their masters, and, having formed themselves into a Kafila, were striving to escape into our provinces by way of Ghuznee and Dera Ismael Khan.

By the middle of June, corn had become comparatively abundant in the city and our camps; but our Commissariat could not yet venture to place the troops on their original footing as to rations. They persevered, however, in collecting grain with great diligence and success, and caused it to be ground at the numerous mills which are turned by the Urghundab. The Bombay troops continued healthy, but sickness amongst the European soldiers from Bengal had increased to a fearful degree. Exposure to heat under canvass in May and June, supervening on a variety of harassing duties, and the fatigue of continued marches, had made a great impression on the constitutions of the men. The flour in the bazars had also been shamefully adulterated by the banians* during the times of extreme scarcity; and the water of nearly all the streams in Affghanistan has a saline impregnation peculiarly hostile to human health. Diarrhœa, dysentery, jaundice, and fever of various types, the last commonly attended with much cerebral deterioration, were daily consigning valuable soldiers to the grave. Notwithstanding these losses and adverse circumstances, all was preparation, during the three last weeks of June, for an advance towards the eastern capital. Treasure to the amount of twenty-two lacs had reached Candahar on the 5th. Its escort, under Colonel Dennie, had made a harassing march at a late season through Cutch Gundava, the Bolan pass, and over the Kozuk. A large supply of grain was likewise obtained from Mooltan by means of a numerous convoy of Lohanee merchants, who became the hired carriers of the government, and arrived at Candahar late in June under their Kafila Bashee, Surwur Khan.

A good deal of useful information was at this time obtained from a French adventurer of low extraction, who, if his autobiography might be believed, had crossed the Balkan in the service of the Turks. He was known to have been more recently employed in the Punjab by the Maha Rajah. He

*Native dealers.

alleged that he had quitted Lahore in disgust, and was now endeavouring, evidently in a state of abject poverty, to make his way back to France by Bombay. As he had now, and on former occasions, travelled with smuggling caravans, whose object was to avoid the imposts of the Affghan and Belooche rulers, he had become acquainted with several bye routes through the Teera mountains, and the country of the Ghiljees between Cabool and Candahar, as well as the road from the latter city to Kelat, and a precipitous defile, by which he affirmed that the Affghan *contrebandiers* travelled from the capital of Mihrab Khan to the town of Gundava.

Grapes, melons, and apples, and several varieties of the cucurbitous tribe have now taken the place, in the bazars of the city, of apricots and plums. But the people confess that the fruits of Candahar are far inferior to those of Cabool, and the heat of the weather renders even the moderate use of them at this season hazardous. The mornings are yet cool, but the mid-day sun is fearfully powerful, and in the evening a species of hot wind begins to blow, which is singularly oppressive. Towards mid-night it commonly lulls, when there is another sudden and chilling change of temperature, against which it is prudent to take precautions before retiring to rest. It is said that the fatal *simoom* often visits Candahar in June and July; but it was never felt whilst the army of the Indus reposed beneath its walls.

The present capital is considered to be little more than coeval with the Suddozye dynasty. One of the few objects of interest in its vicinity are the walls of the ancient city of Candahar. They are to be found about three miles due west of our encampments, at the very foot of a range of mountains of primitive formation, which bound the plains in this direction. The road, perpetually crossed by water-courses, lies over fields of lucerne and clover, planted with rows, and groves of white and red mulberry. The vast and ruinous foundations of the former dwellings extend over an area of near a mile, and are surrounded by a mouldering wall, in which wide and deep breaches have been made by time. There is also a ditch of stagnant water. A portion of these remains are believed by some to belong to the Alexandrian period. The city had been built so close to the mountain as to be completely under command from it. In the centre of the old city is a kind of Acropolis, on which are the thin and spectral ruins of some lofty towers; and near the site of the deserted town, a pathway of more modern date has been elaborated up the side of the adjacent range of mountain. There were no inhabitants visible when I visited it, except about twenty Affghans, who were huddled in a circle around two Moollas, that were taking the lead in the devotions of the party in front of a small mosque.

On the 23rd of June, Shah Shooja, by way of preparation to accompany our further advance, quitted his palace, and took up his residence in the royal tents, which were pitched near the village of Dih Khoju, two miles to the eastward of the city. The wild *feu-de-joie* of his Affghan cavalry, as they escorted him through the Cabool gate, would have induced a stranger to their manners to suppose that there was insurrection within the walls, and that a sharp skirmish was going on in its streets. The undisciplined horse, which have gradually been drawn around the monarch, and taken into pay, already amount to several thousands. Our narrative has now reached the point of general preparation for an advance to Cabool.

OBSERVATIONS.

It is to be feared that a want of skill and perseverance in improving their advantages in war and policy is but too justly imputed to the British as a defect in their national character. The advanced columns of the army of the Indus reached the plains beyond the Gautee range under circumstances of distress almost amounting to disaster. Its cavalry and artillery horses were reduced so low in point of condition by various and protracted privations, that the arm was scarcely effective, and the Commissariat had too good cause to think seriously of the probability of being compelled to have recourse to a yet smaller fractional division of rations. The troops needed repose, food, and some tangible acquisition at least, if they might not be indulged with a victory, to support their spirits, and prove to them that they were not toiling in vain. Doubtless they were fully equal to the task of reducing Candahar, and ardently desired to try their strength against it. But in a political point of view, the abandonment of the capital without a blow by the imbecile and irresolute Barukzyes was a saving of treasure, time, suffering, and blood; in this respect, therefore, substantive gain. Why then was not this advantage followed up? Why were not the fugitive chieftains promptly pursued, and every effort used to secure their persons? Was British India already placed so far beyond the risks of external peril that we could afford to furnish Russia with fresh tools for intrigue, or Shah Shooja's empire so firmly consolidated that we could leave at large, without solicitude, a vanquished pretender to a third of his dominions?

6 / To Herat and Cabul: A Story of the First Afghan War (1902)

G. A. HENTY

G. A. Henty (1832–1902) was a prolific novelist and empire enthusiast whose fiction immortalized the plucky young man as the hero of modern British imperialism. The First Anglo-Afghan War posed a decided challenge to Henty's calling as an imperial booster. He begins his fictional account of the first Afghan campaign with the observation that "in the military history of this country there is no darker page than the destruction of a considerable British force in the terrible defiles between Cabul and Jellalabad in January, 1842." In the pages that follow, he gives one of the most concise, and jingoistic, accounts of the main events of the war. In these excepts (chapter 15, "A Series of Blunders," and chapter 16, "Annihilation of the Army"), Henty dramatizes two of the best-known episodes for a generation of readers who were hungry for imperial fiction, especially the kind of boys' adventure that he was so well-known for.

PREFACE

In the military history of this country there is no darker page than the destruction of a considerable British force in the terrible defiles between Cabul and Jellalabad in January, 1842. Of all the wars in which our troops have taken part never was one entered upon so recklessly or so unjustifiably. The ruler of Afghanistan, Dost Mahomed, was sincerely anxious for our friendship. He was alarmed at the menacing attitude of Russia, which, in conjunction with Persia, was threatening his dominions and intriguing with the princes at Candahar. Our commissioner at Cabul, Mr. Burnes, was con-vinced of the Ameer's honesty of intention, and protested most strongly against the course taken by the Indian government, who determined upon setting up a discredited prince, who had for many years been a fugitive in India, in place of Dost Mahomed.

In spite of his remonstrances, the war was undertaken. Nothing could have been worse than the arrangements for it, and the troops suffered terribly from thirst and want of transport. However, they reached Cabul with comparatively little fighting. Dost Mahomed fled, and the puppet Shah Soojah was set up in his place; but he was only kept there by British bayonets, and for two years he was so protected. Gradually, however, the British force was withdrawn, until only some five thousand troops remained to support him. Well led, they would have been amply sufficient for the purpose, for though the Afghan tribesmen were dangerous among their mountains, they could not for a moment have stood against them in the open field. Unhappily the general was old and infirm, incapable of decision of any kind, and in his imbecile hands the troops, who in October could have met the whole forces of Afghanistan in fight, were kept inactive, while the Afghans pillaged the stores with the provisions for the winter, and insulted and bearded them in every way. Thus a fine body of fighting men were reduced to such depths of discontent and shame that when the unworthy order for retreat before their exulting enemy was given they had lost all confidence in themselves or their officers, and, weakened by hunger and hampered by an enormous train of camp-followers, they went as sheep to the slaughter in the trap the Afghans had prepared for them. It would almost seem that their fate was a punishment for the injustice of the war. Misfortunes have befallen our arms, but never one so dark and disgraceful as this. The shame of the disaster was redeemed only by the heroic garrison of Jellalabad, which, although but one-fourth of the strength of that at Cabul, sallied out after a noble defence and routed the army which Dost Mahomed's son Akbar had assembled for their destruction.

A SERIES OF BLUNDERS

Numerous as had been the blunders, and great the mismanagement up to the 2nd of November, matters might yet have been retrieved had the conduct of affairs been in resolute and energetic hands. Macnaghten was personally a brave and fearless man. Had he at last felt the necessity for strong measures, an attack upon the city would certainly have been attended with success. Now that the first burst of hate and passion had passed,

the inhabitants were filled with apprehension at the punishment that would fall upon them, and none doubted that the British army would at once attack the town. The army itself expected this, and, furious at the treacherous massacre of Sir Alexander Burnes and his comrades, were burning for the order to attack.

The troops were under arms early, but no orders were issued for a forward movement. Some hours later the 35th Regiment of Native Infantry, with two mountain guns, came in from Khoord Cabul, having brushed aside the opposition it had met with on its march. With this valuable addition to the fighting strength in the camp all opposition could have been easily overcome, and yet until three o'clock in the afternoon nothing whatever was done. By this time what could have been effected with comparative ease in the early morning had become a far more difficult operation. Vast numbers of the tribesmen had been pouring into the city since daybreak, and the two miles of plain between the camp and the city, which earlier in the day could have been traversed without a shot being fired, were now covered by a host of fierce enemies; and yet, after wasting so many valuable hours, the general, instead of throwing the whole of the force in the cantonments, and that of Brigadier Shelton at the Bala Hissar, against the city, sent only three companies of infantry and two guns to the attack.

Naturally this handful of men failed; and it was well for them that they did not penetrate into the city, for had they done so they would assuredly have been overwhelmed before they had gone fifty yards. However, the officer in command, seeing the impossibility of the task set him, withdrew his detachment in good order. The result of the day's operation, if it could be so called, was disastrous: the troops, who had until then been eager to be led against the enemy, and confident of success, were irritated and dispirited, and lost all confidence in their commander; while, on the other hand, the Afghans were jubilant over what they considered the cowardice of the enemy. The next day the misfortune invited by the passive attitude of our troops happened. Only eighty men were in charge of the commissariat fort. The little party were commanded by Lieutenant Warren. Early in the day a threatening force of the enemy approached, and Warren sent a messenger urgently asking for reinforcements.

But the Afghans had already occupied an old fort that commanded the road between the camp and the commissariat fort. Considering the enormous importance of the stores, an overwhelming force should have been sent out to drive off the assailants, and to occupy the fort in such strength that it could be held against any assault. Instead of doing this, two companies only of the 44th Regiment were sent. The two captains in command were killed by the fire from the Afghan fort, other officers were wounded, and the men fell so fast that the officer who was senior in command, seeing the impossibility of reaching the store, drew them off. Then an order was issued—which was practically the death-warrant of the army—by General Elphinstone, for a party of cavalry to go out and bring in the little garrison. This party suffered even more severely than the preceding one. From every wall, building, and orchard a storm of musketry broke out, and the troopers, after suffering great loss, again retired. The news that the general intended to abandon the store struck dismay into the officers of the commissariat. Captain Boyd hurried to headquarters, and urged the general to send a force that would sweep away all opposition, and to hold the fort at all hazards. The general promised to send a reinforcement, but no relief was sent.

As night was coming on, Captain Boyd and Captain Johnson again went to the general, and pointed out in the strongest language the result that would follow the abandonment of the stores. The unhappy old man hesitated, but on a letter being brought in from Lieutenant Warren saying that the enemy were mining the walls, and some of the Sepoys, seeing their position was desperate, were deserting, he promised that a strong detachment should be sent at two o'clock in the morning

to storm the Afghan fort and relieve the guard at the commissariat stores. Orders were accordingly issued, but these were presently countermanded, and it was decided that the force should not move until daylight.

By that time it was too late. Warren had repulsed an attack on the walls, but seeing that the enemy were preparing to fire the gate and renew the attack, he retired through a passage that had on the previous day been dug under the wall, and reached the camp in safety. But this was not the only disaster that happened that day. Captain Johnson's store of provisions for the use of the Ameer's troops, on the outskirts of the city, was also attacked. Captain Mackenzie, who was in command of the little garrison there, defended his post throughout the day with the greatest gallantry; but water was scarce and ammunition failing, and large numbers of women and children were in the fort, with great quantities of baggage. Urgent letters were sent asking for reinforcements, but no reinforcements came. Had they arrived the situation would have been saved. The Kuzzilbashes were ready to side with the British. Several of their commanders were with Mackenzie, but when they saw that no help was sent, they refused to join a cause that seemed to them lost. All night the fighting went on, and all next day, until his men were utterly worn out and the ammunition exhausted. No more could be done, and when night came on he moved out of the fort and fought his way to the cantonments—a brilliant action, which showed what could be accomplished by a mere handful of men well led.

While Mackenzie was thus fighting for the stores under his charge, the troops in the cantonments were condemned to see crowds of Afghans looting the stores within four hundred yards of our camp, carrying off the supplies that had been garnered for their subsistence through the winter, and this without a man being set in motion or a gun brought to bear upon the plunderers.

Furious at the imbecility of their leaders, the soldiers clamoured to be led against the enemy.

Unable to resist the demand, the general ordered the 37th Native Infantry to move out; but instead of being led straight against the enemy, the officer in command hesitated and halted, and soon fell back with the indignant Sepoys.

General Elphinstone was already talking of making terms with the enemy, and seemed to despair of victory when no attempt had been made to gain a success. On the 6th, however, a party of the 37th were again sent out under Major Griffiths. Again it was seen what could be done by an energetic officer. The Afghan fort was stormed, the enemy were driven out, and were routed by a party of horse, who dashed at them gallantly. The troops could be no longer restrained, and cavalry, infantry, and artillery poured out; but there was no general plan, and the consequence was, that although desultory fighting went on all day, nothing was accomplished. Had any general plan of operation been laid down, and a combined action fought, the enemy would have been utterly unable to withstand our troops, worked up to fury as these were by the disgraceful inaction that had been forced upon them. In the meantime, starvation would have already stared the troops in the face had not Captains Boyd and Johnson, aided by Angus and other officers of their department, gone out to the native villages and succeeded in purchasing a certain amount of grain. But already the troops were on half rations, and even these scanty supplies could not long be available.

The general, while his troops were out fighting, wrote to Macnaghten, urging that negotiations should be opened with the enemy, and saying, "Our case is not yet desperate, but it is becoming so very fast."

Macnaghten himself was conscious of this, conscious that, under such leading, the situation was fast becoming desperate, and he employed the moonshee, Mohun Lal, who was still in Cabul under the protection of the Kuzzilbash chief, to endeavour to bribe the chiefs of the Ghilzyes. Two lacs of rupees were offered. The chiefs gave a favourable reply, and then Macnaghten, with his usual instability, was seized with a suspicion that they were not sincere, and abruptly broke off the negotiations, thereby mortally offending the Ghilzye chiefs.

Fresh danger was threatening in another direction. Mahomed Akbar Khan, the second son of Dost Mahomed, was on his way with a force from the north, and had already advanced as far as Bamian. Mohun Lal suggested that an emissary should be sent to offer him a large allowance if he would join the British. His suggestion was carried out, and money was spent in other quarters lavishly.

But it was now too late. A quarter of the sum would, a fortnight earlier, have sufficed to satisfy the demands of all the chiefs of the tribesmen. Now that success had encouraged the assailants of our force, and the whole population had taken up arms against us, inspired alike by fanaticism and hatred and thirsting for blood, it was doubtful whether even the chiefs could restrain them had they chosen to do so.

In their letters and journals the officers still spoke with kindness and respect of their unfortunate general. He had been a brave and able soldier, but age and terrible infirmities had rendered him altogether incapacitated for action. He had for months been suffering from gout, and had almost lost the use of his limbs. Only once or twice, after his arrival to assume the command, had he been able to sit on horseback; for the most part he was wholly unable to walk. Sometimes he was confined altogether to his couch; at others he was able to be taken out in a palanquin. His mind was also enfeebled by suffering. On the very day of the first outbreak he had been a little better, and had mounted his horse; but he had suffered a very severe fall, and was carried back to his quarters.

It was altogether inexcusable that Lord Auckland, against the advice of the commander-in-chief and the remonstrances of his other military advisers, should have appointed such a man to a command which, beyond all others in India, demanded the greatest amount of energy and activity. There were many men who might have been worthily selected, men with a knowledge of the political conditions of Afghanistan, of the feelings of the people, of their language and of their country.

General Elphinstone knew nothing of these things, and depended entirely upon the advice of others. Had he relied solely upon that of Macnaghten, things might have gone differently, but he asked advice from all around him, and took the last that was offered, only to change his mind again when he heard the opinion of a fresh counsellor. He was himself conscious that the position was too onerous for him, and sent down a medical certificate of his incapacity for action, and requested to be relieved. The request had been granted, and he was to have returned to India with Macnaghten, but unhappily no other officer had been appointed to succeed him. It is upon Lord Auckland, rather than upon the unfortunate officer, who, in the teeth of the advice of his counsellors and of all common sense, was thrust into a position for which he was wholly unsuited, that the blame of the catastrophe of Cabul should be laid.

Macnaghten, in hopes that Brigadier Shelton, a brave officer, but hot-tempered and obstinate, would be able to influence the general and to put an end to the deplorable indecision that paralysed the army, persuaded Elphinstone to send for him to come in from the Bala Hissar to the camp and bring in with him a regiment of the Ameer's troops. He came into the cantonment on the 9th, and his arrival was hailed with the greatest satisfaction, as it was believed that at last something would be done. Unfortunately, however, Shelton's energy and the general's weakness were as oil and water. No two men were less calculated to pull together. Shelton enforced his arguments with a vehemence that seemed to the general insubordinate in the extreme; while the brigadier, on the other hand, was unable to make allowance for the physical and mental weakness of the general, and was maddened by the manner in which orders that had but an hour before been issued were countermanded.

On the morning of the 10th the enemy mustered in great force, and, occupying a small fort within musket-shot of the defences, opened a galling fire. Macnaghten only obtained the general's consent to a party going out to capture the fort by telling him that unless he gave the order he should himself take the responsibility of doing so, for that at any risk the fort must be captured. Thereupon Shelton was instructed to take two thousand men and attack it. When they were on the point of starting Elphinstone countermanded the orders. Shelton, in a fury, laid the case before the envoy, who was as eager as himself, and the general was again persuaded to give the order and the force advanced.

It was intended to blow open the gate with powder, but by some accident only a wicket by the side of the main entrance was blown in. Led by Colonel Mackrell the storming party, consisting of two companies of Europeans and four of native infantry, advanced. They could with difficulty make their way through the narrow entrance, for they were exposed as they did so to a heavy musketry fire, but two officers and a few soldiers pushed through, and the garrison, believing that the whole column was following them, fled through the opposite gate. But unhappily they were not followed. A body of Afghan cavalry threatened to attack the storming party outside, and these, native and British alike, were seized with an unaccountable panic and fled. In vain their officers endeavoured to arrest their flight. The events of the previous week had terribly demoralized them. Shelton set them a noble example by remaining on horseback alone, and at last shamed them into returning. Again the Afghan horse approached, and again they fled. Again Shelton's expostulations and example brought them back. The guns in the cantonments drove the Afghans off, and Shelton led his men up to the capture of the fort.

In the meantime the handful of men who had entered the fort had been engaged in a desperate struggle for life. The Afghans, discovering how small was the number of their assailants, re-entered the fort and fell upon them in overwhelming numbers. When Shelton's force entered, Colonel Mackrell had fallen mortally wounded, and was carried into the cantonments to die. Lieutenant Bird, with two Sepoys, were the sole survivors. They had, when the enemy poured in, taken possession of a stable and barricaded themselves there, and had successfully repulsed every attack. When they were rescued their ammunition was almost exhausted, but they were uninjured, and no fewer than thirty dead Afghans lying in front of the stable bore mute testimony to the steadiness and accuracy of their aim.

Several small forts were abandoned by the enemy, and a quantity of grain was found in them, but as no measures were taken to convey it into the camp, it was lost again when the troops retired. Desultory fighting went on all the afternoon without any decisive results, and the next two or three days passed quietly.

In the meantime the moonshee was making every effort to bring over some of the chiefs to our side. Macnaghten was sending off letter after letter to the political officer with Sale, urging the necessity for an instant advance of the force at Jellalabad. On the 13th the enemy occupied a hill within range of the cantonment, and, planting two guns there, opened a steady fire. Macnaghten spent hours in endeavouring to persuade the general and brigadier of the absolute necessity for driving the enemy off the hill, but without success, and it was not until he took the responsibility upon himself that a detachment under Shelton was ordered to be sent. It was then four o'clock in the afternoon. The troops advanced in three columns, and the infantry rushed forward with such impetuosity that the two guns with them could not arrive in time to herald their attack. The detachment poured in a volley within ten yards' distance, but

they were unsteady from their exertions in mounting the hill, and their fire took no effect. A minute later the Afghan cavalry charged down upon them. The attack was unexpected, the men in confusion, and the Afghans rode through and through the ranks. The British troops retreated down the slope, where they re-formed behind the reserve; the guns opened fire with great effect, and the infantry again marched up the hill.

Our cavalry now came into action and drove the enemy before them. The infantry carried the height, and the enemy fled, abandoning their guns. It was now getting dark. A party of the Ameer's infantry removed one of the guns; but the Afghan marksmen were keeping up a heavy musketry fire, and the troops, British as well as Sepoys, were so demoralized that they refused to advance and carry off the other. It was therefore spiked and rolled down the hill, while the smaller gun was brought by the Ameer's troops into the cantonment. The enemy, now strongly reinforced, attempted to intercept the retreat, but were beaten off.

On the 15th Major Pottinger and another officer came in wounded, and reported that the Ghoorka regiment that had been retiring from Kohistan had been entirely destroyed. They defended themselves courageously against overwhelming forces, and held the barracks they occupied until maddened by thirst; then they rushed to a stream, where the enemy fell upon them and cut them to pieces, the two mounted officers alone escaping after innumerable dangers. On the 17th Macnaghten heard that there was no hope whatever of assistance from Sale, who was himself surrounded with difficulties. He now urged that the force should all retire to the Bala Hissar, behind whose strong walls they could have maintained themselves. But Shelton vehemently opposed the step, which would have saved the army from destruction, urging that the abandonment of the cantonments would be an acknowledgment of defeat.

On the 23rd of November the enemy again appeared on the hill from which they had been driven; and a strong force moved out against it. Strangely enough, however, they only took one gun with them. The day was disgraceful as well as disastrous, for the British force was signally defeated and the gun was lost, and the troops reentered the cantonment in headlong flight, hotly pursued by the Afghans till they reached the protection of the earthworks. Their conduct showed how completely the imbecility and vacillation of their commanders, and the effect of the insufficient rations on which they had to subsist, had destroyed the *moral* of the troops. The men who a month before could have driven the Afghans before them like sheep, were now unable to cope with them even when in superior numbers.

On the 24th Elphinstone addressed a letter to Macnaghten stating his opinion that their position could no longer be maintained, and that he should at once enter into negotiations with the enemy. He accordingly sent a message to the insurgent chiefs inviting them to send in a deputation to discuss the conditions of the treaty. Two of their leaders came in, but as they demanded that the British should surrender at discretion, giving themselves up, with all their arms, ammunition, and treasure, as prisoners of war, Macnaghten resolutely rejected the offered terms.

Angus had been constantly employed from the day he reached the cantonments. His work was to go out with small parties of the natives employed by the commissariat to bring in the grain that Boyd and Johnson had purchased. There was no slight risk in the work, for although the villagers were glad to sell their corn on good terms, the party who fetched it ran the risk of being cut off by any band of tribesmen they might encounter.

Of an evening he talked over the situation and prospects with the two officers. Absorbed in work as they all were, they were less influenced by the feeling of hopelessness than those who had nothing to do but to rage over the trap into which they had fallen through the incapacity of their leaders.

Still, they did not attempt to disguise from themselves the magnitude of the danger.

"I have no faith in any treaty that could be made," Boyd said. "An Afghan is only bound by his word as long as it pays him to keep it. They will take Macnaghten's money, and will promise that we shall be allowed to go down the passes without molestation; but I am mistaken indeed if we shall not be attacked the moment we enter them. If they do so, few of us will ever get through. The men are weak now from want of sufficient food. They are utterly dispirited and demoralized, as is shown by their shameful flight yesterday. Besides, they will be encumbered with a host of camp-followers, women, and children. I am still of opinion that our only hope is to take refuge in the Bala Hissar, and Shelton's vehement opposition has already put a stop to that. For myself, I would rather that they attacked us here, even if the attack meant our annihilation. It would be better to die so than cooped up hopelessly in the passes. At best the march would be a terrible one. The cold is severe already, and we hear that the snow is deep in the passes; not so deep as to render them impracticable, but deep enough to render the passage a terrible one."

"Of course we are bound to stay with the rest and do our best to the end. Were it not for that, we three might escape. We all speak the language well enough to pass as natives. You, indeed, have already done so. However, of course that is not to be thought of; indeed, it would probably amount to the same thing in the end, for we could scarcely hope to reach either Jellalabad or Candahar."

"No, it is not to be thought of, Johnson," his companion said. "We have to do our duty to the last. I still hope that the general may yet have an hour of inspiration and deliver battle in good order. I believe that the troops would fight well if they did but see that they were properly handled."

On the following day they learned that Akbar Khan had arrived. He was greeted with great enthusiasm and much firing of guns. Macnaghten had a faint hope that he would side with us, as his father, mother, and brothers were in our hands in India; but, on the other hand, he had every reason for bitter animosity against the British, who had, without any ground for complaint, invaded the country and dethroned his father. The prince bore the reputation of being frank, generous, and far brighter and more cheerful than the majority of his countrymen; at the same time he was passionate and impulsive, given to sudden bursts of anger. The wrongs that he and his family had suffered were, indeed, at present predominant in his mind. For two years he himself had been an exile from his country. His father, who had tried so hard to gain the friendship of the British, had been dethroned by them; and as it was notorious that their captives were always honourably treated, he felt that no action upon his part would recoil upon their heads.

He himself was now the heir to the throne if he could win it. He was extremely popular among the people, who hailed his advent as giving them a leader whom they could rely upon, under whom the chiefs of the tribesmen could lay aside their mutual jealousy and animosity and join in the effort to drive the foe for ever from their country. He did not, however, at once assume the chief authority. The Nawab Mahomed Zemaun Khan, a cousin of Dost Mahomed, had been proclaimed Ameer by the tribesmen, and all orders were sent forth in his name. He was a man of humane and honourable nature, of polished manners, and affable address.

As soon as he learned the state of affairs, Akbar Khan took immediate steps to prevent further supplies being taken into camp. He burned the villages where grain had been sold, and placed bands of men to attack any parties coming out from the camp to purchase grain. Day after day passed, messengers came and went between Macnaghten and the Nawab, but nothing was done; the food supply dwindled; only three days' rations remained in camp.

The supplies doled out were scarcely sufficient to keep life together. The oxen and other baggage animals were in such a state of starvation as to be wholly unfit for service. The store of fuel had long been used up, some men died of cold, and all suffered much. Macnaghten was still hopeful, and early in December again urged a retirement, but in vain. The enemy had now guns planted in several positions, and kept up an almost constant cannonade on the camp. On the 8th there were but three days' half-rations left, and the general informed Macnaghten by letter that it was absolutely necessary to surrender upon the best terms that could be obtained; and the three senior officers also signed the letter, saying that they concurred in it. On the 11th there was but one day's food left for the fighting men, the camp-followers were starving. Again and again Macnaghten urged that a force should sally out and at all costs bring in provisions, but the general knew that the men could not be relied upon to fight. The time had come when even Macnaghten saw that all hope had gone save in surrender. He drew out the rough draft of a treaty, and met the leading chiefs of the Afghans at about a mile from the river.

By this treaty the British were to evacuate Afghanistan. They were to be supplied with provisions for the journey, Shah Soojah was to abdicate, and to have the option of accompanying them; but if he did so, his wife and family were to remain as hostages until Dost Mahomed and his family were released. The troops at Jellalabad were also to retire, as well as those at Ghuznee and Candahar. Four British officers were to be left as hostages, to return to India on the arrival of Dost Mahomed and his family on the frontier. The conference lasted two hours, and its main stipulations were agreed to. The meeting then broke up, on the understanding that the British troops were to evacuate the cantonments in three days, and that provisions should in the meantime be sent in. The treaty was a humiliating one, but Macnaghten was not to blame for it. When the three military chiefs had declared that there was nothing for it but surrender, he was forced to make the best arrangement he could, and the terms of the treaty were as good as could have been expected in the circumstances.

When the conference broke up, Captain Trevor, one of Macnaghten's staff, accompanied the chief to the city as a hostage for the sincerity of the envoy. On the 11th the Bala Hissar was evacuated. Akbar Khan pledged himself to conduct the garrison safely to the cantonments, and kept his promise, succeeding in inducing the crowds of horsemen who gathered round to let the little detachment pass. The provisions, however, were not sent in as agreed, and the chiefs refused to send them until the garrisons were withdrawn from the forts they occupied round the cantonments. The parties were each suspicious of the other's good faith. On the 18th snow began to fall heavily. Macnaghten tried desperately to win over some of the chiefs, lavishing money among them. The Afghans made fresh demands, and demanded more hostages, and Lieutenants Conolly and Airey were handed over to them.

On the 22nd Akbar Khan sent in fresh proposals, to the effect that the British were to remain in Afghanistan till the spring, and then to withdraw as if of their own free-will. Shah Soojah was to remain as Ameer, and Akbar as his minister. As a reward for these services Akbar was to receive an annuity of £40,000 and a bonus of £300,000. Macnaghten accepted the terms, and agreed to meet Akbar. The offer was so strange that Elphinstone and others thought that it was probably a plot. Macnaghten replied that he did not think that it was so, but in any case he would go. After breakfast he sent for the officers of his staff, Lawrence, Mackenzie, and Trevor, who had returned, and begged them to accompany him to the meeting. An hour later they set out with a few horsemen. As they rode on Macnaghten admitted to his officers that he was well aware that it was a dangerous enterprise, but that he was playing for a heavy stake and the prize was worth the risk. "At all events," he said, "a thousand deaths are preferable to the life I have of late been leading."

The parties met at some hillocks six hundred yards from the cantonments, where some horse-cloths had been spread upon the snow by Akbar Khan's servants. Macnaghten presented to Akbar a splendid horse he had admired. They dismounted, and Macnaghten took his place on the blankets. Trevor, Mackenzie, and Lawrence sat behind him. Suddenly the envoy and his companions were violently seized from behind. The three officers were dragged away, and each compelled to mount horses ridden by Afghan chiefs, who rode off through the crowd. Trevor unfortunately slipped from his insecure seat, and was instantly cut to pieces, while the other two reached Mahomed Khan's fort alive. In the meantime the envoy himself was struggling desperately on the ground with Akbar Khan. Exasperated by the resistance of his victim, whom he had only intended to seize, the Afghan's passion blazed out, and drawing from his girdle a pistol, which Macnaghten had given him the day before, he shot him through the body. Instantly his followers closed round and hacked him to pieces.

Thus died a gentleman who, in other circumstances, might have made a great reputation for himself. Possessed of unusual talent, his course was marred by his propensity to believe all that he wished, to disbelieve all that ran counter to his own sanguine projects. During the last month of his life he did all that man could do to avert a catastrophe, but he had been unable to instil his spirit into any of the military commanders, or to induce them to take the only course to redeem the position, by giving battle to the foe that surrounded them. He was the author of the ill-fated expedition to Afghanistan, he was its noblest victim. His peculiar temperament was fatal to him. Even when there was no longer any ground for hope he still continued to be sanguine. He had all along believed in himself, and scoffed at the warnings of men who knew the country and people—of Burnes, Rawlinson, Pottinger, and others.

He was thoroughly sincere; he was always able to convince himself that what he believed must be true, and he acted accordingly. He was not a strong man; had he been so the course of events might have been altered. He deferred in every way to Shah Soojah's wishes, however much these might be opposed to his own judgment. He allowed him to misgovern the country, to drive the natives to desperation by the exactions of his tax-gatherers, and to excite the bitterest animosity of the chiefs by the arrogance with which he treated them. A strong man would have put a stop to all this—would have intimated to the Ameer that he held the throne solely by the assistance of British bayonets, and that unless he followed British counsels he would at once yield to the oft-repeated wishes of the Indian government and order the retirement of the troops.

ANNIHILATION OF THE ARMY

In terrible confusion the crowd of fugitives—they were now nothing more—all entered the terrible pass. The Ghilzyes at once commenced their attack. In vain did Akbar Khan and his chiefs endeavour to restrain the fanatics. From the hillsides, from every rocky crag, they opened a murderous fire. That day three thousand men fell, either from the musket fire or from the knives of the Afghans. The dooly-bearers had all deserted on the first day, the greater portion of the camels and ponies had been captured. So far the ladies had escaped; they all rode next to the advanced guard, as this was considered the safest point, for the soldiers here maintained some sort of order, and the Afghans, therefore, devoted their attention to the helpless crowd in the rear. Again the column halted in the snow.

In the morning the camp-followers made another rush ahead, but the troops, who were ordered to march at ten o'clock, did not move, for in spite of all the remonstrances of the officers, the general countermanded the order, believing that Akbar Khan would send in provisions and troops to protect them. Another terrible night was passed, and then Captain Skinner rode into camp with a new proposal from Akbar Khan, namely, that all the English ladies of the force should be placed under his charge, and that they might be accompanied by their husbands. Pottinger, remembering that Akbar Khan's family were in the hands of the British, and believing that he was sincere in his wish to save the ladies and children from destruction, sanctioned the proposal. Elphinstone at once accepted it. It was the choice of two evils. On the one hand Akbar Khan had proved faithless, and on the other certain death awaited the ladies. They were insufficiently clad, had scarcely tasted food since they left Cabul, and had passed three terrible nights in the snow. Undoubtedly it was the wiser course to trust them to Akbar Khan. Accordingly a party of Afghan horse rode in, and Lady Macnaghten, Lady Sale, and ten other ladies, some twenty children, and eight officers rode away under their escort.

The next morning the survivors started. The Sepoys had already lost the greater portion of their numbers; the remainder threw away their guns, which they could no longer use owing to their hands being frost-bitten, and joined the disorganized rabble in front. They were attacked in a narrow gorge, and the pass was soon choked with dead and dying. Not a single Sepoy survived. Of the sixteen thousand men, soldiers and camp-followers, that had left Cabul four days before, not more than a quarter were now alive. Akbar Khan watched the slaughter that was going on, declaring that he was powerless to restrain the Ghilzyes, whom even their own chiefs could not control. He advised that the remnant of the British army should lay down their arms and place themselves under his protection. The general very properly refused the offer, for Akbar Khan had already acknowledged that he was incapable of restraining the tribesmen.

The march was continued. The rear-guard was commanded by Shelton, and nobly they did their work, repulsing several attacks of the enemy, and giving time for those ahead to pursue their way. Before daybreak they started again in hopes that they might reach Jugduluk that day. Despair gave the soldiers strength, and they moved off quietly in order to obtain a start of the camp-followers, who paralysed their action. The latter, however, were soon on their feet, and as usual endeavoured to push on ahead of the troops. For some miles the retreat was uninterrupted, but presently a heavy fire opened on the rearguard. The camp-followers then rushed in a tumultuous crowd past the troops, and when, a little later, the head of the column was attacked, they again fled to the rear, not only hampering the movements of the soldiers, but carrying many of them away by the impetus of their rush. Steadily until day broke, the Afghan marksmen maintained their fire. Soon afterwards the advanced guard reached a village ten miles from Jugduluk, and halting only till the rearguard came up, again pushed forward. Shelton, with a handful of the rear-guard, kept the Afghans at bay, and covered the retreat until all arrived at Jugduluk, where they took their post behind some ruined walls. There was, however, little rest for them; the Afghans, in ever-increasing numbers, posted themselves on the heights and opened a terrible fire. Three bullocks were found among the camp-followers; these were instantly killed and served out to the famishing soldiers, who devoured them raw. Again Akbar's party approached, and Captain Skinner went out to remonstrate with him for permitting the continued attacks, but the Afghan prince declared himself incapable of repressing his men, as his orders were disregarded.

A handful of the 44th Regiment issued out and made a gallant rush at the enemy and drove them back, but as the main body did not follow their example, they again retired behind the ruined walls. All night long and through the next day the force remained at Jugduluk. Akbar Khan sent in a message inviting the general, Shelton, and Captain Johnson to a conference, and promised to send in provisions. This promise he as usual broke, and insisted on retaining the three officers as hostages.

The conference was resumed the next morning. Akbar now seemed in earnest in his desire to put a stop to the slaughter; but the petty chiefs of the tribes between Jugduluk and Jellalabad were now present, and these would listen neither to his entreaties nor commands, nor to the offer of large sums of money. They thirsted for blood, and were determined to extirpate the infidels. Mahomed Shah Khan, to whose daughter Akbar was married, then came forward and asked whether the British would pay two lacs of rupees for safe-conduct to Jellalabad. The general agreed to this, and it seemed that at last the safety of the survivors was ensured. At eight o'clock in the evening the survivors, who now numbered but a hundred and twenty of the 44th and twenty-five artillerymen, again set forth. No provisions had been sent in during the two days' halt, and all were terribly reduced by famine. The Afghans rushed down among the camp-followers, killing them unresistingly. The soldiers, however, held together, and, bayonet in hand, drove off their assailants until they reached the Jugduluk Pass. They struggled up the narrow and terribly steep ascent until when near the summit they came upon a barricade composed of bushes and branches of trees. Here the column was thrown into great confusion, the camp-followers crowding upon the soldiers. The latter fought with desperation, while the Afghans massacred the unresisting camp-followers.

Twelve officers fell here. Their number was large in proportion to that of the men. They had been no better clothed, and had suffered equally from cold and hunger; but they did not give way to the depression that during the first two marches had reigned among the troops. They were upheld, too, by the feeling of responsibility, and the necessity of keeping up an appearance of cheerfulness and hopefulness in order to encourage the men. After desperate fighting some twenty officers and twenty-five soldiers managed to break their way through the barricade, and at daybreak reached Gundamuck. There were but two rounds of ammunition remaining in the men's pouches. Most of them were already wounded, but they were resolute not to lay down their arms, and when called upon to do so they refused. Then the mob of Afghans rushed down upon them. One officer and a few privates were taken prisoners, but seven officers succeeded in cutting their way through, and being mounted, left the Afghans behind them, and reached Futtehbad, but sixteen miles from Jellalabad. Here, however, they were attacked by the peasantry. Two were cut down at once; the others rode off, but were pursued and overtaken. Four of them were killed, and one only, Dr. Brydon, reached Jellalabad alive, the sole survivor of four thousand five hundred fighting men and twelve thousand camp-followers, with the exception only of those who had been taken over by Akbar as hostages.

This, the greatest disaster that ever befell a British army, was due to the vacillation and weakness that had characterized every action since the murder of Sir Alexander Burnes. Had the force pressed forward at once on the morning when it left its cantonment, the greater portion would probably have reached Jellalabad, but two days had been lost before the army reached Khoord Cabul Pass, about ten miles from the city. There were fresh halts, fresh delays, fresh futile negotiations again and again, and during the time thus thrown away the enemy from all the mountains round were gathering in the passes to oppose them, and building the fatal barricade in the pass of Jugduluk. Had the force pushed forward with only an occasional halt of a few hours, they would not have been enfeebled by hunger. By slaying the baggage animals an abundance of food could have been obtained for all, the opposition they encountered would have been comparatively feeble, and cold

would have been their only formidable antagonist. Truly it seemed that a curse had fallen upon the army; that it was Divine retribution for a most unjust and iniquitous war.

Each day Angus and his followers had been taken along, always being halted in positions whence they could see the terrible tragedy that was being enacted. Angus was half-mad with grief and with fury that he was not in his place among the troops. Azim in vain endeavoured to comfort him, by pointing out that it was not his fault that he was not there, but that he had been sent away from the army by the order of his superior; and that even had he not been taken prisoner, he would not be a sharer in what was going on in the pass.

"That is true, Azim, but it is a poor consolation to me. I feel sure that Pottinger foresaw what would happen, and that it was as an act of friendship, in giving me a chance of getting through safely, that he sent me down. It was no doubt kindly meant, but I would a thousand times rather have shared the fate of the rest."

"Well, master, for my part I own that I am glad we are up here. I have no wish to be killed, especially as it would do no good to anyone. Why should a man throw away his life? Allah has given it to us, and we shall die when our time comes. But it would be wicked to throw it away uselessly."

"It is all very well to talk like that, Azim, when one is in safety, but when one sees one's comrades being slaughtered, a man would not be worthy of the name did he not long to be with them and to die fighting by their side. Indeed, we know not at present whether our lives are to be saved. We know not into whose hands we have fallen, or why we should thus be taken along to be spectators of this massacre. The whole thing is bewildering to me."

They now generally conversed in Persian. Their guards, although keeping as strict a watch as ever on them, interfered with them but little. Fortunately the worst scenes took place at night, and were therefore hidden from those on the hill, the incessant rattle of musketry alone telling of the relentless pursuit. On the night of the 12th the roar of fire had been louder than ever. At last it ceased suddenly. Angus and his guards alike remained awake, Angus listening in agony to the sounds of the combat, the Afghans talking together in low tones.

"What do you think has happened?" he asked them when some minutes had passed without the sound of a shot being heard.

"Either Akbar Khan has succeeded in persuading the Ghilzye chiefs to spare what few there are left of the infidels, or the last man has been slain."

Angus felt that the latter was by far the more probable solution, and throwing himself down on the ground he burst into tears. The eight days of mental suffering had shaken him terribly, and now, feeling that his worst fears had been realized, he broke down altogether. Before daybreak his captors moved some distance farther up into the mountains, and by the cautious manner in which they made their way, often pausing to look back and round, Angus concluded that they were desirous of avoiding all contact with their countrymen. He had indeed before observed how careful they were to avoid the Afghans scattered on the hillside, and he now concluded that they must be taking him to the tower of the chief, to be dealt with as he might direct, either shot at once or held by him as a hostage, for whose delivery he might obtain a handsome sum should the British again advance up the passes.

All day they travelled among the hills. At last they came upon a large village. There were no men about, doubtless all had gone to take part in the fray. The women came out and eagerly questioned them as to the fighting on the night before.

"We know nothing," the leader said. "We believe that the last of the infidels has fallen, but we know nothing for certain."

Without pausing they took the two prisoners, whose appearance had created no surprise, as they were taken for natives, to the chief's tower, a much larger building than the abodes of most of the petty chiefs. Standing upon a crag of rock, it overlooked the village; entrance was only obtainable by a ladder leading to a door some thirty feet above the rock. Their coming had been observed. An old man stood at the door.

"So you are back, Suffyd?"

"Yes, as you see. Has the chief returned?"

"No; it is two weeks since we saw him last. He started then with all the fighting men from here and the other villages; but I expect it will not be long before he returns, for, from what we have heard, the work must be nearly done."

The party ascended the ladder, and the leader spoke a word or two with the old man, who looked greatly surprised. The captives were taken into a room, which by its furnishing was evidently one of the chief's private apartments.

"You are free to move about the house," the leader said, "but you must not leave it."

In a few minutes a woman entered, bringing a dish of boiled grain with portions of mutton in it. She gave the usual Afghan salutation. She was followed by another woman with a jug of water, two mugs, and a bottle. These were placed on a low table, and then without another word they left the room. A minute later they returned with a large earthenware dish full of burning charcoal.

"This is a good beginning, Azim," Angus said, his spirits rising at the sight of the hot food; for although they had not been actually starved, they had been on extremely short rations when their supply of flour was exhausted, their captors being, like themselves, reduced to a handful of unground grain each day. "This does not look as if they meant to cut our throats. Evidently our Afghan is acting under orders. Those orders must have been that we were to be well treated."

They ate a hearty meal; then Angus said:

"See what there is in that bottle, Azim."

The cork had already been taken out, and Azim poured some of the liquor into a tin, and handed it to his master. The latter smelt it.

"It is Afghan spirits," he said, "the same as they sell in the bazaars in Cabul."

He filled it up with water, and drank it off.

"Now, Azim, do you do the same."

Azim, who was not a very strict Mohammedan, and had more than once tasted the forbidden drink at Cabul, needed no pressing.

"Well, master," he said, as he put the cup down, "after all this is better than lying dead and frozen down in the pass."

Angus, warmed with the good meal and by the draught that he had taken, could not disagree with his follower.

"I begin to think that you are right, Azim, though I did not believe so yesterday. It is certain that had I joined my countrymen I should have perished with them, and assuredly I have been saved from eight days of awful suffering and from death—if, indeed, we are saved from death."

"I think we can feel certain of that, master. This is not the way the Afghans treat a man whose throat they intend to cut. They certainly do not make a pillau for him, or provide him with a bottle of spirits."

"Do you know, I have been thinking, Azim," Angus said after a short silence, "that if it had been possible for Sadut Khan to know that we intended to leave camp in disguise, this might be his work again. But he could not have known it. No one but you and I, and Major Pottinger, and the three or four officers to whom I said good-bye, knew anything about it. Besides, he would have sent the men who captured us before, and who knew us by sight. And even supposing, which seems to be impossible, that this was his doing, why not have sent us here straight, instead of taking eight days to do a journey that could have been made easily in two, and forcing me to witness the awful scenes in the passes? It is all most extraordinary."

"However, there is no question, sir, that whoever our captor may be, he has been the means of saving our lives."

"There can be no doubt of that, Azim; and though I may not feel that at present, I shall in the future be very grateful to him. Even if he were to have us shot directly he comes here, I should still be grateful, for it would be a sudden death and not a lingering one, as it has been to those below. Well, it is of no use puzzling ourselves over the matter. I suppose we shall learn how it all came about when the chief, whoever he be, returns here. In the meantime we are certainly a great deal better off than we have been for the past two months in cantonments."

"That we are, master. To begin with, I am warm for the first time since the winter set in; and in the next place, I have had a good meal, and do not feel that I could grumble at anything. As to your mission, you said yourself that nothing could come of it, even if you succeeded in getting through, so that in that respect nothing has been lost by our journey being so suddenly brought to an end."

The next day some of the men who had been away with their chief returned, and the old man in charge told Angus that only one man out of all who had started from Cabul had reached Jellalabad, but that several officers had been taken as hostages, including the two generals, Major Pottinger and Captain Johnson, and two others; also, that all the ladies and children, and the ladies' husbands, had accepted the protection of Akbar.

It was a relief, indeed, to Angus to find that his friends Pottinger and Johnson had been saved, and as Captain Boyd was one of the married officers, he also must have escaped the massacre. As to the fate of Elphinstone and Shelton he was indifferent, it was to them that the misfortune that had befallen the army was largely due; but the thought that his three greatest friends had escaped gave him much pleasure. With these exceptions, that but one man out of sixteen thousand five hundred should have escaped was appalling. That the loss had been terrible he was well aware, but he was hardly prepared for the total annihilation of the force.

Another two days passed. They continued to be well fed and treated, and the women who waited upon them seemed to regard them as guests rather than as captives, talking freely with them, and only being silent when Angus endeavoured to find out the name of their chief. It was evident that on this point they had orders to keep silent. On the third day they heard a stir in the village, and shouts of acclamation and welcome. The room in which they were confined was at the back of the house, and they were therefore unable to obtain a view of what was passing.

"We shall learn our fate now, Azim," Angus said.

"I have no fear of its being a bad one, master. We cannot doubt that orders were given that we should be well treated. If we are kept prisoners till the spring, for my part I shall not grumble, if they continue to treat us as well as they have been doing."

They heard the sound of many footsteps and loud talking, then the door opened and Sadut Khan entered. He advanced with both hands outstretched to Angus.

"My dear friend," he said, "how thankful I am that you have been saved where so many have perished!"

"And so it is you, chief, to whom I owe my life?" Angus said, returning the warm grasp of Sadut's hand. "I did not thank you at first, for it seemed to me shameful that an English officer should not share in the fate of his comrades."

Sadut smiled. "But in no case would you have shared their fate. It is not from that I have saved you, but from being killed on your way down. Knowing that the passes were full of our people, I was sure that you must have been taken and murdered. No story you could have told would have availed you. You were not a Ghilzye, nor a member of any of the tribes there, and you would assuredly have been detected and killed had I not saved you."

"That is so, Sadut; and although at first I was half-mad at being unable to join my countrymen, I saw before the end came that, had I done so, my life would have been thrown away uselessly."

"Exactly; and that was why I ordered that you should be enabled to see all that passed. From what I had seen of you, I was sure that at first you would bitterly resent being taken prisoner, and that even if you knew into whose hands you had fallen you would resist; and it was for that reason that I did not this time employ Hassan and his followers to seize you, though all through your journey they kept close at hand, to use my name and authority should any party of tribesmen meet you—not that I had much fear of your detection had they done so. The men with you had orders that in case they did meet such a party, they were to treat you both, not as captives, but as forming part of their own band. Still, it was as well that Hassan should be at hand in case of need."

"I thank you with all my heart, Sadut. I could not have done so at first, but I can do so now; you have indeed saved my life. A few days ago that seemed to me as nothing, for I felt that I was dishonoured in looking on at the massacre of my countrymen. I have had time to think it over since, and I now know that the view I took was exaggerated. Could I have joined them it was plainly my duty to have done so, but if I was a prisoner no blame could attach to me. Have you, chief, taken part in this terrible business?"

"No. With twenty of my own horsemen I rode with Akbar, who is my friend and relative, but I had no intention of drawing my sword against your people. I knew that they had been promised protection, and I thought that Akbar and his force were going to escort them. His word had been given, and I did not think he would withdraw it.

"I do not think it was his intention to do so. He could have done much more than he did, but he could not have saved the fugitives. The Nawab was alone among the Afghan chiefs in the sincerity of his assurances. Akbar had no influence with the Ghilzye chiefs, and even had he influenced them they could not have restrained their tribesmen and the Ghazees. The die was cast. It was Allah's will that those who had invaded the country without any pretext, dethroned Dost Mahomed, who had eagerly sought their alliance, and forced a man we all hated upon us, should meet their fate. Over and over again we implored Akbar, for the sake of his pledge and his word, to assist your people; even if, in his efforts to do so, he fell; then his name would go down as long as our nation existed as one who died in defence of his oath and his honour. He was all along irresolute. At times he did his best short of attacking the Ghilzyes, at other times he held aloof altogether from the scene. At any rate, I can feel that my honour is not soiled. I was not one of those who signed the treaty, but I have done my best to prevent that treaty from being violated. Had your people sallied out from the cantonments and given us battle, I should have fought against them. But even had there been no treaty, I would not have taken part in the massacre of men who were practically defenceless, and who were in no way responsible for the crime of their government."

"I am glad to hear you say so, chief. I should have been grieved indeed had you taken part in so treacherous and terrible a massacre. But how did you learn that I was going to try to make my way down to Jellalabad? That I have never been able to understand."

"I kept a watch over you the whole time, my friend. Either Hassan, or one of his men who knew you, was always in the camp, dressed as one of the camp followers."

"But even then I cannot imagine how he could have told that I was going. I knew it myself but a few hours before I started, and only Major Pottinger and three or four of my friends were aware of it."

"My watch was a good one," the chief said, "and when two Afghans issued from your tent you may be sure the news was quickly brought to the men who had for some days been lying in readiness, and who were prepared to repeat the adventure in the city."

Suddenly, to the astonishment of Angus, Azim threw himself on his knees. "Master!" he exclaimed, "you can kill me, but I own that it was I who betrayed you. I had met Hassan in the camp, and he told me that assuredly no white man would escape alive, that it was settled that all should be attacked and slain in the passes. He said that Sadut Khan had resolved to save you, but that to do this with certainty it would be necessary that he should be informed as to your movements, and where you would ride when the army started. He said that unless I helped them it might be impossible to save you. Then I agreed to do so, and met him or one of his men every day. As soon as you had left the tent after telling me of your expedition, I ran to the spot where I knew I should find Hassan, and told him that we were going alone. He said at once that it would be certain death were you to try to go down the pass, and that you must be carried off as soon as you had left the camp. I knew well that you would be greatly angered, and that if you suspected me you would kill me for my treachery; but that was nothing compared to your life, and so I turned traitor to you, and am willing now that you should order me to be taken out and beheaded."

Angus held out his hand to his faithful follower. "I should have been angry at first—grieved and angry too, but I cannot be angry now. You did what you believed to be best for me, and I acknowledge that it has turned out so. Your treachery was but an act of fidelity, and undoubtedly was the means of saving my life. You did wrong, but it was with the best intentions. You ought to have confided in me."

"But I knew that if I did so you would not have consented."

"That is true enough; still, I was the best judge of what was consistent with my honour. However, next to Sadut Khan I owe you my life, and it would be but poor gratitude were I to reproach you. Let us say no more about it. I shall remember always that you saved my life, and shall forget that you somewhat betrayed my trust. I have for four years past regarded you as my friend rather than as my servant, and I shall esteem you even more so in the future."

Azim retired with tears of joy in his eyes. Sadut and Angus had a long talk together. As if by mutual consent, the subject of the late events was avoided, and the conversation was upon their journey across the Bamian, and Sadut's doings since that time.

"I stayed at Khooloom until the governor, whom we had trusted implicitly, handed over Dost Mahomed's family and mine to your people. I happened to be away at the time, and on my return two days later was warned by Hassan of what had taken place. When Dost returned from captivity among the Turkomans, of course I joined him and accompanied him to Kohistan, and fought by his side in the battle of Purwandurrah. The Ameer had said no word even to me of his intention to surrender, and I was thunder-struck when I heard that he had given himself up. I remained there, and took part in the attack on the Ghoorka regiment at Charekar. After that I returned home. My fortress, as you know, lies far to the west among the Momunds. This place does not belong to me, but to the husband of a sister of mine. She is at present at my place with her husband, who is ill; and as I wished to be nearer to the scene of action, he begged me to use his fort as a residence. I desired to hold myself aloof from the negotiations, as I knew that most of the chiefs were open at any moment to betray the cause for British gold. Still, I was often down in the city, where I own the house to which you were taken. I no longer hated your people as infidels—your kindness to me showed me that there was goodness in your religion as well as in mine—but I was still ready to fight against them as the invaders of my country."

"And now, chief, what do you propose to do with me?"

"That is for you to decide, my friend. I know what you will say, but, though I may regret it deeply, I shall certainly offer no opposition. You are my guest, and it is not for me to dictate to you. I should be happy if you would stay with me till these troubles have passed, but I place myself wholly at your disposal, whatever you may decide upon."

"Thank you, indeed! It is clear to me that if it is in my power I should immediately rejoin our forces."

"I was sure that that would be your wish, and I will send you down with a strong escort to Peshawur."

"I would rather join Sale at Jellalabad."

Sadut Khan shook his head. "In that case," he said, "I shall have rescued you in vain. Sale's force is already besieged, and it will be but a repetition of Cabul. By orders of Akbar Khan, the Ghilzye chiefs have all risen. The town is practically without fortifications, though I hear that the white soldiers have been labouring hard to put the place in a state of defence. But if the army at Cabul could not withstand us, still less will Sale's force, which is only a third of its strength, hold Jellalabad."

"You forget, chief, that they are commanded by a man, and not by an utterly incapable person. They are not dispirited by forced inaction or want of food. I do not say that Jellalabad may not be taken, but I feel sure that it will offer a sturdy resistance, and the news of what has happened in the passes will only fill the soldiers with fury. At any rate, Sale's is the only force that remains of the army to which I was attached, and it is there that it is my duty, with your permission, to go. I am sure that were you in my place that would also be your decision."

"So be it," Sadut said after a long pause. "Were you to go to Peshawur you might meet your death there also, as doubtless a force will endeavour to relieve Jellalabad, and in that case you would certainly go with them. They will never force their way through the Khyber Pass. From what I hear the Sepoys at Peshawur are almost in a state of mutiny. The Sikhs have sapped their loyalty, and have assured them that they will never be able to force the pass; and when they do move forward they cannot be depended upon to stand by the British troops, so that your danger may be as great one way as another. However, Jellalabad is your choice and not mine. The citadel there is strong, and when the town is captured, as it certainly will be soon, the troops can retire there, and may hold out until they make terms and are allowed to return to India."

"I do not think they will make terms, Sadut. They have had a terrible lesson as to the manner in which treaties are respected by the greater portion of your chiefs, and are not likely to trust again to any promises, but will hold out until they have fired their last cartridge."

"They cannot hope to defend themselves," Sadut said positively. "Akbar Khan will himself head the army."

"I do not think, Sadut, that you know yet what a British soldier can do when well led. There has been no great battle fought since we entered Afghanistan, and you must not judge them by the small fights that took place round Cabul; the soldiers there had lost heart and confidence in their commander. It will be a very different thing when you meet them confident in themselves and in their leaders. Believe me, your hosts, however large, do not frighten them. You know how they have overcome many of the best fighting races in India, and that in the teeth of odds as great as can be brought against them here. I say not a word against the courage of your people, but they want discipline and training, and even a host of men, fighting each for himself, cannot withstand the charge of well disciplined soldiers."

"Why did they not come up the passes, then, to aid their friends?"

"Because they were deficient in carriage, they were in a country altogether hostile to them, they had many sick, and must have left a strong force to guard them. There may have been other reasons of which I know not, but these are sufficient. For a force to enter these passes without animals to carry their food and their wounded would have been madness. And I believe that Sale has not more than twelve hundred bayonets, a force sufficient to do wonders in the plains, but which could hardly fight their way up the passes against thousands of good marksmen, as the Afghans assuredly are, armed with guns which carry much farther than their own, and firing in safety behind inaccessible rocks. But whether Jellalabad can resist all attacks, as I believe, or whether the place falls, is a matter which does not affect my resolution. It is my duty to be there, and if you will afford me means of getting there I will assuredly go."

"We will start to-morrow, then, and the sooner we are off the better. The news of what has happened in the passes will spread like a flame through the country, and every fighting man will turn out to complete the work. There is a pathway from here which goes straight down to Gundamuck. I will ride with you with half a dozen of my followers; there are plenty of ponies on the hills. Certainly no questions will be asked, no suspicions can arise. When we get near Jellalabad we shall see how you can best enter. I will ride round the place with you. As I am a friend of Akbar's, it will be supposed that I am examining the place to see where an attack had best be made. There are many orchards and small villages round. When we are as near the town as we can get, you can slip from your horse as we go through an orchard. Keep under cover in the gardens until close to the walls. When you get within musket-shot you can tie a white cloth to your gun, and you will then be safe."

This plan was carried out, and two days later, after a grateful parting from his preserver, Angus stood at the edge of the moat opposite one of the gates.

7

A Journal of Disasters
in Affghanistan (1843)

FLORENTIA SALE

Lady Florentia Sale (1790–1853) was the wife of Major General Robert Sale, who commanded the garrison at Jalalabad—a sufficiently heroic feat to earn him the Order of the Bath. She was also a chronicler of the occupation, the retreat, and the captivity in her own right. According to her account, Sale's journal was only preserved in the heat of insurrection and retreat because she had the presence of mind to bundle her notes in a bag and tie it to her waist the morning she was forced to flee Kabul. Similar to the anonymous female captive who wrote for *Bentley's Miscellany* (see chapter 8), Sale was skeptical of many so-called eye-witness accounts that she implied were drawn from memory, unlike her regular diary entries. Perhaps because her husband was an officer, her account focuses on battles and political intrigue. Generally upbeat and full of vigor, her writing rarely displays fear or despair; the one exception is her apprehension at the prospect that the city, a tinderbox of "flat-roofed and mud-roofed houses," will be burned to the ground by the rebels.

INTRODUCTION

I have not only daily noted down events as they occurred, but often have done so hourly. I have also given the reports of the day, the only information we possessed; also such news as was telegraphed from the Bala Hissar, or sent in by the King or by Capt. Conolly to the Envoy; and many other reports brought by Affghan gentlemen of Capt. Sturt's* acquaintance, and by others of lower degree, who having had dealings with him in the engineer department and public works, and having received kindness from him, gave him such intelligence and warning as was in their power: all of which he communicated [to his superior officers] at different times; but the warnings were not attended to; and as when he gave his advice it was seldom adhered to, he became disgusted, and contented himself with zealously performing his duties and making himself generally useful, acting the part of an artillery

*Lady Sale's son-in-law.

officer as well as that of an engineer. Had poor Sturt's life been spared, it was his intention to have worked up my Rough Notes, and to have added much valuable information: he was too much over-worked to afford leisure to give me assistance at the time. His plans, drawings, &c., with his public and private papers, were lost, except a note or two that were, just a few days before we left Cabul, put with my Journal. I believe several people kept an account of these proceedings, but all except myself lost all they had written; and had recourse to memory afterwards. I lost every thing except the clothes I wore; and therefore it may appear strange that I should have saved these papers. The mystery is, however, easily solved. After every thing was packed on the night before we left Cabul, I sat up to add a few lines to the events of the day, and the next morning I put them in a small bag and tied them round my waist. I am indebted to Capt. Souter, of H. M. 44th Regiment, for a plan, from recollection, of the cantonment and forts. The inaccuracies, if any, are but trifling; and it is sufficiently clear to indicate the positions of the principal places alluded to.

A much better narrative of past events might have been written, even by myself; but I have pre-ferred keeping my Journal as originally written, when events were fresh, and men's minds were bi-assed by the reports of the day, and even hour.

It is easy to argue on the wisdom or folly of con-duct after the catastrophe has taken place. With regard therefore to our chiefs, I shall only say that the Envoy has deeply paid for his attempt to out diplomatize the Affghans. Gen. Elphinstone, con-scious that his powers of mind had become en-feebled with those of his body, finding there was no hope of Gen. Nott's arrival to assume the com-mand, called in another officer to his aid, who had but one object in view (to get back, at all hazards, to Hindostan). He averred that a retreat to the Bala Hissar was impossible, as we should have to fight our way (for one mile and a half)! If we could not accomplish that, how were we to get through a week's march to Jellalabad? Once in the Bala His-

sar, which would have been easily defended by one thousand men, we should have had plenty of troops for foraging purposes; and the village of Ben-i-shehr, just under the Bala Hissar, would have given us a twelvemonth's provisions if we had only made the demonstration of a night march, to have the appearance of taking them by force. Sal-lies from thence might also have been made into the town, where there was always a party, particu-larly the Kuzzilbashes, who would have covertly assisted us, until our returning fortunes permitted them to do so openly.

Independent of ———'s determination to return to India, he often refused to give any opinion when asked for it by the General, a cautious measure whereby he probably hoped to escape the obloquy that he expected would attach to the council of war, composed of Gen. Elphinstone, Brig. Shelton, Brig. Anquetil, and Col. Chambers. I might say nomi-nally composed; numerically it was much more ex-tended. Capt. Grant, with cold caution, obstructed every enterprise, and threw all possible difficulties in the way; Capt. Bellew was full of doubts and suggestions, all tending to hamper and retard op-erations; and numbers of young men gave much gratuitous advice; in fact, the greater part of the night was spent in confusing the General's ideas, instead of allowing a sick man time by rest to in-vigorate his powers. Brig. Shelton was in the habit of taking his rezai with him, and lying on the floor during these discussions, when sleep, whether real or feigned, was a resource against replying to dis-agreeable questions. Major Thain, a sincere friend and good adviser of the General's, withdrew in disgust from the council: and Sturt, who was ever ready to do any thing or give his opinion when asked, from the same feeling no longer proffered it.

As a proof that Sir William Macnaghten's confi-dence in Shah Shoojah was latterly much shaken, he wrote to the Governor of India, proposing that, if it really should be proved that His Majesty was acting treacherously against us, the Dost should be restored to his country. But it is very doubtful whether this despatch ever reached the Governor-General.

I shall not refer back to many small insurrections that took place, but only allude to the events that immediately preceded the grand insurrection at Cabul.

I believe I have indifferently written the name of a village as Dehmaru and Behmaru; it is called both, but Behmaru is the correct name, signifying the husbandless: Dehmaru would be the Husband's Village. It takes its name from a romantic legend of a girl of rank betrothed to a chief who was said to have been slain in combat, and she consequently pined away and died also; but the lover recovered from his wounds, and placed a stone, said to be one of those white ones that look like women in Bourkhor, over her grave on the Behmaru hill; and when he died he was buried beside her, with a similar stone to mark the spot.

CABUL

September, 1841.—Sir William Macnaghten obtained a force to be sent out to the Zoormut country. A chief, contemptuously designated as a robber, was said to have gone into the town of Zaho beyond Gurdez. The information given to Capt. Hay, commanding one of the Shah's corps, represented the place as contemptible. He went there with some few troops supported by guns, found that the place was much stronger than he had supposed, and that he could not do anything against it, and that he was fired at from six forts. On this intelligence reaching Cabul, a large force was sent out on the 28th of September, under Col. Oliver of the 5th, consisting of half of Capt. Abbott's battery, two iron nine-pounder guns, a wing of the 44th Queen's, the 5th N. I., Capt. Warburton's guns, Capt. Backhouse's mountain train, Anderson's horse, the Kohistan corps, and two others of the Shah's, with the King's sappers and miners and the Hindostanee sappers and miners under Capt. Sturt, as sole engineer.

The first day's march was through the city, with narrow streets and sharp turnings, very unfavorable for guns, as was also a bad road afterwards, a nullah, and a steep ascent; all which circumstances kept them from getting into camp until late in the evening; after that the road was good, with the exception of the Al-Timor pass, which was very steep. It rises 9600 feet above the level of the sea. The crest was represented as being as much as a man on horseback could surmount, and the artillery would never have been got over it had not the natives given their assistance: 800 of them dragged the guns up. The great difficulty (as far as I could learn) lay, not so much in the acclivity, as in the roughness of the road, which was perfectly filled with huge blocks of stone. Here it was dreadfully cold, and snow fell. Beyond this pass the people of the country fled, abandoning their property, and consequently their suffering must be very great in the approaching winter.

The chiefs declared that they were ready to submit, but the orders were peremptory to destroy the forts that had fired on the Shah's troops. Lieut. John Conolly and Lieut. Burnet (54th) chupao'd Akram Khan, riding sixty miles at night with 300 horsemen. They surprised the chief, his wives, and families; it was however done through the treachery of the chief's son-in-law, who disclosed his retreat. The Shah has ordered Akram Khan's execution. Whilst these events were going on, disturbances had broken out near Cabul, where much had occurred to incite the chiefs to rise. In former times, under the feudal system, when the sovereign of Cabul required troops, each bold chieftain came forward with his retainers; but these vassals had been taken from them, and were embodied in corps commanded by British officers, to whom they owed no affection, and only paid a forced obedience, whilst their hearts were with their national religion; their chief's power was now greatly limited, and the chouk guaranteed to them was withheld on the plea that the Company had commanded retrenchments. But the saving required by Government was a curtailment of those expences which were defrayed by its own rupees, whereas the 40,000 rupees now the subject of dispute were, in fact, no saving at all to us, as that money was never paid by the Company, but was the chouk or money excused to the chiefs out of the revenue or dues owing to the King, on condition of their enforcing the submission of the petty chiefs and the payment of their rents. This sum whether paid to Shah Shoojah or not, would never have replenished the Hon. Company's coffers; and by upholding the Shah in such an act of aggression we compromised our faith, and caused a pretty general insurrection, said to be headed by Meer Musjude.

The Kohistanee chiefs are urged on by the Dooranee Chiefs in Cabul, and all the country about Tézeen and Bhoodkhak is in a state of revolt. It is only wonderful this did not take place sooner.

The Indian government have for some time been constantly writing regarding the enormous expenditure in Affghanistan, every dāk has reiterated retrench; but instead of lessening the political expences and making deductions in that department, they commenced by cutting off these 40,000 rupees from the chiefs.

Affairs having assumed this gloomy appearance, the Envoy sent in all haste for the force under Col. Oliver to return as quickly as possible, leaving it to Capt. Macgregor's diplomatic ability to patch up the Zaho business as best he might, and come to the rescue with his advice regarding the Tézeenites, with whoso customs, &c. he had much familiarity. Macgregor strongly advised the not stirring up a hornet's nest, and wished to try what he could do by diplomacy. Valour, however, was the order of the day; and various were the suggestions of the politicals. One plan was, that Gen. Sale's brigade, on its way down to the provinces, should make a detour via Nigerow. The troops were not to fight but only by their presence to overawe the Nigerowians, whilst some neighbouring tribes, who had a blood feud with them, should make the attack. Plans of the country were sent in, with imaginary roads drawn on them from various points, whilst supervening obstacles to the march of an army, such as hills and passes, were omitted. The scheme was not considered feasible, in consequence of the advanced state of the season, it being now October, and from the apprehension that the cold would destroy the camels requisite to carry the tents and provisions.

9th October.—The 35th N. I., commanded by Col. Monteath, C. B., with two six-pounder guns under Lieut. Dawes, were suddenly sent at a day's notice to Bhoodkhak, partly as being the first march towards the provinces (they forming a part of Sale's, or the 1st brigade), and partly in consequence of the disturbances.

11th.—The 13th light infantry, commanded by Lieut.-Col. Dennie, C. B., were also sent at a few hours' notice to Bhoodkhak; but as they were not to proceed on their march until the arrival of Capt. Abbott with his guns, I remained at Cabul with my daughter, Mrs. Sturt, who had been staying with us during her husband's absence with Col. Oliver's force; and Sale took his departure from Cabul, fully expecting me to follow him in three days at the latest.

12th.—The 13th and 35th, with the two guns under Dawes, moved forward, the whole under Sale, their object being to go through the Khoord Cabul pass, and place the 35th N. I. in an advanced position at Khoord Cabul, after which the 13th were to fall back again on Bhoodkhak. This movement was effected, but with considerable loss. The Khoord Cabul is a narrow defile, enclosed by high and rugged rocks; it is said that the number of the enemy did not exceed 60 men, but they possessed considerable advantage over our troops in their knowledge of the country and in the positions they took up; for until they commenced firing, not a man was known to be there. They were concealed behind rocks and stones, and by a stone breastwork that they had hastily thrown up, behind which, on our troops entering the pass, they laid in wait, and appeared to pick off the officers in particular. The number of the enemy were, however, underrated, as I am assured there were fully 200 of them. The 35th lost, in killed and wounded, about 40 men; and Capt. Younghusband, of the same corps, was badly wounded in the foot. The 13th had 8 men killed and 19 wounded. Gen. Sale was wounded in the left leg; the ball entered near the ankle, shivered the small bone, and was taken out from the skin on the other side where it had lodged. Lieut. Mein of the 13th, while leading his company up to the breastwork, was severely and dangerously wounded in the head; the skull was fractured by the ball, which entered it. Lieut. Oakes, of the same regiment, had also a very narrow escape, being wounded in the head also. It rained very heavily that night, and the 13th had the full benefit of it, for they were out all night, having two alertes; one of the sentries was mortally wounded, being shot on his post. Exertions were made to discover the persons who fired on our sentries: three men were seized who had in their possession the soldier's belt, which was a tolerable evidence of criminality; but the Envoy wrote to say, that the people about the King said that those men were good men and true, and they were to be released without any punishment!

13th.—Two companies of the 37th N. I. and two guns under Mr. Waller, were sent to reinforce the 13th at Bhoodkhak, leaving only the remainder of the 37th in cantonments, and no guns. Should there be a rising in Cabul, we should be entirely without the means of defence. The Shah's troops have moved from their camp behind, to Siah Sung, for protection, as, from the force which has gone with Col. Oliver, they have not guards enough to protect their camp, or the stores left there: their sentries are fired on constantly. Lieut. Mayne, of the Shah's service, was reported to have been shot when going his rounds last night, but it was a mistake; the suwar who accompanied him was the sufferer.

A poor woman, a Mrs. Smith, the wife of a conductor, was travelling up the Bolan pass to Kandahar, with a few suwars as a guard. She was attacked by the Belooches; the suwars fled, Mrs. Smith got out of her palkee and ran a short distance, but was soon overtaken and killed; the body was not plundered, and her rings were found on her fingers, and her earrings in her ears; not that they committed the act from hatred to the Feringhees and disdain of plunder, but that, according to the superstition of these tribes, it is a most unlucky circumstance to kill a woman; and finding their victim of the gentle sex, they fled, and left her as she fell.

17th.—Col. Oliver's force returned; Capt. Abbott's guns have had their carriages much damaged; the spokes of sundry wheels are absent, thanks to the acclivities and declivities of the Al-Timor pass, so that he requires a few days to put all to rights before he can go to join Sale with the 37th: when they do so, the brigade will move on on Tézeen.

18th.—The enemy came down (a chupao or night attack), 400 strong, on Khoord Cabul, where an action was fought with great loss on both sides; Lieut. Jenkins of the 35th was mortally wounded, and lingered in great agony, having been shot through the spine. Col. Monteath sent to Sale for reinforcements, who despatched to him the two companies of the 37th that had lately arrived at Bhoodkhak.

19th.—The remainder of the 37th marched from Cabul to Bhoodkhak; also Capt. Abbott and his guns, and the Shah's sappers and miners under Capt. Broadfoot. Sale and Sturt have agreed that I am to remain with him and my daughter at Cabul, and to come on with the Envoy, who is anxious to go to his government at Bombay, and Gen. Elphinstone, who returns to the provinces in consequence of ill health.

Sale's brigade is to move on to Khoord Cabul to-morrow. Seventy-seven of the wounded men from thence and Bhoodkhak have come in to cantonments, as also Lieut. Mein, of the 13th. It appears that the Hazir Bash, the escort sent by the King with Capt. Trevor to Capt. Macgregor (political agent), were the people who let the Ghilzyes into the 35th's camp; they were partly of the same tribe, and whilst the rest were fighting, these ever-ready gentlemen did a little work of their own, cutting down surwans and hamstringing camels. Whilst they were thus employed Capt. Wyndham came up with a company of the 35th, and fired into the midst, putting them to rout. Col. Monteath turned these people out of his camp as unsafe to be trusted; the Envoy has ordered them to be sent back to Cabul, and to be kindly treated, and will not believe them to be in fault. The Hazir Bash, as their name imports, are "aye ready for the field," but I fear that just now—

"At a word it may be understood,
They are ready for evil and not for good,"

like Walter Scott's goblin page.

20th.—Lieut. Jenkins's body was brought to Capt. Sturt's house; he died just after he was placed in the dhooley, and was thus saved the additional pain of the journey.

21st.—Lieut. Jenkins's funeral took place. As the 35th lost ninety camels, and fifty more were sent in with the sick and wounded, the force is detained until more camels can reach them from Cabul.

23d.—Much firing has been heard, and great anxiety prevails. All the forts about Cabul are empty, and the Juwans have gone (it is said) to aid in the fight against us at Tézeen: Sale writes that the report is, that the people at Tézeen say they are unable to cope with us in battle, but that they intend to plunder and annoy the force on its way down.

24th.—Sturt sent me a note before I was dressed this morning to inform me, that at Tézeen one small fort had been evacuated, and that Lieut. E. King, of the 13th light infantry, was killed. In the course of the morning I heard that the 13th, having expended their ammunition, were obliged to retreat; that poor King, being the last man to do so, was shot dead on the spot. The men could not stop to take up his body then, but they returned shortly after, and obtained it before the enemy had time to do more than take off his jacket. He was a gallant high-spirited young man, universally beloved, and consequently is much lamented. He was interred under a tent at night, lest the Affghans should recognise the grave and disinter the body. We afterwards were informed that the attack was made on the rear guard before they quitted their ground; that the enemy cut in, in rear of the baggage, took ninety camels with all the treasure of the 13th, a large quantity of ammunition, and other stores.

Gen. Elphinstone told me, that Sale had been very imprudent in using his leg, and had consequently been suffering a great deal of pain, but that the remedies applied had given him relief; he expressed great regret that he had not communicated any information to me, taking it for granted that the Envoy had done so, if I had not a letter from Sale himself; but he was wounded, and with plenty of military occupation, could not always find time to write me many particulars, as he had to send his despatches off as quickly as possible to the General.

A letter from a friend with the force that was sent from Kandahar mentions, that the force had arrived at the extreme point of their tour (Dehwarah) on the 15th of October, and that they were to set out on their return the following day. Capt. Leeson, of the 42d, in temporary command of the Shah's 1st cavalry regiment, was to march twenty-five miles and over a pass (the Kotilla Meercha), to be out of the way of the others, on account of the scarcity of water. The troops had not had any thing to do, nor was there even a chance of their having a foe to contend with, for the people of that part of the country got such a lesson in the fight of Secunderabad, that the chiefs could not have collected 200 men; the forts were mere shells, their walls of no thickness.

28th.—Sale has written me that he arrived at Seh Baba on the 26th at 1 P.M.; that the rear guard was fired on a mile from camp, and three men wounded. They were in a snug post for the night. His leg was doing well, and all inflammation had subsided. They had grain and bhoosa in plenty. Capt. Grant tells me that a chief goes on daily in advance, to keep the country quiet, and bring in grain.

29th.—We hear that since the force left Khoord Cabul, they have never pitched a tent. The rear guard has been attacked daily, and the bivouack fired on every night. The camels are dying forty of a night from cold and starvation. Lieut. Jennings (13th) has been wounded severely in the arm, the bone broken, and the ball went through into his side. Lieut. Rattray (13th) wounded, and a sergeant killed and 3 men wounded; 4 or 5 Sipahees* of the 35th wounded.

30th.—A small dâk has come in for the Envoy and General only, and that only newspapers; the Envoy sent orders to have the dâk sent by a private path, which succeeded.

It seems that the terms made with the chiefs of Tézeen were, the remission of the money which gave rise to the dispute. They were required to call out the *Ooloos*, which they represented would be attended with considerable expense, so they received 10,000 rupees to enable them to do so, when they pocketed the money, but omitted calling out the militia! Macgregor writes that he suspects the chiefs are at the bottom of all the plundering and attacks on our force, though they profess to have nothing to do with it, and that the depredators are the robber-tribes.

Last night as the cavalry videttes went their rounds at Siah Sung, a party of men rushed out of a cave and fired at them; some were taken prisoners; part of them were Affghans, but four were Hindostances, and one of them was a Chuprassy of Capt. Bygrave, who endeavoured to excuse

*Commonly written Sepoys.

himself by saying, he fired at the party supposing them to be Affghans, but could give no reason for being there himself.

Mr. Melville was attacked last evening, but set spurs to his horse and galloped off, on which the Affghans set up a shout; this is the fourth attempt on the part of the Affghans to assassinate British officers within a short time. I before mentioned Mr. Mayne's escape; Dr. Metcalfe was also nearly cut down; and Lieut. Waller, of the Artillery, was wounded on the head whilst riding close to the Siah Sung camp.

31st.—The invalids, whose march had been countermanded, are again under Orders to go out to Siah Sung on Tuesday, to be in readiness to march on Wednesday the 3d of next month. When the barracks for the men and the officers' quarters were erected in the Cabul cantonment, a committee assembled to value them and fix the house rent, both for them and for the two houses to be occupied by the Commander of the forces and the second in command. It was fixed at ten per cent on the actual outlay as specified by the engineers' department. We paid ours monthly, as did the 13th, through the regimental paymaster. The 35th also paid their rent monthly. There was some dispute regarding it with some others, in consequence of the rooms not being all quite finished; but as Capt. Sturt was not ordered to collect the money, but only to pay over whatever he received, the business remained in abeyance. An inquiry is now making about the house rent that has not been paid by the officers who have gone away, so I feel quite delighted that Sale and I are out of the scrape. Brig. Shelton has written officially to the General, to say that it is very hard that he is kept at Siah Sung, when there is a good house in cantonments to which he has a right, and applies officially to the General to give him up either his own house or ours. Now, as long as Brig. Shelton's duty keeps him at Siah Sung, he has no business in cantonments. This is Sunday: both the General and I expect to march on Wednesday, so, *par complaisance*, we neither of us expected to be turned out; however, if we do not go, we both intend vacating our habitations, when our house will be made over to Capt. Sturt, to undergo repairs, so as to be ready for the reception of the next Commander of the forces. Gen. Nott has been written to, to come up immediately, and Gen. Elphinstone is to give up the command to him from the 1st of Nov. The reason that our house is in future to be appropriated by the chief arises from its being the best and most commodious. Sir Willoughby Cotton gave his plan, and Sale his, when the houses were built; and Sir Willoughby living *en garçon* had omitted many little comforts that we had considered indispensable. Added to which, Sale had a *shohe* for gardening, and had an excellent kitchen-garden; whilst I cultivated flowers that were the admiration of the Affghan gentlemen who came to see us. My sweet peas and geraniums were much admired, but they were all eager to obtain the seed of the edible pea, which flourished well; and by being sown as soon as the frost was over we had plenty of succession crops, and we still have peas growing which we hope, if not cut off by frost, will give a crop next month.

The potatoes thrive well, and will be a very valuable addition to the cuisine. The cauliflowers, artichokes, and turnip radishes are very fine, and peculiarly mild in their flavour; they are all from seed we brought with us from our garden at Kurnaul. The Cabul lettuces are hairy and inferior to those cultivated by us; but the Cabul cabbages are superior, being milder, and the red cabbage from English seed grows well.

Regarding the fruits of Affghanistan, I should not be believed were I to state the truth. Selected grapes off a bunch of those in the Kohistan have been known to weigh 200 grains; the largest I ever weighed myself was 127 grains. It was the kind denominated the Bull's Eye by the English; I believe the natives call it the Hoosseinee-Angoor; its form is nearly round, and the taste very luscious; it is of a kind not generally purchaseable. At Kardunah they grow in great perfection. Those I ate were sent as a present from a native gentleman to Captain Sturt, as were also some very delicious pears from Turkistan. The largest peaches I have myself weighed turned the scale at fifteen rupees, and were fully equal in juiciness and flavour to those of the English hothouse. The finest sort are in the Kohistan, but are so delicate they will not bear carriage to Cabul. I have been assured by my friends who have been there in the peach season that the best fruit of the kind at my table was quite inferior to those above mentioned. The Orleans blue plum is excellent. There is a green one resembling in appearance a greengage, but very tasteless. There are also many other kinds, with a great variety of melons, Water, Musk, and Surda, which is accounted the best.

It is reported that Sale's brigade are very badly off for carriage and provisions, and we have here no camels to send to them. The 37th N. I. and the Shah's sappers and miners are ordered back to the Huft Kotul, to await the arrival of the invalids at that place. It is now said that, from the difficulty experienced in procuring carriage, the sick and wounded must be left here.

In the evening we heard that the Envoy had received a hurried note from Capt. Macgregor, by which it appears that between Jugdaluk and Soorkhab the troops were attacked by about 400 men; that ours were unable to force the hills. The enemy left the pass open, by which the brigade proceeded; but they came down in force on the rearguard, who are stated to have been panic-struck. Our loss is stated at ninety killed and wounded. Capt. Wyndham of the 35th killed, and Lieut. Coombes severely wounded; Lieuts. Rattray and Halcombe of the 13th Light Infantry wounded. There has been great loss of baggage and camels; seventy of the latter carried off, which were returned to us on paying ten rupees each for the Hindostances, and twenty each for the Affghan animals. This is instituting a premium for plunder, but it was caused by dire necessity.

There were no despatches for the General, nor letters for me, but we hope to receive further accounts to-morrow.

1st November.—No letters from camp, which has caused both surprise and anxiety.

2d.—Last night a party of Kohistances entered the city; a large body of horsemen were also seen proceeding towards the city from the road that leads by the Shah's camp behind Siah Sung.

This morning, early, all was in commotion in Cabul; the shops were plundered, and the people were all fighting.

Our Affghan servant, Mahomed Ali, who used to sleep in the city, when he passed out to come to my house in the morning was threatened, and reviled as the chuprassy of the Feringhee General, who, they asserted, had been beaten at Tézeen, and that all his troops had run away, and he with them!

The Shah resides in the Bala Hissar, and his guns from that fortress were constantly firing; the Affghans in the city were doing the same from six in the morning. Capt. Sturt hearing that Capt. Johnson's (paymaster to the Shah's force) house and treasury in the city were attacked, as also Sir Alexander Burnes's, went to Gen. Elphinstone, who sent him with an important message, first to Brig. Shelton at Siah Sung, and afterwards to the King to concert with him measures for the defence of that fortress. Just as he entered the precincts of the palace, he was stabbed in three places by a young man well dressed, who escaped into a building close by, where he was protected by the gates being shut. Fortunately for my son-in-law, Capt. Lawrence had been sent to the King by the Envoy, and he kindly procured a palkee, and sent Sturt home with a strong guard of fifty lancers, but they were obliged to make a long detour by Siah Sung. In the mean time, Lawrence came to tell me all that had passed, and to break the bad news to my daughter, Mrs. Sturt.

Lawrence (military secretary to the Envoy) had had a very narrow escape himself. An Affghan, grinding his teeth, and grinning with rage and hatred of the Feringhees, aimed a blow at him with a sword, which Lawrence parried, and putting spurs to his horse he escaped: one of his suwars received a cut in the leg, which was revenged by another horseman shooting the fellow.

It was Lawrence who came to tell me of Sale's wound; he is always kind and friendly, though he has now been twice the herald of ill news. It struck me as probable that the suwars would take Sturt to his own house; and as he and my daughter were staying with me, there would not even be a bed to place him on there. I therefore determined not to lose time by waiting till the bearers could get my palkee ready, but took my chuttah and walked off as fast as I could towards Sturt's house. I fortunately met Major Thain (aide-de-camp to Gen. Elphinstone), for I soon saw a crowd of about fifty suwars in his compound. Thain ran on, and told the bearers to bring him on to my house. I cannot describe how shocked I felt when I saw poor Sturt; for Lawrence, fearing to alarm us, had said he was only slightly wounded. He had been stabbed deeply in the shoulder and side, and on the face (the latter wound striking on the bone just missed the temple): he was covered with blood issuing from his mouth, and was unable to articulate. From the wounds in the face and shoulder, the nerves were affected; the mouth would not open, the tongue was swollen and paralysed, and he was ghastly and faint from loss of blood. He could not lie down, from the blood choking him; and had to sit up in the palkee as best he might, without a pillow to lean against. With some difficulty and great pain he was supported up stairs, and laid on his bed, when Dr. Harcourt dressed his wounds, which having been inflicted about ten o'clock, now at one were cold and stiff with clotted blood. The tongue was paralysed, and the nerves of the throat affected, so that he could neither swallow nor articulate; and the choking sensation of the blood in his throat was most painful to witness. He was better towards evening; and by his wife's unremitting attention in assisting him to get rid of the clotted blood from his mouth by incessant applications of warm wet cloths, he was by eleven at night able to utter a tolerably articulate sound. With what joy did we hear him faintly utter *bet-ter;* and he really seemed to enjoy a tea-spoonful of water, which we got into his mouth by a drop or two at a time, painful as it was to him to swallow it.

It was most gratifying to see the attention and kind feeling manifested on the occasion by the sergeants of the engineer department, and their anxiety (particularly Sergeant Deane's) to make themselves useful to Sturt.

Capt. Warburton, Capt. Johnson, and Capt. Troup were all fortunately in cantonments; for their houses in the city were plundered and burnt. At Johnson's (the King's treasury) the guard of forty men was massacred, as also all his servants but one, who luckily was not at home. The insurgents looted a lakh and 70,000 rupees of public property, and Johnson lost above 10,000 rupees of his own property.

There were of course various reports. We first heard that, on the affair breaking out, Sir A. Burnes went over to the Wuzeer's to ascertain what could be done; and that he was safe there, excepting having been shot in the leg. The King, from the Bala Hissar, sent intelligence to the Envoy "that Burnes was all right;" but a few hours afterwards the King acknowledged that he did not know any thing of him, neither did the Envoy at seven in the evening, when Capt. Lawrence and Capt. John Conolly came to inquire after Sturt's health. Our only hopes of Burnes' safety rest on the possibility of his having obtained refuge in some harem. His brother's fate is as yet unknown. Capt. Broadfoot was shot in the breast, and killed. He was breakfasting with the two Burnes's: before he fell he had killed six men with his own hand. Capt. Drummond is protected by Osmar Khan, Kariez-i-Umeer, chief of a domain, the first stage from Cabul towards the Kohistan. Capt. Mackenzie, political assistant to Capt. Mackeson at Peshawur, came up to Cabul some time since; and when Lieut. Milne (in the Commissariat) was sent to Khelat-i-Gilzie, Mackenzie

took his place in the Shah's commissariat. He was located in a fort divided into two by the range of Commissariat Grodowns,—one side inhabited by Brig. Anquetil, commanding the Shah's forces, the other by Mackenzie, who (the Brigadier being in cantonments) held out in both, with some sappers and miners, a few of the Shah's 6th Regt., and 130 Juzailchees: the latter are good men, and mostly Usufzyes. In this fort were stored 8000 maunds of ottah and wheat. Capt. Trevor hopes to defend his tower as long as it is not fired. Another report states that Trevor, his wife, and one child, have escaped, whilst his six other children have been murdered. Another, that he has escaped, but that his wife and seven children are all murdered.

The Kuzzilbash quarter of the city is said to be all quiet. Nai'b Shureef's son has been killed in some of the scuffles in the city. Abdoollah Khan, Amenoollah Khan, and a few other Dooranee chiefs, are said to be the instigators of the insurrection.

The King (who resides in the Bala Hissar) says if the rebellion is not all over to-morrow morning, he will burn the city,—by no means an easy task: the houses are all flat-roofed and mud-roofed. It is true Cabul has been burnt three times before, and therefore what has been may occur again. By throwing shells into the houses you may fire them; and the individual house fired, being ceiled with wood, blazes fiercely until the roof falls in, and the mud and dust smother the fire without danger to the adjacent buildings. The King has also declared that if the Meer Akor (who protected the man that stabbed Sturt) does not give the assassin up, he will hang the Meer Akor himself. It appears a very strange circumstance that troops were not immediately sent into the city to quell the affair in the commencement; but we seem to sit quietly with our hands folded, and look on. On the breaking out of the insurrection the King sent Campbell's Hindostanee regiment into the city, with some guns, who maintained an arduous conflict for some time against the rebels; but being wholly unsupported, were obliged eventually to give way, when the greater part of them were cut to pieces, and several of their guns were captured.

The state of supineness and fancied security of those in power in cantonments is the result of deference to the opinions of Lord Auckland, whose sovereign will and pleasure it is that tranquillity do reign in Affghanistan; in fact, it is reported at Government House, Calcutta, that the lawless Affghans are as peaceable as London citizens; and this being decided by the powers that be, why should we be on the alert?

8

"English Captives at Cabul" (1843)

This account, published in *Bentley's Miscellany* in 1843, is a remarkable archive of the experience of one of the women taken captive by the allies of Akbar Khan in the wake of the British retreat from Kabul in January of 1842. Not only does this anonymous author offer a worm's-eye view of the food, lodgings, and general conditions the captives suffered, but she also gives us glimpses into the smallest of details—from the insects that invaded their clothes to the sweet-meats that Sultan Jan, an Afghan chief, brought for the children on a visit to the captors. She details the cut and thrust of postoccupation battles alongside the birth of children in captivity, as well as in the context of frequent earthquakes.

Whether inadvertently or not, she also casts doubt on the veracity of her own account. Noting the "scribbling mania" that erupted among those who were witness to the insurrection and final days in Kabul, she suggests that many of the "so-called facts" in these memoirs were true "only in the writers' imaginations." Given the authors who published in *Bentley's Miscellany*—from Charles Dickens to Wilkie Collins to Edgar Allan Poe—her readers would likely have been keen consumers of both historical-drama and realist fiction.

Our arrangements for passing the night at the fort of Koord Cabul did not enable us to make that division of apartments which would have been otherwise so desirable: however, this was not of so much importance as if we had had any *toilette à faire*. The garments we wore by day could not be dispensed with at night; and a little half-frozen water (or, perhaps it should be, half-thawed snow), by way of ablution, afforded our sole preparation for the coming day. To return,—we made our arrangements for the night. These arrangements consisted simply in apportioning our small apartments so that all should have an equal share, clearing them of such little accumulations of dirt, &c. as our limited means admitted of. (The Affghans, we found to our cost, are not more particular in the cleanliness of their dwellings than of their persons.) Each family then spread some of their lighter clothes on the bare ground, reserving the warmest as a covering. That our couches were free from snow, and that we had a roof and walls to protect us from the night-blast, was considered a comparative luxury: so much do our notions of luxury depend on comparison! It was surprising with what readiness all parties, in the absence of servants, lent their assistance to these little works of necessity. Assigning the warmest places to the children, we now, with many most anxious thoughts of our friends with the force, prepared ourselves for sleep. Many of the party, worn out by the fatigue and excitement of the last few days, were already wrapt in slumber, when we were all aroused by the not unwelcome tidings that our dinner—unwonted sound!—was coming. Most of us were in darkness. The smoke from our wood-fires had been found so unpleasant, that, grateful as their warmth would have proved, we had allowed them to go out; but now we blew up the smouldering embers to a blaze, and sat on the ground in eager anticipation of our meal. An Affghan brought to each party a large flaring tallow-candle, of about the dimensions of a stout man's arm; he was followed by a second, bearing a load of the bread of the country,—raised wheaten cakes, flat, and somewhat of an oval form, about half an inch thick, and from eight to ten inches in diameter. These were first distributed. Then two more men appeared, bearing between them a smoking caldron of "pillau," consisting of about a bushel, or more, of boiled rice, in which a small sheep had been stewed to a consistency that admitted of its being easily pulled to pieces with the fingers. A few metal dishes were brought; and this mess was portioned off with that most primitive of all instruments, the hand, to the different parties. Salt is not always an ingredient in Affghan repasts; but, when we asked for it, a large lump of rock-salt was brought, which, after bruising between two stones, we sprinkled over our food. We now clustered round our several messes, and took our first lesson in dispensing with the use of knives and forks. Under other circumstances I doubt not that we should have been greatly amused at our own awkward attempts to convey our food to our mouths without spilling; and truly our gipsy-like appearance must have been altogether ludicrous to unconcerned spectators. Although dipping our fingers in the dish became afterwards a sufficiently familiar operation, still there were very few among us who could ever attain to any degree of proficiency in this Eastern practice.

The night must have been well advanced before we again composed ourselves to sleep. Soundly as some of us may have slept, we all awoke with the earliest dawn. None but the truly wretched can know fully how to appreciate that most merciful of blessings, sleep; or with what sorrowing hearts we poor prisoners were again roused to the full consciousness of our situation, our helpless dependence on the pleasure of a race of semi-barbarians, whose will was almost their only law, and in whose creed mercy finds no place. We again found difficulty in persuading our jailors to provide us with water wherewith to wash, or to convince them that cleanliness was at all necessary to comfort. The remains of our last night's repast served us for breakfast; which meal we despatched rather hastily, not knowing how soon we might be called upon to move. This, we were told, depended on the Sirdar's orders, and that a messenger had been sent to learn his pleasure regarding us. About ten o'clock we were informed that we were to remain where we were till to-morrow. A follower of the Sirdar, named Moossa, was established as our master of the ceremonies. Although he certainly rendered us many services, he proved, as indeed are all his race, a most "salt-butter knave." This man Moossa, or Moossa Khan, as he was by courtesy styled, was believed to be the son of a Cabul butcher. He had, by his unscrupulous performance of all kinds of service, and acting as a too ready tool in furthering his employer's wishes, whether good or evil, worked himself into a certain degree of the Sirdar's confidence. When negotiations were first opened by Sir William Macnaghten, Moossa had been sent into cantonments as a sort of hostage for the good faith of the Cabul chiefs, and had been treated during his stay, as Sir William's guest, with a certain degree of courtesy and consideration. He had, consequently, become acquainted with some of the gentlemen who were now prisoners; and had still, it is to be hoped, as far as his uneducated nature would permit, a proper remembrance of the kindness he had experienced at their hands. Certain it is that he was useful to us, and particularly desirous to render Lady Macnaghten's situation as comfortable as possible.

Some of our party had begun to feel the effect of the glare from the snow upon their eyes: this exhibited itself in the form of a severe smarting sensation, and partial blindness. Moossa Khan's servant applied the universal Eastern remedy of soorma, (black antimony,) introduced under the eyelids. The relief was almost immediate.

We were informed that, when we moved, we should have to march nearly the whole day; and it was considered expedient to make ourselves as little remarkable as possible, that we might be less likely to attract the notice of any stray parties of Affghans. With this intent, turbans and "chogas" (Affghan cloaks) were put in requisition, and all who could obtain these articles did so. It was considered more than likely, that, when Lady Sale was wounded, she had been mistaken for one of the opposite sex, from the circumstance of her wearing an officer's foraging-cap, as the Affghans have a superstitious prejudice against killing a woman; and no other lady was touched, although, from the circumstance of several travelling in panniers, their progress through the enemy's fire was considerably slower than her ladyship's. We were, of course, anxious in our inquiries whether General Elphinstone's force had been supplied with provisions, according to agreement on our going over, and also whether it had marched. On these points we could get no satisfactory replies; but we were led to believe that the force had marched. Some fancied they heard firing; but, if so, it was too indistinct to be certain about. We saw nothing of the Sirdar, or his cousin, Sooltan Jan, to-day; indeed, with the exception of the occasional presence of Moossa, and two or three menials, we were left entirely to our own meditations at that period,—probably one of the least agreeable occupations we could have found. In the evening we had our mess of pillau served out to us as before; and, although some have since grumbled at the plainness of our fare, I believe at the time all partook of it with tolerable zest. In truth, a few days' starvation and the biting frost had whetted our appetites to an exceeding keenness, and it was evident that this national dish was the best fare the little fort afforded; and it was no fault of our entertainers, if their less polished customs did not enable them to supply our artificial wants, such as clean tablecloths, knives, forks, &c. Our arrangements for the night were much the same as on the day previous.

As our fatigue wore off, we naturally became more sensible of the hardness of our couch, and the scantiness of our covering. The children accommodated themselves to their new situation in every respect more easily than their parents. This was but natural: but, from beginning to end of our trials, it was a demonstrated fact, that throughout the whole party patience was exemplified in an inverse ratio to years; and the young and the delicate set an example of meek resignation and Christian fortitude that some of the seniors would have done well to imitate.

On the 11th, we had scarcely finished our morning meal when Moossa hinted to us to get ready for an immediate move. Our preparations occupied only a few minutes; but it was between 10 and 11 A.M. before we left the fort. Lady Macnaghten, and Mrs. Anderson with her infant, were in panniers on the same camel; Mrs. Trevor and her servant (a soldier's wife, Mrs. Smith) were on another; the rest of the party rode on horseback, the children mostly mounted before and behind Affghan horsemen. The situation of several of our party claimed peculiar sympathy. Most had suffered in some way from the fortune of war. Lady Macnagh-ten, Mrs. Trevor, and Mrs. Sturt had all, within a few days, been made widows; Lady Sale was still suffering from the wound in her arm; Mrs. Anderson and Mrs. Mainwaring both had young babies; the former, weak and ill, was compelled to endure the rough motion of a camel and a badly-adjusted pannier. Her conveyance, however, rough as it was, to a certain extent afforded means of privacy, and thus enabled her to make some return for Mrs. Mainwaring's generosity in having taken charge of one of her children on a former occasion, by allowing Mrs. Mainwaring's infant to share with her own in that endearing office which none but mothers can perform. It is a pleasing retrospect to reflect, that adversity on this occasion did not prove that grave of finer feelings for which it so often has the credit. If there were any of our small party who, during their misfortunes, did not rise in general estimation, it must be borne in mind that their ordeal was of no ordinary nature. During our captivity, patience, generosity, forbearance, courage,—all the Christian virtues,—were daily put to the severest test; and most gratifying is it to record, that, if any were found wanting, they were but the exceptions to the general rule. Mrs. Mainwaring was very badly off for a conveyance; another camel was not to be had, and a side-saddle out of the question. In this difficulty it was suggested that the seat which would the least incommode her would be on the top of the load of a baggage-pony. This she eventually adopted, and, under Providence, without serious inconvenience or accident. Major Pottinger and Captain Troup were both sufferers from wounds, and ill capable of riding. There was, however, no alternative. The former had a ball in the leg, which to this day (eighteen months since he received it) causes him much trouble and annoyance. Captain Troup was wounded in the elbow. His wound, though at the time most painful, has since healed, and the arm is as well as ever.

Just as we were about to start, Sooltan Jan made his appearance among us. He was very reserved in his replies to our questions; but told us our destination for to-day was Teyzeen (about sixteen miles on the road to Jalalabad). We scarcely believed this, as we expected to be taken back to Cabul. I should mention that Sooltan Jan and Moossa were very urgent for the ladies to conceal their faces, giving their silk handkerchiefs to some of them for that purpose. Our order of march was simple enough; about two scores of horsemen in the van, a similar number in the rear, and our unhappy selves in the centre. On quitting the fort, all were most anxious to see which road we were to take; and it was with something like hope that we found our direction was really towards Teyzeen. It may be easily supposed that all were too much occupied with their own thoughts to enter much into conversation. Our progress was very slow, and it was past mid-day before we reached the spot where we had parted from the force. It would have been impossible for the most unpractised eye not to recognise it: it was literally strewed with the dead and the dying, of all colours, age, and sex. Most were stripped naked; none but the poorest of the poor had been allowed to retain their clothes. Not a particle of baggage or camp-equipage of the most trifling description was to be seen; even the shoes from the dead horses' feet had all contributed to the plunder of the insatiable Affghans. This was an awful sight!—so many of those who a few hours before were marching with us, now stiff and cold. But this was to have been expected. We had experienced the murderous fire through which our troops had passed two days previously; and that numbers should have died of their wounds, fatigue, hunger, and cold, was no matter of surprise.

We continued our sad journey. On reaching the main road leading to Teyzeen we indulged a hope that we were clear of these sad proofs of man's mortality; and, indeed, we proceeded for about three miles from the encamping ground to the spot whence we had been recalled two days before, without seeing more than three or four corpses.

But at this spot the road suddenly narrows, and leads through a pass called the Tungee Tareekee, between high hills. We had no sooner entered this pass than all our hopes were fearfully crushed. In every direction, on both sides of the road, lay in clusters the corpses of Europeans and natives,—officers, soldiers, and camp-followers. It was impossible to avert the eyes from these dreadful sights; and, sickening and fearful as they were, we had to endure them for many a weary mile. Most of the bodies were stripped of their clothes, and all the Europeans gashed with ghastly wounds,—from their regularity, evidently inflicted after death.

As we proceeded on our way, after getting some distance beyond this pass, the road again became comparatively clear of such scenes, and we were again visited with something like a hope that these acts of slaughter had been confined to the narrow passes. We reached the Huft Kotul (a name given to seven exceedingly steep descents). Here we found the snow had undergone a partial thaw, and, having been again frozen, the surface was dangerously slippery. Even the Affghans, whose horses are the surest-footed in the world, were obliged to ride with caution. How the camels descended with safety has always been to me a wonder. The ladies who were on horseback, and some of the gentlemen, dismounted to walk; but not before some accidents had happened. Mrs. Boyd had a fall, fortunately not a severe one; and Major Pottinger, whose wounded leg made riding a torture to him, also got a fall, which hurt him considerably.

We reached the bottom of these descents without further accident; but now again we were doomed to witness similar frightful sights to those of the morning. For three miles the road leads along the bed of a stream between hills, and at every twenty yards of this distance lay the bodies of our slaughtered soldiers. Many a well-known face did we pass this day!—many a friend, whose pulses lately beat as freely as our own, now sleeping in the icy arms of Death! It is not intended to dwell upon horrors, or the sights of this day's march would furnish matter for lengthy pages. As the sun was setting, our party reached the fort at Teyzeen, into which we were ushered with every show of kindness. It was amusing to see the Affghan chief, Sooltan Jan, assisting in carrying into the inner fort (the door was too small for a camel) the camel-panniers of Lady Macnaghten and Mrs. Anderson. This was a matter of surprise to many, knowing the estimation in which females are held by Affghans; but the act was voluntary, and was repeated several times afterwards on similar occasions. Nor was it only a pretence, in compliment to Lady Macnaghten; for Sooltan Jan, though handsome, was sturdy, and carried at least his own share of the load, calling lustily to his assistants to follow his example, and exert themselves.

At Teyzeen we found Lieutenant Melville. He mentioned that, being wounded, he had asked and obtained General Elphinstone's permission to go over and remain with Mahommed Ukbur Khan. He also gave us many particulars respecting the army after we had been separated from it; but those details are not suited to the present narrative. We may, however, observe, that the army having been dreadfully harassed on the 10th, on its march from Khoord Cabul to Teyzeen, General Elphinstone had made two endeavours, by communicating with the Sirdar, to save the small remnant of his force. The Sirdar's proposals were, however, such as the general could not accept; so, after halting for a few hours at Teyzeen, he had pushed on at nightfall. The Sirdar had received intelligence of his march, and moved off also, it was supposed in pursuit, at about midnight.

This night our quarters were rather scanty. The families were divided into two rooms, the bachelors contenting themselves with a sort of open corridor, or verandah. This, however, had become of less consequence, as we had descended from the region of snow; and, though the air was still piercing cold, it was not so bitterly intense as it had been on the higher level of Cabul. Our evening meal was late before it arrived; but come it did, and, as before, we did full justice to it. We were, however, put to sad shifts for light. The Cabul tallow-candles were here not procurable; and it was only by the greatest ingenuity that we manufactured a light to eat by. The fatigue of the day—we had been upwards of seven hours marching—made us regardless of the hardness of our couch; and most of us were glad to rest both mind and body, harassed and wearied as we were by the scenes and labours of the day. In the morning it again appeared to be a matter of doubt whether we were to pass the day at Teyzeen or to move forward. To be in readiness for the latter possibility, we made our breakfast without delay. By this time we had ascertained fully what our means were: they were limited enough. One had saved a candle, another a needle and some thread, a third could muster a bottle or two of wine, and a fourth some tea! The happy individual who boasted the last-named beverage deserves not only well of his country, (a good and gallant officer was Captain G. St. P. Lawrence,) but particularly so of us; for his activity in preparing hot water, and dispensing to each a share of his prize, was beyond all commendation.—And here let me remark on our good-fortune in having Captain Lawrence with us. He understood sufficient of the language to make known all our wants; and, as the late Sir William Macnaghten's secretary, had become well known among the Affghans, among whom his high spirits and good-humour under difficulties had gained him some slight influence. Many of our party were also deeply indebted to him for clothes. He had, through the means of good servants, saved all his baggage, and dispensed with a liberal hand the contents of his trunks. More than one of our children were dressed in a Guernsey from Lawrence's stores, the elastic web reaching from their shoulders to their heels. His shirts, socks, trowsers, handkerchiefs, and towels became honoured by fairer wearers than ever was dreamt of in the philosophy of their manufacturers. Oh! a truly motley group were we!

We were again on the move by 9 A.M.; our destination Surroobee, a small fort, distant eighteen miles; our order of march the same as before. Mr. Melville was added to our party. We had scarcely proceeded a mile when we were joined by Dr. Magrath of the 37th N. I. He had been made prisoner while attempting to rally part of our force, and was sent as another addition to our party. We were rejoiced to see him, for a report had reached us of his death. We passed a few dead bodies, and fancied we could distinguish small groups of Hindoostanees in nooks in the hills. We wearied ourselves in conjecture as to the fate of the force. If the Sirdar had really gone in pursuit of them, he had not come up with them for the first twelve miles; beyond this, our road lay in a different direction from that taken by the troops. Nothing of interest occurred to us during the march. We moved very slowly, halting every now and then, as if our conductors were expecting some one. In fact, several of the Teyzeen chiefs did join us before we reached Surroobee. It was dusk before we dismounted from our steeds. The same activity was again shown by the Affghans in carrying the ladies into the fort.

Our accommodation at Surroobee consisted of only one room, which was given up to the families; the bachelors, as before, betaking themselves to the verandahs. We had no sooner got into the fort than rain and sleet began to fall, and most thankful were we that we were sheltered; for how, in such a climate, could any one have existed in wet clothes? In a shed close to the room where we were lodged was a young woman baking bread. She had a fine crackling fire in her oven, and was willing to accommodate us with a few loaves for a handsome remuneration. Our party was hungry, the warm bread tempting, and, in consequence, some found more fault than usual with our pillau, which arrived in due course.—Some of our servants joined us at this fort. Poor wretches! they were more than half starved both by cold and hunger. They said they had given us up for lost from the moment we left the camp, but God had ordained it otherwise; and that, for the future, they would link their fate to ours, if we would allow them. They were too glad to receive from us the morsels of bread and pillau we could spare; and both Hindoos and Mahommedans seemed to forget the prevailing prejudice of Hindoostan. We were much confined for room, and badly off for light: we were, however, tired, and "innocent sleep soon knitted up the ravelled sleeve of care."

This morning, the 13th, we were moved off earlier than usual. Indeed, we had scarcely time to discuss a mug of tea; for, with no milk to cool it, and in a metal mug without a handle, it required some time to drink it. We were to march to-day by a route which none of our party had ever travelled: our destination was Jugdulluk. At starting, we struck immediately into the hills to the eastward. The march of the preceding day had been almost free from snow; but, as soon as we again approached the hills, we found them covered with one sheet of snow, some eighteen inches deep. No trace of a road was left; but the Affghans seemed well acquainted with the way. It was very slow travelling for the camels; but these beasts, under the guidance of Affghans, seem capable of double the exertion, and to be endowed with twice the instinct they display when led by Hindoostanees. We had frequent occasion to remark this fact before our journey ended. It took us till near midday to complete our toilsome ascent; after which the road sloped gradually, with occasional strong undulations, down to Jugdulluk. About five miles from the latter place we fell into the track the army had taken; and about this spot we fell in with a few returning Affghan horsemen. From them we learned the woful tidings, that, with the exception of four officers, the Cabul force had been annihilated! Disbelief was the most prominent of our feelings; but this gave way to serious misgivings as we advanced. Dead bodies began to dot the road-

side; for the last two miles the corpses of the fated band, Europeans and natives, lay promiscuously side by side; scores of wretched men, sepoys and camp-followers, were seen in groups on the sides of the hills. They seemed to have been left by the Affghans to their fate, which would most probably prove a lingering death from cold and hunger. Most of them appeared unable to move, having their limbs badly frost-bitten. We reached Jugdulluk a little after sunset. Here we again met the Sirdar; his reception of us was, as before, urbane and courteous. We had scarcely dismounted, when we saw Captain Johnson, commissariat officer of the late Shah's force. From him we learnt that General Elphinstone, Brigadier Shelton, and himself were the last of the Cabul army. On the evening that they marched from Teyzeen their progress was unopposed, or nearly so, till within a short distance of Jugdulluk. Here, however, the Sirdar, by a short cut across the hills, had contrived to place himself in advance of them. The hills were crowded with the enemy, whose terrible juzzails wrought sad havoc amongst our men, who, worn out by cold, and hunger, and incessant toil, could offer no resistance. A communication was again made to Mahommed Ukbur Khan, who, under some pretext of treaty, enticed the three above-named officers to a conference, from which they were not allowed to return. The little remnant of the army attempted to recruit exhausted nature by a meal on horse-flesh. They halted the next day; but, towards evening, finding that their officers did not return, they became impatient, and moved off without orders towards Jalalabad. Their fate is too well known.

The only preparation for our reception consisted of the outer fly of a single-pole tent, raised on only half a pole, so that the sides nearly touched the ground. The impossibility of so large a party finding shelter in such a confined space was brought to the notice of the Sirdar, who, consequently, sent a small Affghan tent, about twelve feet by six. Into this Lady Macnaghten, and Major

Boyd's and Captain Anderson's families crept. The bachelors shifted for themselves, and contrived to procure another tent. At the usual time—about two hours after dark—our pillau was brought; but we were all too much distressed in mind to care for food. When the arrangement was originally made for separating us from the force, it was with heavy hearts that we found ourselves compelled to acquiesce, and we were borne up with the hope that our trials would be short; but many there were among us on this sad night who deeply grieved that they had not been allowed to share the fate of the army. We knew not for what we were reserved; and may God pardon us if we felt not thankful for the life He had preserved! This was certainly the most wretched night we had passed. It is true that many of us had had our individual misfortunes to contend with; but hope for the future had been our support. Now hope seemed crushed; and so deeply were all affected by the general disaster, that, had any one at the time thought of a happier future, it may be doubted if his anticipations would have found even a welcome among us. The army was annihilated, our friends were numbered with the dead; and that we too might be allowed speedily to share their fate appeared the greatest blessing that could await us.

On the morning of the 14th we started early; General Elphinstone, Brigadier Shelton, and Captain Johnson being with us. The Sirdar himself, accompanied by several Ghilgie chiefs, and some two hundred followers, formed our escort. We expected to follow the road to Jalalabad; but our conductors, choosing a different direction, entered one of the several passes which lead from Jugdulluk, and pursued a north-eastern course. For the first two miles we passed great numbers of Hindoostanees perishing by the road-side. Our route was a very wild one. The first few miles may be said to have been a defile, at the end of which we entered upon an open and good road. This, however, was not to continue. We reached a second defile, ascending over broken fragments of rock for several miles. At length we approached a ghat, to ascend which appeared to our unsophisticated sense a feat that none but a wild goat would attempt. However, we had much to learn; for not only did the Affghan horsemen ride over it with apparent ease, but even our camels surmounted the toilsome and dangerous ascent without accident. From the summit of this ghat the view was most magnificent: in the distance, mountains that touch the sky, covered with their perpetual snow; ranges of smaller hills and valleys, stretching away from us as far as the eye could reach; while around us, on every peak that commanded the road we travelled, were perched Affghan horsemen, in the picturesque garb of the nation. How they had gained their perilous positions seemed to us a wonder. We passed on unmolested; but the Sirdar had thought it necessary to take every precaution for our safety. Under other circumstances, how much this journey might have been enjoyed! overwhelmed as nearly all our senses were by our melancholy situation, it was yet impossible not to be struck with admiration at scenery so truly grand. The descent from the ghat, though much less difficult than the ascent, was tedious; and night was closing in before we reached our halting-place, near a small fort, situated in a valley called Kutzi-Mohammed Ali Khan. The owner of the fort objected rather coarsely to admitting the Caffres (infidels) within his walls; we were, therefore, compelled to take up our abode near a small grove of trees outside. The weather had been threatening during the latter part of the day, and it now began to blow almost a gale, with appearance of an approaching fall of rain. Not a tent was provided, and the gentlemen had to set their invention to work to make arrangements for the night. Some were too weary to waste much time in the selection of a spot whereon to sleep; but, making the most of cloaks and "poshteens,"* threw themselves down, and

---

*A sheep-skin tanned with the wool on, making a very warm cloak.

were soon insensible to all the troubles of this world; others contrived to form a shelter from the blast, by putting together the camel-panniers, pack-saddles, &c. However, our fears about the weather proved ungrounded. About ten o'clock the wind went down, and the night remained calm and clear. Our pillau was later than usual to night, and but few remained awake to partake of it.

We were on the move again a little after sunrise. At starting, we had to cross two branches of a stream, called the Punjsheir. The first of these was shallow; the second deep, and at the ford very rapid, indeed a perfect torrent. The Sirdar again accompanied our party, and set the example to his followers in giving assistance to cross the stream. The Sirdar placed his horse by the side of Lady Macnaghten's camel, and, with his hand steadying the pannier, spoke in broken Hindoostanee words of assurance. One lady, who wanted confidence in her steed, was carried across the stream behind an Affghan. Several horsemen were placed in the stream below the ford, to assist servants and others, who, crossing on foot, might have been carried away by the torrent. Indeed, this last arrangement saved more than one poor wretch from a watery grave. In labours of this sort, the contrast between the Affghan and Hindoostanee is most striking. Instead of the apathy with which the latter would have witnessed such a scene, the Affghan was all energy and activity; and, though the stream was deep and icy-cold, was urging his horse whenever he could be useful. The rest of the road to-day, a distance of some sixteen miles, was good and level. At about 2 P.M. we entered the valley of Loghman: a most beautiful valley it is, well watered, and dotted through its whole extent by orchards and thriving villages. As we passed through some of the latter, the inhabitants clustered around us. The women in some of them were anxious to see the ladies' faces,—a curiosity that was readily gratified; but some of these groups were less quiet in their demeanour, using most insulting and threatening language, and by their whole demeanour

proving the expediency of our passing quickly by them. There was some delay in the selection of a fort for us to halt in, and it was about three o'clock before we found ourselves within the walls of Teergurhee. It was perhaps well for us that the delay was no greater; for there was an evident commotion in the valley, and our conductors hurried us in as fast as they could. Teergurhee is a small mud-fort, attached to a considerable village. It was supposed that we should have had to remain some days here, and we were, consequently, much annoyed to find our quarters very confined. We had more room, certainly, than we had had at any previous halting-place; but still it was much too limited for either health or comfort. We got our pillau earlier than usual; and Moossa treated Lady Macnaghten to a curry!

On the morrow (16th) we halted. This was Sunday; nor were we unmindful of the duties of Christians on such a day. Several had been fortunate enough to save prayer-books; nor was the Bible wanting among us; and some, at least, with thankful hearts and chastened spirits acknowledged at the throne of Grace the mercy so lately vouchsafed us. This halt was most grateful to us all: it gave us the much-desired opportunity of a luxurious wash. None know the extent of such an enjoyment but those who have been for days deprived of the indulgence. At this place a few more of our servants joined us; most of them were frost-bitten. How they had survived the general massacre, or how crawled on to this spot, appeared wonderful. Some scores of our late camp-followers had found their way to this village, where were settled a number of Hindoo bungahs, (originally from Shikarpore,) who gave them daily distributions of bread in charity. How these unfortunates had escaped the general massacre, or who had directed their steps to this spot, some twenty miles off the direct road to Jalalabad, we never could ascertain.

During the day we heard several shots fired; we could not exactly learn the cause, but were told that it was the Sirdar's followers quelling some riot that had occurred in the village on our account. Several men were said to have been killed—*pour encourager les autres*, but we could see nothing of what was going on. We got our pillau, as usual, in the evening; and Moossa supplied another curry to Lady Macnaghten.

On the 17th it was rumoured that the people of the valley were very ill-disposed towards us; and, fearing their clamour might end in open violence, the Sirdar deemed it advisable to remove us to a place of greater security. We were, consequently, warned to prepare ourselves for another move. We were soon ready: but numbers of the Affghans had assembled for the purpose of plundering us as we left the fort; and it was, consequently, considered necessary to detain us until the Sirdar had collected some matchlock-men for our protection. This he did, to the number of about three hundred. In the course of an hour (about twelve o'clock) we moved out. The Sirdar Sooltan Jan and Mahommed Shah Khan (father-in-law to Mahommed Ukbur), and a very powerful chief of the Ghilgies, were at the gate waiting for us. They and their followers were most liberal in the application of sticks and whips to keep off the crowd, which, however, they did effectually; and we commenced our march, without any annoyance beyond a volley of maledictions from the *canaille*.

Such scenes as these naturally caused great anxiety and excitement among our party; but we were helpless in the hands of the Philistines, and our only course was to eat quietly as much dirt as our tormentors chose to set before us. We had only five or six miles to travel. The country around us was very beautiful. The Sirdar's party seemed in high spirits. Several chiefs of less note joined in the cavalcade. They seemed well disposed to converse with those of the gentlemen who understood their language. They scarcely touched upon the late occurrences, but seemed surprised that we were downcast. They expected that, like true predestinarians, we should consider the events that had passed to have stood conspicuous in the book of

fate, and, therefore, not to have been averted by the endeavours of man; as to ourselves, that we should consider our *kismut** truly happy,—that we had been born under a happy star. From the tenor of their remarks we tried to gather comfort; for why should they congratulate us if they still intended us injury? But our way was dark before us; and I believe there were few amongst us who possessed sufficient philosophy to gaze calmly on the dim futurity.

Between two and three o'clock we reached a new-looking fort, called Budecobad, the property of the above-mentioned Mahommed Shah Khan; by guess I should say it was situated about thirty miles north-west of Jalalabad, and divided from it by the Cabul river. On entering, we were pleased to find the fort very clean. It was about one hundred yards square, with a smaller fort in the centre; leaving between the two a surrounding space of some twenty-five yards, where the chief's retainers lived. The inner fort was for the accommodation of his family: it was very clean; the rooms well raised, six in number; two of them about twenty-four feet by fourteen, the others about fourteen feet square. The whole of this inner fort, with its court-yard about twenty yards square, was given up to our use; and we were told that we should remain here some days, until the road to Jalalabad was safe for travellers! In the centre of some of the rooms were blazing fires; and the whole appearance gave us hope of less discomfort than we had hitherto experienced.

The Sirdar remained in the inner fort for an hour, receiving some of the chiefs, who had come to pay their respects to him. He made one or two of the gentlemen sit by him, and behaved to them as if on a perfect equality. While talking to the chiefs, he amused himself with eating sugar-cane, at the same time sharing it with the gentlemen near him. This sugar-cane feasting appears a favourite pastime with the Affghans. We got our pillau as

*Kismut—fate.

usual, and lay down for the night with the prospect of being a little less uncomfortable than had lately been our lot.

On the 18th we were up betimes; and, some of us having contrived to buy some eggs, we made a slight variety in our morning repast. The Sirdar and Sooltan Jan, who had passed the night in the outer court, came to take their leave of us. Their behaviour was, as usual, perfectly courteous and kind. Lady Macnaghten, understanding that a fine horse belonging to her late husband, and which she had saved, had attracted the notice of some of the chiefs, begged the Sirdar's acceptance of the animal; knowing very well that with the Affghans to admire and to covet are synonymous, and that their ideas of appropriation are on a sliding-scale easily adapted to suit their convenience. The Sirdar had a little "political talk" with Major Pottinger; then, assuring us that we should go to Jalalabad "as soon as the road was safe," he took his departure. Moossa was established our master of the ceremonies. He was a cross-grained, grumpy wretch; but we were now in a fine school for practising the Frenchman's philosophy, "Quand on n'a pas ce qu'on aime, il faut aimer ce qu'on a." If we could not love the Affghans, it was our policy to conceal from them how cordially we hated them. Hitherto occurrences have been detailed daily as they took place; but henceforward days, weeks, and months passed in such cheerless monotony that this narrative may as well assume a less regular form, and advert only occasionally to dates.

We now began to speculate among ourselves on our prospects of liberation. We calculated to the greatest nicety the weeks, days, and hours, that it would take for the news of our disaster to reach Calcutta. We settled the line of conduct the Government *must* pursue, &c. None, I think, ever dreamed of the course of events that really did follow. We set to work, and parched barley for imitation coffee. Some of the gentlemen, with reeds, and pieces of tin-box, contrived to manufacture what they called "hookahs;" while others blistered their hands in attempts to fashion wooden "dudeens." Although in a milder climate than Cabul, the cold was still very great. The children were as happy as the day was long; their health had not suffered by the hard living and long marches, and they played in the court-yard from morning till night. During the day the sun was very pleasant; and the ladies made a promenade on the terraced roof of our dwellings.

On the 20th we were much rejoiced at the removal of Moossa. He was an unaccommodating monster; and, though he did give Lady Macnaghten a curry every night, he made her pay for it by giving him an excellent camel as a parting present. He stole, also, several trifles from others of the party. It was little enough that we had, and to be robbed of that little was hard indeed. Moossa was succeeded by a stout little fellow, who was always called by us "Mirza;" his name was, I believe, "Bahoodeen." Mirza was a Bokhara merchant, but had been a great deal at Cabul, and had become acquainted with several of the officers; among others, with Captain Troup, who had rendered him some little service, and, I believe, got medicine for some of his family who were sick. At all events, we congratulated ourselves on his advent; and I believe that the little fellow did all he could for us. The first thing he did was to get some little stools made, the only substitute he could provide for chairs. Shortly *charpoys** succeeded to the bare ground. Brass dishes and drinking-cups found their way among us; and, in short, we began to assume less of the appearance and habits of savages than hitherto we had done. It must not be supposed that this was the work of a day, or even of weeks; it was, probably, upwards of a month before we could be said to have emerged from our state of barbarism.

After a week's absence, we were honoured by a visit from the Sirdar and his cousin. The object of their visit was supposed to be an interview with

*Charpoys,—small light bedsteads used in the East.

Major Pottinger, for the purpose of getting him to write to General Sale to give up Jalalabad. If such were really the case, they had got hold of the wrong man in Major Pottinger; for, though he would have made any personal sacrifice for the general benefit, I do not think he would have swerved ever so little from the strict line of his duty to the State, to have saved us all from slavery or death. The Sirdar then paid us all a visit, and begged to be informed if there were anything wanting to our comfort (!). Little did he know of our customs, or he never would have insulted us by asking such a question. He again spoke to Mrs. Anderson of her child, and assured her of her being safe in the zenana of Mahommed Zuman Khan (the Barakzye chief, who had charge of the hostages left at Cabul.) We mentioned to the Sirdar our wish to be supplied with the "raw materials," and to prepare our own meals. This was instantly complied with, and thenceforth we ordered our own meals. It was also hinted to the Sirdar that we had expended the few rupees that we happened to have about our persons when we accepted his invitation; he consequently promised to send us money; which pledge he, much to our surprise, redeemed the next day by sending one thousand rupees to be divided amongst us. Our daily rations consisted of rice, flour, mutton, salt, and ghee, with a little milk in the morning. The Sirdar promised us tea, sugar, &c.; but we looked upon this as only a promise.

One of the greatest annoyances that we experienced I have not yet alluded to. It consisted in an attachment to our persons formed by a diminutive insect, which shall be nameless; but which, from sleeping on the floor of rooms lately inhabited by Affghans, and having no change of clothes, had become a serious nuisance. The Sirdar had taken charge of a note or two from us, and promised to send them to Jalalabad; which he did. A few days afterwards we received letters, newspapers, and clothes from our friends there. This was on the 29th; when we also heard of Brigadier Wild's failure in the Khybur Pass, and of Dr. Brydon's having reached Jalalabad. We were more than happy, as may be supposed, to hear from our friends; nor were we less pleased by the method they adopted to assist us in our distress. They had all contributed a something, and furnished forth two goodly trunks of wearing-apparel, soap, towels, &c. In short, we were now likely to have nothing to grumble for. It was the employment of several hours to distribute our riches. Unfortunately, the clothes sent for public distribution were all for the gentlemen. Lady Sale was more fortunate; as Sir Robert had saved all his baggage on his march to Jalalabad, among which was her ladyship's wardrobe, he was able to send her an ample supply. The other ladies were obliged to content themselves with some coarse cloths and chintzes furnished by the Sirdar. He had also sent needles and thread; thus giving occupation to all the sempstresses of the party, who were most industrious in cutting out and sewing together their several lots. Fashion and ornament gave place to utility; and, though our garments were still of the plainest, all could now rejoice in a change of dress.

We had almost given up the hope of hearing that any more of the officers had escaped, when on the 15th of February we were told that the paymaster, Captain Bygrave, was alive; that he had been saved by some petty chief. At first we were disposed to think this was some mistake, originating in Captain Johnson's (the paymaster of Shah Soojah's force) being with us; but in a few days our doubts were dissipated, and we ascertained that Captain Bygrave was not only alive, but that the Sirdar had contrived to get him into his power. About this time we received a visit from three or four of the chiefs. They appeared to have come in a very angry mood. We afterwards learned that they had been sent by the Sirdar, in consequence of a *cossid**having been seized who had been intrusted with

*Cossid,—a messenger.

a letter from some of our party, containing some information which we considered it expedient that the Jalalabad garrison should be possessed of. It was useless to dispute the point; and we were threatened with closer restraint in the event of being again detected in similar attempts. Major Griffiths and Mr. Blewitt, a writer in Captain Johnson's office, were brought in to us by these chiefs. The major was suffering acutely from a bullet-wound in the arm. Both had been treated tolerably well, though their fare had been of the coarsest.

On the 16th we were summoned by the same chiefs to give up all our arms; which, strange to say, we had hitherto been allowed to retain. A remonstrance was offered, based on the disgrace of officers giving up their arms. This was overruled; and, by way of sweetening the unpalatable measure, a list was taken of the different weapons and their owners, and a promise given that they should all be restored to us when we were liberated. In short, we were helpless, and obliged to yield; though, to do the Affghans justice, they offered every excuse they could devise to show that they were guided by necessity, and regretted giving us any annoyance. Thus was another frail hope blasted. The officers had hitherto flattered themselves that, in the event of any demonstration being made in our favour, they might second it by a little diversion within the fort; or, if circumstances proved favourable, that they might resist being carried beyond the reach of our friends. However we might at the time deplore the above circumstance, we may probably attribute our ultimate safety to it: for, some weeks afterwards, events occurred which would have induced us to strike a blow in our own defence; and, had we done so, we should have insured our destruction, as, when we thought help was near us, time has proved to us that we reckoned without our host.

I have said that frequent alarms had rendered us heedless of whatever might happen. We certainly thought so. But our nerves were to be put to a severer trial; our courage proved by an ordeal more trying than we had hitherto experienced or dreamed of. On the 19th of February, after two or three days of unusually sultry weather, at about eleven in the forenoon, a low, rumbling noise, was heard in the far distance: it advanced slowly towards us, and the earth began slightly to tremble. As earthquakes in that part of the world are far from uncommon, and we had all at different periods experienced slight ones, we at first thought nothing of this; but after a few seconds the woodwork of the fort began to crack and rattle, and the earth to undulate with a short to-and-fro motion. Those who at first had laughed now looked serious. The motion increased until it was with difficulty we could walk; the earth seemed from its agitation as if broken into lumps, and we all expected every instant to see it open. The bastions of the fort, and the tops of all the walls, came toppling down; the walls opened in wide fissures; and it seemed to all that our last hour was come,—that we should be either swallowed by the gaping earth, or crushed to death in the falling masses of the surrounding walls. Those who were in the rooms had remained quiet until the shock had become fearful; when all, as it were with a simultaneous rush, made for the stairs. Ladies, children, servants, mothers with their infants, all running together to the same outlet, increased the confusion, and rendered futile their own efforts to escape from the impending danger. The gentlemen had most of them been lying about in the shade in the court-yard. Lady Sale and Brigadier Shelton were walking on the roofs of the rooms; perhaps fortunately for the former that it was so, as the room in which she lived fell in almost one mass. General Elphinstone and Major Pottinger were, from their wounds and ill-health, incapable of making their escape into the court-yard. And now it is most gratifying to record the devotion of a private of the 44th, William Moore, who was acting in the capacity of servant to the general. He resisted the persuasions of the general to save himself, and stayed by his bedside until the shock had ceased, and assistance could be brought to carry the general's charpoy (bedstead) downstairs. When all had met in the yard below, consternation was painted on all faces. The earth continued rumbling and shaking at intervals; and it appeared to us that we were the doomed victims of Almighty wrath. The Affghans seemed in as great trepidation as ourselves.

Mirza's first care, after the shock had subsided, was to look to the gates, and prevent any one from without gaining admittance; for, among a race so bigoted and superstitious, it was to be feared that the Affghans might consider this calamity a visitation on them for allowing "infidels" to find protection in their valley,—as a signal of divine vengeance for not having extirpated all of the hated race who had fallen within their power. However, fortunately for us, no such feeling was openly manifested, though we afterwards learned that it really had existed to a very dangerous extent. In the afternoon a son of Mahommed Shah Khan visited us, and from him we learned, that of all the forts in the valley (some forty or fifty) the one we were in had suffered the least; that indeed there was not another one left habitable, and that there had been a very great loss of life. This proved to be correct, and no one living had ever experienced an earthquake at all equal in violence to that we had just witnessed. Slight tremblings at intervals during the remainder of the day rendered it advisable not to sleep in the rooms, and we were consequently compelled to make arrangements for passing the night in the open air. Mirza had shewn a very proper feeling in getting a small tent pitched in the outer court for the General and Major Pottinger, as their wounds rendered them incapable of shifting for themselves in the event of another shock. During the following night we had shocks at almost every hour; two of them sufficiently alarming to make us all spring from our lowly couches. It is not to be supposed that we slept very soundly; and I believe all were glad when the day broke on the 20th. This was Sunday, and all assembled in the open air to render thanks for the great mercies hitherto vouchsafed us, and to pray for their continuance. Captains Lawrence and Mackenzie were kind enough to officiate on these occasions; and, if we have not become better Christians after the many instances of God's special providence extended towards us, I can only say we ought to be, for never had human beings more to be truly thankful for. In the afternoon Dost Mahommed Khan came to see us, or rather to inspect what damage had been done to the fort. He was much out of humour, and said that his family had been very great sufferers by the earthquake, which had only been caused by their having protected the Caffres.

On the 21st General Elphinstone and Brigadier Shelton had their swords sent back to them by the Sirdar. The former was bedridden, and the latter had lost his right arm, so that our generous enemy had not much to fear from his magnanimity: still, the compliment was felt by all the officers. On the 23rd Captain Bygrave was sent in to join our party. He was dreadfully emaciated from the sufferings he had undergone, and gave a dismal account of his having passed some six days wandering about in the snow without food; at last he gave himself up in a village, and was humanely treated. He had lost the end-joints of all the toes of one foot, and part of the heel of the other, from frost. He was the only one of the officers of our party who had been seriously frost-bitten. Lieutenant Mein had lost the end of one of his toes; but he made very light of the matter. While on this subject, it may be as well to mention that most of the servants who had joined us were more or less frost-bitten. The sufferings of these poor wretches were dreadful. We had no means of rendering them assistance, and the only remedies that could be procured were poultices. Many of these poor creatures died of lockjaw, after some days of excruciating agony. Those who survived recovered very slowly; and it was many weeks before most of them could use their injured limbs.

Towards the end of this month a report reached us that the "Ameer Dost Mahommed Khan" had escaped from his confinement in Hindoostan, and might be daily expected back in his own country. The report received general credit, but proved eventually to be only a finesse of the Sirdar's, to draw, through the influence of his father's name, more followers around himself. The shocks of earthquakes still continued; and, as we considered the rooms we had inhabited very unsafe since they first commenced, we had most of us, in spite of the many inconveniences, preferred passing the night in the court-yard. Every little rumbling sound acted as an alarum to the more timid; and those who had children felt uneasy if they were out of their sight for an instant. By way of palliating these annoyances, some of the gentlemen set to work erecting a range of small huts in the court-yard. It was hoped that, by making them of light and flexible materials, they would bend to the storm, and be less dangerous than the larger buildings. Mirza was very obliging in supplying materials. Captain Lawrence had some servants, who were *au fait* to the work; and in a few days we could boast two or three little tenements, in which we could sleep without the constant dread of being crushed to death. These earthquakes never entirely ceased while we were prisoners; latterly we became less alarmed at them; but the one terrible shock we had witnessed had quite unnerved us, and the least rumbling sound always put us on the *qui vive* for a start.

On the 4th of March we were subjected to a must humiliating and galling insult. Mirza had been sent for on one or two occasions by the Sirdar, and returned on the evening of the 3rd from one of these jaunts; he appeared much vexed at something which had occurred, and told the gentleman that he had no agreeable tidings for us. On the morning of the 4th he told us that the Sirdar had been given to understand that some of us had arms concealed. As Lady Macnaghten and Captain Lawrence were the only two of our party who

had brought any baggage into the fort with them, we were not long in divining that her ladyship's jewels, plate, and shawls were the real objects of the search; in fact, that it was only an excuse to ascertain what valuables her ladyship had contrived to save. It was evident that Mirza was ashamed of the office imposed on him, and he contrived to let Lady Macnaghten have sufficient notice, in order that she might conceal about her person whatever she considered most valuable. However, this was a precaution that she had taken before leaving Cabul, and had constantly worn fastened round her waist jewels to the supposed amount of sixty thousand rupees. It was thought, however, prudent to secure Mirza's good report by a present, and he consequently received a shawl of five hundred rupees' value.

This insulting search was no sooner completed than we were informed that all our sick and maimed servants were to be turned out of the fort. We were all most indignant at such cold-blooded cruelty, for every man would have been murdered as soon as he had set his foot outside the fort. We remonstrated; but were assured that the orders were most positive, and could not be set aside. It was heart-rending to see the many helpless wretches congregated, as it were, for sacrifice; to hear their supplications, to which we were forced to turn a deaf ear. This cruelty was, however, averted; and I believe Captain Lawrence induced Mirza to delay its execution until a reply could be received to a note he was writing to the Sirdar on the subject. The result was, that the measure was allowed to be forgotten; and we have since had much reason to believe that Mahommed Ukbur was totally innocent of this barbarous order, as well as ignorant of the search by which Lady Macnaghten and Captain Lawrence had been insulted. The originator of these acts was Mahommed Shah Khan, a demon incarnate, whose god was avarice, and whose behaviour to us at a later period shewed how little we had to be thankful to him for.

About this time reports became rife that Shah Soojah was sending a force from Cabul to co-operate with the Sirdar against Jalalabad. It was constantly rumoured that thousands of men were assembled in the valley; and every day we were told that the morrow was fixed on for the grand attack on Jalalabad. On the 5th of March, however, we received some communications from our friends at Jalalabad. They spoke with confidence of being able to hold out till reinforced. They told us of General Pollock's arrival at Peshewar, but that he had received orders not to enter the Khybur until all his force should have assembled: in fact, it appeared evident that the Government had begun to see the mistake of pushing on small detachments unsupported, and had at length determined to do what everybody felt they should have done at once,—to send a well-equipped and overwhelming force, which should leave success beyond a doubt. It was through the Sirdar himself that we were enabled to communicate thus with our friends. He had, however, those about him who could read English; and we were, consequently, obliged to be on our guard as to the contents of our letters.

It was about this period that our party were seized with a scribbling mania. Every one seemed occupied in composing "the only true and particular account" of the Cabul insurrection. Diaries were ante-dated, and made to assume the tone and character of memoranda written at the period. Those who had the most retentive memories, or fertile inventions, were likely to prove the most successful in this employment. This *cacoethes* may be attributed chiefly to the newspapers sent us from Jalalabad; they were all teeming with extracts from certain letters written from Cabul, and pretending to detail facts. I say pretending, because these so-called facts were many of them much of the Baron-Munchausen strain, and only had place in the writers' imaginations. I have seen nearly all these narratives; that of Captain Eyre is by far the best. He has been assisted in his relation of facts by those who had been actors in them. He had more ample means of collecting information than the writers of any publication that has yet appeared; and, instead of writing a fictitious journal, he wrote a good, honest, and correct "narrative."

On the 11th of March we had a visit from Dost Mahommed Khan and Imam Verdee. They came for the purpose of having an interview with Major Pottinger and Captain Lawrence, with whom they were a long time closeted. Of course we were most curious to learn the result; but the meeting broke up, and we were left in our ignorance. Both these chiefs appeared much depressed in spirits: however, like true Affghans, they were determined that we should not rejoice while they were sad; and consequently, before they left the fort, they gave us to understand that Ghuznee had fallen, and that all the garrison had been put to the sword. This they did not tell us themselves; but their followers told our servants, and ill-news is proverbial for its speed.

On the 14th we had an increase to our party: Mrs. Boyd presented her husband with a little daughter. Mirza put us all on the alert by sending for a farrier to shoe our horses and ponies. He would, however, answer no questions further than by saying that affairs must soon come to a crisis, and that it is well to be prepared. This evening we also heard of an attempt to assassinate Mahommed Ukbur Khan: he escaped with a severe wound in the arm, and the would-be murderer was said to have been burnt alive. The English were supposed to be the abettors in this attempt; and there were not wanting those among the Affghans to urge the Sirdar to retaliate on us. Indeed, we had few friends among these people; and have since learned, beyond doubt, that the Sirdar had on several occasions resisted the advice, not only of individuals, but of his "council," if he can be said to have had one, to put us to death. However, he turned a deaf ear to their persuasions, and often took occasion to assure us that not a hair of our heads should be injured. The Sirdar, on more occasions than one, spoke with great apparent feeling and regret of the death of Sir William Macnaghten. He used to say that, much as his measures were disliked, he had never heard a word said to his disparagement as a man; that he was a good man; and that, if all the Feringees (Franks, or English) had been like him, there never would have been a rebellion at Cabul. I have never heard that he exactly confessed to having shot the envoy with his own hand, although I believe there is no doubt of the fact; but he was frequently heard to regret the part he had taken in the event, and this long before affairs were turning against him at Jalalabad. Mahommed Ukbur Khan appears to be a man of violent and uncontrollable impulses; but in his cooler moments, and when he has time to reflect, it may be doubted whether his disposition is not more inclined to kindness and humanity than to cold-blooded cruelty.

On the night of the 14th we had a very smart earthquake; but at breakfast-time we were much diverted with a story we heard. A man of Anderson's horse, a Synd, or descendant of the Prophet, had managed to worm himself into Mahommed Shah Khan's confidence, and had been left in one of the Khan's forts with only a few Affghans. He had contrived to steal the key of the strong box, from which he purloined a large bag of rupees, seized a firelock, sprung upon the back of a horse that stood ready saddled, and got safe away. We afterwards heard that he managed to get unscathed within the walls of Jalalabad. It was in consequence of getting no milk for our breakfast that we heard the story,—the man who milked the cows having gone off with the rest in pursuit of the thief! We heard about this time that Moossa had been sent to tamper with the Seikhs,—a proper office for such a villanous wretch. What became of this man we never could learn.

Our time now hung very heavily upon our hands. We had no books, and scarcely any means of amusement. Lady Macnaghten, taking warning from the search her trunks had been subjected to, found occupation for several days in making a bed-covering of the most valuable of her shawls, quilting them in between common chintz, and making it look as much worn and worthless as possible. As usual on such occasions, chess was thought of, and offered some few days' employment in making men and boards. Soft wood, and dough and clay, were put in request for the former; while pieces of red and blue cloth, sewed in cheques, formed the latter. A pack or two of cards, sent from Jalalabad, were well thumbed by the picquet-players; and some strong reeds furnished hoops and sticks for *la grace*. Still, with all our invention, time moved but slowly along, and we tortured every report we heard into every possible shape, us affording more food for our minds, more range for speculation.

On the 19th March we were informed that Mirza was to be relieved from his charge of us. Many of us regretted this; as, altogether, he had behaved well to us, and had assisted us in procuring a number of little things that were necessary to our health and comfort; and I have heard it asserted that he had promised our party his assistance in gaining possession of the fort, in the event of any detachment being sent from Jalalabad for the purpose of liberating us.

On the 25th August, news having previously been received of General Pollock's forward movement, Mahommed Ukbur sent a messenger to prepare us for an immediate march. Ukbur had sworn that General Pollock's advance should be the signal for our removal to Turkistan, where he would distribute us as slaves to the different chiefs. At night a regiment arrived, about four hundred strong, the men composing it being all armed with English muskets, and (having nearly all formerly belonged to different Affghan corps) observing many of the outward forms of discipline. They were commanded by Sala Mahommed Khan, once a Soobadar in Hopkins' regiment, and who had deserted to Ameer Dost Mahommed Khan, previous to Colonel Dennie's action with that chief at Bameean in 1840. For some time previous to our receiving this abrupt summons, sickness had by turns prostrated the strength of almost every individual of our party; and, although the majority were convalescent, two of the ladies (Mrs. Anderson and Mrs. Trevor) were in a state that rendered their removal impracticable. This having been represented to Ukbur Khan, he reluctantly permitted them to remain; and Dr. Campbell was likewise suffered to stay in attendance upon them. At about 10 P.M. the bugles and drums of our new escort summoned us to mount, and we soon found ourselves on the high road to Bameean. At Killa Kazee we were joined by Lieutenants Haughton and Evans, with about forty European soldiers, who had been left at Cabul in hospital under the charge of the latter officer. Wretched and disconsolate, we journeyed on; and, after crossing four steep mountain passes, we arrived on the 3rd September in the valley of Bameean, beyond the Indian Caucasus. Here the European soldiers were lodged in a small dirty fort, about a mile beyond the celebrated Boodist images; whilst the ladies and officers were permitted to remain in their tents outside until the 9th September, when Sala Mahommed obliged us to remove into another fort, about one hundred yards from that containing the soldiers. The change was greatly for the worse; for the wretched hovels into which we were crammed, having been recently inhabited by cows, goats, and sheep, teemed with vermin, and retained the unswept remains of filth. A few rays of light penetrated through small holes in the roof, which just sufficed to rescue the apartments from the stigma of absolute darkness.

On Sunday, September 11th, Sala Mahommed having received a positive order from Ukbur Khan for our instant march to Kooloom, the desperate state of our condition induced Major Pottinger to sound him with the offer of a bribe for our release. Captain Johnson volunteered to be agent in the matter, and found our keeper more accessible than was expected. This man had hitherto kept aloof from every attempt at friendly intercourse with the prisoners; towards whom his manner had been invariably haughty, and his language harsh. Great was our astonishment, therefore, to learn, as we did in the course of the day, that he had been seduced from his allegiance to Ukbur, and brought over to our side. Meanwhile the rapid advance of the two English armies upon Cabul, and the probable defeat of Ukbur, led us to expect that chief's arrival amongst us as likely to happen at any moment. It was, therefore, necessary to be prepared against any sudden surprise. The Huzareh chiefs in the neighbourhood were sounded, and found favourable to our scheme. The men composing our guard were gained over by a promise of four months' pay. A new governor was set up over the provinces by Major Pottinger, the existing governor, Zoolficar Khan, being too much in Ukbur's interest to be trusted. Presents and promises were distributed in all directions; and with so much success, that on the 13th of September we had assurances of aid from all the chiefs between the Sir Chushm and Lygham, bodies of whose armed followers were said to have been posted along the road to keep the passes.

On the 16th of September the country was considered sufficiently safe to admit of our setting out on our return towards Cabul. We had only proceeded a few miles, when a messenger met us with news of General Pollock's victory over Ukbur; which cheering intelligence was shortly afterwards confirmed by a note from Sir Richmond Shakespear, who was hastening to our assistance with six hundred Kuzzilbash horsemen.

On the 17th we re-crossed the Kaloo Ghat, and encamped about three miles from its base. We had been here about two hours, when horsemen were descried descending the pass of Hajeeguk. Instantly Sala Mahommed's men were on the alert, and formed up in line. Judge of our joy when the banner of the Kuzzilbash was distinguished streaming in the air; and imagine, if you can, with what emotions of delight and gratitude we eagerly pressed forward to greet our gallant countryman, Sir Richmond Shakespear, who soon came galloping up to where we stood. For the first time after nine months of miserable thraldom, in the clutches of an unprincipled savage, we felt the blessedness of freedom. A heavy load of care had been removed from our breasts, and from that moment we were altered beings. To God be all the glory, for He alone could bring it to pass!

But there was danger still around us. Ukbur, and other powerful chiefs, were still at large, and might have followers and influence sufficient to intercept our flight. Sir Richmond, therefore, having written to General Pollock for a brigade to meet us, hurried us on by forced marches of twenty-five and thirty miles a day. Recrossing the Hajeeguk and Oonai passes, we entered the beautiful valley of Maidan on the 20th of September; and, as we approached the town of Kot-Ashroo, a body of English dragoons and native cavalry came suddenly upon our view, picketed in some adjoining field.

All doubt was now at an end; we were once more under the safeguard of British troops. General Sale was there in person; and his happiness at regaining his long-lost wife and daughter can readily be imagined. The gallant veteran's countenance was an index to his feelings; and apathetic indeed must have been the heart that failed to sympathise with his holy joy. The camp was still a few miles further on; and we formed a procession of glad spirits as we moved along towards the pass of Suffet Khak, whose heights we could discern crowned with British bayonets. These we found to be a part of the brave 13th light infantry, who, as the ladies successively ascended the hill, raised three hearty cheers of welcome to each of them,—sounds never to be forgotten, producing a thrill of ecstasy through the whole frame. The mountain-guns under Captain Backhouse wound up the scene with a royal salute.

On the following evening we reached General Pollock's camp at Cabul, where the horse-artillery guns uttered similar sounds of public exultation. Such was the history of our wonderful deliverance. Had Sala Mahommed Khan proved incorruptible, no effort of our army could have saved us; and, in gaining over him and the Huzareh chiefs, Major Pottinger was mainly instrumental. To him and Sir R. Shakespear the highest praise is due. General Pollock also, I verily believe, did his best; and our efforts would have been of small avail but for his victorious march on Cabul. To him, likewise, we ought therefore to be grateful; but above all to Heaven.

9 / *The Life of the Amir Dost Mohammed Khan* (1846)

MOHAN LAL

Mohan Lal (1812–77) was a student in the first English class at Persian College, Delhi, in 1828 and a *munshi* (native interpreter) for Sir Alexander Burnes in Afghanistan. This selection from Lal's two-volume *Life of the Amir Dost Mohammed Khan of Kabul* is part dynastic genealogy, part clan-warfare history. Dost Mohammad, the emir of Afghanistan (1793–1863), was arguably one of the most important players in central Asia in the nineteenth century—so powerful that he was able to keep British, Russian, Persian, and Turkistan ambassadors waiting in his court and hold the whole fate of Afghanistan in the balance. In this excerpt we see what a fearless warrior Lal thought Dost Mohammad was—as when he throws himself in the way of a Persian caravan, seizes its booty, and proceeds to lay siege to Kandahar. We also see what a wise and prudent leader Lal thought Dost Mohammad could be when he held a council of war to assess the optimum strategy for besting Shah Shuja. Though Dost Mohammad was ultimately unable to prevent Shah Shuja from being crowned at the hands of the British, Lal shows how critical a role Mohammad played in shaping the geopolitical terrain in which the First Anglo-Afghan War took place.

Abdal was the first and founder of the Abdali tribe. He left three sons, namely, Fofal, Barak, and Alako. If I were to mention the names and lineal descent of the offspring of Fofal and Alako, it would lengthen this book too much. The very valuable account of the kingdom of Kabul, by the Honourable Mountstuart Elphinstone, contains a correct and minute description of their descendants, as well as botanical, mineral, and animal information concerning that territory. In short, this interesting work has been a guide to many, and is as useful to travellers in Afghanistan as the mariner's compass is to voyagers on the seas. This honourable gentleman has made an everlasting impression on the minds of the people of Central Asia of his most amiable, kind, and noble disposition. It is a source of great pride to the travellers of Europe or British India to hear his name even into the remotest parts of Afghanistan with respect and tone of affection from the lips of those who are in general unaware of the names of the distinguished men of their own country. His generosity has gained for him the immortal name of "Hatim Tai,"* and his talents as a statesman the high appellation of "Socrates."† I can without any hesitation say that it was the name of "Ulfrishteen" (Elphinstone) which was the passport for the "army of the Indus" to march through Afghanistan without any opposition. The valuable books of the late Captain Arthur Conolly and of Sir Alexander Burnes give us descriptions which also add to our knowledge of this celebrated and far-extended tribe. My object is to write about the early life, rise, and government of Dost Mohammed Khan, mentioning the names of his immediate predecessors, the sons of Barak, and not the sons of Fofal and of Alako.

Haji Jamal Khan, grandfather of Dost Mohammed Khan, was son of Usaf, son of Yaru, son of Mohammed, son of Omar Khan, son of Khizar Khan, son of Ismail, son of Nek, son of Daru, son of Saifal, son of Barak, the second son of Abdal. Tradition says that through successive generations Abdal descended from the Israelitish household; but to speak the truth, the origin of the Afghans is so obscure, that no one, even among the oldest and most clever of the tribe, can give satisfactory information on this point. Some of the Afghans, recognising their descent from the children of Israel, feel ashamed of their being related by blood to the Jews, upon whom they look as infidels. Concerning the obscurity of the true descent of the Afghans, if curiosity induces any one to desire to know more on that difficult subject, I can safely refer to and justly quote from the highly esteemed book by the Honourable Mountstuart Elphinstone: "After this cursory notice of the facts relating to the Afghans which are ascertained by authentic history, we may now examine what they

say of themselves. The account they give of their own origin is worthy of attention, and has already attracted the notice of an eminent Orientalist. They maintain that they are descended from Afghan, the son of Irmia, or Berkia, son of Saul, king of Israel, and all their histories of their nation begin with relating the transactions of the Jews from Abraham down to the captivity. Their narrative of those transactions appears to agree with that of the other Mohammedans; and though interspersed with some wild fables, does not essentially differ from the Scripture. After the captivity (they allege that) part of the children of Afghan withdrew to the mountains of Ghore, and part to the neighbourhood of Mecca, in Arabia.

"So far this account is destitute of probability. It is known that ten of the twelve tribes remained in the East after the return of their brethren to Judea, and the supposition that the Afghans are their descendants explains easily the disappearance of the one people and the appearance of the other. The rest of the story is confirmed by the fact that the Jews were very numerous in Arabia at the time of Mohammed, and the principal division of them bore the appellation of Khyber, which is still a district in Afghanistan, if not of an Afghan tribe. The theory is plausible, and may be true; but when closely examined, it will appear to rest on a vague tradition alone; and even that tradition is clouded with many inconsistencies and contradictions.

"The Afghan historians proceed to relate that the children of Israel, both in Ghore and in Arabia, preserved their knowledge of the unity of God and the purity of their religious belief, and that on the appearance of the last and greatest of the prophets (Mohammed) the Afghans of Ghore listened to the invitation of their Arabian brethren, the chief of whom was Khauled (or Caled), son of Waleed, so famous for his conquest of Syria, and marched to the aid of the true faith, under the command of Kyse, afterwards surnamed Abdoolresheed. The Arabian historians, on the contrary, bring the descent of Khauled from a well known

*Famous for unlimited bounties in the old Persian histories.
†Celebrated minister and adviser of Alexander the Great.

tribe of their own nation, omit the name of Kyse on their list of the prophets, companions, or allies,* and are entirely silent on the subject of the Afghan succours. Even the Afghan historians, although they describe their countrymen as a numerous people during their Arabian campaign, and though it appears from a sarcasm attributed by those historians to the Prophet (who declared Pushtoo to be the language of hell), that they already spoke their national and peculiar tongue, yet do not scruple in another place to derive the whole nation from the loins of the very Kyse who commanded during the period of the above-mentioned transactions.

"If any other argument were required to disprove this part of the history, it is furnished by the Afghan historians themselves, who state that Saul was the forty-fifth in descent from Abraham, and Kyse the thirty-seventh from Saul. The first of these genealogies is utterly inconsistent with those of the Sacred Writings, and the second allows only thirty-seven generations for a period of sixteen hundred years. If to these facts we add that Saul had no son named either Irmia or Berkia, and that if the existence of his grandson Afghan be admitted, no trace of that patriarch's name remains among his descendants; and if we consider the easy faith with which all rude nations receive accounts favourable to their own antiquity, I fear we must class the descent of the Afghans from the Jews with that of the Romans and the British from the Trojans, and that of the Irish from the Milesians or Bramins."

It must be borne in mind that the Honourable Mountstuart Elphinstone's mission terminated at Peshavar, and that he was never himself in Kabul. But the information given in his account of that kingdom, as well as its immediate neighbourhood and more distant dominions, is so correct, and everything is described in such a manner, that all

*Ansaur, "Assisters."

readers would at once think the honourable gentleman had himself been in the capital, had traversed the whole country, and examined all its wonders personally. Above all, his sojourn in Peshavar, while negotiating with the late Shah Shuja, his constant communication, directly and indirectly, with the people of all ranks, and his civil and liberal manners towards every one, created a most wonderful and noble reversion of respect for the generosity, truth, and justice of the British nation in the hearts of the inhabitants of that part of Asia, and on this account all European travellers have been well treated, and many of the Afghan chiefs offered their homage to Lord Keane when advancing upon Cabul. This high-minded gentleman describes the Barakzais, the tribe of Dost Mohammed Khan, as follows:— "The next clan to the Populzye, which it far exceeds in numbers, is the Baurekzyes. This great clan inhabits the country south of Candahar, the valley of Urghessaun, the banks of the Helmud, and the dry plains which that river divides. Those near Candahar, and many of those in Urghessaun and on the Helmud, are led by the fertility of their soil to agriculture, and the industry of others has even produced caureezes and cultivation in the midst of the desert, but the greater part of the tribe is composed of shepherds. They are a spirited and warlike clan, and as Fatah Khan is now their chief, they make a much more conspicuous figure than any other tribe among the Afghans. At present the grand vizier and almost all the great officers of state are Baurekzyes, and they owe their elevation to the courage and attachment of their clan.

"Their numbers are not less than thirty thousand families."

When the Sarfraz Khan was murdered he left twenty-one sons and several daughters. If I did not mention that they had different mothers, it might puzzle the reader to consider that so many children were born from one mother. The celebrated Vazir Fatah Khan, afterwards entitled Shah

Dost by Mahmud Shah, was the eldest son of Sarfraz Khan. He, Taimur Quli Khan, and Mohammed Azim Khan were brothers from one mother, who belonged to the Nusrat Khail clan. Then Navabs Asad Khan, Samad Khan, and Turrahbaz Khan were born from the Barakzai mother. The seventh son of the Sarfraz Khan was Ata Mohammed Khan, who was the real brother of Yar Mohammed Khan, of Sultan Mohammed Khan, of Said Mohammed Khan, and of Pir Mohammed Khan. Their mother was from the Alakozai family. Purdil Khan, who was the twelfth son of the Sarfraz Khan, was brother to Sherdil, to Kohindil, and to Mehardil Khan. These descended from their mother of the Idu Khail clan of the Hutak Ghilzai. The well known Navab Jabbar Khan is said to be the seventeenth son of the Sarfraz, and is the only one from his mother, of whom mention is made in the book of Mr. Vigne. The reputation of her character stands now high. Jumma Khan was born from an Afghan slave girl. Aslam Khan's mother was also a slave of the tribe of Kafar Siahposh. The hero of my tale, Dost Mohammed Khan, was the twentieth, and his younger brother, Amir Mohammed Khan, was the twenty-first son of the Sarfraz Khan; their mother being from the Siah Mansur family, a branch of the Persian tribe, which was looked upon with disgrace and contempt, by the others, the Afghan wives of the Sarfraz Khan.

I must safely say that the mother of Dost Mohammed was the favourite wife of Sarfraz Khan. She accompanied him in the various campaigns, and would not allow him to rise early and march long after sunrise. For this she was blessed by the troops and camp followers, who did not like to start earlier in cold.

When the Sarfraz was no more, Fatah Khan, with the sons of his own uncles, namely, Abdul Salam, Abdul Vahid, Mohammed Rahim Khan Amin-ul-mulk, and two other confidential men, made their escape through one of the bulwarks of the city of Qandhar to Girishk, and took up their abode in the fort named Sadat. After a short stay in that place, he went through Sistan to Persia, and joined Mahmud Shah in Kirman, whither he had fled through fear of Zaman Shah. These were the days in which the descendants and family of Payandah Khan suffered most miserably. They were begging from morning till night for pieces of bread. Many were prisoners, and others had taken shelter in the mausoleum of the late Ahmad Shah, with the view of gaining food which was daily distributed for charity's sake. No doubt my hero was included in the company and shared their miseries.

Abdul Majid Khan, son of the uncle of Dost Mohammed Khan, asserting his claim, after the Afghan custom, to inherit the widow of the nearest relation, forced the widowed mother of the latter to marry him. His brother Abdulamin Khan married the sister of Dost Mohammed Khan in the same forcible manner. While these unfortunate events were taking place in the family of the Sarfraz Khan, Dost Mahommed Khan, with his younger brother Amir Mohammed Khan, lived four years in one of the forts of Maruf, which belonged to the new husband of his mother, called Abdulmajid Khan. At this time he was from seven to eight years of age.

Meanwhile Fatah Khan returned with Mahmud Shah from Persia, and encamped in the village of Amirbaldan, situated in the vicinity of Sistan. In this place he met with Mirakhor, who was one of the chiefs of Shah Zaman, and governor of Qandhar. The Mirakhor, without gaining any information of the strength of Fatah Khan's force, was overawed by the reputation of his rival's celebrated bravery, and was compelled to flee, leaving his tents and camp equipage in possession of Mahmud Shah. Now the stars of the descendants of the Sarfraz began to shine.

When the reign of Shah Zaman was at an end, Fatah Khan placed Mahmud Shah on the throne of Kabul, and admitted Dost Mohammed Khan into all the secrets of each party. This promising young man was in attendance upon him at all times, and never went to sleep till Fatah was gone to his bed. He stood before him all the day with his hands closed, a token of respect among the Afghans. It was not an unusual occurrence, that when Fatah Khan was in his sleeping-room, Dost Mohammed Khan stood watching his safety.

After some time had passed, Shah Shuja prepared an army to proceed against Mahmud Shah and Fatah Khan at Kabul, and to revenge the outrage done by them to his brother Shah Zaman. On hearing this, Fatah Khan and Prince Kam Ran, son of Mahmud Shah, quitted Kabul to check him. Near the village of Ishpan the armies fought with each other. In the beginning of the battle the warriors of Fatah Khan became dispirited, but at length Shah Shuja was routed and overcome. Whatever royal property and treasures were left to him by the late kings fell into the hands of the followers of Fatah Khan, and many of them were very much enriched. Shah Shuja fled, and the Vazir Fatah Khan, flushed with success, went down to Peshavar for the purpose of collecting the revenue of that place. At this time Mahmud Shah had very little force in Kabul, which induced Abdulrahim Khan Ghilzai to make the Logar people his partizans, and to rebel against his Majesty. He set out for Kabul, and the king, being alarmed, released Mukhtar-ud-daulah, Ahmad Khan Nurzai, and Akram Khan Ghilzai from custody, and sent them to oppose the refractory chief. These chiefs collected about three thousand men, while the enemy was at the head of twenty thousand horse and foot. A hard fight ensued between the Ghilzai rebels and the Durranis of the king, who lost Taj Mohammed Khan, Akram Khan Ghilzai, and Sher Mohammed Khan, who had much influence in the kingdom. Finally the Durranis were victorious; and the rebels, after losing numerous followers, retired to their native villages. The heads of the dead were cut off and brought by the Durranis into the presence of Mahmud Shah. He ordered them to be heaped up outside the palace, on the cliff known by the name of "Tapaikhaki-balkh."

While peace was thus being established on the southern side, a fresh rebellion broke out in the East. "Fatah Khan Babakarzai" took up his residence in the house of the priests of "Ozbin," and besought them to take up his cause. They assembled a large body of plunderers, and with the aid of Jabbar Khail and the Ahmadzai tribe, which in all amounted to about forty thousand men, they came with the above-mentioned rebel, and made breastworks near "Munar Chakri" to fight with the king's forces. The Vazir Fatah Khan moved with an army to punish this refractory multitude, which, after a little fighting, was defeated and dispersed. The Vazir cut off nearly one hundred heads of the rebels and brought them into the city. After this he went to collect the revenues of the country of Bannu, and on his way back was surprised by the arrival of the news that Prince Qaisar of Herat, being unable to wage war with the prince Haji Firoz, had fled, and had sought refuge and aid from the king of Persia; and that after passing some time in that country, he had marched to seize on the city of Qandhar. On this he immediately joined Prince Kam Ran at Qandhar, and marched to check the progress of Qaisar. They met and fought with each other at Kokran, in which place Akram Khan Ghilzai was killed on the part of Kam Ran, and Prince Qaisar was taken prisoner and carried to Kabul.

While Fatah Khan was engaged in suppressing the aforesaid disorders in the kingdom, the enterprising Dost Mohammed Khan was with him. His heroic conduct and persevering energy of mind were very pleasing in the eyes of the Vazir, and were the subject of jealousy of his older and younger brothers. His age at this time was fourteen years. As his intrepidity was the topic of the warrior's conversation, his beauty also rendered him a favourite with the people in those days.

After that time the Vazir Fatah Khan, along with Dost Mohammed Khan, directed his course back to Kabul. This afforded a favourable opportunity for Shah Shuja at Peshavar, who, finding that the territory of Qandhar was left without forces, proceeded through the Vazir's country to take it if possible. Akram Khan Barakzai, Mohammed Ali Khan, and Mir Akbar were then with his Majesty. No sooner had Fatah Khan and Dost Mohammed Khan heard of the movement of Shah Shuja towards Qandhar, then they set out to assist Prince Kam Ran against his Majesty. When they reached that place they confined Ghafur Khan Barakzai, Saidel Khan Alakozai, and Khojah Mohammed Khan Badozai, believing that they were likely to go over to Shah Shuja. This intelligence alarmed Mukhtar-ud-daulah, who thought that the daily increasing power of Fatah Khan would some day ruin him; and to prevent this evil he excited the Mirvaiz, Khojah Khanji and Sayad Ashraf to take his part.

The seditious Mirvaiz assembled the inhabitants (Sunnis) of Kabul, and on religious pretence excited their animosity against the Kuzilbashes (Shias). He added that Mahmud Shah and Fatah Khan, contrary to their own religion, are protectors of the Shias, the annihilation of which tribe is incumbent on the Sunnis' faith. As the greater part of the Qizilbash force was advancing with Fatah Khan and Dost Mohammed Khan towards Qandhar, the Mirvaiz, finding their part of the town weakened in its defence, ordered the Kabul, Kohistan, and Ghilzai people to make a sudden attack on it; and one of the divisions of the Qizilbash fort, occupied by the Khafis, was plundered, and Shah Mahmud besieged in Bala Hissar. At last his Majesty was taken prisoner, and Shah Shuja planted on the throne.

As soon as Fatah Khan was informed of his master's dethronement, he quitted Qandhar immediately with Dost Mohammed Khan, to fight with Shah Shuja in Kabul. About four miles from the city a battle took place between Shah Shuja and Fatah Khan, in which the latter was beaten, and compelled to join Prince Kam Ran at Qandhar. Shah Shuja being victorious returned to Kabul.

As Navab Asad Khan, uncle of Dost, was a prisoner in the Bala Hisar of Kabul, Mukhtar-ud-daulah supplicated his Majesty to release him, and allow him to be his guest. The Shah complied with his request, and Mukhtar-ud-daulah did every honour to Asad Khan. The Nawab being desirous to destroy all feelings of animosity between the Sadozai and Barakzai family, wished to make matrimonial connexions among them; consequently the sister of Dost Mohammed Khan was married to Shah Shuja. After this his Majesty requested Navab Asad Khan, Gul Mohammed Khan, the brother of Mukhtar-ud-daulah and Dost Mohammed Khan, to go to the Vazir Fatah Khan at Qandhar, and after assuring him of every attention and respect on the part of the king to induce him to relinquish all designs of supporting Mahmud Shah, and to attach himself to Shah Shuja. The latter also made an oath to restore him to the rank and privileges of his late father the Sarfraz Khan, and to treat him with all due consideration. The aforesaid chiefs went down to Qandhar, and delivered the messages of the king to Fatah Khan, who was pleased with this unexpected condescension in Shah Shuja, and immediately marched for Kabul. Prince Kam Ran was broken-hearted at this unhappy turn of affairs, and was obliged to take refuge in Hirat.

When the intelligence of Fatah Khan's departure from Qandhar reached Mukhtar-ud-daulah at Kabul, he went down to meet him at Ghazni, and conducted him to the presence of the king. Fatah Khan did not receive the favours of his Majesty as stipulated, nor was the Ghilzai division of the army placed under his charge. He was nearly two months in the house of Mukhtar-ud-daulah, who treated him with distinction and civility. In the meantime Akram Khan advised Shah Shuja to proceed to Peshavar, and there to put Fatah Khan and Mukhtar-ud-daulah into custody, and so to save himself from all fear of injury from them. One of the men who was aware of this secret went and said to Mukhtar-ud-daulah that Akram Khan and Shah Shuja had contrived to ruin them. Mukhtar-ud-daulah was lost in wonder at such ungrateful contrivances of Shuja, whom he had shortly before made king, after dethroning Mahmud Shah. He said to himself, that if he were to rebel openly just now, to prevent the ill designs of his antagonist, it would bring a load of disgrace to his own long-earned reputation. He therefore advanced seventy thousand rupees secretly to Fatah Khan, and told him to wait in Kabul on the excuse of procuring a marching equipage, while he himself would go with Shuja to Peshavar. He added also, that when Fatah Khan should receive the news of the Shah's arrival in Tezin, he should immediately commence proceedings as a foe to the king, and should cause the release of the chiefs, namely: Baqar Khan, Ibrahim Khan, Mirza Abul Qasim Khan, and Mardan Khan, and convey them to Shah Zadah Qaisar at Qandhar. These chiefs were the friends of Shah Mahmud, and therefore had been put into confinement by Shah Shuja. While Mukhtar and Fatah Khan were planning these proceedings against Shah Shuja, they entered into an agreement with each other, that the friends and enemies of the one should be friends and enemies of the other, and both should join when an antagonist appeared against either of them.

No sooner had Shah Shuja reached Tezin on his way to Jalalabad then he heard of the hostile views of Mukhtar and Fatah Khan. Immediately he issued orders that a strong cavalry force should return to Kabul, and bring the captive nobles of Shah Mahmud to his presence, along with the guard already with them. Before this cavalry had reached Kabul the brave Fatah Khan took all the chiefs out of custody, and conducted them to Qandhar, through Lahogard. Shah Zadah Qaisar was ruling in Qandhar at that time, and Ahmad Khan Nurzai was his minister. Fatah Khan, after long marches, reached the "Edgah" gate of Qandhar at midnight, and bribed the guard to report his arrival secretly to Agha Idrak, then confidential eunuch of the Shah Zadah. When he heard this he

instantly waited upon Qaisar, and mentioned the arrival of Fatah Khan, with this message, "If the Shah Zadah had any intention of becoming a king, this seemed a good opportunity, and he (Fatah Khan) would place him on the throne; otherwise he should send him a quiet and plain answer."

Fatah and Dost took immediate steps to intrigue with their former master, Prince Qaisar, against Prince Kam Ran, whom they, when every thing was in their own favour, turned out of the city; and they then invited the former to take his place. In these times of agitation Dost failed also in the respect which was due to the royal household, and omitted no opportunity to plunder and rob the royal ladies. After the Shah Zadah Qaisar, with the assistance of Fatah Khan and Dost Mohammed Khan, had seized the government of Qandhar, his royal highness dispatched Mohammed Ali Khan, and Mir Akbar, to Shah Shuja and Mukhtar-ud-daulah, and proposed that if he would allow him the possession of Qandhar, Shikarpur, and their dependencies, he would destroy Kam Ran, with Haji Firozuddin. He also suggested that if his Majesty suspected the attachment of his royal highness, and the fidelity of Fatah Khan and of Dost Mohammed Khan, he would immediately send their brother Mohammed Azim Khan as a hostage to the Shah.

Shah Shuja-ul-Mulk did not accept the offers of Shah Zadah, but continued his march to Qandhar. When the royal camp was near a village called "Chishmah Shadi," Dost Mohammed and Fatah Khan fled from the city to Frah, and the Shah Zadah, in company with Khowajah Mohammed Khan, proceeded to take shelter in "Dehlah." This intelligence disappointed his Majesty, who set out by express to get the Shah Zadah if possible. Mukhtar-ud-daulah secretly conveyed the news to the Shah Zadah, who quitted "Dehlah," to secure himself in some distant and out of the way place.

On this Shah Shuja entered the city of Qandhar, and offered the most kind and honourable treatment to Dost Mohammed and Fatah Khan, who

immediately waited upon him. Four days afterwards Shah Zaman and Mukhtar-ud-daulah went
and brought Shah Zadah Qaisar with Khowajah
Mohammed Khan into the presence of his Majesty, who pardoned them for their past misdeeds
and restored the government of Qandhar to them.
Shah Shuja, in company with Dost Mohammed
and Fatah Khan, proceeded to Sindh, where he received the usual tribute from the Meers, and bent
his course by the Derajat and Peshavar to Kabul.

Meanwhile the Mir Alam Khan was deprived of
the governorship of Derah Ghazi Khan, and Ata
Mohammed Khan Nurzai was placed by Shah
Shuja in that important situation. This alarmed
Dost Mohammed and Fatah Khan to such an extent, that they found no safety for their persons
but in flying towards Hirat. The Mir Alam also
fled at the head of some good and brave cavalry,
and gained employment under Shah Zadah Qaisar in Qandhar. In Hirat Dost Mohammed and
Fatah Khan did all in their power to induce Shah
Zadah Haji Firoz to attack Qandhar and Kabul,
but he did not comply with their request. He said
he had not ambition to rule the kingdom of Afghanistan, and was well satisfied with the present
possession of Hirat.

The refusal of Shah Zadah Haji Firoz broke the
hearts of Dost Mohammed and Fatah Khan, and
even compelled them to return to Shah Zadah Qaisar at Qandhar. Here Khowajah Mohammed Khan
Fofalzai, with the friendly assistance of the Mir
Alam Khan Nurzai, began to insult Dost Mohammed and Fatah Khan with dispute about equality,
and intrigued with Shah Zaman, who at this time
was living with his son Shah Zadah Qaisar in Qandhar, to put them both in confinement.

With this view Shah Zaman begged the confidential servants of Shah Zadah Qaisar, who were
the Mir Alam Khan Nurzai and Shah Navaz Khan
Achakzai, to call upon Dost Mohammed and
Fatah Khan, and state on the part of his Majesty
that they should give him a grand entertainment.
The quick-sighted Dost Mohammed Khan discovered the real object of the pretended familiarity and base affection of Shah Zaman, and both
brothers apparently showed themselves highly
honoured by such favour of Shah Zaman. They
made preparations for three different entertain-
ments; one on their own part, the second from
Navab Asad Khan, and the third from Mohammed Azim Khan.

Upon the one hand Fatah Khan was preparing
everything pompously to receive Shah Zaman in
the beautiful garden of Maranjan, as if he were not
aware of the conspiracy, and on the other, the active Dost Mohammed was secretly engaged in
adding to the number of his body guard, and kept
a piercing eye on all sides to secure the safety of
his brother, Fatah Khan, and of himself, in case
the conspirators should dare to injure them. His
celerity and readiness to meet any blow showed
Shah Zaman and Shah Zadah Qaisar the impossibility of making them the victims of the conspiracy,
and therefore to remove every suspicion from the
minds of Dost Mohammed and Fatah Khan, the
Shah conferred the dress of honour on them.
Thus the watchfulness of the hero of my tale frus-
trated the designs of the conspirators, who in great
despair made all possible schemes to gain their
mean object during the day, but availed nothing.

At last Shah Zaman and Shah Zadah Qaisar left
the entertainment, and on returning to the palace
gave orders that no chief should enter the court-
yard accompanied by more than five attendants.
During twenty days Fatah Khan managed to take
about one hundred men with him, when he was
waiting upon Shah Zadah, and thus secured his
safety for such a period. At length, the Shah Zadah
concealed some of his strong men in his garden,
when he gave orders that his nobles should wait to
pay their respects. This was done, and suddenly
the Mir Alam Khan, the nephew of the Sardar
Ahmad Khan, surnamed Saifuddaulah, lifted up
Fatah Khan and threw him down on the ground,
which broke two of his teeth, and immediately
they made him a prisoner. After this the friends of

Fatah Khan, namely, Navab Asad Khan, Mirza Mohammed Raza, and Agha Mehndi, were similarly treated; but the brave Dost Mohammed was fortunately aware of the impending danger, and lost no time, but called his followers, who amounted to about five hundred men. It was not in the power of Shah Zadah to catch Dost Mohammed Khan, when thus protected.

It was impossible for a man like Dost Mohammed Khan to see his brother, Fatah Khan, suffering in custody without using his utmost energy to obtain the freedom of the dear captive. At the head of his followers he made a bold rush into the outer gate of the palace, but on reaching the door of the residence of the Shah Zadah, where Fatah Khan was confined, he was disappointed to observe that it was shut, and not only strongly defended, but all the walls and towers filled with matchlock men. They all at once fired at him, and he, having no means to ascend the walls, relinquished the attack. However, he besieged the palace; on which the Shah Zadah ordered Khowajah Mohammed Khan and the other chiefs to shut the gates of the city, and thus cut off the means of escape from Dost Mohammed Khan when thus reduced in the number of his adherents. One of the friends of Mohammed Azim Khan secretly sent this news to the Dost, and added also that the chiefs, with five hundred men each, had been ordered to take charge of the different gates and towers of the city against him.

When the intelligence of the defeat of Shah Zadah reached the Imperial court of Shah Shuja, he proceeded quickly in person to defend the city of Qandhar. On this, Fatah Khan and the Mir Alam Khan made preparations to oppose the progress of his Majesty. Since there was no other person so qualified as Dost Mohammed Khan, both in conducting political affairs and in the energetic duties of a field-marshal, the whole party unanimously elected the lion of my subject to undertake that important post.

The field-marshal, Dost Mohammed, with his accustomed alacrity and perseverance, led his troops to oppose Shah Shuja, whom he met near Qarahbagh, or rather in Obeh. A battle ensued, and both parties fought desperately, when the Sardar Ahmad Khan Nurzai became the medium of a negotiation between the Shah and Dost Mohammed Khan. War was changed into peace, on which Dost Mohammed returned to Girishk, and Shah Shuja, after replacing Shah Zadah Qaisar in the government of Qandhar, moved back to Kabul with Mukhtar-ud-daulah.

It was not long after the arrival of Shah Shuja in Kabul that his Majesty was surrounded with new difficulties, and thought to have recourse to the services of the brave Dost Mohammed and of Fatah Khan. The affairs of the capital took a most frightful aspect. The prime minister, Mukhtar-ud-daulah, in junction with the celebrated hypocrite, the Mir Vaiz, the priest of Kabul, rebelled against his royal master, with the view to recognise Shah Zadah Qaisar, governor of Qandhar, as sovereign of Afghanistan. When this cheerless information reached the ears of his Majesty, he immediately sent a deputation consisting of the Durrani nobles of the realm, namely, the Sardar Madad Khan Ishaqzai, Ahmad Khan Nurzai, some members of the royal family, and holy descendants of the Prophet the Sadats, as well as other "Aq Saqal," silver-bearded people of respectability, to Dost Mohammed and Fatah Khan in Girishk.

The deputation of the Shah, after engaging and pledging themselves for the personal safety and good treatment of Dost Mohammed and of Fatah Khan, conducted them to Qandhar. As soon as this report spread in the country, Mukhtar-ud-daulah and the Mir Vaiz, as well as their followers, relinquished all their rebellious designs for the time. Shah Shuja felt very anxious to secure the closer alliance of Dost Mohammed and of Fatah Khan, and therefore he himself met them in Qandhar. His Majesty gave them every assurance of his favour and attachment, and delivered to them a sealed engagement written on the holy leaf of the "Qoran," and at the same time conferred the title of "Sardar i Sardaran" (chief of chiefs) upon Fatah Khan: he also gave a most valuable dress of honour, along with a superior horse with gold trappings, to Dost, and one lakh of rupees for their expenses.

After Shah Shuja had succeeded in obtaining the good will and services of Dost and Fatah Khan, he proceeded to raise tribute from the Meers of Sindh; but the Sindhians made preparations to fight with the Shah. On this the nobles of the court, namely, Akram Khan, &c. &c., petitioned the Shah to make peace on getting five lakhs of rupees from them; while the hero Dost Mohammed and Fatah Khan, relying on their intrepidity and sagacity, begged the Shah not to lend an ear to the proposals of Akram, but to leave the whole affair to their arrangement. They also added that, without using arms and sacrificing lives, they would get from the Meers and fill the royal coffers with thirty lakhs of rupees. However, Akram foolishly prevailed on his Majesty to follow his counsel; and going secretly to the Meers at night, brought only five lakhs of rupees, and made an arrangement with them.

This proceeding of Akram Khan, which was nothing but a tissue of folly and crooked understanding, not only showed the weakness of the Shah's powers to the Sindhians and caused a loss of twenty-five lakhs of rupees to the royal treasury, but it also excited the extreme displeasure of Dost Mohammed and Fatah Khan. They deeply lamented the damage sustained by the ill counsel of Akram Khan, and became exceedingly wrathful, that the Shah, instead of paying attention to their advantageous advice, followed that of their inferior and fool.

Dost Mohammed and Fatah Khan were so much disgusted with the above-mentioned proceedings, that they left Haidarabad and came up to Shikarpur. Hither the Shah followed them and apologized to them. He swore that nothing of the kind should happen in future, and that all the affairs of his government, whether internal or external, should be adjusted by their guidance. As nature had cultivated noble and independent notions in the head and heart of Dost, he therefore could not be estranged by ill usage of this kind, but was determined to oblige and serve the Shah evidently and openly, and agreed to fight with Shah Zadah Qaisar, Mukhtar-ud-daulah, and Mir Vaiz, who had again assumed the character of enemies to the Shah.

When Dost Mohammed and Fatah were informed of the hostile movements of Shah Shuja, they raised a large army, and under the royal shadow of Shah Mahmud and of Shah Zadah Kam Ran, set out to oppose Shah Shuja. Dost Mohammed volunteered to be the head of the advanced guard, and was accompanied by his stepbrother Purdil Khan, and also by Nur Mohammed Khan, the brother of Khowajah Mohammed Khan, who was slain in the late battle of Tahkal, in Peshavar. The very moment he had reached Kalat i Ghilzai, Nur Mohammed Khan went over to Shah Shuja, and Ata Mohammed Khan Nurzai and Yahya Khan Bamzai, who were commanders of large bodies of troops, fled towards Dehlah and Murghab.

At the time these sad desertions took place, and the leader of the advanced guard remained alone, Shuja would not have hesitated a moment to seize and destroy him (Dost Mohammed) by surprise, but he knew his brave heart and wise head, and therefore avoided a skirmish with him. It is said by the people that at this crisis Dost Mohammed was afraid of Shah Shuja, because he was deserted and alone, and the Shah was afraid of the talents and heroism of Dost, lest he might cause dissension among his followers. These fears, entertained on both sides, prevented an immediate contest, and afforded a favourable opportunity to Dost Mohammed Khan to retrace his steps and join his brother Fatah Khan.

On the approach of Shuja's army, Mahmud Shah, being aided only by Fatah Khan and Dost Mohammed, found himself too weak to fight with Shah Shuja, and therefore in this low spirit he fled to Girishk.

After some time Dost Mohammed and Fatah Khan left Girishk and went to Sabzvar, where they remained for three months. During their sojourn in this place they were informed that Shah Shuja had left Qandhar for Kabul, and appointed Shah Zadah Yunas, with Azam Khan Nasakhchibashi and the Mir Alam Khan, governor of the former city.

Meanwhile Dost Mohammed and Fatah Khan heard that two large caravans were to pass near Khashrod, one from Qandhar to Persia, and the other from the latter country to the former. On this they placed themselves on the road of the caravans, and the very moment they encountered with them every article fell into the possession of these noble highway-men. They gained plenty of money by this plunder from the merchants. Immediately after this they raised an army and prepared themselves to attack Qandhar.

Dost Mohammed and Fatah Khan met no opposition on the line of their march to Qandhar, which place they fortunately took with little trouble. The governor of this place fled, and joined his master Shah Shuja in Derajat; and Mir Alam Khan, the lieutenant-governor, being a relative of Pir Mohammed Khan Alakozai, threw himself on the protection of Shah Mahmud, who was again made nominal king by Dost and Fatah. After arranging the government affairs of Qandhar, Dost Mohammed and Fatah Khan proceeded to take Kabul, under favour of the name of Shah Mahmud. They succeeded in gaining possession of this capital, and sent Mohammed Azim Khan towards Peshavar to oppose Shah Shuja.

While Mohammed Azim Khan was encamped at Balabagh to intercept the progress of Shah Shuja, Dost Mohammed and Fatah Khan were strengthening themselves and weakening their adversaries in Kabul. Among them was the Mir Alam Khan, whom they confined and treated with barbarous cruelty. Shah Shuja, at the head of twenty-five thousand men, proceeded from Peshavar to Kabul. When the royal army reached Jalalabad, Mohammed Azim Khan, finding himself unable to oppose his Majesty, left the highway and took shelter in the different skirts of the Sufaid Koh.

No sooner had the above-mentioned intelligence reached Dost Mohammed and Fatah Khan then they marched down to Surkhab to bring Mahmud Shah with them. These three enterprising men had no more than three thousand soldiers, and knew the strength of the army they were going to fight with; but Dost Mohammed's bravery, mingled with policy, was always depended upon, and generally productive of the results of victory. On their arrival in the vicinity of the Lukhi of Surkhab, they thought that if the Durrani chiefs should cause the release of the Mir Alam Khan, he would probably succeed in joining Shah Shuja, and desertions might take place among the followers on both sides. To prevent this anticipated misfortune, Dost Mohammed and Fatah Khan murdered the poor prisoner.

Now Dost Mohammed and Fatah Khan held a council of war with their subordinate chiefs in the presence of Shah Mahmud, and stated that it was most contrary to the rules of policy and of war to appear in the open field with a small force of three thousand before a monarch or enemy of twenty-five thousand well mounted cavalry and well equipped infantry. The only thing they think now advisable to preserve warlike fame and gain honour is to avoid a general action, and then with determined spirit to attack the enemy by surprise. They also proposed that, until the enemy were perfectly routed, they should not divide themselves into small bodies, and commence to plunder their respective antagonists, as was usual with the Afghans, because this would cause great confusion among them, and probably the enemy would get the benefit of it. They also added that, though the enemy exceeded them in power and number of men, none of them ought to be disheartened and go over to him, believing that the victory would always attend his army, because such conduct would not only cause a disgraceful name for the man himself who should do so, but would also dishearten the rest of their followers.

These counsels of Dost Mohammed Khan were applauded by Mahmud Shah, Fatah Khan, and the chiefs, on which they left everything of peace and war to his sound and wise management. He remained all day concealed in the bushes or "lukhi," and about evening he marched with all his forces. He made a long march under cover of the darkness of night, and about five in the morning he attacked the Sardar Madad Khan, Azam Khan, and Ghafur Khan, who commanded ten thousand foot and horse, and had been sent as an advanced brigade. Persons who were present in the field of battle told me that it was out of the power of any man's tongue to describe the matchless alacrity, prowess, and steadiness of Dost Mohammed Khan in this grand battle. In one moment he was seen making a havoc in the lines of the enemy, and then, forcing his way back, he was observed to encourage his followers to fight; and another time he was perceived to restore order among the undisciplined soldiers. Madad Khan and Azam Khan, commanding the opposite forces, now felt the narrowness of their situation, and at the same time were panic-struck to see that Dost Mohammed was causing great slaughter in their army, which was already much reduced in number and in power. At length Dost Mohammed Khan routed and dispersed the enemy, who suffered exceedingly both in men and in baggage.

When the report of the defeat of the strong royal force under Madad Khan, &c. &c., by a small body of troops under the personal command of Dost Mohammed Khan reached the camp of Shah Shuja, it not only incensed his Majesty, but alarmed him much, and made him proceed in person to check the progress of Dost Mohammed Khan. Shah Shuja had still fifteen thousand good soldiers under the command of the celebrated Akram Khan, who made the King believe that Shah Mahmud's forces were only three thousand men, and that they would not stand before him; and also that Dost Mohammed would soon lose the name of victorious, which he lately obtained in consequence of the ill management of Madad Khan. It appears that Akram Khan was either jealous, or had foolish brains to suppose that he could beat an army headed by Dost Mohammed Khan, who was never once known to leave a field of battle without gaining the victory, except some foresighted policy had induced him to do so. However, Shah Shuja made all necessary arrangements for waging war with Mahmud Shah and Fatah Khan, evidently proud of the superiority of his army, yet in heart extremely fearful of the energies of Dost Mohammed Khan. I heard from several credible people in Afghanistan that at this time of the war Shah Shuja said confidentially to his minister, that while Dost Mohammed is not captured, the victory is not to be expected; and while he is alive the crown will not be on his (Shuja's) head.* The forces on both sides were arrayed in the field, those of Shah Shuja commanded by the Sardar Akram Khan, and those of Shah Mahmud were guided by the personal and heroic directions of Dost Mohammed Khan. A battle ensued, and after a severe conflict the Sardar Akram Khan was killed, with many hundreds of Shuja's army. Some say that the deceased was cut down by Dost himself; and others add that he had received a ball from some of his own followers. The fall of such a high nobleman in the field, with so many hundred followers, produced an alarming feeling in the forces of Shuja. His Majesty was also himself frightened, and at last compelled to flee. All the rest of his followers also dispersed.

Shah Mahmud and Fatah Khan, happy in their success, and proud of the victory gained by their

---

*This appears to be a wonderful and true prophecy.

brave adherent Dost Mohammed Khan, returned to Kabul, and Mahmud was placed on the throne and acknowledged as King of Afghanistan. Fatah Khan, the elder brother of Dost Mohammed Khan, was appointed prime minister of the Shah, and he gave the charge of various important situations to his brothers. Since the qualifications for conducting war, unshaken courage and persevering generalship, as well as the talents for administering the affairs of the realm, prudent foresight and sound policy, were shining on the forehead of Dost Mohammed Khan, Mahmud Shah and the Vizir considered his presence with themselves of much value, and consequently he was selected as next person to the Vazir, but in reality he was first in everything.

The Afghan Wars (1896)

ARCHIBALD FORBES

Published at the end of the nineteenth century, when the British were still dealing with a restive North-West Frontier, Archibald Forbes's history of the first two Anglo-Afghan Wars is quite skeptical of British intentions, let alone capacity, in the region. Forbes (1838–1900) was a British war correspondent who covered everything from the Franco-Prussian War (1870) to the Battle of Isandlwana (1879), chiefly for the *Daily News*. In this passage he tells of "the road to ruin" (Sir William Macnaghten's assassination at the hands of Akbar Khan) and "the catastrophe" (the escape from Kabul) in dark and fatalistic terms. Note his distrust of both Macnaghten and Mohan Lal (see chapter 9), who loom almost as sinister as the assassins themselves. As for the retreat, Forbes recounts one "fresh butchery" after another, capturing both the "surging concourse of miserable followers" and the "cool deadly rancor" with which the doomed British troops who led the followers fought death to the last.

The ill-omened evacuation by our doomed people of the cantonments wherein for two months they had undergone every extremity of humiliation and contumely, was begun on the dreary winter morning of January 6th, 1842. Snow lay deep on plain and hill-side; the cruel cold, penetrating through the warmest clothing, bit fiercely into the debilitated and thinly clad frames of the sepoys and the great horde of camp followers. The military force which marched out of cantonments consisted of about 4500 armed men, of whom about 690 were Europeans, 2840 native soldiers on foot, and 970 native cavalrymen. The gallant troop of Company's Horse-Artillery marched out with its full complement of six guns, to which with three pieces of the mountain train the artillery arm of the departing force was restricted by the degrading terms imposed by the Afghan chiefs. In good heart and resolutely commanded, a body of disciplined troops thus constituted and of a fighting strength so respectable, might have been trusted not only to hold its own against Afghan onslaught but if necessary to take the offensive with success. But alas, the heart of the hapless force had gone to water, its discipline was a wreck, its chiefs were feeble and apathetic; its steps were dogged by the incubus of some 12,000 camp followers with a great company of women and children. The awful fate brooded over its forlorn banners of expiating by its utter annihilation, the wretched folly and sinister prosecution of the enterprise whose deserved failure was to be branded yet deeper on the gloomiest page of our national history, by the impending catastrophe of which the dark shadow already lay upon the blighted column.

The advance began to move out from cantonments at nine A.M. The march was delayed at the river by the non-completion of the temporary bridge, and the whole of the advance was not across until after noon. The main body under Shelton, which was accompanied by the ladies, invalids, and sick, slowly followed. It as well as the advance was disorganised from the first by the throngs of camp followers with the baggage, who could not be prevented from mixing themselves up with the troops. The Afghans occupied the cantonments as portion after portion was evacuated by our people, rending the air with their exulting cries and committing every kind of atrocity. It was late in the afternoon before the long train of camels following the main body had cleared the cantonments; and meanwhile the rear-guard was massed outside in the space between the rampart and the canal, among the chaos of already abandoned baggage. It was exposed there to a vicious jezail fire poured into it by the Afghans, who abandoned the pleasures of plunder and arson for the yet greater joy of slaughtering the Feringhees. When the rear-guard moved away in the twilight, an officer and fifty men were left dead in the snow, the victims of the Afghan fire from the rampart of the cantonment; and owing to casualties in the gun teams it had been found necessary to spike and abandon two of the horse-artillery guns.

The rear-guard, cut into from behind by the pestilent ghazees, found its route encumbered with heaps of abandoned baggage around which swarmed Afghan plunderers. Other Afghans, greedier for blood than for booty, were hacking and slaying among the numberless sepoys and camp followers who had dropped out of the column, and were lying or sitting on the wayside in apathetic despair, waiting for death and careless whether it came to them by knife or by cold. Babes lay on the snow abandoned by their mothers, themselves prostrate and dying a few hundred yards further on. It was not until two o'clock of the following morning that the rear-guard reached the straggling and irregular bivouac in which its comrades lay in the snow at the end of the first short march of six miles. Its weary progress had been illuminated by the conflagration raging in the cantonments, which had been fired by the Afghan fanatics, rabid to erase every relic of the detested unbelievers.

It was a night of bitter cold. Out in the open among the snow soldiers and camp followers, foodless, fireless, and shelterless, froze to death in numbers, and numbers more were frost-bitten. The cheery morning noise of ordinary camp life was unheard in the mournful bivouac. Captain Lawrence outlines a melancholy picture. "The silence of the men betrayed their despair and torpor. In the morning I found lying close to me, stiff, cold, and quite dead, in full regimentals, with his sword drawn in his hand, an old grey-haired conductor named Macgregor, who, utterly exhausted, had lain down there silently to die." Already defection had set in. One of the Shah's infantry regiments and his detachment of sappers and miners had deserted bodily, partly during the march of the previous day, partly in the course of the night.

No orders were given out, no bugle sounded the march, on the morning of the 7th. The column heaved itself forward sluggishly, a mere mob of soldiers, camp followers and cattle, destitute of any semblance of order or discipline. Quite half the sepoys were already unfit for duty; in hundreds they drifted in among the non-combatants and increased the confusion. The advance of the previous day was now the rear-guard. After plundering the abandoned baggage the Afghans set to harassing the rear-guard, whose progress was delayed by the disorderly multitude blocking the road in front. The three mountain guns, temporarily separated from the infantry, were captured by a sudden Afghan rush. In vain Anquetil strove to rouse the 44th to make an effort for their recapture. Green was more successful with his handful of artillerymen, who followed him and the Brigadier and spiked the pieces, but being unsupported were compelled a second time to abandon them. On this march it became necessary also, from the exhaustion of their teams, to spike and abandon two more of the horse-artillery guns; so that there now remained with the force only a couple of six-pounders. While the rear-guard was in action a body of Afghan horse charged on the flank, right into the heart of the baggage column, swept away much plunder, and spread confusion and dismay far and wide. The rear of the column would probably have been entirely cut off, but that reinforcements from the advance under Shelton pushed back the enemy, and by crowning the lateral heights kept open the thoroughfare. At Bootkhak was found Akbar Khan, who professed to have been commissioned to escort the force to Jellalabad, and who blamed our people for having marched out prematurely from the cantonments. He insisted on the halt of the column at Bootkhak until the following morning when he would provide supplies, but he demanded an immediate subsidy of 15,000 rupees and that Pottinger, Lawrence and Mackenzie should be given up to him as hostages that the force would not march beyond Tezeen until tidings should arrive that Sale had evacuated Jellalabad. Those officers by the General's instructions joined the Afghan chief on the following morning, and Akbar's financial requisition was obsequiously fulfilled. After two days' marching our people, who had brought out with them provisions for but five and a half days expecting within that time to reach Jellalabad, were only ten miles forward on their march.

Another night passed with its train of horrors—starvation, cold, exhaustion, death. Lady Sale relates that scarcely any of the baggage now remained; that there was no food for man or beast; that snow lay a foot deep on the ground; that even water from the adjacent stream was difficult to obtain, as the carriers were fired on in fetching it; and that she thought herself fortunate in being sheltered in a small tent in which "we slept nine, all touching each other." Daylight brought merely a more bitter realisation of utter misery. Eyre expresses his wonderment at the effect of two nights' exposure to the frost in disorganising the force. "It had so nipped even the strongest men as to completely prostrate their powers and incapacitate them for service; even the cavalry, who suffered less than the rest, were obliged to be lifted on their horses." In fact, only a few hundred serviceable men remained. At the sound of hostile fire the living struggled to their feet from their lairs in the snow, stiffened with cold, all but unable to move or hold a weapon, leaving many of their more fortunate comrades stark in death. A turmoil of confusion reigned. The Afghans were firing into the rear of the mass and there was a wild rush of camp followers to the front, who stripped the baggage cattle of their loads and carried the animals off, leaving the ground strewn with ammunition, treasure, plate, and other property. The ladies were no longer carried in litters and palanquins, for their bearers were mostly dead; they sat in the bullet fire packed into panniers slung on camels, invalids as some of them were—one poor lady with her baby only five days old. Mess stores were being recklessly distributed, and Lady Sale honestly acknowledges that, as she sat on her horse in the cold she felt very grateful for a tumbler of sherry, which at any other time would have made her "very unladylike," but which now merely warmed her. Cups full of sherry were drunk by young children without in the least affecting their heads, so strong on them was the hold of the cold.

It was not until noon that the living mass of

men and animals was once more in motion. The troops were in utter disorganisation; the baggage was mixed up with the advance guard; the camp followers were pushing ahead in precipitate panic. The task before the wretched congeries of people was to thread the stupendous gorge of the Khoord Cabul pass—a defile about five miles long, hemmed in on either hand by steeply scarped hills. Down the bottom of the ravine dashed a mountain torrent, whose edges were lined with thick layers of ice on which had formed glacier-like masses of snow. The "Jaws of Death" were barely entered when the slaughter began. With the advance rode several Afghan chiefs, whose followers by their command shouted to the Ghilzais lining the heights to hold their fire, but the tribesmen gave no heed to the mandate. Lady Sale rode with the chiefs. The Ghilzai fire at fifty yards was close and deadly. The men of the advance fell fast. Lady Sale had a bullet in her arm and three more through her dress. But the weight of the hostile fire fell on the main column, the baggage escort, and the rear-guard. Some of the ladies, who mostly were on camels which were led with the column, had strange adventures. On one camel was quite a group. In one of its panniers were Mrs Boyd and her little son, in the other Mrs Mainwaring with her own infant and Mrs Anderson's eldest child. The camel fell, shot. A Hindustanee trooper took up Mrs Boyd *en croupe* and carried her through in safety; another horseman behind whom her son rode, was killed and the boy fell into Afghan hands. The Anderson girl shared the same fate. Mrs Mainwaring with her baby in her arms attempted to mount a baggage pony, but the load upset and she pursued her way on foot. An Afghan horseman rode at her, threatened her with his sword, and tried to drag away the shawl in which she carried her child. She was rescued by a sepoy grenadier who shot the Afghan dead and then conducted the poor lady along the pass through the dead and dying, through, also, the close fire which struck down people near to her,

almost to the exit of the pass, when a bullet killed the chivalrous sepoy and Mrs Mainwaring had to continue her tramp to the bivouac alone.

A very fierce attack was made on the rear-guard, consisting of the 44th. In the narrow throat of the pass the regiment was compelled to halt by a block in front, and in this stationary position suffered severely. A flanking fire told heavily on the handful of European infantry. The belated stragglers masked their fire, and at length the soldiers fell back firing volleys indiscriminately into the stragglers and the Afghans. Near the exit of the pass a commanding position was maintained by some detachments which still held together, strengthened by the only gun now remaining, the last but one having been abandoned in the gorge. Under cover of this stand the rear of the mass gradually drifted forward while the Afghan pursuit was checked, and at length all the surviving force reached the camping ground. There had been left dead in the pass about 500 soldiers and over 2500 camp followers.

Akbar and the chiefs, taking the hostages with them, rode forward on the track of the retreating force. Akbar professed that his object was to stop the firing, but Mackenzie writes that Pottinger said to him: "Mackenzie, remember if I am killed that I heard Akbar Khan shout 'Slay them!' in Pushtoo, although in Persian he called out to stop the firing." The hostages had to be hidden away from the ferocious ghazees among rocks in the ravine until near evening, when in passing through the region of the heaviest slaughter they "came upon one sight of horror after another. All the bodies were stripped. There were children cut in two. Hindustanee women as well as men—some frozen to death, some literally chopped to pieces, many with their throats cut from ear to ear."

Snow fell all night on the unfortunates gathered tentless on the Khoord Cabul camping ground. On the morning of the 9th the confused and disorderly march was resumed, but after a mile had been traversed a halt for the day was ordered at the instance of Akbar Khan, who sent into camp by Captain Skinner a proposal that the ladies and children, with whose deplorable condition he professed with apparent sincerity to sympathise, should be made over to his protection, and that the married officers should accompany their wives; he pledging himself to preserve the party from further hardships and dangers and afford its members safe escort through the passes in rear of the force. The General had little faith in the Sirdar, but he was fain to give his consent to an arrangement which promised alleviation to the wretchedness of the ladies, scarce any of whom had tasted a meal since leaving Cabul. Some, still weak from childbirth, were nursing infants only a few days old; other poor creatures were momentarily apprehending the pangs of motherhood. There were invalids whose only attire as they rode in the camel panniers or shivered on the snow, was the nightdresses they wore when leaving the cantonments in their palanquins, and none possessed anything save the clothes on their backs. It is not surprising, then, that dark and doubtful as was the future to which they were consigning themselves, the ladies preferred its risks and chances to the awful certainties which lay before the doomed column. The Afghan chief had cunningly made it a condition of his proffer that the husbands should accompany their wives, and if there was a struggle in the breasts of the former between public and private duties, the General humanely decided the issue by ordering them to share the fortunes of their families.

Akbar Khan sent in no supplies, and the march was resumed on the morning of the 10th by a force attenuated by starvation, cold, and despair, diminished further by extensive desertion. After much exertion the advance, consisting of all that remained of the 44th, the solitary gun, and a detachment of cavalry, forced a passage to the front through the rabble of camp followers, and marched unmolested for about two miles until the Tunghee Tariki was reached, a deep gorge not more than ten feet wide. Men fell fast in the horrid defile,

struck down by the Afghan fire from the heights; but the pass if narrow was short, and the advance having struggled through it moved on to the halting-place at Kubbar-i-Jubbar and waited there for the arrival of the main body. But that body was never to emerge from out the shambles in the narrow throat of the Tunghee Tariki. The advance was to learn from the few stragglers who reached it the ghastly truth that it now was all that remained of the strong brigade which four days before had marched out from the Cabul cantonments. The slaughter from the Afghan fire had blocked the gorge with dead and dying. The Ghilzai tribesmen, at the turn into the pen at the other end of which was the blocked gorge, had closed up fiercely. Then the steep slopes suddenly swarmed with Afghans rushing sword in hand down to the work of butchery, and the massacre stinted not while living victims remained. The rear-guard regiment of sepoys was exterminated, save for two or three desperately wounded officers who contrived to reach the advance.

The remnant of the army consisted now of about seventy files of the 44th, about 100 troopers, and a detachment of horse-artillery with a single gun. The General sent to Akbar Khan to remonstrate with him on the attack he had allowed to be made after having guaranteed that the force should meet with no further molestation. Akbar protested his regret, and pleaded his inability to control the wild Ghilzai hillmen, over whom in their lust for blood and plunder, their own chiefs had lost all control; but he was willing to guarantee the safe conduct to Jellalabad of the European officers and men if they would lay down their arms and commit themselves wholly into his hands. This sinister proposal the General refused, and the march was continued, led in disorder by the remnant of the camp followers. In the steep descent from the Huft Kotul into the Tezeen ravine, the soldiers following the rabble at some distance came suddenly on a fresh butchery. The Afghans had suddenly fallen on the confused throng, and the descent was covered with dead and dying.

During the march from Kubbar-i-Jubbar to the Tezeen valley Shelton's dogged valour had mainly saved the force from destruction. With a few staunch soldiers of his own regiment the one-armed veteran, restored now to his proper *métier* of stubborn fighting man, had covered the rear and repelled the Ghilzai assaults with persevering energy and dauntless fortitude. And he it was who now suggested, since Akbar Khan still held to his stipulation that the force should lay down its arms, that a resolute effort should be made to press on to Jugdulluk by a rapid night march of four-and-twenty miles, in the hope of clearing the passes in that vicinity before the enemy should have time to occupy them.

That the attempt would prove successful was doubtful, since the force was already exhausted; but it was the last chance and Shelton's suggestion was adopted. In the early moonlight the march silently began, an ill omen marking the start in the shape of the forced abandonment of the last gun. Fatal delay occurred between Seh Baba and Kutti Sung because of a panic among the camp followers who, scared by a few shots, drifted backwards and forwards in a mass, retarding the progress of the column and for the time entirely arresting the advance of Shelton's and his rear-guard. The force could not close up until the morning, ten miles short of Jugdulluk, and already the Afghans were swarming on every adjacent height. All the way down the broken slope to Jugdulluk the little column trudged through the gauntlet of jezail fire which lined the road with dead and wounded. Shelton and his rear-guard handful performed wonders, again and again fending off with close fire and levelled bayonets the fierce rushes of Ghilzais charging sword in hand. The harassed advance reached Jugdulluk in the afternoon of the 11th, and took post behind some ruins on a height by the roadside, the surviving officers forming line in support of the gallant rear-guard struggling

forward through its environment of assailants. As Shelton and his brave fellows burst through the cordon they were greeted by cheers from the knoll. But there was no rest for the exhausted people, for the Afghans promptly occupied commanding positions whence they maintained a fire from which the ruins afforded but scant protection. To men parched with thirst the stream at the foot of their knoll was but a tantalising aggravation, for to attempt to reach it was certain death. The snow they devoured only increased their sufferings, and but little stay was afforded by the raw flesh of a few gun bullocks. Throughout the day volley after volley was poured down upon the weary band by the inexorable enemy. Frequent sallies were made and the heights were cleared, but the positions were soon reoccupied and the ruthless fire was renewed.

Captain Skinner, summoned by Akbar, brought back a message that General Elphinstone should visit him to take part in a conference, and that Brigadier Shelton and Captain Johnson should be given over as hostages for the evacuation of Jellalabad. Compliance was held to be imperative, and the temporary command was entrusted to Brigadier Anquetil. Akbar was extremely hospitable to his compulsory guests; but he insisted on including the General among his hostages, and was not moved by Elphinstone's representations that he would prefer death to the disgrace of being separated from his command in its time of peril. The Ghilzai chiefs came into conference burning with hatred against the British, and revelling in the anticipated delights of slaughtering them. Akbar seemed sincere in his effort to conciliate them, but was long unsuccessful. Their hatred seemed indeed stronger than their greed; but at length toward nightfall Akbar announced that pacific arrangements had been accepted by the tribes, and that what remained of the force should be allowed to march unmolested to Jellalabad.

How futile was the compact, if indeed there was any compact, was soon revealed. The day among the ruins on the knoll had passed in dark and cruel suspense—in hunger, thirst, and exhaustion, in the presence of frequent death; and as the evening fell, in anguish and all but utter despair. As darkness set in the conviction enforced itself that to remain longer in the accursed place was madness; and the little band, leaving behind perforce the sick and wounded, marched out, resolute to push through or die fighting. In the valley the only molestation at first was a desultory fire from the camping Ghilzais, who were rather taken by surprise, but soon became wide awake to their opportunities. Some hurried forward to occupy the pass rising from the valley to the Jugdulluk crest; others, hanging on the rear and flanks of the column encumbered with its fatal incubus of camp followers, mixed among the unarmed throng with their deadly knives, and killed and plundered with the dexterity of long practice. Throughout the tedious march up the steeply rising defile a spattering fire came from the rocks and ridges flanking the track, all but blocked by the surging concourse of miserable followers. The advance had to employ cruel measures to force its way through the chaos toward the crest. As it is approached from the Jugdulluk direction the flanking elevations recede and merge in the transverse ridge, which is crowned by a low-cut abrupt rocky upheaval, worn down somewhat by the friction of traffic where the road passes over the crest. Just here the tribesmen had constructed a formidable abatis of prickly brushwood which stretched athwart the road and dammed back the fugitives in the shallow oval basin between the termination of the ravine and the summit of the ridge. In this trap were caught our hapless people and the swarm of their native followers, and now the end was very near. From behind the barrier and around the lip of the great trap, the hillmen fired their hardest into the seething mass of soldiers and followers writhing in the awful Gehenna on which the calm moon shone down. On the edges of this whirlpool of death the fell Ghilzais were stabbing and hacking

with the ferocious industry inspired by thirst for blood and lust for plunder. It is among the characteristics of our diverse-natured race to die game, and even to thrill with a strange fierce joy when hope of escape from death has all but passed away and there remains only to sell life at the highest possible premium of exchange. Among our people, face to face with death on the rocky Jugdulluk, officers and soldiers alike fought with cool deadly rancour. The brigadier and the private engaged in the same fierce *mêlée*, fought side by side and fell side by side. Stalwart Captain Dodgin of the 44th slew five Afghans before he fell. Captain Nicholl of the horse-artillery, gunless now, rallied to him the few staunch gunners who were all that remained to him of his noble and historic troop, and led them on to share with him a heroic death.

All did not perish on the rugged summit of the Jugdulluk. The barrier was finally broken through, and a scant remnant of the force wrought out its escape from the slaughter-pit. Small detachments, harassed by sudden onslaughts and delayed by reluctance to desert wounded comrades, were trudging in the darkness down the long slope to the Soorkhab. The morning of the 13th dawned near Gundamuk on the straggling group of some twenty officers and forty-five European soldiers. Its march arrested by sharp attacks, the little band moved aside to occupy a defensive position on an adjacent hillock. A local sirdar invited the senior officer to consult with him as to a pacific arrangement, and while Major Griffiths was absent on this errand there was a temporary suspension of hostilities. The Afghans meanwhile swarmed around the detachment with a pretence of friendship, but presently attempts were made to snatch from the soldiers their arms. This conduct was sternly resented, and the Afghans were forced back. They ascended an adjacent elevation and set themselves to the work of deliberately picking off officer after officer, man after man. The few rounds remaining in the pouches of the soldiers were soon exhausted, but the detachment stood fast and calmly awaited the inevitable end. Rush after rush was driven back from its steadfast front, but at last, nearly all being killed or wounded, a final onset of the enemy sword in hand terminated the struggle and completed the dismal tragedy. Captain Souter of the 44th with three or four privates all of whom as well as himself were wounded, was spared and carried into captivity; he saved the colours of his regiment, which he had tied round his waist before leaving Jugdulluk. A group of mounted officers had pushed forward as soon as they had cleared the barrier on the crest. Six only reached Futtehabad in safety. There they were treacherously offered food, and while they halted a few moments to eat two were cut down. Of the four who rode away three were overtaken and killed within four miles of Jellalabad; one officer alone survived to reach that haven of refuge.

The ladies, the married officers, and the original hostages, followed Akbar Khan down the passes toward Jugdulluk, pursuing the line of retreat strewn with its ghastly tokens of slaughter, and recognising almost at every step the bodies of friends and comrades. At Jugdulluk they found General Elphinstone, Brigadier Shelton, and Captain Johnson, and learned the fate which had overtaken the marching force. On the following day Akbar quitted Jugdulluk with his hostages and the ladies, all of whom were virtually prisoners, and rode away through the mountains in a northerly direction. On the fourth day the fort of Budiabad in the Lughman valley was reached, where Akbar left the prisoners while he went to attempt the reduction of Jellalabad.

PART III

The Second Anglo-Afghan War, 1878–1880: Imperial Insecurities, Global Stakes

Competing diplomatic missions were again the pretext for the outbreak of hostilities in 1878. Despite the promises of the Gorchakov Circular, Russian overtures to the emir of Afghanistan—Dost Mohammad Khan's son Sher Ali Khan—sparked British concern, and forty thousand troops were dispatched to settle the question. Sher Ali died at Mazar-i-Sharif on his way to seek political asylum in Russia, to be succeeded by his son Mohammad Yaqub Khan. With the Treaty of Gandamak in 1879, Yakub relinquished control of foreign affairs and ceded significant portions of the North-West Frontier to the British in exchange for an annual subsidy and the withdrawal of the British Army. Once again, an uprising in Kabul and the murder of a British agent, Sir Pierre Cavagnari, provoked a new phase of the war. The British favored Yakub's cousin, Abdur Rahman Khan, whom they installed as emir—but not before significant struggle, especially at Maiwand in 1880. A grandson of Dost Mohammad, Abdur Rahman held Afghanistan until his death in 1901 by keeping numerous rebels fiercely in check, including his cousin Yakub and peoples such as the Hazara, who were seeking their autonomy from the latest Afghan dynastic power.

11

"Gorchakov Circular" (1864)

Prince Alexander Gorchakov (1798–1883), head of foreign affairs, seeks to explain Russia's position on central Asia as a matter of national security in his famous circular. British officials and other specialists who knew of the document cited it most often as evidence that Russian promises to cease and desist from territorial expansion in central Asia were not to be trusted, especially in the face of what was to become the Second Anglo-Afghan War. But the text also leaves an impression of the fragility and defensiveness of Russian rule over native peoples—a geopolitical insecurity that later observers (see chapter 17) were to note with varying degrees of sympathy and relish.

The position of Russia in Central Asia is that of all civilized states which are brought into contact with half-savage nomad populations possessing no fixed social organization.

In such cases, the more civilized state is forced in the interest of the security of its frontier, and its commercial relations, to exercise a certain ascendancy over their turbulent and undesirable neighbors. Raids and acts of pillage must be put down. To do this, the tribes on the frontier must be reduced to a state of submission. This result once attained, these tribes take to more peaceful habits, but are in turn exposed to the attacks of the more distant tribes against whom the State is bound to protect them. Hence the necessity of distant, costly, and periodically recurring expeditions against an enemy whom his social organization makes it im-

possible to seize. If, the robbers once punished, the expedition is withdrawn, the lesson is soon forgotten; its withdrawal is put down to weakness. It is a peculiarity of Asiatics to respect nothing but visible and palpable force. The moral force of reasoning has no hold on them.

In order to put a stop to this state of permanent disorder, fortified posts are established in the midst of these hostile tribes, and an influence is brought to bear on them by degrees to a state of submission. But other more distant tribes beyond this outer line come in turn to threaten the same dangers, and necessitate the same measures of repression. The State is thus forced to choose between two alternatives—either to give up this endless labor, and to abandon its frontier to perpetual disturbance, or to plunge deeper and deeper into barbarous countries, when the difficulties and expenses increase with every step in advance.

Such has been the fate of every country which has found itself in a similar position. The United States in America, France in Algeria, Holland in her Colonies, England in India: all have been forced by imperious necessity into this onward march, where the greatest difficulty is to know where to stop.

Such have been the reasons which have led the Imperial Government to take up, first, a position resting, on one side, on the Syr-Daria [river], on the other, the Lake of Issik Kul, to strengthen these lines by advanced forts.

It has been judged indispensable that our two fortified lines, one extending from China to the Lake of Issik Kul, the other from the Sea of Aral, along the Syr-Daria, should be united by fortified points, so that all posts should be in a position of mutual support leaving no gap through which nomad tribes might make their inroads and depradations with impunity.

Our original frontier line along the Syr-Daria to Fort Perovsky, on the one side, and on the other, to Lake Issik Kul, had the drawback of being almost on the verge of the desert. It was broken by a wide gap between the two extreme points; it did not offer sufficient resources to our troops, and left unsettled tribes over the back with which any settled arrangement became impossible.

In spite of our unwillingness to extend our frontier, these motives have been powerful enough to induce the Imperial Government to establish this line between Issik Kul and the Syr-Daria by fortifying the town of Khemkend, lately occupied by us. This line gives us a fertile country, partly inhabited by Kirghiz tribes, which have already accepted our rule, and it therefore offers favorable conditions for colonization, and the supply of provisions to our garrisons. In the second place, it puts us in the neighborhood of the agricultural and commercial populations of Kokand.

Such are the interests which inspire the policy of our august master (Alexander II) in Central Asia.

It is needless for me to lay stress on the interest which Russia evidently has not to increase her territory, and, above all, to avoid raising complications on her frontiers, which cannot but delay and paralyze her domestic development. Very frequently of late years the civilizations of these countries, which are her neighbors on the continent of Asia, has been assigned to Russia as her special mission.

12

"The Russian Foreign Policy in Asia" (1877)

EUGENE SCHUYLER

Eugene Schuyler (1840–90) was the first American diplomat to visit central Asia. As secretary to the U.S. legation in St. Petersburg, his book *Turkistan*, from which this excerpt is drawn, went into five editions in Britain within three years of its publication and two in the United States. Schuyler was an unlikely Russophile. He was a lawyer in New York City in 1863 with a PhD from Yale in philology when he met some naval officers connected to the Russian fleet and became intrigued with the language and the place. By 1867 he was the U.S. consul in Moscow, having learned Russian from an Orthodox priest.[1]

Here Schuyler tracks the struggle between Britain and Russia in central Asia, drawing on example after example to demonstrate that Russia had no intention of moving in on India. More specifically, he defends the Gorchakov circular and calls English attitudes toward Russia "undignified." He has well-defined views of Russian forms of colonization, specifically with respect to natives and how best to govern them over the long-term. His detailed accounts of rebellions in 1863 and 1875 give him the opportunity to analyze Russian strengths and weaknesses in the face of civil unrest and religious war.

The policy of Russia cannot be concluded merely from the Conquests and extensions of territory, without taking into account the causes of these movements. Yet this is what is usually done; and the fact that since the Crimean war Russia has annexed considerable portions of the three khanates of Bukhara, Khokand, and Khiva is put forward as a proof of a scheming policy and of a plot to dominate the whole of Asia. With much greater force might it be said that the extension of British rule in Asia is the result of a long-matured and traditional policy of Asiatic conquest; yet no one who knows how the spread of British rule in India and in the adjacent countries has been brought about would think of accusing the English Government of such a design. Why, then, should such accusations be brought against Russia? Simply because there is a widely spread belief in Western Europe—and irrational ideas of this kind are often hardest to eradicate—that as Russia is governed (so it is thought) by a single will, and as the political steps of Russia are taken without the publicity which attends such measures in constitutional countries, Russian statesmen are almost preternaturally wise and skilful, and that there exists a traditional and hereditary policy. Such a policy would be difficult enough anywhere, and it does not and has not existed in Russia; in fact not only in Asiatic but in other Eastern as well as in European affairs Russia is guided by no policy whatever, except so far as yearly and almost daily changing circumstances may dictate. Were it to be generally admitted,—I will not say as true, but even as possible,—that Russia had no foreign policy except that of carrying out such views as might for the moment seem advantageous, the present situation of affairs both in Europe and Asia might be more easily understood and difficulties might be better avoided.

It seems, therefore, exceedingly unfair towards Russia to bring up the Circular issued by Prince Gortchakof after the capture of Tchimkent as a proof of the bad feeling of the Russian Government in its dealings with Central Asia. Under ordinary circumstances such a step as that taken by Russia in 1864 for rounding off her frontier and filling up the gaps between the lines of the Syr Darya and of Siberia would have excited no remark and would have needed no explanation. But England had always been jealous of the independence of the Central Asiatic Khanates; and the English press,—with a feeling which would seem to imply that it believed the English hold on India to be weaker than it really is,—immediately raised a cry of alarm, as if this were an advance made towards wresting that great empire from English hands. Prince Gortchakof, therefore, thought it best to explain the object of the movement in a circular which he issued to the different Russian embassies and legations. In that circular the Prince set forth what were undoubtedly the true reasons for the Russian advance. He also stated that there was no intention of advancing further, for this campaign had been undertaken purely to prevent the necessity of subsequent campaigns. "We find ourselves," he said, "in face of a more solid, more compact, less unsettled, and better organised society; and this marks with geographical precision the limits to which interest and reason prescribe us to advance, and at which we must halt, because, on the one hand, any further extension of our rule meeting henceforth, not with unstable communities, like independent nomad tribes, but with more regularly constituted states, would exact considerable efforts and would draw us on from annexation to annexation into infinite complications; while, on the other hand, having henceforth for neighbours such states, notwithstanding their backward condition and the instability of their political action, we can nevertheless be assured that to the common advantage regular relations will one day be substituted for the disorders which have hitherto paralysed the progress of these countries."

There would seem to be no ground for charging Russia with duplicity in this Circular, for there is nothing in it which was not at the time generally believed. Its great fault was in believing that the home authorities, with the peculiar system of government which prevails in Russia, would be able to control the movements of the generals in command, and in thinking that the Khanates of Central Asia were well-organised states, that political relations might be had with them, and that they would be amenable to reason or would respect the obligations of treaties. Prince Gortchakof could not then know that General Tchernaief, in violation of orders, would the next summer attack and capture Tashkent. He was misinformed also as to the value of the country annexed. One thing, however, he saw clearly,—although the efforts necessary were much less considerable than he had supposed,—that a further extension of rule over the Khanates would lead from annexation to annexation and to infinite complications. How some of these annexations were brought about and why some of these attacks took place I shall endeavour to explain.

I referred above to the peculiar constitution of the Russian Government. This has a more important bearing on the Asiatic policy of the Empire than has been generally supposed. Each minister being independent and responsible only to the Emperor, there is no Cabinet, properly so called, and can be no united policy. The councils of ministers do not so much discuss questions of policy as questions of detail, the solution of which depends upon two or three ministers jointly. Sometimes a subject is deemed so important that a special commission is appointed to study it and to come to a conclusion, which may or may not be ratified by the Emperor. Still, even in this case, as each minister has the right of a personal audience with the Emperor, when he can explain in detail all his arguments for the proposed measure, the decision of the commission may be set aside almost as soon as it is made. A striking instance of this occurred in the formation of the Trans-Caspian military district The plan for the establishment of this district was opposed both by Prince Gortchakof and by the Minister of Finance, the one on political and the other on financial grounds, and it was rejected by a large majority in the commission specially appointed to consider it. Yet the united influence of the Grand-Duke Michael and of the Minister of War was so strong as to obtain the Imperial sanction to the scheme but a few days after.

It will be seen from this one example that it is possible for a measure to be put into operation although it may be contrary to the ideas and desires of the Foreign Office. But this is not an isolated case; such things are of constant occurrence. The difficulty in such cases is that in the end no one is responsible, not even the Government, for it is guided by no settled policy. As matters now stand there are five distinct rulers over large provinces in Asia, all of whom have differing interests, and some of whom are in constant rivalry, if not in actual bad relations with each other. All are nominally dependent in military matters upon the Minister of War; all are practically independent of the Foreign Office; all have the right of reporting personally and *vivâ voce* to the Emperor, and really acknowledge no other authority. These are the Grand Duke Michael, the brother of the Emperor, and the Lieutenant of the Caucasus, and the Governors-General of Orenburg, of Turkistan, of Eastern and of Western Siberia. The Governors-General of Turkistan, of Eastern and of Western Siberia, on account of the affairs of Kuldja, have to do with Chinese officials, and in spite of telegraphs and post-roads each of them pursues a policy which at times differs from that of each of the others, as well as from that of the Russian Minister at Pekin, who acts under the direct instructions of the Foreign Office. The Governors-General of Western Siberia, of Turkistan, and of Orenburg have different methods for the government of the Kirghiz, who are nearly equally divided between the three provinces. General Kryzhanofsky and General Kaufmann, as is well known, look at the affairs of the Steppe and of the Central Asiatic Khanates from entirely different and almost irreconcilable points of view. The Grand Duke Michael, to whom the Trans-Caspian district has lately been subjected, has still different ideas, and in his anxiety to find some occupation for the large army placed under his orders frequently makes propositions to the Ministry of War, which, on account of foreign complications that would arise, are as often rejected by the Emperor on the advice of Prince Gortchakof; and yet almost without exception they are merely adjourned and not utterly forbidden, for we see that the Grand Duke is sometimes allowed to carry out his plans on a smaller scale than he at first intended, as well as to take steps for larger projects, and we know the great influence which both the Grand Duke and the Minister of War have with the Emperor.

The fears of English remonstrances and of diplomatic complications have had great influence on the Russian policy in Asia. The Foreign Office has been exceedingly annoyed by the persistent manner in which, on each movement of troops, questions have been asked in Parliament, or the British Ambassador has hinted or stated to Prince Gortchakof his desire to know the reasons for such a step; and not un-frequently movements quite insignificant in themselves have been forbidden for fear of English remonstrances. This has not been unnoticed in the Russian press. A recent book on Central Asia says, "This has caused us to explain to England every one of our movements, to quiet her with regard to our intentions and to define our policy. This cannot but have its effect on our actions, which receive a tinge of indecision and display a possible fear of awakening vain apprehensions on the part of our rival. The wish to quiet the English disbelief in us and to give no cause for English protests has made us look through our fingers at many greater or less breaches of international law on the part of Khiva, Bukhara, and Kashgar. England would never have permitted half of these wrongs and insults. Our moderation, however, has been vain. In the eyes of Englishmen we have won nothing, and if England for a time appears to believe in us and to be friendly, the feeling is not sincere."

It is impossible to believe that there is any settled intention on the part of the Russian Government of making an attack on India, or even of preparing the way for it, nor is there any desire for the possession of India. Young men in the army of Turkistan, whose only thought is for advancement and decorations, may, indeed, talk loudly; but the men who control the policy have no such thought. What might happen in case of a war between Russia and England on other questions is, indeed, hard to say. If Russia could then—easily for herself—make a diversion on India she would certainly be justified in doing so, but the position of Russian affairs in Turkistan is hardly such as to allow her to do so for many years to come, to say nothing of the distance of Turkistan from European Russia, the bad communications, and the intervening deserts and mountains between Turkistan and India, which would render such a movement ex-

ceedingly difficult, if not impossible. The only danger to India from Russia lies through Persia. Experience has proved that all invasions of India have come through Afghanistan, and Afghanistan can only be approached by Russia through Persia.

The Emperor Paul, from his hatred of the English and his sympathy with Napoleon, did, indeed, propose an expedition to India, but his plan was so wild that even Napoleon laughed at it. His idea was that Russia should concentrate in Astrakhan 25,000 regular troops and 2,000 Cossacks. France was also to send a body of 35,000 men up the Danube to the Black Sea, when they were to be conveyed in ships to Taganrog, and were then to march to the Volga and sail to Astrakhan. From there both armies were to go to Astrabad, and it was expected that the troops could march from Astrakhan to the Indus in forty-five days. Napoleon having refused to consent to this expedition, Paul resolved on undertaking it with his own means; and in order not to make the conquest too much of a burden upon the Government, he intended to effect it by means of the Don Cossacks alone, to whom he presented India in a letter of January 12 (24) to General Orlof, the Ataman of the Don Cossacks, in which he said: "All the wealth of India will be your reward for this expedition." The Cossacks were to march from Orenburg to Khiva and Bukhara, and thence to the Indus. Several other letters with new orders succeeded, and Orlof promised to undertake the expedition and carry it out successfully. The Cossacks prepared for their march, which was fixed for the beginning of May, when on the night of March 23 the Emperor Paul suddenly died, and the change of Government put a stop to the whole plan.

In the early part of the Crimean war another project for the invasion of India was presented to the Emperor Nicholas by General Duhamel, but Russia's attention was too much taken up with what was passing on the Danube and in the Crimea to pay much attention to it. The success of such an expedition would, of course, depend upon which country had the preponderance in Persia, for it is only with the consent if not the active co-operation of Persia that such a plan would stand the slightest chance of fulfilment.

Apprehensions for the safety of her Indian possessions led England to engage in the only negotiations on the subject of Central Asia which have yet taken place. They were begun in the early part of 1869 by Lord Clarendon, who in a conference with Baron Brunnow, the Russian Ambassador, said that while Her Majesty's Government had not the slightest cause for alarm in the rapid progress of Russia in Central Asia, yet something must be done to allay the excitement and the suspicions of the British public and the British press. He therefore proposed what became known as the "neutral zone," that there should be a strip of territory between Russia and the Indian possessions the neutrality of which should be guaranteed by both parties. Prince Gortchakof received this suggestion in very good part, and proposed that Afghanistan be selected as that zone. This, however, did not suit the views of the Indian Government, which was by no means desirous of having Afghanistan remain neutral,—so far at least as England was concerned. Subsequently Lord Clarendon had an interview at Heidelburg with Prince Gortchakof on this subject, and still later in the autumn of the same year Mr. Forsyth, as the representative of the Indian Government, visited St. Petersburg, and held several conferences with Prince Gortchakof, and other Russian ministers. It was found that a neutral zone in its strict sense was impossible. The idea of the Indian Government then was to establish on the frontier of each country a girdle of semi-independent states, those nearest India—Afghanistan, Khelat, and Yarkand (Kashgar)—to be subject to British influence, and those on the other side of the Oxus, including Bukhara and Khokand, to be subject to that of Russia. As the plan of independent or semi-independent states was found an impossible one, it was barely proposed to Russia, and after several conferences it

was substantially agreed, that "Afghanistan should be completely outside the sphere within which Russia should be called upon to exercise her influence," while it was understood that all the countries to the north of that should be considered to be under Russian influence, and that no interference should be made there by England. The only question to decide was as to the actual boundaries of Afghanistan, it being agreed that all the countries in the effective possession of Shir Ali Khan, and which had formerly recognised the sovereignty of Dost Mohammed, should be considered as Afghanistan, and it was arranged that the memoranda and papers on this subject should be submitted to General Kaufmann, as the person nearest the spot capable of judging the question, in order that he might report to the Russian Government what the actual boundaries of the country were. The matter drifted on, for no reports were received from General Kaufmann, who seemed to find it exceedingly difficult to ascertain the real boundaries of Afghanistan, in spite of the pressing reminder of Sir Andrew Buchannan in the autumn of 1871. Finally, on October 17, 1872, Lord Granville wrote a dispatch to Lord Augustus Loftus, for communication to the Russian Government, in which it was stated that the English Government not having received any information from Russia, had been obliged to make up their minds from the best information they could receive, and had concluded *to consider* as fully belonging to the Amir of Kabul:—"1. Badakshan, with its dependent district of Vakhan, from the Sarikul (Woods' Lake) on the east, to the junction of the Koktcha River, with the Oxus (or Penja), forming the northern boundary of this Afghan province throughout its entire extent. 2. Afghan Turkistan, comprising the districts of Kunduz, Khulm, and Balkh, the northern boundary of which would be the line of the Oxus from the junction of the Koktcha River to the post of Khoja Saleh inclusive, on the high road from Bukhara to Balkh. Nothing to be claimed by the Afghan Amir on the left bank of the Oxus below Khoja Saleh. 3. The internal districts of Aksha, Seripul, Maimena, Shibberjan, and Andkhoi, the latter of which would be the extreme Afghan frontier possession to the north west, the desert beyond belonging to independent tribes of Turkomans. 4. The Western Afghan frontier, between the dependencies of Herat and those of the Persian province of Khorassan, is well known, and need not here be defined."

This despatch brought out a reply from Prince Gortchakof, conveying the report of General Kaufmann, and a memorandum by Mr. Struve, who claimed that Badakshan and Vakhan were not subject to the rule of Shir Ali Khan. Prince Gortchakof, therefore, objected to having them included within the limits of Afghanistan under his objection. He, however, subsequently withdrew his objection, as he said, to please the English cabinet. He added, 'We are more inclined to this act of courtesy, as the English Government engages to use all its influence with Shir Ali, in order to induce him to maintain a peaceful attitude, as well as to insist on his giving up all measures of aggression or further conquest. This influence is indispensable. It is based not only on the material and moral ascendancy of England, but also on the subsidies for which Shir Ali is indebted to her. Such being the case, we see in this assurance a real guarantee for the maintenance of peace.' When this correspondence came to be published, some alarm was felt as to the obligation of England, implied in the last paragraph of Prince Gortchakof's note, to maintain Shir Ali's peaceful attitude and to restrain him from all measures of aggression or further conquest. It was said that this committed England to an armed intervention for the preservation of peace. Mr. Gladstone, in a speech in Parliament (April 23, 1873), repudiated this responsibility, saying that the influence of England was only to be exercised by means of friendly advice. The Russians looked upon this as a formal repudiation of the whole transaction on the part of the English Government, for it was evident that

Russia would not guarantee the inviolability of Afghanistan territory, if the English did not agree that they would compel the Amir to respect the territory on the other side of the Oxus,—territory which is now Bukharan, but what will probably some day be Russian. The "Official Gazette," remarking on Mr. Gladstone's explanation, said: 'If England has preserved her freedom of action Russia has also preserved hers, and consequently the two Governments have not in reality pledged themselves to any inconvenient obligations which might have the effect of placing them in false relations.' In reality, therefore, the matter remains exactly where it was before the negotiations of 1869 and 1872 were begun, except that an agreement has been brought about as to what are the boundaries of Afghanistan. Unless some new arrangement should be made, Russia has a perfect right, in case of troubles on the Oxus, to cross it and inflict punishment upon the troops and provinces of Shir Ali.

The attitude of England toward Russia with regard to Central Asia, can hardly be called a dignified one. There are constant questions, protests, demands for explanations, and even threats—at least in the newspapers and in Parliament—but nothing ever is done. Outcries were made about the expedition to Khiva, but when the occupation had once become a fait accompli, the same men and the same journals said that no harm was done. Again there were outcries and questions about the possibility of a Russian movement on Kashgar. Now, after Khokand is occupied, the conquest of Kashgar is looked upon as not so alarming after all. At present there is a similar uneasiness about Merv, and the Russophobist party are using all their efforts to show, either that the Russians must not be allowed to take Merv, or if they do take it, that Herat must be occupied. In all probability Merv will be occupied by the Russians, and in all probability the English Government will do nothing at all. It would seem wiser and more dignified, instead of subjecting the Russian Foreign Office to constant petty annoyances, to allow the Russians plainly to understand what limits they could not pass in their onward movement. A state of mutual suspicion bodes no good to the relations of any Governments.

One of the great causes of the Russian advance in Central Asia, and one of the greatest difficulties with which the Foreign Office has had to deal, has been the full powers granted to General Kaufmann to carry on diplomatic relations with the neighbouring states. Whatever reason might have existed for this at first, now that the post-roads are in better order, and that the telegraph is completed to Tashkent and Hodjent, the policy of Turkistan should certainly be entirely governed by that of the Government at St. Petersburg. These powers, however, General Kaufmann has regarded as the apple of his eye. There are the best reasons to believe that full details of the actual state of the relations between the Khanates and Tashkent have not always been communicated to the Home Government, and that at times formal permission has been asked and explanations have been given only after military expeditions have actually started. The policy which has prevailed at Tashkent, so far as it can be distinct from the policy at St. Petersburg, has been a purely personal one. The great desire of the Governor-General has been to play the part of pacificator of Central Asia. With this view treaties were made with various states—which were far from being kept—by which, in the opinion of many—not only at St. Petersburg but even in Tashkent, to say nothing of those abroad who followed the movements,—the surrounding Khanates were reduced to vassalage. How far this is true may be seen from the late war with Khokand. It being supposed that both Khokand and Bukhara were perfectly subdued, and were ready to carry out all the wishes of the Government, the campaign against Khiva was undertaken without great necessity, but to round off the whole with a successful military expedition, which would put down the last elements of disorder in Central Asia. . . .

In forming a judgment on the methods and the results of the Russian policy in Asia, it may be of use to consider the relations of Russia with each country separately.

FIRST—KHOKAND

By the campaign of Tchernaief in 1864–5, and the subsequent capture of Hodjent in 1866, the Khan of Khokand was restricted to a very small portion of his former territory,—which had at one time extended west to the mouth of the Syr Darya, and north almost to Vierny,—and was left to govern a small fertile territory completely surrounded by mountains, except on the western side near Hodjent. At that time the Russians proposed to occupy also the province of Namangan, thus limiting the Khokandian rule to the south of the rivers Syr Darya and Naryn, and General Romanofsky himself was desirous of rectifying his then irregular frontier by occupying the city of Khokand and by the conquest of the whole country. But the shrewd advice of Ata Bek caused the Khan to send envoys to congratulate the Russians on the capture of Hodjent from the Bukharans; and as there had been no actual cause for war except the feeling supposed to prevail in Khokand, General Romanofsky was reluctantly compelled to abandon the project. He was soon afterwards removed, and as the policy indicated by the Government at St. Petersburg was always against fresh conquests, and as nothing occurred on the side of Khokand of such great importance as to render a war absolutely necessary, the country remained unattacked until the rebellion of 1875 made Russian interference imperative.

On his arrival at Tashkent late in the autumn of 1867, General Kaufmann informed Khudayar Khan of his accession to power, and requested him to send an envoy to conclude a treaty of commerce. Subsequently, on account of the movements of troops in Khokand and fears of a change in Russian policy, he was obliged to write the

Khan an assuring letter. To this the Khan replied with an autograph letter and an envoy, who assured General Kaufmann that the movements of troops were only the usual autumn manœuvres caused by the distribution of winter clothing. General Kaufmann informed the envoy in plain terms of the demands which he had to make with regard to the rights of Russian traders, and the diminution of the duties, and sent by him a copy of the treaty which he proposed. A small Russian mission went to Khokand at the same time for the purpose of investigating to some extent the resources of the country. To the conditions of the treaty the Khan would not at first consent, maintaining that he could not allow Russian merchants to travel freely over the country, as he could not guarantee them against attacks from the more fanatical of his subjects. In addition to this he desired to send an embassy to St. Petersburg, and, if this could not be allowed, at all events to obtain a letter directly from the Emperor, assuring him of peace and friendship, which would be a guarantee of good relations independently of the change of the Russian governors, for, with all the respect he had for them, he could not but notice that in the course of three years there had been four Russian commanders, each of whom had proposed his own conditions for peace.

General Kaufmann replied to the Khan formally and decisively in a letter of January 29 (February 10), 1868. "The great Russian Tsar never allows any dissension between the Khans and the people in the countries neighbouring to us. Your Highness writes that you cannot answer for the crimes of some of your subjects with regard to Russian traders. To this I reply, either they must obey your commands or they do not acknowledge your authority over them. A nation must have a head. Those of your people who, in spite of your commands, do harm to Russian merchants, must then obey my orders. I cannot allow unruly and independent people in the neighbourhood. The general quiet demands that they shall submit ei-

ther to you or to me." To Mirza Hakim, one of the envoys, General Kaufmann spoke in strong terms of the indecision of the Khan, and said that if he had wished to occupy the Khanate he would not have wasted time and words, but would before that have moved his troops and ended the whole matter. At last the Khan withdrew from his pretensions of carrying on direct relations with St. Petersburg, and agreed not only to accept the Treaty of General Kaufmann as the representative of the Emperor, but to sign it as well. The main privileges secured by the treaty were five: 1. The right of Russian merchants to visit all the towns in the Khanate; 2. That of establishing caravanserais and depôts for goods where they wished; 3. That of having *caravan-bashis* or commercial agents in all the towns of the Khanate; 4. The reduction of the customs duties to 2½ per cent, and the rendering them equal both for Christians and Mussulmans, and, 5. The free passage through Khokand of Russian caravans desiring to go into the neighbouring countries. The treaty was finally signed, and was approved by the Emperor in November 1868.

This treaty was never carefully observed. Additional duties on cotton and silk were imposed [. . .] and difficulties were placed in the way of freely travelling in the country. The Russian merchants resident in Khokand were kept under the severest restrictions, and one was even attacked and nearly killed, an offence which was condoned by a small compensation paid by the Khan.

In the Russian campaign against Samarkand, the attitude of the Khan was anything but favourable to the Russians, and his troops were kept ready while he was on the watch for an occasion to attack the Russians in the rear. The speedy capture of Samarkand, and the reports from the Russian camp of his envoy Mirza Hakim, who was greatly under Russian influence, kept him for the moment quiet. The Russians seemed so satisfied with the results that finally, as a mark of satisfaction, General Kaufmann allowed Mirza Hakim to go to St. Petersburg, where he was received by the

Emperor. After his return Khudayar Khan was invested with the order of the first class of St. Stanislas, and a slight difference was made in the title by which the Russians addressed him. A year later, in December 1869, Khudayar made a complaint to the Governor-General against the Amir of Bukhara, saying that in subduing the Beks of Hissar and Kulab, he had fallen upon a vassal of Khokand—Shir Ali, the Bek of Karategin—who had consequently been obliged to take refuge in Khokand. Negotiations were therefore entered into on this subject with the Amir, and he sent to Tashkent as his excuse a letter of Shir Ali, which showed his participation in the disturbances in the Bekship of Hissar. Khudayar declared this letter to be forged, and sent for comparison a genuine letter of Shir Ali. The seal did indeed seem to be a counterfeit one, and the Governor-General proposed to the Amir to return Karategin to its lawful ruler. In the meantime Shir Ali Khan raised some troops and marched into Karategin, but was defeated by the united forces of the Beks of Kulab and Hissar and was taken prisoner.

Wishing to avoid any contest between the rulers of Bukhara and Khokand, because the success of the former would lessen the moral value of the Russian protection received by the latter, General Kaufmann proposed to Khudayar Khan to restore Karategin to its former ruler, Mozaffar Shah, who was kept a prisoner in Khokand, and asked the Amir in return to free Shir Ali. The compromise was accepted by both sides and was immediately put into execution. In this way Karategin was formed into a practically independent state lying between Khokand and Bukhara, and the Russians succeeded in attaining a sort of moral weight and influence in the concerns of that locality. Although the Khokandians claimed a nominal sovereignty over Karategin, it was never enforced, and certainly, of late years especially, since the Kirghiz insurrection, the rulers of Karategin have paid no tribute to the Khan, nor recognised in any way his authority over the country.

After the capture of Shahrisabs in July 1870 Jura Bek and Baba Bek fled to Khokand, but owing to his previous enmity combined with the threatening demands of the Russians, the Khan consented to infringe the laws of hospitality and delivered the fugitives at Tashkent. Mr. Struvé was then sent on a mission to Khokand to thank the Khan for his action and to discuss certain questions which had never been satisfactorily settled. Among these were the regulation of the boundaries, the settlement of the claims of Russian merchants, the explanation of the circumstances which had delayed the return of Mozaffar Shah to Karategin, the appointment of a permanent agent in Khokand, and indemnity for the attack made by the mountaineers on the Cossacks of Colonel Dennet during the expedition in the Upper Zarafshan. This last claim the Khan for some time resisted, but finally, through the advice of the more sensible of his councillors, he yielded, and paid the sum of 5,000 rubles, part of which went to those wounded and to the families of the killed, and the rest to the fund for regimental churches. To the request for permission to appoint a permanent agent the Khan gave his consent, as indeed he had done on one or two previous occasions. But curiously enough, as soon as the consent was obtained the Russian authorities thought no more about it and no permanent agent was ever appointed.

A contrary course would have been much more beneficial to Russian interests, for a resident agent, if a man of ability and well supported, could have succeeded in obtaining a strong moral influence over the Khan, and the Russians would have been sufficiently well informed of the state of the country to have foreseen and prevented the explosion which resulted in the war of 1875. It seemed, however, at that time to General Kaufmann as well as to Mr. Struvé, that the Khan was even then thoroughly a vassal of Russia, and opportunity was taken to propose to him the conquest of Kashgar. Yakub Khan had not at that time been recognised by the Russian Government, which was considerably disquieted by the attitude he had taken, and it was thought to be a very shrewd plan to get rid of him in this way, and instead of two neighbours to have but one. Khudayar Khan could not, however, sum up resolution enough to agree to the proposal, and did nothing more than declare his readiness to act as mediator between Yakub Bek and the Russians.

In 1872 the Khan's eldest son, Nasreddin, Bek of Andijan, was allowed to visit Tashkent, where he remained for about three weeks. Although he engaged there in secret intrigues against the Russians, this visit was thought greatly to strengthen Russian influence in Khokand.

Khudayar Khan, who had never been a popular ruler, and who had twice been driven from the throne on account of his cruelty and rapacity, continually excited discontent among his subjects, and more especially among the nomad tribes of Kiptchaks and Kirghiz who lived in the mountainous regions of the north-east and south-east. Rebellions therefore were frequent, and a revolt broke out in 1873 which, though quelled for the time, was renewed in 1874, and finally, in 1875, terminated in the war which led to the occupation and annexation of the Khanate by Russia.

The policy of the Russian administrators during these insurrections seems to have been a mistaken one. They endeavoured to remain neutral, but they were so insufficiently informed of the position of affairs and of the actual state of feeling in Khokand, that they did not seem to understand that they were looked upon as the protectors and supporters of the Khan; and indeed the Khan would have been dethroned long before had it not been for the fear of the inhabitants that the Russians would immediately march into the country and restore him. The officials at Tashkent did not seem to have sufficient foresight to see that the absorption of the Khanate by Russia was inevitable sooner or later, and that their best plan therefore was gradually to prepare the way for this by gentle means, so that the end might come without a shock. They further believed that the Khan was an obedient vassal, and they lulled themselves into a false security; if they thought at all about annexation, they thought that the fear inspired by their arms throughout Central Asia was such as to render conquest a work of the greatest ease. This would have been true a few years ago, but of late the Russians had lost their moral weight in the country, and the natives of the Russian provinces had become discontented. They had begun to look upon their new rulers as no better than their old. They had published their discontent in letters and petitions to the neighbouring countries, and the people in Khokand had not only resolved to attempt all rather than come under Russian rule, but had begun to believe that the Russians were weaker than they had previously supposed.

At the outbreak of the rebellion in 1873 both Kirghiz and Kiptchaks so hated the Khan that they were inclined to be favourably disposed towards the Russians. Many of them migrated across the boundary and asked the Russians to intervene and dethrone the Khan, and afford them protection. Nor was this movement confined to the nomads. Similar petitions were received from the inhabitants of towns. Had the Russians in the summer of 1873 chosen to occupy Khokand they could have done so without striking a blow, for both nomads and Sarts would have joined them, and the Khan would have been driven into exile at the first news of their advance. General Kolpakofsky saw this, and telegraphed to St. Petersburg for permission to intervene, but the diplomatic storm with regard to the occupation of Khiva was then in full blast and permission was refused.

When the Russians declined to interfere on the side of the nomads it was believed that they maintained the side of the Khan, and as the feeling grew more and more bitter against Khudayar Khan it increased proportionately against the Russians. Finally, in 1875, a step was taken which without a doubt increased the hostile feelings against the Russians and possibly precipitated the conflict.

It was resolved to prepare for an expedition against Kashgar. In order to accomplish that end more speedily, it was desirable to send a part of the troops through Khokand, and Mr. Weinberg, the diplomatic official, was despatched on a mission to Khokand to secure the consent of the Khan to the passage of troops. Colonel Scobelef accompanied him, charged to explore the pass of Terek Davan leading to Kashgar. The mission took as a propitiatory offering to Khudayar Khan a boy of seventeen, named Abdul Kerim Bek, who had been put forward by the Kirghiz as a pretender to the throne. Abdul Kerim had lived in Hodjent all his life, knowing nothing of his extraction until the year before, when he was approached by the Kirghiz, and when he was removed to Tashkent on the complaint of the Khan, while his chief adviser, Abdul Kaum, was sent to Tchimkent. His surrender had never been asked for, and was entirely gratuitous on the part of General Kaufmann. This, like the surrender of Tokhtamysh Bek of Shahrisabs to the Amir of Bukhara, being contrary to the rules of asylum and hospitality which even Central Asiatics recognise, was not only a shameful act on the part of the Russian authorities but it turned out contrary to their expectations; it lowered rather than increased their influence with the natives. In surrendering Abdul Kerim, General Kaufmann, it is true, requested the Khan to be gracious and pardon him, which, indeed, he promised to do. The boy, who was confided to the care of Ata Bek, was lost sight of in the ensuing rebellion.

The Russian mission, with a guard of twenty-two Cossacks and *jigits*, accompanied by Mirza Hakim, the Khokandian envoy, arrived at Khokand on July 25, 1875.

When permission was asked for Colonel Scobelef to make his investigations of the mountain passes, the Khan consented, but said that part of the country was unsafe owing to disorders which had broken out among the nomads, although he had sent 4,000 men against them under the command of Abdurrahman Aftobatcha, and hoped that quiet would soon be restored. The Khan, however, seemed troubled by the course events were taking, and was disposed to listen with calmness to the advice given him by Mr. Weinberg on the part of General Kaufmann with regard to the treatment of his people, who urged upon him more moderation and justice.

A few days later, on July 31, a report reached the capital that Nasreddin, the Khan's eldest son, had gone over to the rebels, and that the cities of Ush, Namangan, Andijan, and Assake were occupied by them. It became known at the same time that the real head of the insurrection was Abdurrahman Aftobatcha, who had been sent to quell it. The next day information was brought that the Khan's brother, Sultan Murad, Bek of Marghilan, had joined the insurgents. They had that day occupied Marghilan and were already within thirty or forty miles of Khokand. Khudayar Khan then resolved to put himself at the head of the troops which remained favourable to him and to march against the insurgents. The Russian envoys unwisely decided to accompany him, thus giving him the appearance of having Russian support. The march was fixed for August 3, but during the preceding night the greater part of the Khan's army, together with his second son, Madamin Bek, abandoned him to join the insurgents. Resistance was no longer to be thought of, and Khudayar Khan decided to place himself under the protection of the Russian envoys and to seek a refuge in Tashkent. The Russian merchants in Khokand, with their clerks and assistants, also joined the mission.

The exit from the city through the excited and angry mob was attended with considerable difficulty, but after a ride of two days under constant attack the party reached Hodjent in safety. The Russians had two jigits killed, while one disappeared. The retreat was a perilous one, for the party fell at one time into an ambuscade, and the soldiers who started with the Khan abandoned him from time to time, and always fired at the Russians as they were leaving. Some of the messengers sent to Hodjent for assistance were killed, but one finally arrived in safety, and a force of troops was immediately despatched to the boundary. The Khan was accompanied by his younger son, Urman, Ata Bek, the Atalyk, Mullah Maaruf, Bek of Sokh and nephew of Khudayar, and a suite of 643 people, many of whom were women. He had also a large train of carts, on which he succeeded in bringing part of his treasure, to the amount of over a million pounds sterling. For the bravery shown during this march each of the Cossacks was subsequently recompensed with the Cross of St. George, and a grant of 14,000 rubles was made by General Kaufmann to cover the loss of baggage and equipments, each Cossack receiving 500 rubles as his indemnity.

Mr. Weinberg insists that a *hazavat* or religious war against the Russians was proclaimed at the opening of the insurrection. This, however, was not believed at the time, and the subsequent friendly overtures to the Russians made it in their opinion improbable. The arrival, however, of the Russian mission, which, by accident, coincided with the opening of the insurrection, the surrender of Abdul Kerim, and the protection afforded to the Khan, his family, and his treasure, all, doubtless, had their weight in inspiring the insurgents with the belief that the Russians were taking the part of the Khan and would endeavour to restore him to the throne. It was, therefore, but natural that they should attempt to gain time in order to be themselves the first in the field.

When Colonel Scobelef and Mr. Weinberg returned from Khokand, General Kaufmann was at Vierny on a tour of inspection, but hastening his departure he arrived in Tashkent on August 12, with the intention of taking such measures as would be necessary for the protection of the frontier. A few hours before his arrival a Khokandian envoy appeared bearing a letter from Nasreddin, who had been elected Khan after the flight of his father, as well as letters from the three chiefs of the insurrection, Abdurrahman Aftobatcha, Mullah Issa Aulié, and Halyk Nazar Parmanatchi. In these papers the causes of the insurrection were stated to be the crimes which Khudayar Khan had committed against the Shariat and his oppression of the people, facts which, it was stated, were necessarily well known to the Governor-General. A desire was expressed to live in peace with the Russians, and a hope was indulged in that there would be no change in the relations between the two countries. General Kaufmann answered the new Khan, with a promise to recognise him as such if he would bind himself to carry out all the treaties and engagements entered into by his father, and would recompense Russian subjects for any losses they had sustained during the rebellion. This answer was returned with some confidence, because the Russians believed the young Nasreddin would prove a pliant tool, as he was known to be good-natured, not fanatical, to have adopted many Russian habits—especially that of drinking vodka—and they thought that from his visit to Tashkent he would have a knowledge of Russian ways and of Russian aims. But, almost at the same time with the letter, emissaries had been sent to stir up the inhabitants on the border, and proclamations had been issued, which were soon circulating throughout the country, calling upon all good inhabitants to rise against the Russian tyrants and to unite with the Khokandians in a war for the faith. As usual on the proclamation of a religious war, a formal summons was sent to the Russians to become Mussulmans.

Long before the campaign in Khokand was actually finished General Kaufmann had gone to St. Petersburg, and General Kolpakofsky, who was now in command, considered it necessary to go personally to Khokand to bring order into the country. To render this easier Nasreddin Khan, Abdurrahman Aftobatcha, and other prominent persons, who had shown great hostility to the Russians, were sent prisoners to Tashkent.

On the anniversary of his accession (March 2) the Emperor signed an order for the annexation of Khokand, and General Kolpakofsky, who had just arrived, proclaimed to the inhabitants that their prayer to become Russian subjects had been granted, and that the whole country was now annexed to Russia, and would be known as the district of Ferghana (its ancient name). It was placed under the rule of General Scobelef.

Soon after this Pulad Bek was captured by an energetic Kirghiz and brought to Marghilan, where he was hanged, on the ground that he had killed twelve Russian soldiers whom he had taken prisoners. The official reports are silent as to any prisoners being taken on either side, but we know from other sources that not only had the road from Namangan to Hodjent been unsafe since the first occupation of that territory, but that marauders had even penetrated within the Russian lines and there captured small bands of people. All the transports from Hodjent to Namangan were compelled to go under a strong escort, and on one occasion two Russian officers with twelve Cossacks had been captured and killed.

It seems that quiet has not entirely been restored even by the annexation, for we find that several tribes of the Kara-Kirghiz—especially the Bogus—refused to take part in the general submission of Khokand and concentrated themselves in Gultcha, under command of Abdullah Bek. General Scobelef was sent there with a considerable force, and succeeded in obtaining the submission of all the Kirghiz chiefs, with the exception of Abdullah Bek and two of his companions, who fled further into the mountains, whither they were pursued by jigits.

The events of this last campaign will probably open the eyes of Russian administrators, who will see that a country which it would have been easy to secure by proper means has been found the hardest of all to take by force of arms; and although this is not so much owing to the warlike character of the nomad population as to the hatred which has grown up of recent years to the Russians and the dislike to falling under their rule, it remains to be seen whether this province, ravaged as it has been by the orders of Russian generals, will be easily governed; and it is to be hoped that this at least will bring the Russians to see the necessity of better administration and of a wiser treatment of the natives.

NOTE

1. Patricia Herlihy, "Ab Oriente ad Ulteriorem Orientem: Eugene Schuyler, Russia, and Central Asia," in *Space, Place, and Power in Modern Russia: Essays in the New Spatial History*, edited by Mark Bassin, Christopher Ely, and Melissa K. Stockdale (DeKalb: Northern Illinois University Press, 2011), 126–27.

13 /   "The Afghan War: A Lecture" (1878)

HANDEL COSSHAM

Handel Cossham (1824–90) was a Liberal member of Parliament and a colliery owner whose speech to the Bath Young Men's Liberal Association in 1878 makes a passionate case against war on the very threshold of the second Afghan campaign. Cossham takes aim at a host of aristocrats, including Benjamin Disraeli (Lord Beaconsfield, whose second ministry was 1874–80), and allows us to see, in the process, the long tradition of war as a political as well as a purely military issue.

Afghanistan in 1878 was part and parcel of the Great Game in central Asia that the British had been playing with Russia for decades. As a Liberal member of Parliament, Cossham wants to win that game every bit as much as his Tory colleagues across the aisle. Yet given Britain's posture at the Congress of Berlin (also 1878), where the great powers professed a commitment to peace and stability, he fears that British involvement in Afghanistan proves that "our hypocrisy and selfishness and subtlety have been exposed before the whole world." For Cossham, in the end, the enduring question was the cost of unnecessary war in Afghanistan. In his view, "the national disgrace, the shame," was to be found "in the crime of spilling blood uselessly."

THE BISHOPS AND THE AFGHAN WAR

Since delivering the following Lecture I have been pained to see the votes of the Bishops on this Question.

There are 26 Bishops in the House of Lords—of these 8 attended and 2 paired—not one of these right rev. gentlemen lifted his voice against this unrighteous war, and only one (the Bishop of Oxford) voted against it! The Bishop of Manchester has spoken against it in the country, but he neither voted nor paired. The Bishops of Bangor, Chichester, Gloucester, Hereford, St. Albans, and St. David's voted *for* the war and for burdening the people of India with the expenses. The Bishops of London and Peterborough paired in the same sense.

It is surely time to free these so called Bishops of the Prince of Peace of political duties and parliamentary responsibility.

WESTON PARK;
DECEMBER 23RD, 1878.

THE AFGHAN WAR

On Tuesday evening Mr. Handel Cossham delivered, at the Guildhall, in connection with the Young Men's Liberal Association, a lecture on "The Afghan War," with especial reference to a speech recently delivered in this city by Lord Bury in defence of the Government. Mr. Parry occupied the chair and was supported by Messrs. Woodrow, Read, Maber, Humphries, Mager, Griffiths Dyer and other members of the Association. There was a large attendance, the Sessions Court being crammed. Very little opposition was manifested though there were a few Conservatives present.

Previous to the lecture Mr. Maber stated that that was the last meeting for this session. He was pleased to announce that during the next year lectures on principal events of interest would be given by Lord John Hervey, Colonel Hayter, M.P., and Mr. Samuel Butler. In the course of a short speech he said he hoped that the example set in Bristol would be followed at the next election at Bath.

The Chairman then called upon Mr. Cossham to commence his lecture.

Mr. Cossham (who was loudly cheered) said:—I think it will be almost impossible for the most sanguine supporters of the Government, and their war policy, now to assert that they have any grounds for thinking that the country is in favour of their policy; almost every constituency that has had an opportunity of expressing its opinion, lately, has given to that policy the most decided negative.

Maldon and Bristol last week have, with equal emphasis and clearness, said to the Government,

and especially to Lord Beaconsfield, "We are sick of your duplicity, your want of frankness, your contempt of Parliament, and your constant tendency to war." I can personally bear testimony that the issue clearly put before the electors by both sides at Bristol was, approval or otherwise, of the Government policy, and the majority of 1,550 is the reply to the challenge by the commercial centre of the West.

My object to-night will be to set before you, as clearly and briefly as I can, the grounds of my opposition to the present Government policy, and especially to the Afghan policy of the Government as indicated, and supported, by Lord Bury yesterday fortnight in Bath. Let me say, however, before contesting the positions taken by his lordship, that I deeply regret he was not heard with attention, and replied to without clamour. It is not only fair play to give every expression on public questions a fair hearing. But our side of every great question will always suffer most when the appeals are to passion and not to reason. We have to convert the nations to our views when we seek changes in national policy, and our appeals must be to reason, and not to passion,—to intelligence, and not to Jingoism.

I have not the advantage of having heard Lord Bury on the 2nd of December. But I have taken care to select the report of his speech from the Tory organs, so that I may not be misled by any coloured reports of his speech by the Liberal organs. First, I desire to enter my protest against the remark of Major Allen, M.P. (the Chairman of the meeting), in saying, "Let us have some 'fun' to-night, but do not let it be all on our side." Now I venture to say that this is not the way to approach a great, and I will say, a solemn question like peace and war. It may seem "fun" to Major Allen that the lives of Englishmen should be sacrificed, and the money of India and England wasted, in an unjust and unnecessary war. But there are many, even on his own side of politics, who regard it as a serious and important subject. They cannot find "fun" in the discussion of it, and I venture to add that any man who can is unworthy to be entrusted with a seat in Parliament. Having said thus much relative to the Chairman's speech, let me now deal with Lord Bury. I see his lordship, in that refined way so characteristic of his class, said there was "some *devilment* in the meeting, but no real mischief." I should like to have the benefit of his lordship's opinion as to who brought the devilment into the meeting, and who has persistently tried to stir up in the minds of the people the war fever, and the excitement and unreason that finds its natural fruit in Jingoism, or appeals to noise, clamour, brute force, and rowdyism. What, let me ask, could be a more notorious appeal to passion and prejudice than the statement of Lord Bury that "when Englishman are put before a foreign enemy we forget that we are Liberals or Tories?" Will his Lordship venture to say that we have no right to ask, first of all, whether a war is just or necessary, before we are what he calls "put in front of an enemy?" Does he mean that Englishmen are to be used as mere machines, and to be put in "front of so-called enemies" at the bidding of Lord Beaconsfield, without having an opportunity of discussing or deciding on the justice of the war? I do not think I misrepresent Lord Bury, or the Tory party, when I say that *is* what they mean, and before I close I will show you that is what they have been doing, and it is against that immoral and unconstitutional sentiment I am here to protest to-night. Again I ask why should Lord Bury state that the Duke of Argyll approves of the "views entertained by the present Government." The noble Duke, I venture to say, knows his own opinion better than Lord Bury does, and, by the bye, the great Scotch Duke is not accustomed to change his coat (politically) as Lord Bury has done; he knows his own mind, and can always give clear expression to his convictions, and nothing can more libel the noble Duke than to say that he at all approves of the Afghan policy of the Government. He may, and no doubt does,

disapprove of Russia obtaining possession ot Afghanistan, and let me say that nothing is so likely to give Russia a predominating influence in Afghanistan as the Tory policy of bluster and bounce that Lord Bury came here to defend. There is no doubt that in dealing with Afghanistan Russia has flattered and said smooth things to the Ameer, while we have threatened and bullied, and the result has been that the door was opened to the Northern Bear and closed to the British Lion. We have ourselves, however, to thank for this. When Lord Northbrook left India the Ameer was no more in favour of Russia than he was of England.

Lord Bury then went on to define the difference between the Liberal policy of the past and the Tory policy of the present Government. That I may not misrepresent his lordship, let me quote his exact words. "The only question," he said, "and the only difference between the two parties is that the late Government believes that if the policy which they inaugurated had been allowed to continue the object which we all have in view would have been obtained without a war, whereas those who differ from them believe that that policy had it been pursued would not have landed us in a position creditable to our arms, but have landed us in disaster." Lord Bury calls this "a fair and impartial account of the difference there is between us." With all due deference, I shall venture to dispute this statement of the issue between the two parties, and to assert that (I hope unintentionally) his lordship has misled himself, and tried to mislead you. I will undertake to prove that not only have the present Government departed from the well-known policy of Lord Lawrence, from 1863 to 1868, and who served during that time under Earl Russell, Lord Derby, and Mr. Disraeli; of Earl Mayo (a Conservative), who served under Mr. Gladstone from 1868 to 1872; and of Lord Northbrook, who served under Mr. Gladstone and Mr. Disraeli, from 1872 to 1876; but that the new policy of the present Government began with the appointment of Lord Lytton in 1876. In order that I may make it clear that there has been a new policy adopted by the present Government, let me ask you to note a few facts. On the 26th of December, 1867, Sir Stafford Northcote, writing to the Indian Government, said, referring to Russian advances in Central Asia, "With regard to the progress of Russia in Central Asia, her Majesty's Government see no reason for any uneasiness, or for any jealousy. The conquests that Russia has made, and apparently is still making, in that region are in our opinion the natural result of the position in which Russia was placed, and afford no ground whatever for representation indicative of suspicion or alarm."

Then January 4th, 1869, I see by the papers that the Indian Government transmitted to the Duke of Argyll a memorandum almost unanimously deprecating any extension of frontier in the direction of Afghanistan; they were even hostile to the occupation of Quettah, and only two out of the ten members of the Indian Council were in favour of asking for a British resident in Cabul.

July 1, 1869, Lord Mayo's Government distinctly told the Ameer that no European officers should be placed as Residents in his cities, so that the present Government have not only changed the policy, but they have distinctly broken the treaty entered into by Lord Mayo (himself a Conservative). And what appears to me to involve a deeper measure of national guilt and national responsibility relative to this promise is this: That Lord Lytton (in order to evade the responsibility which this promise involves) has laid it down that as it was not made in writing and embodied in a treaty, therefore it is not binding on us! And is it come to this? That the word of a British representative in India is to go for nothing? That a promise made in the face of India and the world is not to be regarded?

It appears that even this degradation has to be endured in order to support the Asiatic policy of Lord Beaconsfield.

Again, July 9th, 1869, Sir Stafford Northcote, speaking in the House of Commons on the subject of India, remarked "of all things most to be deprecated was a policy of mystery."

Now, I venture to think it would be impossible to condemn the policy of the present Government more emphatically than to use the words of Sir Stafford Northcote in 1869. And in the same speech he went on to condemn, in noble words, annexations of territory in Afghanistan.

April 22nd, 1873, I also find Sir Stafford Northcote again speaking on Indian matters thus:— "The question was raised in what way were we to proceed in consequence of the advance of Russia, were we to take any forward step or to remain on the defensive?" He (Sir Stafford Northcote) thought the general opinion of the country was in favour of remaining on the defensive.

November 13th, 1873, Shere Ali (writing to Lord Northbrook) says "The friendly declaration of your excellency that you will maintain towards myself the same policy which was followed by Lord Laurence and Lord Mayo, has been the cause of much gratification to me."

Up to this point there has been consistency, unity, and straightforwardness in the policy of England towards the ruler and people of Afghanistan.

But in January, 1875, there begins a change—we see it first in a despatch of Lord Salisbury written to Lord Northbrook, in which he says "I have to instruct you to take measures with as much expedition as the circumstances of the case will permit, for procuring the assent of the Ameer to the establishment of a British resident agency at Herat, and when this is accomplished it may be desirable to take a similar step with reference to Candahar."

Now mark, this is done in direct violation of the pledge given by Lord Mayo in 1869, and in utter violation of the recommendations of the Indian Council.

November 19th, 1875, Lord Salisbury again presses the subject on Lord Northbrook and the Indian authorities thus: "The first step (he writes) toward establishing our relations with the Ameer upon a more satisfactory footing will be to induce him to receive a temporary embassy in his capital," and he adds—and I want you to note this— "There would be many advantages in ostensibly directing it to some object of small political interest, which it will not be difficult for your Excellency to find out, and if need be to *create*."

Here is a clear departure from the traditions of Government with respect to India, and yet Mr. Disraeli said in the House of Commons as late as May 5th, 1876, speaking of Afghanistan, as prime minister, "There are many in that country who wish to be masters, and there are many aspirants to power, but that is not a state of affairs that can, in my opinion, be remedied by force. It is by promoting friendly relations—it is by cherishing communications—and it is by commercial influence, to a great degree, that we must gradually obtain that position in Afghanistan, which I believe would be the natural position for both countries, if they were equally conscious of the independence, the security, and the peace that are involved in that relation."

In the same speech Mr. Disraeli said, "He was not of the school who view the advances of Russia in Asia with those misgivings some do. He thought that Asia was large enough for the destinies of Russia and England." Now, what mystery, what double meaning there is in all this. At the time these peaceful sentiments were uttered Mr. Disraeli was preparing the way for his new policy by sending out Lord Lytton. And hence, on the 10th of May last year, Lord Lytton writes that "he was of opinion that the opportunity and pretext (mark the word!) hitherto wanting for the dispatch of a complimentary mission to Cabul were furnished by his accession to office," and by "the addition which the Queen had been pleased to make to her sovereign titles with special regard to India."

Now in the face of these facts who would have thought that Lord Salisbury would venture to say in the House of Lords, June 15th last year, "We have not tried to force an Envoy upon the Ameer at Cabul, our relations with the Ameer have undergone no material change and there is no reason for apprehension of any change of policy or of disturbance in our Indian Empire. I see the Marquis of Bath (whose honest denunciations of the Government policy entitles him to our gratitude and respect) called attention to this want of candour in his speech on the Afghan war last week in the House of Lords, and Sir Stafford Northcote on the 9th of August last year (just as Parliament was breaking up) said "I can speak with confidence on the general line of policy which I have always considered ought to be followed, and which I believe the Government are fully determined to follow in the matter of our Indian policy." In the same speech he went on to say "I have always demurred to the idea which has been put forward by some that the best way to meet danger is to advance beyond our frontier and have always held that the true lines we ought to lay down for ourselves are these—to strengthen ourselves within our frontiers and do so by a combination of measures, moral and material." He further added "the main lines of our policy are unchanged and I believe the country will be satisfied with, and will wish them to continue." Yes, Sir Stafford is right—the country did, and does, wish the past policy to continue, and had the present Government acted on the lines of that policy, and the distinct pledge given by Sir Stafford Northcote, as the mouthpiece of the Government, to Parliament and the country, we should have been spared the humiliation, the national disgrace, the shame, and the crime of spilling blood uselessly.

Coming back to Lord Bury, I ask how, in the face of the facts that I have referred to could his Lordship venture to say "that the only difference between the policy of the late and the present Government was, that we thought the object could be obtained without war and the present Government did not." The difference between the two policies is not, and never has been, a difference as to how best to carry out the same object. It is a difference that is vital, fundamental and irreconcilable.

The former policy was based on a just, friendly, honest recognition of a neighbour's rights; the other is based on the blustering, bullying, and immoral attempt to make "scientific boundaries" by "removing your neighbour's land-mark," and upon us will come the curse that was pronounced against that crime, unless we repent and make restitution. That I am not overstating my case, let me call your attention to the noble utterances of Lord Carnarvon last week on this subject. He said "that he could not reconcile the war with any notions of right or justice; that the policy that led to it was dangerous, and the object aimed at unsound and illusory; that the rectification of frontier had ruined the second empire in France, and would ruin us if persevered in; that the Government had adopted a policy of acquisition (which is a polite way of describing robbery); that it was an unscrupulous and silly exhibition of power; and though Parliament might sanction, the country would condemn it."

These are weighty words; they contain more weighty charges, and they come from one who, till lately, was a member of the present Government.

I will not follow the historical sketch of Lord Bury as to Russian progress in Asia, &c., except to call attention to the fact that for every mile of territory that Russia has taken in Asia during the last century, we have taken at least 10 miles.

I join issue again with Lord Bury as to the statement that in 1873 the Ameer had become "permanently estranged from the Indian Government, and that he took every opportunity of showing contempt and disregard for the British alliance." The facts will not bear out this statement, and I challenge Lord Bury to prove the correctness of what he stated. That in this statement he is distinctly contradicted by Lord Cranbrook, by Sir Stafford Northcote, and also by the present Prime Minister, I have proved by previous quotations.

Lord Bury goes on to contend "that this altered feeling of the Ameer rendered a change of policy necessary." But facts show that from first to last the change was on our part, and not on the part of the Ameer. He has always objected to European Residents in his cities, and we have pledged ourselves not to enforce it. He is no more opposed to it now than he always has been. But the change is here—We, in violation of our pledges, again and again repeated, have lately tried to force Residents upon him. We have done so, in the most insulting Tory fashion, and the result is, what might have been expected—war, confusion, strife, danger to our Indian Empire, expense, loss of life, and probable future troubles.

Lord Bury went on to speak of the danger to India from Russia, through Cabul. But here again he is at issue with his own chief. Lord Beaconsfield, on the 9th of November last, at the Mansion-House, when, in his pompous way, he told us "the country had a chance to get a little light on public questions; that there was no danger to India from that quarter; and though I am not a military man, and hope I never shall be, yet I think that even I can see that every mile we advance towards Russia on the north-west of India, the easier it will be for Russia to attack us, and the more difficult it will be for England to defend India."

It is clear that Lord Bury has the idea that the reception by the Ameer of Russian envoys, and refusing ours, gives us grounds for war. Now let me put a case. Suppose England refused to allow the Ameer to send agents and representatives to Calcutta; at the same time it allowed Russia to do so. Would that be a cause of war? I think not. In the exercise of the sovereign right of states it is a well-understood principle that consent must be had and obtained before Ambassadors are placed anywhere. Why then should we deny to the Ameer what we claim ourselves? His objection may be unwise, but it is quite understandable. He has seen that our policy in the past has been—first, to send a Mission; second, to interfere with the independence; third, to stir up sectional strife; and fourth, to annex. And Shere Ali, not wishing to be swallowed by the British Lion, has steadily refused our envoys, at the same time seeking to retain our friendship. The blood of this contest is not therefore on the head of the Ameer, as Lord Bury said; it is on the head of Lord Beaconsfield and the present Government.

And here let me ask, do you think this policy is worthy of England, worthy of her power, her fame, her character for fair dealing, because we have, or think we have, a ground of quarrel with Russia, which is a strong power, that we should therefore attack Afghanistan, which is a weak and comparatively defenceless power? My countrymen, this war can bring us naught but dishonour and disgrace; it was begun in the dark, it has been planned and pursued under the guise of deception and falsehood; it is unjust in its aims and will be ruinous in its results.

I venture to join issue with Lord Bury in another statement. He said, "The Russians had been foiled at Berlin." On the contrary, the Russians (through the crooked, vacillating, double dealing policy of the present Government), obtained the sanction of Europe to nearly all they asked for or wanted. We have played Russia's game throughout, and we stand before the world humiliated and despised because we went into the Conference of Berlin professing one thing and doing another. We carried "two faces under one hat," and our hypocrisy and selfishness and subtlety have been exposed before the whole world.

Lord Bury I see in conclusion laid the following unction to his soul, that the war he had come to explain and defend was a "just and necessary war." But if you have followed me thus far I hope I have proved that the war was utterly unnecessary and therefore flagrantly unjust.

I have done with Lord Bury. But now just a word as to the speech of Alderman Gibbs. In moving a resolution approving of the Government policy, he is reported to have said that the war was a "defensive war." May I ask the worthy Alderman to tell me if this is a "defensive" war whoever engaged in an aggressive war? We go into a neighbour's territory who has not attacked us, who has done us no

wrong, we seize his strongholds, desolate his country, murder his subjects, and seek to take his capital, and then roll our pious eyes up and thank God we are only engaged in a "defensive war." But Mr. Gibbs is not satisfied with this, he kindly speaks for our party as well as his own, and says "that had the late Liberal Government been in power they would have done just the same." Let me remind Mr. Gibbs that this is a breach, I hope unintentionally, of the 9th Commandment. It is "bearing false witness against his neighbour." There is no Liberal Government during the last 30 years that would have led us into the false and humiliating position in which we now stand toward the Ameer and the people of Afghanistan. It is only a Beaconsfield and a Salisbury that could place us on the inclined plane towards national disgrace and ruin along which we are now being dragged.

Turning now to the general discussion of the Afghan question, and leaving Lord Bury and the Conservative meeting of a fortnight ago behind, let me deal with one or two points that require attention, and first we are accused of being unpatriotic and disloyal because we venture to challenge the justice of a war in which we are involved. But my reply is that we have been involved in that war without our knowledge, behind our backs, and without our consent.

Even the present Publican Parliament was not consulted; even they are treated as though they could not be trusted and are only called together to ratify what has previously been done. "But look," say some, "at the majorities they command" and that support their policy in Parliament, and I say, yes, look at them, and look till you resolve to turn enough of the docile following that Lord Beaconsfield now has into a minority that will be unable to support such a policy as that which is now ruining our commerce, destroying our industry, and keeping the whole world in feverish excitement. But we "should sink all party interests" say some, "when the question is peace or war." And I should be glad if men would rise above party and passion and prejudice in dealing with this great question. But alas! he must be a sanguine man who expects the great Tory party to do that. What did Sir Alexander Gordon say last week, when defending the views I am advocating to-night? He said that a man on the Conservative side of the House who ventured to assert opinions at variance with his party was so annoyed by the rank and file that it was difficult for him to do so, and the honourable baronet (whose Toryism is of the purest character) had to come over to the freer atmosphere of our side of the house in order to express his opposition to the present war policy of the Government. So you see jingoism is not confined to the pot-house politicians of the country, it is to be found rampant and vulgar, even in the elevated atmosphere of the House of Commons.

3rd. But we are told, "Our prestige in India must be kept up." So say I. But surely that prestige can be best sustained by frank, manly, honourable, and generous conduct. I agree with the noble Christian utterances with which Mr. Gladstone closed his magnificent speech in the House last week, when he said, "That truth and justice are the only sure foundation of international relations, and that there is no possession so precious either for peoples or men as a just and honourable name." What we now possess in India will take all our strength to hold, and all our wisdom to govern wisely. It is a grand inheritance. Some call it the "brightest jewel in the crown" of our Queen. However that may be, it is a fearful responsibility. To hold the destinies of two hundred millions of human beings in our hands is a responsibility the full weight of which I think few of us have estimated. They are a docile people, easy to govern and not difficult to please. But we must not strain their patience too much. As Lord Derby nobly said last week, the great danger to India is not from Russia, but from the heavy pressure of taxation. "There (said the noble lord) two hundred millions of people are compelled to try the dangerous experiment of seeing how little they can live on." Let

those people once be made to feel that life under our rule is hardly worth having—and we have nearly reduced them to that—and then we may look out for an explosion compared with which 1857 will be tame and insignificant. On this financial rock the present Government are fast running our Indian empire, and I call upon every lover of justice—every well-wisher to our fellow subjects in India, to help to hurl from power the men who are thus endangering the most wonderful possession it has ever been the lot of a great nation to possess. And what, let me ask, is more likely to endanger our position in India than the proposal of the Government to use the two millions of money raised this year in India for the purpose of providing a fund against the danger of future famines? And yet, in the face of this solemn obligation entered into with the people of India, they now prefer to waste this money that has been wrung out of the starvation and suffering of the people of India in a dishonourable and unjust war.

4th. But we are told that the Ameer "must be humbled," and what then? Will any man tell me what England or India is to gain by the humiliation of the Ameer? It is the old Tory policy. For 500 years at least, out of the last 800, we have been trying to humble France, and a debt of 800 millions is about all we have to show for that folly. The Court of George III, and that old Tory, Lord North, thought to humble America, and they expended 200 millions of money and wasted thousands of lives to do it, and you have the result to day in a country larger, nearly as rich, and in some respects more powerful than our own; and further, let me frankly add, that America free is worth more to us and the world than America fettered. This policy of "humiliating" those with whom we may differ is a very dangerous one. It draws from the scabbard a sword that cuts both ways, and I think the sharpest edge is shown by history to turn towards the nation that first draws it.

5th. We are told that "the prerogative of declaring war rests with the Crown." I admit this frankly.

But the nation has only submitted to that because, during the last 40 years, at least, the sovereign has been under the guidance of statesmen of both parties, who would not advise her thus to strain the prerogative and endanger the crown. The Duke of Wellington, the late Lord Derby, and Sir Robert Peel on the one side, and Lord Melbourne, Earl Russell, Lord Palmerston, and Mr. Gladstone on the other, were all statesmen who had too much regard for the crown, the constitution, and the country thus to act; they treated Parliament with respect, and the nation with confidence; they tried (each according to his light) to bind the cottage to the throne, and the parliament to the people. It remains for the present Prime Minister to stand alone among English statesmen, to devise a policy that reduces parliament to a nullity, and creates a despotism out of a constitutional government. But parliament supports the Government in this policy. I know it. But let me ask any candid man, do you believe the country will back such a policy? Is there not rather every indication that whenever the country is appealed to the decision will be adverse to the present government and their policy? All I can say is, if they do not believe this, let them try us. This Indian policy, the opposition to Russia, the alliance with the Turk, the bringing Asiatic troops into European warfare, has all been evolved since the last election, and it has been evolved by a man, who is not governed by any of the political traditions of the past, but who, being a sort of half Jew and half Christian, has, I verily believe (as I heard Professor Rogers say the other evening), "forgotten the morality of the old testament, and never learnt the morality of the new."

Let them give us the opportunity of testing it in Bath, and I venture to hope—nay, I almost venture to predict—that Bath, following the spirited example of Maldon and Bristol last week, will return a verdict hostile to Lord Beaconsfield and his policy.

Having dealt with some of the arguments in support of this "spirited foreign policy," let me now deal with a few of the considerations that should I think induce us to reconsider our position.

And 1st, look at the state of the country to-day, with banks failing, commerce crippled, industry starving, and the whole country suffering. How can we look without alarm at the reckless expenditure of national wealth now going on? Hear Mr. Chamberlain. He said last week in the house, "that during the 25 years he had known Birmingham, he had never known trade so depressed," or the people so pinched as they are now. Hear Mr. Burt—than whom no man has earned a higher title to speak on behalf of the working classes. They did themselves honour in returning him, and he has done himself high honour by the way he has represented them. What does he say? "I have mixed with thousands of the working classes during the last few months and they one and all condemn this war as unnecessary and unjust."

The whole Liberal party in Parliament and the country condemn it, all the great military authorities in India condemn it. Every living Viceroy (except Lord Lytton) condemns it; the common sense of the nation condemns it; the empty pockets and still more empty cupboards of the sons of toil, condemn it; and, above all, the great principles of justice, equity, and honesty (which no statesman, and no nation, can afford to ignore) condemn it.

I think, therefore, we should unite with one voice to call on the present Parliament to give back to the people they have betrayed and insulted the power to replace them with men who are in sympathy with the age in which we live—the traditions that have come down to us through centuries—and whose aspirations and hopes are in the direction of Constitutional Government, and not of Asiatic despotism.

2nd. I oppose this war because under any possible condition, and with any conceivable issue, we must be losers. If our arms should (as they did forty years ago) meet with reverses, the effect on our Government in India may be most serious.

We only just saved the Empire twenty-one years ago, and we may not be equally fortunate next time. It is playing with lighted matches in the midst of a magazine of powder; we may come out unhurt, but the chances are against us. But suppose we are ever so successful, what then?—and then? Our troubles would in that case be just beginning. Are we to annex the territory? The present Government say "No," but I cannot forget that they told us twelve months ago they were going into the Berlin Conference to defeat Russia, and to uphold the "territorial integrity of the Ottoman Empire," and then they entered into a secret treaty with Russia to carve a big slice out of Turkey, and into another secret treaty with Turkey to take another slice for ourselves, and then had the impudence to come home and call that "Peace with Honour;" and I must be excused for saying that I think we are justified in receiving with great caution the promises of a Government like that. I cannot forget either that when the present Government took office in 1874, they stated that they were as much opposed to the income-tax as the Liberal Party, and might as safely be trusted to get rid of it. They have kept that pledge by putting 3d. in the £ more on the income-tax. And we have not seen the end of this Tory method of abolishing the income-tax yet.

It is national policy that govern national expenditure, and Toryism means war abroad, poverty at home, bad trade, low wages and general depression.

3rd. I have another ground of objection to urge against this policy of Lord Beaconsfield, and that is that it keeps public attention off home duties. There is a long and ever accumulating list of public questions that must be dealt with before long, and that it would be better to face in a calm and peaceful way than to have them forced upon us by an angry and excited people.

There is the whole question of national expenditure that will have to be dealt with.

There is the land question that will not long remain where it now stands. The farmers have been shamefully betrayed by the present Government.

They were promised "security of tenure," and they have instead a "permissive" law, that nearly every landlord notices himself out of. Surely the time will come when the great farming class will learn, like every other class and section of the country has had to learn—that when they desire any real reform, anything that savours of national justice, and not merely class prejudice and class interest; the hope and anchor of that section of society is with the Liberal Party.

Then there is the great Church question, that will be sure to divide society, and split up parties again and again, before it is finally settled on the basis of religious equality. But there is no use ignoring it, or trying to sail round it. It stands in our path, and meets us at almost every turn. Statesmen are weary of the Priestly claims and Popish tendencies of the clergy; and, from a sense of disgust, will before long help us to lift the Church into a higher life, by freeing her from a control that hinders her progress and lessens her spiritual power.

The universities must be still more thrown open. In some shape popular control will have to be given over the drink traffic. Local self-government will have to be adopted, and Home Rule in the form of local self-government given to Ireland, to Scotland, to Wales, and to our English counties. Above all, the prerogative of the Crown will have to be made consistent with the dignity of Parliament and the safety of the nation, and I venture to think that as a safeguard against the possible tricks of a man like Lord Beaconsfield we shall have to adopt triennial parliaments—these and all similar reforms are now being kept back by the blood and bluster foreign policy of the present Government. I think the nation has become heartily sick of it. We of this generation have never seen Toryism in power before; we have seen them in office but not in power. Mr. Disraeli with a minority behind him and Lord Beaconsfield with a majority in front of him are two different things. We have had a taste of the latter the last five years, and I venture to predict that it will be quite enough to keep the nation from trying the experiment again for the next twenty-five years.

Our duty is clear. By an enlightenment of the public mind—by setting out facts, and urging reasons that are logical and sound—let us try to create a public sentiment against which this bastard imperialism shall dash itself to pieces. Let us seek to impress on the nation that injustice and robbery are as wrong in nations as in individuals—that there is not one code of morals for nations and another for individuals. The great principles of right are not only eternal, but world-wide, and I believe it is our interest—as it is certainly our duty—to recognise and teach the truth "that righteousness exalts a nation, while sin is a disgrace to any people."

Mr. Cossham, who, during the delivery of the lecture was frequently and loudly cheered by the audience, concluded by moving the following resolution:—"That having heard the lecture the meeting was of opinion that the war with Afghanistan was unnecessary and unjust."

Mr. B. W. Weaver moved the following amendment:—"That in the opinion of this meeting the Afghan war is both just and necessary." At the out-set of his remarks he took exception to Mr. Cossham quoting isolated passages in the speeches of Major Allen and Lord Bury, which were delivered amidst the greatest excitement and confusion, and he (Mr. Weaver) contended that the speakers at the Guildhall were, under the circumstances, perfectly justified in making use of the language they did. They had, he said, to take broader views of a great national question than that. Proceeding, he detailed the circumstances leading to the war, and maintained that the Ameer had, by his refusal

to accept an Envoy, insulted the English nation; India being ruled by moral influence and prestige more than by force of armies and navies made it absolutely necessary that the insult should be wiped off, or the English influence in India would be materially weakened. He argued that we were bound to arrest Russian aggression if dangerous to our interests, and contended that it would not be safe for Russian influence to predominate at Cabul. One of the results—not the cause of the war— would be to secure our frontier, and he argued that it was most desirable to form a "scientific frontier," and secure the safety of the Indian Empire. Commenting on the opposition in Parliament, Mr. Weaver quoted from an article in *Saturday's Review* on the Afghan Question. He denied that the result of the Bristol election could be taken as an expression of opinion on the Foreign Policy of the Government. It was rather a victory for the "Home Rulers," who he believed as a rule cared little for the interests of England; he also quoted from the *Saturday Review* in support of his arguments that the return of Mr. Fry for Bristol was no indication of disapproval on the part of the nation of the Foreign Policy of the Government.

Mr. G. Allpass seconded the amendment.

The remarks of Mr. Weaver and Mr. Allpass met with many expressions of dissent, and Mr. Cossham having replied in a speech that was loudly cheered, the resolution, on being put to the meeting, was carried almost unanimously.

A vote of thanks, proposed by Mr. Maber and seconded by Mr. Read, having been accorded to Mr. Cossham for his lecture, the meeting terminated.

"Afghanistan and Its Peoples" (1878) and "Afghan Women and Children" (1880)

If Afghan women scarcely appear in official accounts or soldiers' memoirs, these two newspaper articles are evidence that images of women did circulate deep in the heart of provincial Britain. Readers of the day got information about women's "condition" under Muslim law, their courtship and marriage arrangements, their clothing, and even their complexions. Victorian readers were also invited to make comparisons between "Mohammedan" women and their Christian sisters, in terms of dress and moral purity. The "Cabulese" lady comes in for particular scrutiny in a description that typifies the gendered and sexualized orientalism of the later nineteenth century, when women were chiefly viewed as ornaments and evaluated exclusively according to Western standards.

AFGHANISTAN AND ITS PEOPLES

The obscure but somewhat remarkable country called Afghanistan has recently and suddenly come into prominence before the attention of England, and, indeed, before the world. The daring step taken by the Ameer in the latter part of the month of September, 1878, in refusing passage to the English Mission, at once placed the kingdom of Cabul into antagonism to the British nation. The region which bears the name of Afghanistan is situated in Asia, to the north-west of India. On the east it is bounded by the Punjab, from which it is separated by the mountain wall of the Suliman Range. The wild country of Beloochistan forms the southern boundary. On the west is Persia, a desert extending along the entire Afghan frontier. Afghan Turkestan and Badakshan, also subject to the Ameer of Cabul, are on the north, and form the boundary. The extent of the country is roughly estimated at 600 miles from east to west, and 500 miles from north to south. The physical features of the country are diversified by the greatest extremes. Throughout the entire extent it is mountainous, and its general aspect is that of elevated, flat-bottomed valleys, partially cultivated in the vicinity of the streams, and bounded by bleak mountain spurs. Some of its plains are deserts, others are fertile, the result of irrigation effected by diverting the waters of the rivers during the rain season. The rivers of Afghanistan are not remarkable, excepting for their irregularity and uncertainty. From the nature of the country, thus characterized by such extremes, we might naturally expect a somewhat variable climate. This doubtless is the case in some respects, but the Afghans know nothing of the fickleness of climate with which we are so familiar. In India and Afghanistan, and indeed in most of those Eastern countries, they have what may still be designated the early and latter rain. The most remarkable rainy season in Afghanistan is called the S.W. monsoon, which extends from Africa to the southern peninsula of Asia, and deluges within certain limits all the intermediate countries for the dreary period of four months in the year. In Southern India it commences about the end of May, and reaches Afghanistan a little later. The "latter" rain falls in winter, and assumes the form of rain or snow according to the temperature of the place. It extends over all Afghanistan, and as far west as the Hellespont, and is of much greater importance to husbandry than the south-west monsoon, except in some particular districts. The temperature of the country of course varies according to the situation of the place. At Cabul, for instance, the winter is vigorous, and the snow lies for two or three months. During most of this time the people keep indoors, and sleep close to their stoves. While at Jalalabad the winter and climate assume more of an Indian character, and in summer the heat is very great, the thermometer standing for days as high as 112 to 113 deg. Upon the whole, therefore, the temperature may be pronounced moderate, the average heat being greater than in this country and less than in India. That it is healthful appears from the fact that diseases are few. Fevers and agues are common in winter, and are more or less felt in spring. Colds are somewhat more frequent and dangerous in winter. Small-pox, it appears, is about the most fatal; and opthalmia, a disease which affects the eyes, is a very common complaint. These are the principle diseases which af-

flict the Afghans, and in their consequences might be greatly modified but for their ignorance of medical sciences.

The People

All the fruits of Europe, except the gooseberry and strawberry, are found in Afghanistan, and the absence of these is amply compensated for by the water melon and pomegranate. Wheat and barley are also cultivated, as are maize, tobacco, cotton, rice, sesamum, and the pania christie. Among trees, the olive, the mulberry, the oak, cedar, walnut, and the pine abound. The origin of the Afghans, like that of the ancient Britons and many other nations, is wrapped in mystery. The derivation of the name Afghan even is uncertain, but it is probably of modern origin. It is said to be known to the Afghans themselves through the Persian language. Their own name for their nation is Pooshtoon. The Arabs call them Solimanee. Though mystery shrouds the origin of this people there is no lack of opinions on the subject. By the majority of the Eastern writers they are regarded and believed to be the descendants of one of the lost 10 tribes of Israel. As a people the Afghans are physically well formed, being tall, robust and active; their olive and sometimes sallow complexions and strongly marked hard features give their countenances a savage expression, which is generally intensified by their practice of tinging the eyelids with antimony, which in their opinion adds force and beauty to the face, and gives a dazzling brilliancy to their fiery blackeyes. Their black beards they cut quite short, and the hair of their head is shaven from the front to the top of the head, the remainder at the sides and back is allowed to grow, and falls in long curls over their shoulders. Born for war, they are brave even to rashness. In manners and in all social habits they are coarse and rude, and know nothing of the rules of politeness or even common civility. Social rank and distinction they totally ignore; they rudely intrude them themselves into the presence and society of those who are in all respects their superiors, and at once, without ceremony, enter into conversation. Idleness is a dominant vice of the people, and the man who steadily works for about a month in the year is almost a model of industry. Like the Turks and the Persians, they take their meals sitting on the ground, with their heels tucked under them, and their fingers are a substitute for knives and forks. They are noted for their hospitality, but it appears not on account of their love for that virtue, but because it is an ancient custom. They are utterly destitute of principle and the words patriotism and honor are but empty sounds. They readily make promises, which they seal by oaths most solemn, and on the slightest pretext perjure themselves with an impudence perfectly inconceivable. The spirit and character of this people and their institutions is correctly expressed in the following terse utterance of an old Afghan:—"we are content with discord; we are content with alarms; we are content with blood; but we will never be content with a master."

Houses and Occupations

One portion of the population inhabit houses, the other dwell in tents, the latter of the two modes of living being generally the more popular. In the matter of architecture and building they show but little advance on their forefathers. Indeed, if we may judge from ruins that strew the valleys and plains which give evidence of skill, energy, and industry, which characterized a past prosperous age, they have evidently deteriorated. In the building of their houses they are like the birds in their erection of their nests, the system and style being exactly those of their forefathers. The material ordinarily used is sun-dried brick; for the houses of the rich, the bricks are burnt. In the former case, the wall is roughly formed with mud and chopped straw. This soon consolidates, as there is little rain. The rough surface is smoothed with a trowel. The dwellings of the wealthy are also plastered. The roof is vaulted somewhat after the shape of a beehive. The houses rarely consist of more than one floor, and while, as at Kandahar, the rooms are decorated with considerable taste, yet compared to European dwellings they appear mean in the extreme. Respecting personal luxuries and indulgences, it appears the habit of snuffing is more popular and extensive than smoking. Their drink is buttermilk or sherbert. In some places they use a liquor made from sheep's milk, which has an enlivening, if not an intoxicating, quality. They are fond of a little social excitement, so as often as a man can afford to kill a sheep he makes a feast. The favorite amusement of the Afghans is the chase, in which they are generally skillful and successful. Races are common, especially in connection with a marriage; when the bridegroom perhaps gives a camel to be run for. In the way of amusement they have various contests, both as a display of strength and skill. The dress of the men varies. Originally it appears to have consisted of a pair of loose trousers and, in dark colored cotton, a large shirt—like a wagoner's frock, but with wider sleeves; a low cap, the sides of which are of black silk or satin, the top or crown of gold brocade, or of some other bright coloured cloth. The boots are of brown leather, laced or buttoned up to the calf. More generally the head is covered by an enormous blue or white turban, and the feet with slippers without quarters. An outer garment or cloak of well tanned sheep skin, with the wool inside, is thrown loosely over the shoulders, and covers most of the body. On the point of dress they are extremely careless. The fashions change but seldom, and often their clothes are rendered disgustingly filthy the first time they are worn by their habits of squatting down on the ground, utterly heedless as to the condition of the place. Many of them never change their garments, not even the shirt, until quite worn out. Washing themselves is an operation of rare occurrence.

Afghan Women

The condition of Afghan Women is better than in India and many other heathen countries, but it varies with the social rank. The women of the upper classes are entirely concealed from the public gaze, not being allowed to go out of their houses; at the same time, they enjoy the comforts and even luxuries which their position affords. Those in less affluent circumstances do the work of the household, while the women of the lower classes share in doing the work of the men. The laws of Mahommedanism allow a husband to beat his wife (of course, if she deserves it), but it is considered discreditable for a man to avail himself of this privilege. Several of the ladies of the upper class learn to read, and some of them evince power and attainments in literature; but it is regarded [as] immodest in a woman to be able to write, as their jealous lords think she might avail herself of this accomplishment to carry out an illicit correspondence. The women in towns when seen are always wrapped in a large white sheet, which covers them from head to feet, and completely hides their figure. A network in the hood enables them to see their way. In the country they go unveiled, but immediately cover their faces when they see a man with whom they are not on the most friendly terms, and seldom enter the public apartment of their own house if a stranger be present. And to their honour be it spoken, their moral purity and integrity puts to shame multitudes of their sex in this Christian country.

Courtship and Marriage

The Afghans, like most other Asiatics, have to purchase their wives, the price varying according to the position of the parties concerned, and the circumstances of the suitor. The effect of this is that while the women, as I have stated, are on the whole kindly treated, yet they are in some measure necessarily regarded as property. A husband can divorce his wife without assigning any reason, but the wife cannot return the compliment. She may sue for a divorce on good grounds, but this is seldom done. If the husband dies before the wife, his relatives receive the price that is paid for her in case of a sec-

ond marriage; but among the Afghans, as among the ancient Jews, it is regarded as incumbent on the brother of the deceased to marry the widow. She is not, however, compelled to marry against her will, and if she have children it is considered most becoming to remain a widow. The common age for marriage is 20 for men, and 15 or 16 for women. But many men are found unmarried at the age of 40, in consequence of being unable to pay for a wife; and women single at the age of 25; when, of course, the former becomes an old bachelor, and the latter attains to the distinction of being an old maid. In all parts of the country, the age at which individuals marry is regulated by their ability to find a wife and maintain a household. Hence, in the case of wealth, betrothal and marriage take place at a ridiculously early age. In towns, men have no opportunity of seeing the women of other families. This, at the outset, must be an extremely embarrassing thing to a man setting out in search of a better half. When a man has thought of a particular young lady, he sends a female relative or neighbor, who, having secured an interview with the person in question, has to report to the suitor the general result. If this be so far satisfactory, the same person next seeks to ascertain the views and feelings of the lady's mother on the subject, and of the family generally as to their approval of the alliance. If all this be favorable, then the "go-between" makes a formal offer on behalf of him for whom he is acting, and makes arrangement as to the day when a public proposal is to be made. At the time appointed the father of the suitor goes with a party of his male relatives to the girl's father, a similar deputation of women waits on her mother, and the offer of marriage is made in the proper form. The suitor then sends a ring, or a shawl, or some other present to his affianced bride whom he has never yet seen, and his father begs the girl's father to accept his son as his servant. All this being done, sweetmeats are brought in, of which both parties partake, after solemnly repeating the Fauteheh, or opening verse of the Koran, and praying for the affianced couple. The girl's father then makes some trifling present to the lover, and from this time the happy pair are considered as we should say engaged. A considerable time may elapse before the marriage is celebrated, the interval being employed by the girl's relations in providing and preparing her dowry, which consists of household furniture and personal ornaments. The bridegroom is also diligently engaged in collecting the other necessary funds to enable him to pay the price of his wife, and to provide whatever else is deemed requisite for the setting up of a household.

Education and Language

The standard of education, as might be expected, is extremely low; and the whole system is defective from beginning to end. Of the poorer classes probably not more than one-fourth can read their own language. The rich generally employ a priest, who is called a Moolah, and who resides in the house, to teach the children. In small villages the priest is also a schoolmaster, to whom, as a salary, a piece of land is allotted, and in addition, he receives a small contribution from his scholars. In larger and more important places the two offices are distinct. In towns there are regular schools, and the masters are sustained by school fees, as in European countries. The sum paid to a school-master about 50 years ago was about 13d a month. The course of study is prescribed by Mohammed-anism. The great prophet Mohammed directed that a child should begin its letters when it was four years four months and four days old. For fever they recommend cold baths, and when possible, in iced water. There is great diversity of opinion among the medical men as to the treatment of wounds. Some of them affirm that they should never be washed, but that the blood and matter should be left to coagulate on the surface to re-form the flesh. For an aperient they use fresh fat, which they derive from the tails of their sheep, and in this we see how nature has kindly provided for this necessity. Four or five pounds of this fat

being melted down, is administered as one dose. In the estimation of an Afghan, every European is a doctor, in whose skill they have unlimited confidence, so that whenever they have the chance, even though in perfect health, they appeal to him for medicine, and having obtained which, no matter what it might be, they swallow there and then, evidently acting on the principle that prevention is better than cure, for he naively says as he dispatches the drug, "I am not ill, but I may become so." But little can be ascertained as to the origin of the language, which they call Pushtoo. Most of the words are from unknown roots. The words relating to religion, government and science are mostly through Arabic, through the Persian. They boast of a few literary men; but in point of mental ability and scholarly attainments they rank very low. They go not beyond a circle of ideas of the narrowest limits. They have neither the genius of creation nor the faculty of imitation. They refuse to learn anything that would enlarge their minds and contribute to their well-being, because it is different from that recommended by their forefathers and teachers. Science they regard as a useless burden, which only fatigues those who pursue it, without adding to their happiness . . .

AFGHAN WOMEN AND CHILDREN

The correspondent of the *Calcutta Pioneer* writes:— "The dress of Afghan women, especially those whose husbands have rank or wealth, is extremely picturesque. A short tight-fitting bodice of green blue or crimson silk confines the bust, but buttons so closely up to the throat that one can only guess at the proportions of shoulders and bosom. The bodice is generally embroidered with gold, and then becomes so stiff and unyielding that it is virtually a corset. In this cold weather the short arms of the sari are continued down to the wrist, and the vest itself is padded with wool for the sake of warmth. Trousers *a la Turc*, baggy and flowing as Fatima's, and tightly fastened at the ankles, a broad silk *kummerbund* of almost endless length, with the ends so disposed that they become skirts, dainty white socks, and a tiny slipper or shoe, gold embroidered—such is the indoor dress of the Cabulese lady while covering and hiding all save feet and ankles is the voluminous white garment drawn over the head and face, and falling to the heels. These veiled beauties have jewelry scattered over their forehead, hands, wrists, arms, and ears; while handsome gold loops secure the yashmak at the back of the head; the hair being slightly drawn from the forehead, and tied lightly into a knot, Grecian fashion. The length of a silk *kummerbund* which circles a lady's waist is something astonishing: one I saw must have been 12 yards long by 18 inches broad, and the end was even then not forthcoming. The slippers and shoes are of Cabulese make, and are very pretty. On a pale green background beautiful patterns were worked with gold and silver thread and part-coloured silk, until the effect is more like that of a fairy slipper than one for daily use. But a stout leather sole is put on, with high heels rudely bound with iron, and then the work of art is complete. The stalls in which their slippers and shoes are made is the gayest in the whole bazaar. A Cabulese lady's foot is so small, almost to deformity, and the baggy trousers by contrast make them appear exceedingly petite. From the few faces seen, and those chiefly of old or *passee* women, it is difficult to judge of the famed beauty Cabulese are said to boast of. The children are, certainly, as a whole, the prettiest I have ever seen. Their complexions are red and white, with a tinge of olive pervading the skin, eyes black and lustrous, well-shaped features, teeth to make a Western beauty envious, and bright, intelligent looks that sadly belie the race to which they belong. Their mothers must be beautiful, for their fathers are generally villainous-looking; the men losing all the pleasing traits which as boys they possessed. The lady I have described as seen in the *zenana* for a moment was certainly handsome, and was far lighter in complexion than a Spaniard; her eyes were really worthy of the praises sung by Hafiz, but the sensuous lips were a little too full and pouting. It was just such a face as one imagines in a harem, and would be in keeping with the languorous life of a voluptuary to whom sensuality is a guiding star. Such faces always lack character, and would soon prove insipid in the eyes of the West. The Cabulese lady, when journeying, is either carried in an elaborate wickerwork cage covered with the inevitable flowing linen, or rides, Amazon fashion, on a pony behind her lord.

15 / "India and Afghanistan" (1879)

R. D. OSBORN

Debates about foreign policy and diplomacy, as well as about the empire more generally, were rife in Victorian journals such as the *Contemporary Review*, which featured contributions by the leading lights of the period, including Cardinal Manning, T. H. Huxley, and William Gladstone. Liberal in tendency and internationalist in scope, the journal was not a slave to party; *Contemporary Review* instead served as a forum for debate on subjects as wide-ranging as theology and philosophy, science and belief, war and art.

In this article on the national-imperial security stakes of Afghanistan for India, Lieutenant Colonel R. D. Osborn lays the blame for the Second Anglo-Afghan War squarely at the feet of the British—not simply in terms of immediate policy but as a result of the first "iniquitous" war forty years earlier. A critic of Lord Edward Bulwer Lytton's "cruel" and "criminal" policy vis-à-vis the emir of Afghanistan, Osborn paints the government as helpless and blind to its own strategic failures. In doing so he raises questions about the defense of India via a "scientific frontier" like Afghanistan, whose stability was predicated on an alliance with a strong and independent indigenous ally—but whose real aim was to fend off the eternal Russian threat. In his cynical view, this means that India will never be secure until Britain makes "offensive and defensive alliance[s] with the barbarian enemies of Russia all over the world." Were that even possible, Osborn nonetheless fears that the war is having the opposite effect: Lytton's policy has not protected India but has placed the very future of the Raj in peril.

When the news arrived that Major Cavagnari and his companions had fallen victims to the fury of the Kabul populace, the *Daily Telegraph* "called aloud, before Heaven, for a punishment which should ring from end to end of the Continent of Asia." It is a pity that so much fine and eloquent indignation should be expended on the Afghans instead of those who are truly responsible for the catastrophe which has evoked it. If ever there was a future event which might be predicted with absolute certainty, it was that Major Cavagnari and his companions would perish precisely as they have done. Twice, within forty years, have we invaded Afghanistan, although on both occasions we have frankly avowed that with the inhabitants of the country we had no cause of quarrel whatever. Nevertheless, we carried fire and sword wherever we went, cutting down their fruit trees, burning their villages, and leaving their women and children shelterless under a winter sky. What could we expect as the fruit of such acts, except that our victims—knowing, as we did, that they were revengeful, passionate, and too ignorant to forecast the consequences of their actions—should retaliate in kind the moment that they had the opportunity? The first invasion of Afghanistan is now known by general consent as "the iniquitous war;" but it is open to question if even that war was so elaborately contrived, or so long laboured for as this—the first act of which has terminated in the slaughter of Major Cavagnari and his escort.

The circumstances which preceded it are briefly these. For eighteen months Lord Lytton had attempted, by alternate threats and cajolery, to prevail upon the Ameer Shere Ali to make a surrender of his independence, and become a vassal of the Indian Empire. These attempts having failed, war was declared against him on the pretence that he had insulted us before all Asia by declining to receive a "friendly" mission sent by the Indian Government. This mission was *not* friendly. It was notorious throughout India that it would go to Kabul charged with an ultimatum which offered the Ameer the choice of war, or the sacrifice of his independence. But even this mission the Ameer never refused to receive—nay, it is certain that he would have received it if the opportunity had been given to him, so great was the value he attached to English friendship. But what the Government of India desired was not the reception of the mission, but a pretext for making war upon the Ameer. It knew that the policy which it meditated in Afghanistan would so completely destroy the sovereignty of the Ameer, that it was impossible he should agree to it. At the same time, it was impossible to declare war against an independent prince, simply because he declined to divest himself of his independence. The war must, somehow or another, be made to appear as if it were due to some act of the Ameer. Consequently, almost from the hour in which the announcement was made that the mission was to start, the Ameer was plied with insults and menaces which, if they were not intended to drive him to some act of overt hostility, had no purpose at all. And when these proved unavailing, Lord Lytton directed Sir Neville Chamberlain to attempt to force his way through the Khyber Pass, without waiting for the permission of the Ameer. In the most courteous manner the Afghan officer, in command at the Khyber, intimated to the mission that, without the sanction of his master, it was impossible to allow it to proceed; and this refusal was instantly telegraphed to England as a deliberate insult which must be wiped out in blood. From first to last, so far as his conduct towards us is concerned, the Ameer was absolutely blameless. During his entire reign his consistent endeavour had been to draw closer the ties of amity between himself and us. The Russian mission had forced its way to Kabul, despite of all his endeavours to hinder its advance; and there can be no question that but for the previous action of Lord Lytton that mission would never have come to Afghanistan. But eighteen months before that occurrence Lord Lytton had withdrawn our Native Agent from the Court of the Ameer. This had been done as a mark of displeasure, and a proof that no alliance of any kind existed between the two States. This proceeding Lord Lytton followed up by the occupation of Quetta, although he was well aware that such an occupation would be interpreted—and rightly—by the Ameer, as a menace to his independence, and the harbinger of war. So it came about that when the Russian mission knocked for admission at the doors of his capital, the Ameer found himself on the one side threatened by Russia, and on the other abandoned and threatened by Lord Lytton. Lord Lytton, in point of fact, is as directly responsible for the entry of the Russian mission to Kabul as he is for the dispatch of his own.

But if Lord Lytton's treatment of the Ameer was cruel and ungenerous, criminal, at least to an equal extent, was his treatment of the people over whom he ruled. At that time there was an appalling amount of suffering all over India. The country had been ravaged by a series of famines. In the Punjab prices were abnormally high. The North-West Provinces were still unrecovered from a dearth, during which the Government of India had exhibited a rapacity and indifference to human suffering which would, with difficulty, be credited in England. Terrible as is the mortality resulting from a famine in India, the death-roll represents but a tenth part of the suffering which such visitations inflict. For every human being that dies, ten are left, without money and without physical strength, to struggle feebly for existence on the margin of the grave. They cannot give a fair day's work for a fair day's wage. They may reckon themselves fortunate if their enfeebled powers can earn just sufficient to keep body and soul together. For all these wretched beings—and last year in Upper India they numbered many millions—the smallest rise of price in the necessities of life means death from hunger. A war, therefore, with the enormous rise of prices which it would immediately produce, was nothing less than a sentence of torture and death passed upon tens of thousands of our own subjects. Undeterred, however, by the warnings of experience, deaf to considerations of humanity and justice, the Government of India started on its wild-goose chase after a "Scientific Frontier." The victims whom it trampled to death in this mad chase have never been numbered—they never can be numbered. The Afghans who died in defence of their village homes form but a hundredth part of them. The residue was composed of our own mute and uncomplaining subjects.

A war thus wantonly commenced resulted in a failure as ignominious as it deserved. Long before the Treaty of Gundamuck the ambitious policy of the Government had become an object of contempt and ridicule all over India. It was known that Lord Lytton and his advisers were at their wit's end to discover something which might be made to do duty as a "Scientific Frontier," and so bring a misjudged enterprise to a conclusion. But it is the peculiarity of our Ministers to believe that they can arrest the inexorable sequence of cause and effect by a dexterous manipulation of the faculty of speech. Lord Beaconsfield appears to have imparted to his colleagues his own belief in the omnipotence of phrases to remove mountains, and make rough places smooth. So the Treaty of Gundamuck was no sooner signed than Ministers and Ministerial journals raised a great hymn of triumph over the wondrous things which they had wrought in Afghanistan. The one solid national advantage to be derived from the sacrifice of Cavagnari and his comrades, is that this method of treating facts will have to be laid aside. Lord Lytton is not likely to appeal again to his "carefully verified facts" as a proof that he is a much wiser man than Lord Lawrence. Lord Cranbrook will not again express his conviction that the "objections (to an English Resident) expressed by Shere Ali will be shown to have been without substantial foundation." Yakoub Khan and his five attendants are all that remain of that "strong, friendly, and independent Afghanistan" which Mr. Stanhope informed the House of Commons had been created by the war. The anguished cry of the *Daily Telegraph* "for a punishment which shall ring from end to end of the Continent of Asia" is the latest expression of the "results incalculably beneficial to the two countries" which, according to Lord Lytton, were to flow from the Peace of Gundamuck.

A failure in policy more signal and more complete than this it is impossible to imagine. But it is to be noted that the Ministerial journals are doing their utmost to save the "Scientific Frontier" from the destruction which has overtaken the projects of the Ministry. And so long as a belief in this Frontier is cherished anywhere, the return to a safe and rational policy is obstructed. In the following pages, therefore, I shall, firstly, endeavour to show that the (so-called) "Scientific Frontier" is as purely fictitious as the "strong, friendly, and independent Afghanistan" which we were told had been created out of chaos by means of the war. And, secondly, I shall discuss the various lines of conduct which lie open to us, when we have occupied Kabul, in order to determine which is best fitted to ensure the stability of our Indian Empire and the contentment of its inhabitants.

THE SCIENTIFIC FRONTIER.

In all the discussions on this Frontier question, a very obvious, but all-important, fact has been persistently forgotten. It is that British rule in India is a rule based upon military supremacy; and that, therefore, our Indian army—English as well as native—is primarily a garrison, having its duties upon the places where it is quartered. We could not withdraw our troops from any part of India without incurring the risk of an outbreak in the districts thus denuded. The "Punjab Frontier Force" has always been a force distinct from the "Army of India," and recognized as having special duties of its own. So far as I know, in the discussions on a "Scientific Frontier" no reference has been made to the above circumstance. The Indian army has been spoken of as if it were so much fighting power, which we were free to concentrate at any point we pleased. And to this oversight is due the hallucination that an improved frontier would enable us to diminish the strength of the Indian garrison (properly so called). The fact is, that before this last war we had almost the very frontier which our situation in India required. If the authority of the Ameer had extended up to the boundaries of our Empire, troubles between the two States must have occurred, resulting inevitably in the extinction of the weaker. The evil of such an extension of territory no one denies; we should not only have had to hold Afghanistan with a strong garrison—certainly not less than twenty thousand men—but we should have been compelled to maintain a frontier force, to guard against aggression from without, either from Russia or Persia. Forty thousand men would have been needed for this double duty, in addition to the pre-existing garrison of India. But by a piece of supreme good fortune the authority of the Ameer did not begin where ours left off. Between us and him were interposed the tribes which dwell in the hills along our North-Western frontier. These tribes acknowledged allegiance neither to him nor to us. Broken up and divided amongst themselves, the worst they could inflict upon us was an occasional raid into our territories; and these we could repress without having to call the Ameer to an account for the lawlessness of his subjects. A few regiments of horse and foot were all that we needed for the defence of our frontier; while as against foreign invasion we possessed a frontier that needed no defence at all. That frontier consisted of the foodless deserts and inaccessible hills of Afghanistan. These were impenetrable to an invader, so long as we retained the friendship and the confidence of the people who dwell among them. Consequently, to quote the language of Sir Henry Rawlinson, "our main object has ever been, since the date of Lord Auckland's famous Simla Manifesto of 1838, to obtain the establishment of a strong, friendly, and independent Power on the North-Western frontier of India, without, however, accepting any crushing liabilities in return." We all know the manner in which Lord Auckland set about obtaining the "strong, friendly, and independent Power," and the "crushing liabilities" we had to accept in consequence. Tutored by experience, we adopted a wiser and more righteous policy, which was producing admirable results.

The difficulty of establishing a stable friendship with Afghanistan arises from the character of the people. It is the habitation, not of a nation, but of a collection of tribes, and the nominal ruler of Afghanistan is never more than the ruler of a party which, for the time, chances to be strongest. Consequently there never existed an authority, recognized as legitimate throughout the country, with which we could enter into diplomatic relations. At the same time, their divided condition crippled the Afghans for all offensive purposes. We had, therefore, nothing to fear in the way of unprovoked aggression, and our obvious policy was to win the confidence of these wild tribes and their chiefs, by carefully abstaining from encroachments on their independence. Such, in fact, has been the policy which every Governor-General has pursued in the interval which divides the "plundering and blundering" of Lord Auckland from the like achievements of Lord Lytton. And it had been attended with the greater success, because under the firm guidance of two remarkable men, Afghanistan had progressed considerably towards the status of an organized kingdom. Shere Ali had diligently trod in the footsteps of his father, the Dost, and it is in these terms that the Government of India describes the rule and policy of the Ameer in the year 1876:

Those officers of our Government who are best acquainted with the affairs of Afghanistan, and the character of the Ameer and his people, consider that the hypothesis that the Ameer may be intimidated or corrupted by Russia (even supposing there was any probability of such an attempt being made) is opposed to his personal character and to the feelings and traditions of his race, and that any attempt to intrigue with factions in Afghanistan, opposed to the Ameer, would defeat itself, and afford the Ameer the strongest motive for at once disclosing to us such proceedings. Whatever may be the discontent created in Afghanistan by taxation, conscription, and other unpopular measures, *there can be no question that the power of the Ameer Shere Ali Khan has been consolidated throughout Afghanistan in a manner unknown since the days of Dost Mahomed, and that the officers entrusted with the administration have shown extraordinary loyalty and devotion to the Ameer's cause.* It was prob-

ably the knowledge of the Ameer's strength that kept the people aloof from Yakoub Khan, in spite of his popularity. At all events, Herat fell to the Ameer without a blow. The rebellion in Salpoora in the extreme West was soon extinguished. The disturbances in Budukshan in the North were speedily suppressed. *Nowhere has intrigue or rebellion been able to make head in the Ameer's dominions.* Even the Char Eimak and the Hazara tribes are learning to appreciate the advantages of a firm rule. . . . But what we wish specially to repeat is that, from the date of the Umballa Durbar to the present time, *the Ameer has unreservedly accepted and acted upon our advice to maintain a peaceful attitude towards his neighbours.* We have no reason to believe that his views are changed.

This "strong, friendly, and independent Power"—this edifice of order and increasing stability—the British Government deliberately destroyed in the insane expectation of finding a "Scientific Frontier" hidden somewhere in the ruins. It is difficult to conceive of an action more impolitic or more cruel. In a month the labours of forty years were obliterated, old hatreds rekindled, and the wounds of 1838, which the wise and gentle treatment of former Viceroys had almost healed, were opened afresh.

We come next to the inquiry as to what this "Scientific Frontier" is, in order to obtain which this act of vandalism was perpetrated. This is a question involved in some obscurity. The *Times* is the great champion of the "Scientific Frontier," but in its columns, as also in Ministerial speeches, it changes colour like a chameleon. Sometimes it is called the "possession of the three highways leading to India," thereby rendering the Empire "invulnerable." At other times it is recommended to us because it protects the trade through the Bolan Pass, and enables us to threaten Kabul. The fact is that the (so-called) "Scientific Frontier"—meaning thereby the frontier we acquired by the Treaty of Gundamuck—is a make-believe, an imposture. It is not the "Scientific Frontier" in pursuit of which we "hunted the Ameer to death" and reduced his territories to a condition of anarchy.

Those who have followed the history of the war

with attention will remember that in September of last year the Calcutta correspondent of the *Times* was smitten with a really marvellous admiration for Lord Lytton. "India," he wrote, "is fortunate in the possession at the present time of a Viceroy specially gifted with broad statesmanlike views, the result partly of most vigilant and profound study, partly of the application of great natural intellectual capacity to the close cultivation of political science and the highest order of statecraft." Here we have the portrait of the lion painted by himself; and it is not surprising that this superb creature should have regarded with considerable scorn the policy of his predecessors who never claimed to be "specially gifted" for the exercise of "the highest order of statecraft." "The present measure," the correspondent went on to say, "for the despatch of a mission to Kabul forms but a single move in an extensive concerted scheme for the protection of India, which is the outcome of a long-devised and elaborately worked-out system of defensive policy." Here we have a fine example of the "puff preliminary." In the issue of the *Times* for the 10th September this "extensive concerted scheme for the protection of India" is detailed at length, and is there plainly set forth as intended for a barrier against Russia:—

> The Indian Government are most anxious to avoid adopting any policy which would bear even the semblance of hostility towards Russia, but the extreme probability of a collision sooner or later cannot be overlooked. It is necessary, therefore, to provide for a strong defensive position to guard against eventualities. From this point of view it is indispensable that we should possess a commanding influence over the triangle of territory formed on the map by Kabul, Ghuznee, and Jellalabad, together with power over the Hindoo Khosh. . . . This triangle we may hope to command with Afghan concurrence if the Ameer is friendly. The strongest frontier line which could be adopted would be along the Hindoo Khosh, from Pamir to Bamian, thence to the south by the Helmund, Girishk, and Kandahar, to the Arabian Sea. It is possible, therefore, that by friendly negotiations some such defensive boundary may be adopted.

Such were the moderate designs entertained by the Indian Government when they dispatched what they called a "friendly mission" to the Court of the Ameer. If Lord Lytton imagined that "friendly negotiations" would obtain these tremendous concessions from the Ameer, it would show that a training in "the highest order of statecraft" does not preserve even a "specially gifted" Viceroy from the credulousness of an infant. But his acts show that he entertained no such belief. He felt, as every one must feel who reads the extract I have made, that demands such as these must be preceded by a war. Hence the menacing letters addressed to the Ameer; hence the rude and insulting manner in which Sir Neville Chamberlain was ordered to attempt an entrance into Afghanistan without awaiting the permission of the Ameer; and hence, finally, the monstrous fiction of a deliberate "insult" inflicted upon us, when, in point of fact, we had been the "insulters" all along. The obvious intention throughout was to obtain a pretext for declaring war, because without a war the "Scientific Frontier" was manifestly unattainable. Lastly, when war had been determined upon, the same "official" correspondent came forward in the *Times* to make known the objects of the impending campaign. "We have," he wrote, "been driven into what will probably be a costly war entirely against our will, and all our endeavours to avoid it. The occasion, therefore, will now be seized to secure for ourselves the various passes piercing the mountain ranges along the whole frontier from the Khyber to the Bolan; and further *strategic measures will be adopted to dominate entirely the Suleiman range and the Hindoo Khosh.*"

It is impossible not to admire the hardihood of this remarkable correspondent when he alleges that the war was "entirely against our will, and all our endeavours to avoid it." But this is not the matter with which I am at present concerned. The official character of these communications will be denied by no one, and they make it clear that the "Scientific Frontier" was intended as a barrier against Russia, and would have made the Hindoo Khosh the external boundary of the Indian Empire. Such a frontier is manifestly the dream of a military specialist, to whose mental vision the Indian Empire, with all its diverse interests, has no existence except as a frontier to be defended against the Russians. And it illustrates the ignorance and precipitate folly which has plunged us in our present difficulties that a project so wild should have been seriously entertained. To have carried it out the subjugation of Afghanistan would have been an indispensable preliminary, and then the civilizing of it, by means of a system of roads and strong garrisons throughout the country; the entire cost of these vast operations being defrayed by a country already taxed to the last point of endurance, heavily burdened with an increasing debt, and ravaged by periodical famines. Such, however, was the "Scientific Frontier" for which a "specially gifted Viceroy," trained in "the highest order of political statecraft," declared war against the Ameer. But the frontier which we obtained at the close of the war, and which Ministers and Ministerial journals would have us believe is the genuine article which they wanted from the beginning, is not only not this frontier, but it has not the smallest resemblance to it.

The new frontier does not differ from the old except in three particulars. We hold the Khyber Pass as far as Lundi Kotal, and we have acquired the right to quarter troops in the Kurram Valley and the Valley of Peshin. Of these the Kurram Valley is a mere cul-de-sac, leading nowhere. But I will not ask of my readers to accept of my judgment on this matter. Among the best known advocates for a forward and aggressive policy in Afghanistan is Dr. Bellew. An accomplished linguist and an experienced traveller, he accompanied Colonel Lumsden's mission to Kandahar in 1857; he was also a member of the mission entrusted with the settlement of the Seistan boundary question, and no man living is better acquainted with the geography and people of Afghanistan. I believe it will not be denied that Lord Lytton, during the recent war, trusted largely in his knowledge and suggestions. He has thus expressed himself on the policy of occupying the Kurram Valley:—

The Kurram Valley would involve the addition of about one hundred and fifty miles of hill frontage to our border, and would bring us into contact with the independent Orakzais, Zaimukhts, Toris, Cabul-Khel, Waziris, and others, against whose hostility and inroads here, as in other parts of the border, we should have to protect our territory. By its possession, as we are now situated, we should be committed to the defence of a long narrow strip of land, a perfect cul-de-sac in the hills, hemmed in by a number of turbulent robber-tribes, who are under no control, and acknowledge no authority. In ordinary times its acquisition would add to the serious difficulties of our position. In times of trouble or disturbance on the border, its possession would prove a positive source of weakness, a dead weight upon our free action. In it we should run the risk of being hemmed in by our foes in the overhanging hills around, of being cut off from our communications with the garrison of Kohat, by the Orakzais on the one side, by the Waziris on the other. These are the disadvantages of the step. In return what advantages should we derive? Not one. With Kurram in our possession we certainly could not flank either the Khyber or the Goleri Pass, because between it and the one, intervenes the impassable snowy range of Sufed Koh; and between it and the other, intervenes the vast routeless hilly tract of the Waziris. From Kurram we could neither command Kabul nor Ghazni, because the route to either is by a several days' march, over stupendous hills and tortuous defiles, in comparison with which the historical Khyber and Bolan Passes, or even the less widely-known Goleri Pass, are as king's highways.

This, I think, is sufficient to dispose of the Kurram Valley. If the old frontier has been rendered "invulnerable," it is not the acquisition of the Kurram Valley which has made it so. There remains the Peshin Valley. This valley is an open tract of country lying almost midway on the line of march between Quetta and Kandahar, but nearer to the former than the latter. Three easy marches from Quetta suffice to place a traveller in the centre of it. It cannot accurately be described as an extension of our frontier, because it is dissevered from it by more than two hundred miles of difficult country. Between the valley and British territory, the lands of the Khan of Khelat are interposed in one direction, and numerous robber-tribes—Kakers, Murrees, Bhoogtees—in another. Until the valley is securely linked to the Indus by a railway from Sukkur to the Bolan Pass—a costly work, which could not be executed in less than seven years—it will be impossible to quarter more than a few thousand men in it—and these for six months of the year will be as completely detached from their base of supply and reinforcement in India, as if a tract of empty space ran between them. So far from ensuring any increased security to India by our premature occupation of this valley, we have only enhanced the chances of a hostile collision with the rulers and people of Afghanistan. We were already in military occupation of Quetta, and until easy and rapid communication had been established between Quetta and the Indus, nothing was to be gained by a yet further advance from our base. As a barrier against Russia this frontier is without meaning, and no better proof of this fact could be adduced than Sir Henry Rawlinson's commentary upon its merits in the Article on the "Results of the Afghan War" which recently appeared in the *Nineteenth Century*:—

> The Afghan settlement is a very good settlement as far as it goes, but it is not immaculate—*it is not complete.* To yield us its full measure of defence, the Treaty must be supplemented by all legitimate precautions and supports. *Persia must be detached from Russia coûte que coûte.* Russia herself must not be left in any uncertainty as to our intentions. She must be made to understand . . . . *that she will not be permitted unopposed to establish herself in strength . . . . even at Abiverd*, nor to commence intrigues against the British power in India. She

might indeed be warned that, if necessary, we were prepared in self-defence to support the Turcomans—with whom she has no legitimate quarrel—with arms or money, or even to turn the tables on her by encouraging the efforts of the Uzbegs to recover their liberty . . . . *It would be almost fatuity at such a moment to withdraw our garrison from Candahar. . . . .* Yacub Khan must be made to see that it is as much for his interest as our own to hold an efficient body of troops in such a position that, on the approach of danger . . . . *they might, with military alacrity, occupy Herat as an auxiliary garrison.*

And what is implied in detaching Persia from Russia he explains in another part of his Essay.

> If Russia, as there is strong reason to believe, is now pushing on to Merv or Sarakhs . . . . with the ultimate hope of occupying Herat, then it might very possibly be a sound policy to extend to Persia the provisions of the Asia Minor Protectorate, or even to support her actively in vindicating her rights upon the frontier of Khorassán.

From all which it would appear that our "Scientific Frontier" is simply good for nothing until it has been supplemented by an offensive and defensive alliance with the barbarian enemies of Russia all over the world. In order to ensure the safety of India, we must protect not only our own "Scientific Frontier," but we must guarantee the Sultan all his Asiatic possessions; we must be ready at any moment to fight for the "integrity and independence" of Persia; we must be prepared to march our troops to Herat, and to show a front against the Russians on the Oxus; we must provide the Tekeh-Turcomans with arms and money, and assist the Uzbegs in their attempts to recover their liberty. Such are the "legitimate precautions and supports" which are requisite to render the new frontier immaculate and complete. But if with a "Scientific Frontier" we remain liable to such tremendous demands as these, it passes imagination to conjecture in what respect we could have been worse off when our frontier was "haphazard."

THE CIRCUMSTANCES OF THE PEACE.

I shall next endeavour to show the circumstances which compelled the Indian Government to acquiesce in a peace which thus left the avowed object of the war unfulfilled. The preparations for the invasion of Afghanistan were on a scale corresponding to the magnitude of the enterprise as explained by the "official" correspondent of the *Times*. Troops were set in motion for the North-West frontier from garrisons in the extreme south of India. Men were sent from England to man heavy gun batteries. In addition to the troops under General Roberts, no less than three columns were formed to invade Afghanistan via Sukkur and the Bolan, and the same number to advance through the Khyber. The force which marched to Kandahar was supplied with four heavy gun batteries, and a fifth was sent up subsequently, although, except upon the supposition that permanent entrenched camps were to be formed in Afghanistan, these heavy guns were simply an encumbrance and a source of danger. But the campaign had barely commenced before the Government became aware that it had utterly miscalculated its cost and difficulty. It is easy enough for an army to enter Afghanistan; it is next to impossible for it to subsist when it has got there. It is easy enough to scatter the Afghans when collected in battle array; it is next to impossible to subjugate them because they never are *so* collected. From these causes our raid into Afghanistan was but little removed from an ignominious failure. If we had not made peace we should have been compelled to evacuate the country from the enormous costliness of retaining troops in it. Under such circumstances, a peace was needed too urgently to allow the Government to stand out for any extraordinary concessions. They took what they could get, which proved to be, as we have seen, the right to place garrisons in the two valleys of Kurram and Peshin. But having gone to war in search of a "Scientific Frontier," no alternative was left to them

except to frankly confess that they had not found it; or to affirm that these two valleys constituted it.

We come now to the causes of our failure. These are all-important, and ought to dissipate for ever the fear of an invasion of India by Russia or any other Power. The plan of the campaign required that Afghanistan should be invaded from three points; but the most important operation was understood to be the advance of General Stewart upon Kandahar. As soon as hostilities appeared inevitable, a small force under General Biddulph had been sent forward to secure Quetta against a sudden attack. General Stewart followed later on, and the two columns numbered upon paper about 20,000 men, with 60 guns. Meanwhile, a third column was ordered to assemble at Sukkur in support, and placed under the command of General Primrose. These extensive preparations were supposed to indicate the determination of the Indian Government to push on as far as Herat. The distance which had to be traversed between Sukkur and Kandahar is, roughly speaking, about four hundred miles, but the country presents extraordinary difficulties. From Sukkur to Jacobabad extends a level tract which, during the rains, is flooded to a depth of seven feet. Between Jacobabad and Dadur—a town situated at the entrance of the Bolan Pass—extends the Sinde desert. Any large force marching across this desert would have to take with them, not only food and forage, but water, for only at intervals of fifteen or twenty miles is the parched and barren soil pierced by a few brackish springs, which just suffice for the needs of the hamlets which have sprung up around them. For six months of the year this desert is literally impassable. A hot wind sweeps across it, which is fatal to man and beast. Only once did the Indian Government venture to send troops across it after this "blast of death" (as the natives call it) had begun to blow. This was in the last Afghan war. Some hundreds of native troops were sent as an escort in charge of supplies, and in four days one hundred Sepoys perished, three hundred camp followers, and (I think) nine officers out of fourteen. Beyond Dadur is the Bolan Pass. This Pass is about eighty miles in length; regular road there is none; what purports to be a road is merely the bed of a stream, which, during the rainy weather, is filled from bank to bank with a volume of rushing water. Neither food nor forage is obtainable in the Pass, and even the camels, when starting from Dadur, had to carry a seven days' supply of food for themselves. Between Quetta and Kandahar the country is open, but neither is food procurable for a large force, nor forage for the horses and camels. From first to last General Stewart's troops were almost wholly fed from India. The winter, luckily, was one of unprecedented mildness. But for this, in place of a march upon Kandahar, a terrible catastrophe could hardly have been averted. In ordinary seasons the snows fall heavily in and around Quetta early in November, and the cold is intense. The Bolan Pass is swept from end to end by hurricanes of wind and rain and snow. At the very time when these storms usually occur we had a dozen regiments and batteries straggling along the whole length of the Bolan Pass. Last year, however, there was neither snow nor hurricane, and our troops got through the Pass in safety. There was no opposition offered to our advance on Kandahar, but, from the want of food and the hardships which had to be endured, no less than twenty thousand camels perished upon the march. This mortality decided the campaign. When General Stewart reached Kandahar the situation was as follows:—The magazines at Quetta were nearly empty. Four months' food was collected at Sukkur, but awaited carriage for its transport to Quetta. The third column under General Primrose was assembling on the Indus, and needed ten thousand camels to enable it to advance. To supply all these wants there were at Sukkur about 1600 camels. In order to lessen the pressure on the Commissariat, General Stewart divided his forces, despatching one column to hunt for supplies in the direction of Giriskh, and sending another with the same object to Khelat-i-Ghilzic. These movements caused the death from cold and hunger of a large additional number of camels, and demonstrated that there was not food in that part of Afghanistan sufficient for a force so large as that collected at Kandahar. Sinde, meanwhile, had been swept so bare of camels that it was impossible to collect a sufficient number for the carriage of food to Quetta before the hot weather had set in, and the march across the desert was barred by "the blast of death." Immediate action was necessary if General Stewart's troops were not to starve; and eight thousand men returned to India, reducing the garrison left at Kandahar to four thousand. This number, it was trusted, the Commissariat would be able to feed during the hot weather. But even this small force was so scantily supplied with carriage that it could not have moved, in a body, for fifty miles in any direction. It was, so to speak, nailed to the spot on which it was encamped. This want of food, far more than the physical difficulties of the country, is and always will be the insuperable obstacle to carrying on extensive military operations in Afghanistan. The people obtain no more from the soil than just suffices for their own wants; and for days together an invading army has to pass over huge wastes with hardly a trace of human habitation, and consequently destitute of food.

Not a little amusing was the revulsion of feeling caused throughout India by the lame and impotent conclusion of the advance on Kandahar. It was a demonstration of the impossibility of an invasion which convinced those who were most reluctant to be convinced. If when we had all India from which to draw our supplies, and with no enemy to oppose us, our utmost efforts had merely sufficed to place four thousand men in Kandahar, and leave them there, isolated and defenceless, it was chimerical to suppose that the Russians could march for double that distance an army capable of attempting the conquest of India. "Kandahar," writes a military correspondent to the *Pioneer*—the official journal of India—"is acknowledged to be a mistake, and it is hoped that a British army will never again be dispatched in that direction; it is a mere waste of men, money, and means, and an unsuitable line for either attack or defence."

And the *Pioneer*, the very purpose of whose existence is to preach the infallibility of the Indian Government, thus endorses the remarks of its correspondent: "The theories about Kandahar are by this time exploded; indeed, there are many critics who have refused to adopt them from the very beginning; believing against General Hamley, that the main road into Afghanistan, whether we march as defenders of the Kabul Ameer or as avengers, must lie past Peshawur and Jelalabad."

The failure on the Kandahar side placed the Indian Government in an extremely difficult position. An advance on Herat was plainly out of the question; even one on Ghuznee was beyond the power of General Stewart and his troops. Elsewhere the aspect of affairs was hardly less cheering. The expedition in the Kurram Valley had resulted in the somewhat ignominious retreat out of Khost. We had about 15,000 men holding the line from the Khyber to Jelalabad; but in effecting this, 14,000 camels had perished, and several of the regiments had been more than decimated from sickness and exposure. We had not subjugated a rood of territory on which our troops were not actually encamped. The main strength of the Ameer's army was untouched, while all along our Trans-Indus frontier the hill tribes were in a state of dangerous unrest. The hot weather was coming on apace, when cholera and typhoid fever would be added to the number of our enemies. Thirty thousand troops had been set in motion, the garrisons in the interior of India dangerously weakened; three millions of money expended; and this was all that had been achieved. If now Yakoub Khan refused to come to terms, what was to be done? General Brown might be ordered to force his way from Jelalabad to Kabul, but what was he to do when he got there? The cost in money would be certainly heavy—the cost in men, not improbably, heavy also. And if, on our arrival at his capital, Yakoub Khan retired to either Balkh or Herat, we were powerless to follow him. Yakoub Khan, in fact, had the game in his hands. We had shot our bolt and failed. He had simply to decline to make peace, and keep out of our reach. We should then have been compelled either to evacuate the country, or to occupy it with the certainty that a little later on we should be compelled to withdraw, when the drain on the finances of India became too heavy to endure. Sir Henry Rawlinson rightly says, that a very small force can march from one end of Afghanistan to another; but a very large force is requisite permanently to hold it. The tribal divisions which hinder unity of resistance hinder also the achievement of any decisive victory. Each tribe is an independent centre of life, which requires a separate operation for its extinction.

Such was the dilemma in which the Government found themselves involved. It was almost equally disastrous either to withdraw or to advance. If the troops were withdrawn, they would return burdened with the ignominy of failure. If they advanced, it would be into a tangle of military and political embarrassments, the issue of which it was impossible to foresee. There was only one way of escape possible, and that was to relinquish the ambitious projects from which the war originated, and acquiesce in any settlement which the adversary would agree to. The result was the Treaty with Yakoub Khan—a Treaty which I have no hesitation in saying has placed in peril the existence of our Indian Empire.

It is, indeed, impossible to account for the infatuation or the obstinacy which caused the Indian Government to stipulate for the reception of an undefended British Envoy at the Court of a prince in the position of Yakoub Khan. It would have been so easy to have introduced a clause in the Treaty, to the effect that as soon as Yakoub Khan's authority was firmly established an English

Envoy should be accredited to Kabul. This would have saved the political consistency of the Government without exposing the Indian Empire to the tremendous strain and peril of a second Afghan expedition. There was absolutely nothing to be gained, either in India or England, by immediately forcing an English Envoy on the luckless Yakoub; while it enormously enhanced the difficulties with which he had to cope. Nevertheless, in the face of historic precedents, in defiance of multiplied warnings, Lord Lytton deliberately resolved to reproduce, for the edification of Asia, the tragedy of Shah Soojah and Sir William Macnaghten, the only difference being that on this occasion the principal parts were played by Yakoub Khan and Major Cavagnari. The fact is that from first to last in this bad business the chief agents were moving in a world of their own imagining. They appear to have persuaded themselves that they had but to refuse to *see* facts, and the facts would vanish, They had but to publish in the *Times* that Lord Lytton was a "Viceroy specially gifted," and forthwith he would become what he was described to be. They had but to assert that the Afghans had no objection to the presence of a British Envoy at Kabul, and immediately their objections would disappear. The mischief is done now past recall. Hardly even in 1857 was our Indian Empire in a position of greater peril than it is now. The persistent opposition between official acts and official language which has been the distinguishing characteristic of Lord Lytton's administration has created an universal disbelief in the sincerity of our speech and the equity of our intentions. In the circle which surrounds the Viceroy, it seems, indeed, to have become an accepted maxim that it is a matter of indifference whether or not the natives are heartily loyal to our rule. And Sir Alexander Arbuthnot, in his Minute on the Repeal of the Cotton Duties, notes the fact as "a grave political danger." It is a maxim which could not have been formulated except by the agents of a Government who felt that they had

forfeited, past hope of recovery, the confidence of those they were set to rule over. Of the alienation itself there can be no question. The loyalty of the native has, probably, never been at a lower ebb since 1857. And any reverse in Afghanistan might kindle a flame that would spread from one end of India to the other.

But there is nothing to be gained by anticipating greater difficulties than already beset us. I will assume that no additional complications occur—that General Roberts has succeeded without much difficulty in the occupation of Kabul—that General Stewart has possession of Kandahar, and that all we have to determine is what to do with Afghanistan now we have got it. There are but three courses of conduct possible—withdrawal from the country altogether, a return to the arrangements formulated in the Treaty of Gundamuck, or annexation. I will consider the last first.

The danger to India arises not from the existence of any Russian designs against our Empire, but from the belief that such exist. This belief will, so to speak, hybernate for a season; then all at once we find it in full activity, and creating a panic in every heart of which it takes possession. These are the critical moments for the well-being and security of our Indian Empire. In such a period of panic we rushed into the disastrous war in Afghanistan in 1838. Under the influence of like feelings we involved ourselves in the inglorious raid the first act of which has just terminated. On both occasions we have been guilty of assailing a Prince whose only desire was to form an intimate alliance with us. On both occasions we have carried fire and sword among a people with whom we frankly avowed that we had no assignable cause of quarrel. But so long as Afghanistan extended between us and the Russian dominions in Asia it was physically impossible to declare war against Russia. In our unreasoning panic we fell upon the Ameer and his people, because there was no one else to attack. But if we make the Hindoo Khosh our military frontier, then Russia, by assembling a few thousand men upon the Oxus, can, whenever she pleases, agitate India from one end to the other. She will not need to attack. The menace will be sufficient. For we must remember that the undisputed supremacy of British rule in India depends, in the main, upon two conditions, both of which are destroyed if we annex Afghanistan. The one is, that no heavier burden be laid upon the people than they are willing to bear; and the other, the absence of any hope of deliverance. The cost of maintaining our supremacy in Afghanistan *will* make the burden of our rule utterly intolerable alike to our native soldiers and our civil population; the assembling of a Russian army on the frontiers of Afghanistan will provide the hope of deliverance. The hazards and uncertainties of the situation would keep the natives in a state of perpetual unrest. The ambitious and the disaffected would engage in intrigue and conspiracy; trade would languish; the internal development of the country be abruptly arrested; and the Empire would assuredly be wrested from our hands on the occasion of the first European war in which we became involved.

THE TREATY OF GUNDAMUCK.

Annexation being impossible, is it wise, or is it practicable, to return to the provisions of the Treaty of Gundamuck? It is neither wise nor possible, for the simple reason that this Treaty was based upon a fiction. It was grounded upon the utterly false assumption that there existed in Afghanistan a central authority, acknowledged as legitimate by all the people of Afghanistan, with whom we could establish permanent diplomatic relations. There is no such authority. Instances have been adduced of attacks made upon European Embassies in other Oriental countries, and the argument has been put forward, that as, notwithstanding such outbreaks, diplomatic relations have been maintained with Turkey and Persia, there is

no reason to conclude from the fate of Major Cavagnari that they are impossible in Afghanistan. The cases are not parallel. The Ameer of Kabul has no such authority in his capital or throughout his dominions as the Sultan or the Shah. It is possible, though not very probable, that a British Envoy might reside in Kabul without being murdered, but the measure of his utility would depend upon the fluctuating fortunes of the Ameer to whom he was accredited. The only way to obviate this would be to place a force at the disposal of the Envoy, sufficient to put down all insurrectionary movements against the Ameer. But if we undertook this duty, we should become responsible for the character of the civil administration. We could not punish the victims of a cruel or rapacious Ameer, without at the same time cutting off at their source the cruelty and rapacity, by the deposition of an unworthy ruler. And thus, in a very brief time, we should find that virtually we had annexed the country. Facts are stubborn things, and it is worse than useless to fight against them. Those who contend that the murder of Major Cavagnari ought not to be allowed to overturn what they term the "settled policy" of the Ministry, are bound to show in what way this "settled policy" can be carried out. How do they propose to obtain an Ameer towards whom all the sections of the Afghans shall practise a loyal obedience? And if no such Ameer can be obtained, with whom or with what are we to establish diplomatic relations?

THE POLICY OF WITHDRAWAL.

There remains the policy of withdrawal. The surest barrier against foreign aggression in India is to be obtained in the contentment and prosperity of the people. A people thus situated are prompt to repel invasion, and secret intrigue is deprived of the conditions essential to its success. But in order that the people of India should be prosperous and contented, it is absolutely necessary that the financial burdens they have to carry—and especially the military charges—should not be enhanced. It is not possible to advance our military frontier—even to the extent of the (so-called) "Scientific Frontier"—without an enormous enhancement of our military expenditure. And all military expenditure is unprofitable, in the sense that it takes so much from the tax-payer and brings him no material equivalent. Consequently, whatever else this forward policy accomplishes, it cannot fail to impoverish the people and stimulate their discontent. Moreover, the incidents of the war have demonstrated that an invasion of India from Central Asia is physically impossible. We started from the Indus, firmly resolved to march to Herat, if necessary; but when we had reached Kandahar, we found it impossible to advance further. It would be equally impossible for a Russian army to march from Herat to the Indus. There is, therefore, no such reason for a change of frontier as was alleged in justification of the war.

In all probability there is not even a Tory in England who does not in his heart approve of a policy of withdrawal; but there are, he would say, difficulties in the way. There are. After all the glowing eulogies they have pronounced upon themselves, it will not be pleasant or easy for Ministers to transfer these eulogies to their opponents. It will be extremely disagreeable for a "specially gifted Viceroy" to have to confess that his chiefest gift was a gigantic capacity for blundering. But if India is to be preserved to the nation, there is no escape from this unpleasant alternative. Either Ministers must acknowledge an error that is now patent to all the world, or India must be saddled with the heavy costs and the incalculable risks of an annexation of Afghanistan. These risks, it must be remembered, are not transitory, but enduring; and if we accept them, we must be prepared for a doom of absolute effacement in the politics of Europe. The argument which will be urged against withdrawing from Afghanistan is, of course, the old familiar one—the loss of prestige. This is an argument impossible to refute because the exact worth of prestige is an unknown quantity, as to which no two people are agreed. But whatever be its value, to rush upon ruin and destruction in order to preserve our prestige is an act of insanity. It is as if a man should commit suicide in order to preserve his reputation for courage. When we retired from Afghanistan in 1842, we frankly confessed the mistake we had committed, and I am not aware that any evil resulted from the confession. The wrongs that we had done left behind them a legacy of evil, but not the confession of those wrongs. And so it is now. The frontier policy of Lord Lytton has ruined our reputation for justice, truthfulness, and generosity, and the stain of that policy must cling to us for ever. We shall not conceal or efface it by laying a crushing burden upon our native subjects and upon future generations of Englishmen, in order to evade the humiliation of a confession. On the contrary, we make what reparation is still in our power when, in the interests of both, we refuse to annex Afghanistan.

ROBERT D. OSBORN,
LIEUTENANT-COLONEL.

16 / From the *Spectator*

"The Magnitude of the Afghan War," "The Disaster in Candahar," "Abdurrahman Khan," "The First Lesson of Candahar," "The Rumour from Cabul," and "The Death of Abdurrahman Khan"

The *Spectator*, which has been in continuous publication since 1828, was owned by a journalist, Meredith Townsend, and was one of the most important organs of the nineteenth-century periodical press—not least because then, as now, it rarely eschewed controversy, taking up the most contentious issues of the day. In this series of editorials and commentaries published in the *Spectator* during the last year of the Second Anglo-Afghan War, we get a sense of how events unfolded for readers in the metropole in real time. The fits and starts of battle, the skirmishes and reverses and minor triumphs, and the figure of Abdur Rahman Khan (ca. 1840–1901) are all in evidence, as is the expectation that under General Roberts, the city of Candahar should have been taken with greater dispatch. Down to the Abdur Rahman's death in 1901, his value as an ally and a ruler was an issue, as was the question of what kind of disorder might follow the demise of such an awesome central Asian strongman.

THE MAGNITUDE OF THE AFGHAN WAR

We wish to bring strongly before the public a fact in connection with the Afghan War which demands the closest attention of the country, and which neither party will, we believe, attempt to deny on any party ground. This is the magnitude of the operations, which has not yet been sufficiently realised. Modern Indian wars, those beyond the frontier excepted, notwithstanding a general impression to the contrary, have hitherto been usually short. The first Sikh war lasted only a few months, the second Sikh war was over within the year, the conquest of Pegu was substantially effected in a few weeks, and the last Persian war could almost be computed in days. Even the great war with the Mutineers only lasted two years. This Afghan affair has already involved two campaigns, separated only by a few weeks of nominal truce; and a third is to begin in the spring, while the force involved is perpetually growing larger. The officials in India state as little as they can, and we do not pretend to know the secrets of the Cabinet, which possibly may be rather dragged than leading in the matter; but every account from the spot represents a third campaign as already resolved upon. General Roberts, besides holding Cabul, making his long communications with India safe, and clearing the hill country round him, which is swarming with possible enemies, is to attack and capture Ghazni, a fortress which is the last stronghold of the Afghans in the south, and may be tenaciously defended—we do not say it will be, for we will not again assume that Afghans will act like other soldiers and if defended will require a heavy siege train for its reduction. He must also either simultaneously or subsequently ensure the obedience of Bamian. At the same time, Sir Donald Stewart, with or without Persian auxiliaries, is to occupy Herat, a fortress unusually strong for Asia, as Eldred Pottinger's defence of it showed, held by some 10,000 Afghan troops, and likely to be protected by any force that Abdurrahman Khan, the heir of Dost Mahommed, may succeed in getting together in the country round Balkh. We, of course, vouch for none of these statements as to coming operations, but they are repeated on the spot in every variety of form, and are supported by the facts officially acknowledged, that a strong reserve division is being formed at Peshawar; that the gaps in General Roberts's and General Bright's columns are being supplied; that a corps of observation is being pushed forward from Candahar to Girishk, obviously to command the crossing of the Helmund; and that another strong brigade has been dispatched from Bombay, where troops are not just now too plentiful. If these accounts are correct and these designs are entertained, the subjugation of Afghanistan is to be continued, and the forces employed across the Indus cannot be reduced. Lord Lytton himself, in a formal proclamation to the people of India, estimated the strength of these forces at 42,000 men of all arms, and though he had an interest in quoting the paper strength rather than the real strength, still, a reserve division and a new brigade have been added, and Sir F. Haines will have had three months in which to push up recruits and absentees. Heavy drafts of men leave England by every steamer, and all officers on leave serving with regiments beyond the Indus have been ordered to rejoin. It is the duty of the Indian Government to see that its forces in front are strengthened to the utmost limit that transport and commissariat difficulties will allow, and we do not suppose the military departments, badly as we think of their policy and their judgment, have lost all military traditions. We are, therefore, justified in believing ourselves well within the truth when we say that it is intended this spring to employ a well-appointed army of 45,000 men in reducing Afghanistan, in garrisoning its fortresses, and in maintaining its communications intact through an unusually difficult and dangerous hill country, pierced by few passes, and occupied by tribes who, on the best official evidence, dispose of 100,000 fighting men.

We have not, we think, said a word which our most bitter opponents will deny, and need not say that we have no objection to raise to the magnitude of the force. If the work is to be done at all, there will not be a man too many. Indeed we should greatly prefer to see a further reserve of 5,000 Europeans stationed along the railway line between Allahabad and Rawal Pindee, and kept ready for an instant advance. Lord Lawrence held that the work would occupy 30,000 Europeans, and we have as yet only 14,000 Europeans actually on the ground, even if "the ground" is held to include the whole region between the Indus and the Helmund. But we wish our readers to see that we are not engaged in trifling operations or movements of routine, but are employing an army large even for Indian precedent, larger than we ever sent to the Crimea, larger than any force we could land in any part of Europe, upon a task which natural difficulties, the hostility of the people, and the immense extent of country to be traversed—Afghanistan is, according to the best authorities, as large as the German Empire—render one of formidable difficulty. There is every probability that with such a force the work will be done, but there is no probability that it will be done quickly or without heavy loss in officers, or that when done, a large reduction of the force can be safely accomplished at once. If Afghanistan is to be British in any sense, it must be garrisoned, and garrisoned in such force that local insurrections can be put down without separate expeditions from the Peninsula, which are too embarrassing to the Departments and to the general arrangements for the garrisoning of India, to be incessantly repeated.

We are, therefore, on the facts supposed, employing an unusually large army, on an unusually difficult task, for a period unusually ill-defined, but sure to be very considerable; and must, of course, while we are doing the work, keep the Army and its reserves thoroughly supplied with all the requisites of war, men specially included. Surely an enterprise of this magnitude should demand the close attention of Parliament, not only for its cost, which must be enormous, not only for its drain of men, which, the scale of our establishments being remembered, must be considerable, but for the kind of mortgage it places upon the energy both of India and the Empire. The enterprise involves for India the imprisonment of more than a fourth of her nominal strength and more than a third of her available strength, in a position where, unless the Generals retreat, they can be of no practical service within the Peninsula itself. That is to say, if any disturbance, say, in Hyderabad, threatened order in India, the Government would have only two-thirds of its regular strength available for its repression. In reality, it would have much less, for the Military Department, quite wisely, is using in Afghanistan only picked regiments, more especially in cavalry, and half of those which remain, deprived of their support and leadership, would be comparatively, if not positively, unserviceable. Even in the event of any European enterprise, which is quite possible if our friend the Turk continues so exceedingly refractory, the occupation of the Indian Army, in such a way that it could not endure withdrawals, and that no picked native regiments could be sent either into Egypt

or Asiatic Turkey, would be a very serious deduction from British strength, or be a serious addition to the exertions which the kingdom would be called upon to make. This is not a country which finds it easy to wage two wars at the same time, more especially when in one of them defeat cannot be risked, because it might involve a general insurrection. Of course, no embarrassing incident may occur, and if the conquest of Afghanistan is essential to our national existence the risk must be run but would it not be advisable to take some ordinary precautions, to add, for example, twenty thousand men to the strength of the Army? It is true, such an addition would be expensive, and would make fresh taxation necessary, and would make sensible Tories ask anxiously what we are doing with a great army up there in the clouds beyond the furthest boundaries of the Empire; but still, if the work is necessary, and can be proved to be necessary, and has become more necessary than ever since the Russians were defeated in the Turcoman desert—all of which things Tories are alleging every day—the consequent sacrifices should be made to secure the national safety and the prestige of the Imperial arms. The Government seems to shrink from the duty, but surely their shrinking can be only temporary? It is not to be conceived that this proud Ministry, which secured "peace with honour"—and Cyprus, which has redeemed the national position in the world—especially at Constantinople—and which has solidified an "emasculated Army" and a "phantom Fleet," shrinks, merely out of terror of an election, from measures indispensable to replace that proportion of its fighting strength new to be shut up in Central Asia. It should not so risk the future of the country and the Empire. If, however, Ministers should so risk it, if they should resolve that their dangerous wars should be cheap wars, if they should be more careful to appear to win glory easily than to strengthen the solid power of the country, would it not be advisable for sensible Tories to communicate to them the energy they lack, and inform them that the work to be done, being both noble and indispensable, the country will submit to any needful sacrifice of self? True, if that course were taken, the country would realise, as it has not realised, what was being done; and a few Tories or even, possibly, many Tories would lose their seats but what is that to Ministers who act so exclusively from a sense of duty, who go to war with such reluctance, but who, being in it, are determined so to wage it as to increase the glory of an ancient empire and an illustrious reign? We do not think that soldiers who understand the coming campaign doubt that the war will be a serious one, even though the fighting should not be heavy, and would ask sensible men of both parties whether it would not be wise to make a large and immediate addition to our strength. They may reply, indeed, in proportion to their ability they will reply, that the war is a perfectly needless waste of resources not at all too extensive for our duties, is at once a blunder and a crime; but they will be wandering from the point. The Tory assumption is that Afghanistan must be conquered, and that the Government is going to conquer it brilliantly, and with completeness. We accept that assumption, and ask only that, as in the conquest a large army will be locked up, the needful addition should be made to our muster roll of effectives. If that is not done, and anything goes wrong, the country will see that Ministers have been gambling with its soldiers and its treasure.

THE DISASTER IN CANDAHAR

Men reap what they have sown. The British have under taken no enterprise in Asia so unjustifiable as the second invasion of Afghanistan, and have suffered in none so much loss or such deep humiliation. We described the country a fortnight since as a morass, from which the Government must extricate itself; but we ought rather to have called it a quicksand from which extrication might prove impossible. Every step the nation takes to escape

seems to land its feet in a yet more tenacious sand. The first rush was no sooner over, and a semblance of peace secured by the extorted Treaty of Gundamuk, than the murder of the Resident compelled us to commence a second and far more extensive campaign. That was no sooner terminated, after a terrible expenditure both of money and lives, and a new Native Government acknowledged, and a withdrawal into India arranged, than a frightful disaster once more renders it imperative not only to stand fast, but to increase the already large army which is exhausting the resources of India in an admittedly sterile effort. Providence seems to mock at our efforts to undo the mischief we have wrought, and to insist that the nation, for once, shall see and hear the full consequences of its crime. There is even a kind of dramatic completeness in the method of our punishment. The nominal object of our invasion—in reality, a gross instance of buccaneering—was to force the Afghans to admit a British Resident in Cabul; and because we succeeded, because the Resident was at last accepted, we were dragged into a second war, employing sixty thousand men. We were still unwilling to retire without something to show for all the lives and money expended, and therefore kept Candahar in our own hands, or those of our vassal; and because we kept it, we have again to employ our whole strength to avenge a defeat which, unavenged, may turn the whole course of history. Not a man can quit Afghanistan until Ayoub Khan's army has been scattered, and it will be well if we have not Afghanistan to reconquer, in a campaign to which all that have preceded it will seem like trifles.

As we pointed out some time since, the formal announcement that the British had decided to dismember Afghanistan, and keep its richest province under their own control, exasperated the Army at Herat beyond endurance. The soldiery knew perfectly well that the Candaharees, apart from a few traders, desired no foreign rule; they held Shere Ali, the new Wali, to be either a traitor or a fool; they foresaw quite clearly that the British would never rest in Candahar, and they resolved not to surrender the old kingdom without a struggle. Whether they compelled Ayoub Khan to march, or whether that Prince, who, though indolent, has been trusted by his family with great commands, saw that his hour had come, is not yet known. At all events, he marched on Candahar, and with the results which he and his soldiery had at once foreseen. The force swelled at every step, the moment they reached the Helmund the Wali's army mutinied and joined them, and from every part of Afghanistan the fighting men gathered to Ayoub Khan, till the British Viceroy was informed and reported to London that Ayoub Khan had in a few days been joined by 4,000 "Ghazis," or fanatics, the nickname by which the English describe the picked irregulars of the nationalist party. Altogether he found himself in command of 12,000 men. On the 23rd inst. the main body crossed the river, and found before them a British Division of all arms, terribly attenuated in numbers, and supported only by a body of the Wali's cavalry, who may or may not have proved faithful, but who must have been constant objects of suspicion. So perversely confident were the Indian authorities in the "friendliness" of the Candaharees, who must necessarily like subjugation by men able to build railways, that even when Sir Donald Stewart had been despatched from Candahar to take Ghazni and strengthen the British in Cabul, the Reserve Division, organised in Bombay by Sir R. Temple's forethought, was not ordered to advance, and the province was left in charge of a garrison, we fear, less than 3,500 strong, with a most dangerously low proportion of European effectives. We do not believe that, allowing for the sick, there were 1,500 white men in all in Candahar; and when General Burrows advanced to the Helmund to meet Ayoub Khan, half of these must have been left in the city, which otherwise, although so "friendly," was certain to rise behind him. It is true, General Phayre, with his strong Reserve Division—still too weak in Europeans—was ordered forward as soon as Ayoub's intentions were known;

but he was stopped by the floods in the Bolan, and the unfortunate General in Candahar was compelled to meet the enemy, and hold down the city with a force hardly exceeding an ordinary brigade. Of course he did it, as he would have marched, being ordered, to Khiva, but he must have known from the moment the Wali's army revolted that his safety hung upon a single contingency. The Afghans might display the "cowardice" of which, whenever they decline fighting, they are accused, and then Ayoub Khan would be driven back across the Helmund, and his army would melt away, as such armies do, into the villages. On the other hand, the Afghans might fight as they fought Sir Donald Stewart outside Ghazni, charging right up to the General in command; and then, with such thin regiments and so few Europeans, there would be no hope. The die went against the British. Under that intermittent impulse, which the most experienced Generals can neither understand nor forecast, which perplexed our leaders forty years ago as it perplexes them now, the Afghans elected to fight, and the catastrophe reported to the House of Commons by Lord Hartington occurred. "General Burrows's Brigade was annihilated,"—or rather, as was subsequently ascertained, partly destroyed, partly driven in little parties back to Candahar. Whether the British were overwhelmed by a rush of numbers, whether the Wali's cavalry betrayed them, or whether they were surrounded, we do not know—we can be sure only that they fought well; in any case, they were crushed, only driblets escaping to warn General Primrose, who had been left in command at Candahar, of the great disaster. He withdrew his men at once into the citadel, where he will most likely be surrounded by Ayoub Khan's army and the fighting toughs of Candahar, and where he must remain until General Phayre, with the Reserve Division, can relieve him, or until—if that be necessary—General Donald Stewart, renouncing the idea of withdrawal by the Khyber and the Shuturgardan, fights his way back past Ghazni once more to Candahar. Fortunately, he is one of the most experienced and able, as well as one of the most daring of British officers, and will do all that can be done; but for many days, perhaps weeks, the British people must be divided between pity for the fallen, and suspense as to, the fate of those who survive, and who, while they survive, uphold the Flag in Candahar. General Primrose appears to be confident that he can hold his citadel till October, unless the water gives out—a very serious doubt to throw out—and it is possible that if General Phayre can be reinforced in time by even one regiment of Europeans, he may force his way rapidly through Ayoub Khan's army, swelled, as it will be, by victory, and the junction of the tribes round Pisheen. The time of captivity of the 2,000 men in the Citadel may otherwise be long. The season is too early for forced marches, the transport for Candahar is insufficient, and it may well be weeks before General Phayre's command, should it prove insufficient, can be swollen into an army.

It is easy to exaggerate, but it is useless to conceal the seriousness of the situation. The Afghans, for the first time in their history, have defeated us, not after a capitulation or by treachery, but in the field. They will not consider this disparity of numbers, or any other circumstance, except this, that they have destroyed a British "army"—it was not a British army, but a Native brigade, with a handful of Europeans to assist it—which thought itself able to cope with them. The news will spread in a few days throughout Afghanistan, and in a few days every man of one of the vainest races in the world, as well as one of the bravest, will deem the Afghans the equals of the English. It is most fortunate that the new Ameer, Abdurrahman Khan, knows something of European politics, and much of the strength of the English, for his knowledge may induce him to remain faithful, and so, earn, once for all, the confidence of the great Southern Power upon which he must be in future dependent. But nothing will keep the Afghan soldiery from a victorious General's standard, and there is some fear of a popular movement in favour of the nation precipitating itself upon Sir Donald Stewart's force, and attempting to drive the detested white men beyond the Passes at once. That movement might not in itself be exceedingly formidable. The British in Afghanistan and the Passes are strong enough to meet any force the Afghans can collect; they are well commanded, and they may be able, while the enemy is so elated, to deliver a crushing blow. But it must not be forgotten that the British have been preparing for withdrawal; that their Cavalry has already started; that the Sepoy force, certain regiments, like the Guides, excepted, is neither in good heart nor in good health, and that the rising, if it occurs at all will be nearly universal. Such a movement is always most perplexing to a small army which suddenly finds itself in an enemy's country, unable to collect a ton of forage without a skirmish, or to rely on obtaining anything except from its own magazines and transport train, and possibly obliged to fight for every mile of its communications. Even should this calamity be spared us, and the Ameer, as is quite possible, feel more jealousy of Ayoub Khan than of the retreating British, the disaster still breaks up all arrangements, makes it impossible to retire without victory, and compels us, unless General Phayre is suddenly and strikingly successful, to fight a campaign beyond the Bolan, just when, after three years of harassing warfare, India was longing for and expecting peace. Lord Hartington had not announced the completion of arrangements for evacuating Afghanistan by seventy-two hours, when he was ordering reinforcements from England to meet a turn in Afghan affairs.

ABDURRAHMAN KHAN

The political sky grows brighter in Cabul, so much brighter as to throw out the blackness of the prospect in Candahar into painful relief. None of the details are as yet accurately known, but it is manifest from the result that Lord Ripon has been negotiating in Eastern Afghanistan with patience, skill, and success. He evidently decided that Abdurrahman Khan, as the only Pretender not involved in the late struggles, and popular in the provinces to which British influence does not reach, would be the preferable candidate for the vacant throne. As against any candidate except Yakoob Khan, he was obviously in the right, Moosa Khan being a mere child, and Hashim unpopular with Sirdars whose assistance is indispensable, and Yakoob himself was weighted by one heavy disability. Like most Afghans, he is vindictive; he is accused of having threatened Sirdars for whom the British extorted an amnesty, and he is suspected of harbouring hatreds which he would gratify at the earliest possible moment, to the discredit of British promises of protection. Abdurrahman, therefore, was preferred, and after tedious negotiations, which threatened at one time to break down in consequence of differences about Candahar, an agreement was arranged, and Abdurrahman was invited to visit Cabul as Ameer of Afghanistan. It remained, however, to secure to him a quiet occupation of the throne, at least for a period sufficient to enable the British army to retire, and this was effected with great skill. The hatred of the Afghans is towards the British as Europeans, Infidels, and invaders, rather than towards any special descendant of Dost Mahommed; and once aware that the British would retire if Abdurrahman were elected, the friends of Yakoob Khan unanimously accepted him. Mahmoud Jan, the soldier who reduced us to such straits in Sherpore, and who expected to be Regent under Moosa Khan; the Moullah Mooshki-Alam, the head of the fanatical party; and Asmutoollah Khan, the unsubdued chief of the Ghilzais, or second most powerful of the eastern clans, all agreed to the selection, threw over Yakoob Khan, and started to pay their devoirs to the new Ameer at Charikar, in Kohistan. With their defection Yakoob Khan's chance faded away, and even his moral claim, which, as against us, is irresistible, became, as against his cousin, materially

diminished, Abdurrahman, who is, be it remembered, the legitimate head of the dynasty, according to European, though not according to Asiatic ideas, having acquired a new title from what is virtually a popular election. Mahmoud Jan and the rest have steadily fought the British, and are not so far under their influence as to obey a Pretender they cordially dislike; while behind them stand all the more formidable fighting men, Ghilsais, Kohistanees, and Pathans of the Khyber. With such support and British favour, Abdurrahman can rule; and his public acknowledgment as Ameer, which took place on Thursday, was a wise act. All the accounts of his personal character yet received are favourable. He is described on all hands as a reasonable man with whom it is possible to do business, as acquainted with politics, and as free from personal rancours; while his past history shows him a good soldier, and his present enterprise a man both of courage and decision. He may rule Afghanistan fairly well, especially if he can organise a guard strong enough to resist attack from any single clan; and at all events, with his accession any excuse for stationing British troops in Eastern Afghanistan ends. Preparations are therefore making for departure. The sick have been sent home, the European cavalry are on their way, and all is reported ready for the stupid piece of vandalism, the blowing-up of the defences of the capital, with which it is our custom to ingratiate ourselves with the peoples we restore to freedom. The Army will, it is stated, have evacuated Afghanistan before September, to the immense relief of all who compose it; of the European privates, who are harassed and uncomfortable; of the Sepoys, who are discontented, almost to mutiny, and who suffer, through some unexplained cause, believed to be a peculiarity of climate, from morbid depression; and of the European officers, who, besides the annoyances incidental to any campaign, have to get through much inglorious work, and undergo the permanent risk of individual assassinations. It is not pleasant, even to the bravest officer, to know that of any three men he sees two would stab him if they get a chance; and one may make the attempt, chance or none.

The prospect of escaping from the Afghan imbroglio, and of confining the consequent waste of treasure to twenty millions, is, however, broken by the intelligence from Candahar. On Saturday a telegram was received in London which shows that if we are to remain there at all, we must completely garrison the country, for our friendship destroys any native ruler. Ayoub Khan, in advancing from Herat, did not depend upon his ability to defeat the Wali, Shere Ali, but on the reluctance of his opponent's troops to fight for the Infidels' nominee, and the result proved that he was right. The moment the Heratees arrived within striking distance of the Wali's force, the latter's infantry— that is, his whole army, except his personal guard of cavalry, who were probably bound to him by clan ties—seized his guns and set off to join the enemy. General Burrows, of course, sent cavalry in pursuit, who "dispersed the mutineers"—that is, compelled them to join Ayoub in detachments and small parties, instead of in regiments; but he was obliged to fall back thirty miles, and the incident has a most serious political meaning. So detested are the British even in Candahar, where they are supposed to be popular, and probably are popular with the powerless trading classes, that the native ruler is paralysed by their favour, and would, if they withdrew, be at once handed over by his own soldiers to any enemy unconnected with Europeans. If the British garrison were withdrawn, the fighting men in the province and city would at once proclaim Abdurrahman, the body of the people would obey as usual, and the British would be compelled either to acquiesce, or to reconquer the province by an army which the Ameer might be compelled by opinion to resist in arms. We are, in fact, if we remain, compelled to guarantee Shere Ali not only against external attack, but against revolution among his own soldiery and subjects. We must support him in any

tyranny he chooses to perpetrate, subdue any revolt, even if thoroughly justified, and guard him besides with at least 5,000 men from any external attack. In return, we receive a right to keep a cantonment in Candahar on the watch till the Russians or somebody else invade India through Afghanistan, a contingency about as probable as a German invasion of Great Britain through Ireland. We obtain nothing else, for the revenue will go to the Wali; there is no trade worth protecting, and the Candaharees will not enter the Indian native regiments. At the same time, as Candahar is the best province of Afghanistan, we make of Abdurrahman and his successors inevitable enemies, whose first preoccupation must be to regain their territory. Considering the distance of Candahar from India, the fact that the Beloochees hold our communications always at their mercy, and the extreme dislike of the Sepoys to service beyond the Passes, the position must be regarded as nearly hopeless, and justifiable only until we can persuade the Wali to come to an agreement with his natural superior, the Ameer of Afghanistan. Under such an agreement, we might, after allowing Shere Ali money enough to keep up a personal guard, retire, and once more quit the mountains and the Afghan sea of intrigue, insurrection, and assassinations. The Government would, no doubt, in that complete retirement, acknowledge that it had failed; but then failure was inevitable, and is the admitted central fact of the position. We have expended twenty millions and have lost hundreds of valuable lives in an endeavour to fight Russia without declaring war on her, and the total result is that the name of the Afghan Ameer is Abdurrahman, instead of Shere Ali. The Russians are no further off, the Afghans are no more friendly, and we have no new strength in India, either for defence or attack; indeed we are slightly weaker, for, in consequence of the waste beyond the Hills, we must either reduce the Army or we must increase taxation, and with it the possible discontent of the body of the people.

THE FIRST LESSON OF CANDAHAR

The defeat near Kushk-i-Nakud was a severe one, but it will not be an unmitigated disaster, if it teaches British statesmen and Generals one great lesson. In advancing beyond India, we leave behind the two must important conditions of Indian warfare. The first of these, made evident in a century of almost constant war, is that when European troops are opposed to Indian soldiers, we need never count heads. If the General is able, his soldiers fed, and his ammunition sufficient, disparity of numbers makes no difference. Bad information, slow marching, careless dispositions, every deficiency, has proved unimportant, in [the] presence of the inestimable advantage that, once opposite the enemy, the British can always defeat him, though the odds are ten or even twenty to one. At Plassey, Clive, with 900 Europeans and 2,100 native Sepoys and eight light field-pieces, defeated an army of 50,000 men, with a numerous and powerful artillery. At Cutwah, 650 Europeans and 1,200 natives defeated Meer Cassim, with 30,000 men disciplined by Europeans. At Assaye, the Duke of Wellington, with only 4,500 men, of whom only two regiments and some artillerymen were British, defeated Sindiah's splendid army of 16,000 infantry, disciplined by De Boigne, and 20,000 cavalry, with a host of Irregulars. At Meeanee, Sir Charles Napier, with but one English regiment and only 2,000 men in all, defeated 30,000 or 35,000 Beloochees, who left their guns in our hands, with 6,000 dead on the field. In almost all our great victories, we were hopelessly outnumbered. Indeed, had it not been so, the conquest of India would have been impossible. Till 1857 we never had, in the whole peninsula, as many Englishmen as obeyed Wellington at Waterloo, and never were able by any exertion to concentrate 50,000 trained men for a pitched battle. As a rule, any native Prince, however petty, could outnumber us, and any province, however feeble, could overwhelm any garrison we could station within its confines; while India, as a whole, could have hurled us, if its population would only have flung handfuls of sand. We won, in despite of numbers and in contempt of numbers, *through the* inherent superiority in battle of our fighting-men. Once outside India, that primary condition of our dominion is no longer present. We have beaten Afghans repeatedly, and sometimes against terrible odds, but when they decide to fight, the result, when the odds are heavy, is no longer certain. Charasiab was doubtful for an hour. We were beaten when we retired into Sherpore, though the fact was concealed and forgotten in subsequent success. In Sir Donald Stewart's last fight the Afghan charge broke the Europeans, and now in the recent battle we have been avowedly defeated, with a loss of one clear half of all the men seriously engaged. As every defeat, however small, means in Asia serious danger, and as a great defeat might involve destruction, we must outside India count heads, must employ adequate forces, must believe it needful to be at least one-half our enemy in numbers. That necessity fearfully increases the costliness in life, as well as treasure, of every campaign and of every occupation. We have to employ armies, where brigades would have sufficed in India itself, used divisions where battalions would anywhere to the south have been trusted to win the day. It will take more men to recover our mastery at Candahar than Wellington in India ever commanded, and we could not hold Afghanistan safely without as many Europeans as hold all India from the Kistna to the Sutlej. The demand on us, too, in such a war is exaggerated by the second change. Within India, a trained native soldier under European officers, and supported by European regiments, is worth, at least, three native soldiers not placed under those conditions, He is as good for everything but a "pounding march," such as seldom occurs, as a European. The Sepoy in English service is a different and a superior man to the Sepoy in native service, and this not only in discipline, for in 1858 our new native levies defeated our oldest native regiments in revolt, but from a change in his idea of his own powers. He gains a self-confidence which his whole people seem, somehow, to have lost. Outside India, this advantage disappears. There are picked native regiments, such as the Guides and a few others, which are as good as any regiments in the world, which would, perhaps, stand fairly up against Germans, or Englishmen, or Frenchmen but the mass of the Sepoys are hardly the equals, certainly not the superiors of Afghans. If we had to conquer Afghanistan without Europeans, the General would require as many soldiers as his enemy, and then would not be perfectly certain of success. It comes, therefore, to this, that we must either trust small armies of Europeans perfectly appointed, armies we cannot spare under our existing organisation, or raise our composite armies to a size which will make every campaign as costly and as exhausting as if it were fought in Europe. Already we are employing in Afghanistan as many men as in the Sikh wars, and we are not decidedly successful.

It is quite evident from Colonel St. John's account why General Burrows was defeated. He fought as he would have fought in India against a native army, and as his superiors in Bombay, it is evident, from the statements previously published there, expected him to fight. He knew nothing about Ayoub Khan's strength, not even the number of his guns, and probably cared nothing. He was a British General in command of a British composite army, and whether his opponent had 4,000 men or 14,000 mattered nothing, we had always won against any odds, and we should win. The heavy impression evidently made by his adversary's twenty gun's amazed him, but he had still the never-failing resource, an attack by British soldiers, and he attacked. The Afghans, however, are not Indians; they charge, and their charge was too much for the Sepoys to resist. Outnumbered by three or four to one, and by men who are individually their superiors, the native infantry broke and fled, and in their flight disorganised the 650

Europeans behind them, a mere handful, and forced them also to retreat, losing, in desperate but brief resistance, two-thirds of their entire number. The cavalry appear to have fled before, and the retreat of the infantry, huddled upon a single road, which they refused, in spite of their officers' commands, to quit, must have been a hideous rout, for they were pursued for ten miles, and fled on for forty, reaching the Argandeb, forty miles away, in twenty-four hours, a march which nothing but desperate extremity would have got out of them. Without food, or even water, the men dropped at every step; and though the Afghans— who were probably unaware of the completeness of their own victory—did not pursue "vigorously," when the army re-entered Candahar one-half of the total infantry and seventy-five per cent of the Europeans had been lost, a proportion almost without a precedent, in a battle not followed by a surrender on the field. Many of the officers are only reported missing; but though a straggler or two may turn up, soldiers in uniform "missing" in Afghanistan are lost men—as every "friendly" Candaharee villager would have a knife for beaten Infidels too weary for self-defence; or for Indians who, under Infidel command, had presumed to invade his country.

We are happy to perceive that the meaning of the affair has not been hidden either from Sir Frederick Haines, the Commander-in-Chief or General Donald Stewart, commanding at Cabul. We hear no more of single regiments of Europeans "on their way to Candahar," or of small divisions with half regiments of English infantry ordered to relieve this beleaguered garrison. If water does not fail him, General Primrose can hold out for three months; and if water does fail him, it will fail in the very beginning of the siege, the besiegers cutting the aqueduct and leaving him dependent on his wells. General Phayre has, therefore, been ordered to wait for European reinforcements, which as Bombay has no more to spare, have been sent up from Bengal, and cannot reach him before August 20th, at earliest. At the same time, General Roberts has been directed to take a powerful force, an army, in fact, of 9,000 men from Cabul, and march as rapidly as may be on Candahar. He will probably have to win a battle near Ghuzni, which even Afghan generalship will not suffer him to pass without an engagement; but his force will relieve and carry on the small garrison of Khelat-i-Ghilaye, and when his junction has been effected with General Phayre, should have from 14,000 to 15,000 men, one-third of them Europeans, with whom to encounter Ayoub Khan, and an army which by that time will have doubled, or reached 30,000 men. These are reasonable odds, and with a General like General Roberts this Government of India ought, by the middle of October, to have driven Ayoub Khan back to Herat, and to be as securely in possession of Candahar as before. That is all it will have attained. At an expense of about two millions—for the war is now costing 700,000 a month, without allowing for the unheard-of-prices General Phayre will have to pay for transport—the position will have been retrieved, and the Ministry enabled to decide whether they will retire, or retain Candahar till Ayoub Khan has once more collected a force sufficient to make it indispensable to guard the line of the Helmand. It is the specialty of war in Afghanistan that victory or defeat produces always the same result—a certainty that the very next incident will compel us to do all this work over again. We have imagined the best result possible, but there is no certainty that the moment General Stewart has defeated Ayoub Khan, Abdurrahman, relieved of his rival, may not declare war or that the troops, pronouncing him too friendly to the Infidel, may not, by the easy expedient of assassination, clear the way for a leader more ready to drive the white men back to the Plains. There is nothing to do but go on, for we must relieve Candahar, and must defeat Ayoub Khan; but the work, costly and exasperating as it is, must necessarily be sterile.

THE RUMOUR FROM CABUL

We have no means as yet—Friday afternoon—of knowing whether the rumour of an insurrection in Cabul and of the murder of Abdurrahman Khan is true or not. Judging on prima facie evidence, we should say it was true, but the evidence is too imperfect for a definite opinion. The Calcutta correspondent of the Times, telegraphing on Thursday, denies the story; but he acknowledges that nothing is known of affairs in Cabul beyond the 16th inst., a fortnight ago—that is, in such matters, a century. It is certain that the Commissioner of Peshawur has ascertained that natives believe the rumour, that the Viceroy acknowledges a suspension of information from Cabul, and that the Civil and Military Gazette of Lahore, a journal which has the sense to employ Persian news writers, thinks the story substantially correct. The first information of the murder of Sir Louis Cavagnari was received in the same way, and any Persian or Hindoo dealer in the Cabul Bazaar who had business relations with Peshawur would have no difficulty in sending the facts through the Khyber to his correspondent. He would not exaggerate either, though, as his object would be to enable his friend to sweep the bazaar of certain Afghan goods, he might send away his messenger too early, and before the ultimate result of the struggle had declared itself. As to the meaning of the revolt, it can have but one, if it has occurred at all, namely, that the national party in Cabul, enraged at Abdurrahman's friendliness to the British, have put him to death, and intend either to raise Moosa Khan, Yakoob's son, to the throne, or, still more probably, to elect Ayoub Khan, the only Barukhzye who has defeated the white Infidel in the open field. He has always had a strong party in Cabul, he has not given personal offence to the Sirdars, and he may very easily have purchased the "party of Ghuzni," which has not submitted to the Ameer. Of course, the scene being Afghanistan, the first object would be to assassinate Abdurrahman; and it has all along been stated, with curious persistency, that the Ameer, for reasons not given, is unpopular with his personal guard, the men who accompanied him from Balkh. In a revolt of this kind their fidelity would be everything, and if he has been murdered, it has failed.

We must wait for the facts, and as yet the only fact is a disturbance so serious as to suspend communication between Cabul and Peshawur; but we should like our readers to reflect for a moment on what the rumour, if true—and it may easily be true—would mean. It would mean that the error of the Government in remaining in Candahar six months after General Roberts had given them the opportunity of retiring, was about to involve a fourth Afghan campaign, of the same exhausting and utterly sterile kind. If we were out of Candahar, Afghan revolts would matter no more to us than South American wars. It would be nothing to us which Barukhzye ruled or how he ruled, whether he was elected by acclaim, or whether he became sovereign through the "natural selection" demonstrated by killing all his competitors. The Afghans cannot attack us, and are no more to us than any other clans beyond our frontier who prefer to settle dynastic disputes, like European Legitimists in Spain or Portugal, by the sword. If Abdurrahman kills Ayoub, so much the better; and if Ayoub kills Abdurrahman, where is the harm to us? Ayoub does not hate Englishmen worse than the Sultan, nor was Lieutenant Maclaine a person we were more bound to avenge than Mr. Ogle, but we have not declared war on Mr. Ogle's account. We could have refused, if that were thought wise, to recognise Ayoub, and shut the Passes against him, and then have waited until the next revolt had brought up somebody else. As, however, we have, in the teeth of commonsense, political morality, and our own interests, chosen to remain in Candahar, we may now have to wage another costly campaign. The first idea of any nationalist Ameer, and especially of Ayoub, must be

to recover Candahar; and as we cannot retreat before menace, we must await attack, defeat the enemy, and in all human probability drive him from his throne, before we can be even approximately safe. That operation will cost us five millions, five thousand European soldiers, wounded, invalided, or sent to hospital, and continued disaffection in our Sepoy Army. And what do we gain by it all? Our opponents in this controversy are never tired of accusing the Liberals of sentimentality and fanaticism; but in this instance, though Liberals hate buccaneering even for "Imperial" objects, they are defending the policy of hard, unsentimental sense. They ask, with Bismarck, why English bones are to be broken and English sovereigns wasted, in order that one barbarian may rule instead of another on a valueless bit of the Central-Asian plateau. There never was such folly since Napoleon III invaded Mexico, to enable the Latin race to strengthen itself against some future aggression from their Anglo-Saxon neighbours. Ayoub Khan is a Russian nominee? So they said Abdurrahman Khan was; and he is, according to this story, murdered,—as Ayoub also will be, if he shows a desire to play into the hands of any Infidel whatsoever. If we are to conquer Afghanistan in the interest of Europe and civilisation, well and good, though Europe might find more profitable work; but to conquer it in order to substitute one Afghan for another, or one "friendly" to England for one friendly to Russia, is [a] childish waste of power. Whichever he is, he will either hate all wearers of the hat with impartial and implacable malignity, or he will be killed for not hating them enough. Of all British delusions, the most absurd and the most ruinous is that Mahommedans of Central Asia can be induced to love one set of white-faced Christians better than another, or regard any of them in any light but that in which Kurds regard Armenians or Greeks—as people to be shot down, plundered, or expelled, as may be most convenient for the day.

THE DEATH OF ABDURRAHMAN KHAN

The death of Abdurrahman Khan, the Ameer of Afghanistan, is undoubtedly a misfortune, though its extent depends upon several unknown quantities. It is the necessity of the Indian Empire that Afghanistan should be in strong and friendly hands, and the late Ameer was both. The eldest son of the eldest son of Dost Mahommed, Abdurrahman Khan was in English ideas the legitimate head of he Barukhzye dynasty, and even in Mussulman opinion might advance a reasonable, if not exactly a final, claim to the throne. He did advance it; but he was defeated by his uncle Shere Ali, best described as an Afghan Saul, who had been nominated his successor by Dost Mahommed. Abdurrahman fled into Central Asia to the protection of General Kaufman, and for eleven years was compelled to eat his heart out in idleness while waiting his opportunity, as at once guest and prisoner in Samarcand. He was well treated, and learned much; but intercourse does not always produce friendship, and he never loved the Russians. His chance did not come till 1879, when he was thirty-nine years old, and by that time he had become a very terrible man. Sprung from the fiercest house in Central Asia, with an Usbeg-Tartar for mother, dominated by ambition, with a hard and sarcastic temperament, not at all unlike that of Frederick the Great, and a sense at once of defeat and betrayal, Abdurrahman returned to Afghanistan a man of iron, resolved to pour death out of a bucket sooner than be successfully resisted. The East has often produced such men, as Italy did in the time of the Renaissance, and among them Abdurrahman Khan was probably at once the ablest and the most cruel. For four years he struggled against a thousand enemies, his own kinsmen, the great clan chiefs, the soldiers whom Afghanistan is always throwing up; and partly by treachery, partly by ruthless cruelty, he so prevailed that in 1883 he might have said, with Marshal Narvaez, "I cannot forgive my enemies for I have killed them all." Then the British Government, which had always favored his claims, perceived that there was at last a true ruler in Afghanistan, and resolved to help him consolidate his power. The weakness of each successive Ameer had been the want of a standing army, a want arising from deficient revenue, and a subsidy of £120,000 (afterwards £180,000) a year removed this difficulty from the Ameer's path. With an Army of twenty thousand men dependent only on himself, with a sleepless industry like that of Philipp II, never resting from his work, never pardoning and never striking except once for all, the Ameer raised a new local revenue, and spread such a fear of him throughout his dominions, which cover an area half as large again as France, that, as English observers report, his own highest satraps, men invested with power of life and death, could hardly muster courage to open an unexpected letter. A great peace fell upon the land, so that for the first time in centuries strangers could traverse it in safety, and the people could cultivate their valleys without the certainty that others than themselves would reap their crops. Whether Abdurrahman cared to "civilize" his people may be doubted, his "works," his roads, his arsenals, etc., being chiefly intended to consolidate his own power but he did care for order, and he secured it, often by cruelties which Ivan the Terrible would have thought extreme. Still, he secured it, and with it also external peace. What his real feeling towards either English or Russians was will always remain unknown—he probably hated both, though in unequal degrees—but from the moment when he was firm in the saddle he appears to have decided that the great Empire to the south was less to be dreaded than the great Empire to the North, and that he should stick to the former. The money helped, no doubt, for it gave him precisely the force he needed; but there was also keen political insight. England, he saw clearly, did not want Russian territory, while Russia did or might want territory in India. It was safer, therefore, to adhere to the Power which had no temptation to cross his own dominion, and then seize it to "defend communications." At all events, he made up his mind, and in spite of many vexations, especially some evidence that the British hardly regarded Afghanistan as he himself did, as a great power in Asia, he remained from 1883 to his death a loyal, though a difficult and sharply sarcastic friend.

The question now is whether he founded anything, whether, that is, his power was due solely to his personal abilities and terrible character, or whether he established a real throne which could be transmitted in safety to his successor. He certainly endeavored to do so. He intended obviously to leave his scepter to his eldest son Habibullah who is, unfortunately for himself, Royal, as Central Asia counts Royalty, only on one side, but whom his father trusted as fully as it was in his nature to trust anyone. He left him when only seventeen for two years as his Viceroy in Kabul; he has for four years made him Chancellor, as we say in Europe, that is, intermediary between himself and his great officers; and four years ago he gave him authority even over the Treasury, a subject on which Asiatic Sovereigns are always jealous. These great powers Habibullah is believed to have used wisely, certainly to his father's contentment; and if he inherits anything of the Ameer's tiger will, he may pass through the troublous times which will inevitably follow the tyrant's death with honor and success. He will, however, have to show the qualities that keep thrones, for with the lifting of the flagstone all the frogs will jump. Every element of disorder in Afghanistan, all the men who think they should be greater, all the clans which have been crushed, all the banditti longing for license, will think their time has arrived, and that they must try conclusions with the ruler of Kabul, which, again, possesses one of the most dangerous mobs in the world. The sinews of rebellion in Afghanistan have, however, been cut, if not cut through, and our main fear now is reduced to a single question. Can a man who for thirteen years never offended a master like Abdurrahman Khan be possessed of a strong character of his own? It is possible, for the awe of Abdurrahman Khan must have been on Habibullah as on the rest of Afghan mankind; he may have concealed his real self; and if he is a strong man all may go well, even from the first. That he will be on the side of the British we have no doubt, for the subsidy will be needed to keep his Army devoted to his cause. Even the Janissaries needed regular pay, and the Albanians mutiny when they do not get it.

It is fortunate that the event, in itself disastrous, finds India in the hands of a Viceroy who will pursue his own policy, or that of the Cabinet, without regarding the hundred policies which the military party in India will press on his attention, and fortunate, too, that that policy cannot be a rash one. The object, with South Africa still on our hands, clearly is to avoid war if possible, but to strengthen the hands of the new Ameer when he is at once seated by every means at our disposal. It will be much to him to be acknowledged at once, more to receive an advance upon his subsidy, most of all to be able to assure his chiefs that the great Empire of the South will not tolerate anarchy within Afghanistan itself. Until that arises there is no danger from Russia, whose hands are full while her Treasury is empty, and it is to suppress that that Lord Curzon will, we doubt not, direct all his energies. He cannot alter the character of Habibullah, whatever it may be; but if the new Ameer has the making of a ruler in him, a question which six months will determine, he can materially smooth his path. The death of Abdurrahman Khan occurs at an unlucky moment for us, if only for the encouragement it will give the Boers; but the situation is easy compared with that produced by the murder of Sir Louis Cavagnari. *Then*, almost before we could draw breath, we had to invade.

PART IV

The Great Game, 1880–1919

Border disputes, specifically over the demarcation of the North-West Frontier, continued to erupt in the wake of the end of the Second Anglo-Afghan War. Some, such as the contest between Russia and Afghanistan at Panjdeh in 1885, came perilously close to all-out war, in part because of the British government's determination to extend its influence in central Asia by using its Afghan ally as a proxy—a position that Abdur Rahman Khan firmly resisted. The result was the Anglo-Russian Demarcation Commission, which fixed the border in 1887, and the establishment of the Durand Line in 1893, via which the British negotiated the border between British India and Afghanistan with the emir. Insecurities plagued imperial policymakers until century's end and beyond. Though officially neutral during World War I, Afghanistan accepted delegates from a Turkish and German mission, fueling decades of suspicion about Afghanistan's loyalty to the British. Like many others subject to British imperial power, if not rule, the emir, Habibullah Khan, sought a seat at the Treaty of Versailles table at the end of the war; he was assassinated in February 1919. His successor, Amanullah Khan, decided to try to invade British India, and the British declared war. Though its manpower was weakened in the aftermath of the Great War, Britain had the tactical advantage of the Royal Air Force. Ultimately, the Durand Line was reaffirmed and Afghanistan became an independent state, though it was far from settled. Both Europeans and Afghans continued to struggle against local tribesmen seeking their own interests in the region well into the twentieth century.

17 / Russia in Central Asia (1889)

GEORGE NATHANIEL CURZON

At the conclusion to *Russia in Central Asia* (1889), George Nathaniel Curzon (1859–1925) was prepared to acknowledge the benefits that Russian imperialism had brought to the region, and even to admire Russia's capacity to quiet the "terrible terrors of the desert." He was particularly enthusiastic about Russia's success in imposing its military will on the populations it sought to rule. He even went so far as to suggest that the peoples Russia colonized had "loyally" accepted their dominion, though he rejected claims that the Russians were more successful in this regard than the British in India.

Curzon, who was later viceroy of India (1899–1905) and foreign secretary (1919–24), gained invaluable knowledge of empire in his early travels and research in central Asia and Persia. In this excerpt, he lays out central Asia as a case study in imperial tactics: an opportunity to assess Russia's success and failure and to hold British examples up to comparative scrutiny—what he calls "the contrast of rival methods" in fields such as native education, military strategy, protocols of rule, and schemes for improvement, both cultural and material. His grudging admiration for Russian imperial accomplishment makes an instructive contrast with Sir Robert Wilson's fears about a marauding Russian hegemon seventy years earlier.

First, then, it cannot be doubted that Russia has conferred great and substantial advantages upon the Central Asian regions which she has reduced to her sway. Those who have read descriptions of the state of the country from the Caspian to the Amu Daria, in the pre-Russian days of rapine and raid, when agriculture was devastated, life and property rendered insecure, and entire populations were swept off under circumstances of unheard-of barbarity into a life-long servitude, can form some idea of the extent of the revolution by which peace and order and returning prosperity have been given to these desolated tracts; and the traveller, who once dared not move abroad without a powerful escort, is enabled to wander with impunity over the unfrequented plain. The experiences of Vambéry, of MacGregor, of Valentine Baker, and of every English voyager in or near the Turkoman country, contrasted with my own modest narrative, illustrate the immensity of the boon. At a comparatively recent date the members of the Boundary Commission reported that, till within three or four years before their visit, Turkoman marauders used to scour the country as far as Farrah, 150 miles south of Herat, that between Sarakhs and Kuhsan the land was utterly depopulated, and that raiding-parties were pushed to the very walls of Meshed. Except among the Persian Turkomans of the Atrek border, the *alaman* may be said now to be a thing of the past.

Let me quote here the words of Sir Henry Rawlinson on the subject, spoken at a meeting of the Royal Geographical Society in 1882:—

> No one will question but that the extension of Russian arms to the east of the Caspian has been of immense benefit to the country. The substitution, indeed, of Russian rule for that of the Kirghiz, Uzbegs, and Turkomans throughout a large portion of Central Asia has been an unmixed blessing to humanity. The execrable slave trade, with its concomitant horrors, has been abolished, brigandage has been suppressed, and Mahometan fanaticism and cruelty have been generally mitigated and controlled. Commerce at the same time has been rendered more secure, local arts and manufactures have been encouraged, and the wants of the inhabitants have been everywhere more seriously regarded than is usual under Asiatic rulers.

This is at once a significant and a handsome admission, coming, as it does, from one whom Russian writers are never tired of representing as choragus of the choir of English Russophobes and Jingoes. Voyaging through the country myself, and seeing on all sides the mouldering fortalices and towers that spoke so eloquently of the savage tenure of the past, I could not repress a feeling of gratitude to those who had substituted peace for chronic warfare, and order for barbaric anarchy. The desolation from which the land still suffers is the product of natural causes, whose operation may be checked but cannot be altogether reversed; and not of human passions, which were so long and ruthlessly devoted to making still more terrible the terrors of the desert. If we still meet with but a scanty population, if the towns are more like villages, and the villages like clusters of hovels, and if civilisation is still in an embryonic stage, let us remember that it is only a decade since there was neither sedentary population, nor town, nor civilisation; and that thus a land is being slowly won to the service of man which man himself has hitherto rendered a byword and a curse. The Russian eagle may at first have alighted upon the eastern shores of the Caspian with murderous beak and sharpened talons, but, her appetite once satisfied, she has shown that she also came with healing in her wings.

Turning to the dominion of Russia and the means by which it is assured, I make with equal pleasure the acknowledgment that it appeared to me to be firmly and fairly established, and to be loyally accepted by the conquered races. Though we hear a good deal in books of the fanaticism of Mussulman populations, and might expect still more from the resentment of deposed authority, or the revenge of baffled licence, revolts do not occur and mutinies are not apprehended among the subjugated peoples. I attribute this to several reasons: to the ferocious severity of the original blow; to the powerlessness of resistance against the tight military grip that is kept by Russia upon the country; and to the certainty, which a long course of Russian conduct has reasonably inspired, that she will never retreat. A few words about each of these.

The terrifying effect of such a massacre as Geok Tepe survives for generations. The story is repeated from father to son, and from son to grandson, losing none of its horror in the process of lineal transmission. The ruined walls of the fortress remain to add a melancholy emphasis to the tale. Meanwhile, though the fathers were slain, the sons have grown up into contented citizenship.

Several of the survivors stand high in the service of the conqueror. A new generation has heard with a shudder the tale of national downfall, but itself only remembers a later order, and can scarcely imagine a time when the Ouroussi were not masters in the land.

The second reason, viz. the overpowering military strength of Russia in the country, is even more cogent in its application, and must be held to detract somewhat from the brilliancy of her achievement. The proportion of soldiers to subjects in Transcaspia and Turkestan (figures of which, contrasted with those of British India, I gave in an earlier chapter) is such as to render any attempt at opposition a fiasco. Russian Central Asia is indeed one vast armed camp, and the traveller, who in the course of several weeks' journey scarcely sets eyes upon a Russian civilian, comes away with respect for the discretion, but without much surprise at the peaceful attitude, of the people. When the Russians boasted to me, as they habitually did, of their own popularity, contrasted with British odium in India, I could not help remembering that I had seen a great Indian city of 80,000 inhabitants, and a hotbed of idolatrous superstition, held in peaceful control by four English civilians, without the aid of a single red-coat. I could not help recalling the lacs of rupees, amounting to hundreds of thousands of pounds sterling, spontaneously offered by Indian princes, in order that this very popularity, of which I now heard so much, might not be brought any nearer to their doors, but that the familiar odium might continue to be their lot. Nor could I forget Lord Dufferin's offer to the Punjabi chiefs, that their irregular troops should, under native command, but by the aid of British instruction, be turned into disciplined battalions, and presented with breechloading rifles and batteries of guns. Recalling these facts, and comparing them with what I saw in Transcaspia, I did not feel that the inequality was precisely what my Russian friends supposed.

A conviction of the permanence of Russia and of Russian conquests is a third and important element in explaining the bases of her power. A forward movement, whether voluntarily undertaken, or beneath the pressure of circumstances, is seldom repented of and never receded from. No return tickets are issued to a punitive foray of Cossacks. Advance is inexorably followed by annexation. '*J'y suis, j'y reste,*' is the watchword of the Russian vanguard. There is no likelihood of 'making it so hot' for Russia that, for sake of peace, or economy, or men's lives, she will waver or fall back. A hornets' nest raised about her head is followed, not by a hasty withdrawal of the intruding member, but by a wholesale extermination of the insects. How different from the English method, which shrinks from annexation as from a spectre; which publishes to the world, including the guilty party, its chivalrous design of Retribution followed by Retreat, and which, instead of reaping from a frontier campaign the legitimate harvest of assured peace and good government in the future, leaves the smouldering embers of revenge in the ruins of burnt villages and desolated crops, certain, sooner or later, to burst out into a fresh conflagration!

It would be unfair, however, both to Russian character and to Russian policy, to suggest that it is owing solely to prudential reasons that there is no visible antagonism to her sway. Such calculations may ensure its stability, but they do not explain its favour. I gladly, therefore, add the recognition that, so far as I was able to ascertain, Russian dominion is not merely accepted by, but is acceptable to the bulk of her Asiatic subjects, and that the ruling class, though feared, is also personally esteemed. Russia unquestionably possesses a remarkable gift for enlisting the allegiance and attracting even the friendship of those whom she has subdued by force of arms, a faculty which is to be attributed as much to the defects as to the excellences of her character. Let me first mention the latter.

The extreme frankness and amiability of Russian

manners cover a genuine *bonhomie* and a good-humoured *insouciance*, which render it easy for them to make friends and which disarm the suspicion even of a beaten foe. The Russian fraternises in the true sense of the word. He is guiltless of that air of conscious superiority and gloomy hauteur, which does more to inflame animosity than cruelty may have done to kindle it, and he does not shrink from entering into social and domestic relations with alien or inferior races. His own unconquerable carelessness renders it easy for him to adopt a laissez-faire attitude towards others, and the tolerance with which he has treated the religious practices, the social customs, and the local prejudices of his Asiatic fellow-subjects is less the outcome of diplomatic calculation than it is of ingrained nonchalance.

A remarkable feature of the Russification of Central Asia is the employment given by the conqueror to her former opponents on the field of battle. I mentioned in an earlier chapter the spectacle of which I was a witness at Baku, where the four Khan of Merv were assembled in Russian uniform to greet the Czar. This is but a casual illustration of a method that Russia has consistently employed, and which is a branch of the larger theory of Massacre followed by Embraces that was so candidly avowed by Skobeleff. The chiefs are sent to St. Petersburg to excite their wonderment, and are covered with decorations to gratify their vanity. When they come back they are confirmed in their posts or offices, and are presently rewarded with an increased prerogative. Their small number is, of course, a reason why they may be so employed with impunity. The English have never shown a capacity to avail themselves of the services of their former enemies on a similar scale. I remember reading only a short time ago an account given by an old Boer of the British annexation of the Transvaal, and the troubles, culminating in Majuba Hill, that ensued. His explanation of the discontent and rebellion was a very simple one, and probably contained a good deal of truth.

"If you had made *maaters* [chums]," he said, "with Oom Paul [Kruger], and a few others of our leading men, and given them posts, and if you had listened a little to them, and had not been so terribly *hoogmoedaag* [high and mighty], all would have gone well." The "high and mighty" policy has been at the root of a good many English failures, just as its converse has been responsible for a good many Russian successes.

With the followers a not less successful policy is adopted than towards the chiefs. As soon as fighting is over they are invited back to their homesteads, and to the security of undisputed possession tempered by a moderate taxation. The peasant is satisfied, because, under more scientific management, he gets so many cubic feet more water from his canals and so many bushels more grain from his land. The merchant is pleased, because he sells his wool or his cotton at a bigger price than he realised before. All are amenable to the comfort and utility and cheapness of Russian manufactured articles, in contrast with the clumsy and primitive furniture of their previous lives. Above all, security is a boon which none can depreciate; and if the extinction of the *alaman* is a cause of regret to a few scores or hundreds, it is an unmixed blessing to thousands. Russian authority presents itself to the native populations in the twofold guise of liberty and despotism: liberty, because in many respects they enjoy a freedom which they never knew before; despotism, centred in the image of the Great White Czar, which is an inalienable attribute of government to the Oriental mind.

We may trace indeed, in the panorama of Russian advance, a uniform procession of figures and succession of acts, implying something more than a merely adventitious series of events. First comes the Cossack, brave in combat and affable in occupation, at once the instrument of conquest and the guarantee of retention. Next follow the merchant and the pedlar, spreading out before astonished eyes the novel wares, the glittering gewgaws, and the cheap conveniences of Europe. A new and lucrative market is opened for native produce. Prompt payment in hard cash proves to be a seductive innovation. Presently appear the priest with his vestments and icons, conferring a divine benediction upon the newly established order; the *tchinovnik* and kindred symptoms of organised settlement; the liquor-shop and its vodka, to expedite, even while debasing, the assimilative process; the official and tax collector, as the final stamp of Imperial Supremacy. Then when a few years, or sometimes only months, have gone by, imposing barracks rise, postal and telegraph offices are built, a railway is laid, colonists are invited, the old times are forgotten, and an air of drowsy quiescence settles down upon the spot that a decade before was scoured by predatory bands or precariously peopled by vagabond tribes.

On the other hand, the Russians have been aided in the work of pacification by qualities which, though discreditable to civilised peoples, are familiar by immemorial usage as well as by national instinct to Oriental tribes. To an unrefined race such as the latter a want of refinement is not shocking. To peoples with whom lying is no disgrace (*vide* Alikhanoff's description of the Turkomans, quoted in Chapter V.) untruthfulness presents no novelty. To a society trained in theft and dishonesty (*vide* O'Donovan's 'Merv Oasis,' *passim*) corruption is no crime. The conquest of Central Asia is a conquest of Orientals by Orientals, of cognate character by cognate character. It is the fusing of strong with weaker metal, but it is not the expulsion of an impure by a purer element. Civilised Europe has not marched forth to vanquish barbarian Asia. This is no nineteenth-century crusade of manners or morals; but barbarian Asia, after a sojourn in civilised Europe, returns upon its former footsteps to reclaim its own kith and kin. Assimilation is less remarkable when rulers are severed from subjects by a gap of but a few centuries, and when no impassable chasm of intellect or character intervenes. A system backward in Europe is forward in Central Asia; stagnation

here is dizzy progress there; and coarser agencies are better fitted for the work of redemption than a more polished instrument.

No more striking illustration of the policy of laissez-faire, of which I have spoken, can be given than the attitude which Russia has throughout adopted towards those institutions which are commonly the rallying-ground of prejudice and superstition among Mahometans, namely, the religion and the education of the native peoples. The former she has absolutely left alone. The Mullahs have been allowed to teach and preach the Koran; the dervishes alone have been restrained in their fanatical importunities; mosques have even, in some cases, been repaired by Russian means; and at one time the Government actually went so far as to build mosques itself for the conciliation of the Kirghiz. No Russian propaganda has been tolerated in Central Asia; proselytism is tabooed; and it is a curious but significant fact that we find Russian writers boasting that their Church has never despatched a missionary to Central Asia nor made an Asiatic convert. From one point of view this policy has had the most satisfactory results; for the bigotry, which persecution or even covert hostility might have sharpened, has sunk into an indifference which will pave the way to a more thorough political union. But how different is this system from that of the English Church, whose missionary activity is the wonder, if unfortunately it is not the redemption, of foreign lands, and which aspires to create converts almost before it has made citizens! There is this broad difference between the problem which has confronted the two nations in Central Asia—that the Russians have so far come into contact with only one, and that a Monotheistic creed; while the English have found themselves plunged into a weltering sea of Pagan superstition and blind idolatry.

The contrast between the rival methods is nowhere more conspicuous than in the field of native education. If England has recognised a special and primary obligation in her dealings with conquered peoples it has always been in the education and development of the young. Indeed, her lavish distribution of the resources of culture and knowledge in India is the main cause of the difficulties with which her administration is now confronted. Wisdom is justified of her children, and those who have caught the glamour of nineteenth-century learning are not content to sink back into the slough of primordial ignorance. The Russians have proceeded upon very different lines. The educational habits and institutions of their Mussulman subjects have been left untouched. The *mektebs*, or primary schools, and the *medresses*, or high schools, still communicate their straitened and stinted learning, their senseless lessons by rote, and their palsied philosophy, to thousands of Russian subjects, whom not an effort is made to lift on to a higher plane of intellectual development. The Government does not even supervise the collection or distribution of the *vakufs*, or religious endowments; and large sums of money are annually left to the discretion of unlettered Mullahs and priests. That a better era, however, is dawning, and that Russia is beginning to recognise her duties towards those with whose rule she is charged, may be gathered from the details which I quoted in an earlier chapter upon Tashkent.

Such, broadly speaking, have been the means by which Russia has gained her position, and having gained it, has made it secure: namely, overwhelming military superiority; a resolute policy; the gift of material advantages; equable and tolerant administration; personal popularity; and a calculating prudence. Let me add thereto that, in the process, the conquerors have exhibited qualities of a very high order, commanding respect and admiration. The Russian soldier is perhaps the most faithful modern parallel to the Spartan. He would let the wolf tear at his vitals without uttering a groan. Endued with great hardihood and power of self-sacrifice, possessed of a blind but inspiring devotion to duty, he takes his orders silently and executes them promptly. The child of a

Northern and Arctic clime, he serves without a murmur in fervid deserts and under excruciating suns. Encamped in the wilderness, he builds huts and houses that recall memories of home, and with singing and merriment he peoples the solitude with cheerful fancies. Above all, he is animated by a lofty pride of birth, and by an unfaltering faith in the destiny of his country. It is of such stuff that heroes and great nations alike are made, and by such hands that empires have commonly been built.

Other considerations, however, there are which must also be taken into view. Apart from difficulties arising from the nature and climate of the country, it cannot be contended that, in their career of Central Asian conquest, the Russians have been confronted with any very formidable obstacles. The only two critical military operations in which they have been engaged were the native attempt to recapture the citadel of Samarkand in 1868, after Kaufmann had marched away in pursuit of the Bokharan army, leaving only a small garrison behind; and the siege of Geok Tepe. The former was a heroic performance; the latter was, to some extent, an artificial success; for Skobeleff's one fear, based on a wide knowledge of Oriental adversaries, was lest the Turkomans should escape him by flight, before he could administer the necessary lesson. As it was, the siege reflected at least as much credit upon the Tekkes as it did upon the Russians; for the former, with no guns, and only inferior rifles, exposed to a murderous artillery fire behind the worst possible defence in the world—viz. a walled enclosure in a level plain, with higher ground in the possession of the enemy—exhibited a gallantry beyond praise. The earlier fights with Kirghiz, Khokandians, and Bokhariots were mostly "walks over," and must ordinarily have degenerated into a rout almost from the start, if the ludicrous disproportion of slain, returned in the Russian official reports of the engagements, be accepted as true. So far the Russians in their advance have not met one genuinely warlike people or fought one serious battle. Their prodigious prestige has had the effect of Joshua's trumpets before the walls of Jericho. No one knew this better than Skobeleff, who told an amusing story of the capture of Ura Tepe by Romanovski in 1866. When the *aksakals* (grey-beards) of the town were brought before the Russian commander they kept asking: "But where are the giants that breathed out fire?" Romanovski discreetly answered that he had sent the giants back to Russia, but would recall them at the first necessity.

This is one among many contrasts between Russian and British conquests in Asia. England only won India after terrific battles, and only holds it by the allegiance of warlike peoples. Indeed, she is far safer in the masculine hands of Sikhs and Mahrattas and Rajputs, than among her tenderly reared nurseries of hot-house Babus. Great, however, as was the task set before England in comparison with Russia, in acquisition, still greater is the strain of retention. The English are thousands of miles from home, and are severed therefrom by continents and oceans. The Russians are still in Russia. From St. Petersburg to Tashkent, or from Odessa to Merv, a Russian never leaves Russian soil; he is still in the fatherland, speaking the same language and observing the same customs. The expansion of Russia is the natural growth of the parent stem, whose stately circumference swells larger and larger each year. The expansion of England is the throwing out of a majestic branch which exhausts and may even ultimately break off from the maternal trunk. Or, to adopt another metaphor, Russia, in unrolling the skein of her destiny, keeps one end of it fast held in her own hand, and is in unbroken connection with the other extremity. England has divided her skein into a multitude of threads, and has scattered them broadcast over the globe. In Central Asia the Russians are residents as well as rulers. In India the English are a relief band of occupants, leaseholders of a twenty years' term, yearning for the expiration of their contract, and for the ship that will bear them home. In Turkestan and Transcaspia Russians are more obvious to the naked eye than are their subjects, and, as I have said, Russian soldiers are far more obvious than Russian civilians. In India the English are swallowed up in a mighty ocean of humanity. You may travel for days, if at any distance from the railway, and never catch sight of a white man; and your *rara avis* when you find him will not have scarlet plumage.

A further contrast is presented by the relative security or insecurity of the two dominions. Many and different enemies have it in their power to wreak mischief upon India. With an extensive and for the most part defenceless seaboard, she is exposed to hostile navies. Her commerce finds a hundred different outlets, not one of which is safe from attack. Upon the north and north-west she is galled and worried by the stings of fanatical tribes. Russia alone can drive her into a ferment by moving a single *sotnia* of Cossacks a few furlongs. On the other hand, the Russian Empire in Central Asia is impregnable. Every avenue of approach is in her own hands; there is no enemy at her gates. No Armada can threaten where there are no seas; no hostile army can operate at such a gigantic distance from its base. England can do her no positive injury. Her commerce is overland and cannot be touched; her communications are secure and cannot be severed. We have no interest in further advance. Our hands are full. Russia is growing and spreading, is headstrong and young; and rash fingers are never wanting to beckon her on. Aggression may be sense for her; it is folly for us. The utmost we hope for is to arrest her before the Rubicon of our honour is reached; the least we desire is to provoke her to plunge into the stream.

18

"The Amir's Homily" (1891)

RUDYARD KIPLING

Rudyard Kipling, whose writings about the Raj have left a rich archive of fact and fiction that has influenced generations of readers and historians, was preoccupied with the human drama of imperial rule. In this 1891 short story, set in Abdur Rahman Khan's court, Kipling (1865–1936) represents the emir of Afghanistan as a merciless ruler whose authority "covers the most turbulent race under the stars." In contrast to the clear-thinking, polished statesman who comes across in Abdur Rahman's autobiography (see chapter 19), Kipling's version of the Afghan ruler is cold and unforgiving; Abdur Rahman's cult of personality casts a long shadow over petitioners, to whom he shows little mercy. Though the thief seeking amnesty is the center of the story, we should not fail to take note of Kipling's representation of the emir's attitude toward women, as evidenced in the tale of the wife seeking divorce. She exits cursing the emir under her breath when the divorce is cruelly rejected, setting the stage for Abdur Rahman's final, thunderous denial—a performance that earns him Kipling's mock admiration as a man of honor.

His Royal Highness Abdur Rahman, Amir of Afghanistan, G.C.S.I., and trusted ally of Her Imperial Majesty the Queen of England and Empress of India, is a gentleman for whom all right-thinking people should have a profound regard. Like most other rulers, he governs not as he would but as he can, and the mantle of his authority covers the most turbulent race under the stars. To the Afghan neither life, property, law, nor kingship are sacred when his own lusts prompt him to rebel. He is a thief by instinct, a murderer by heredity and training, and frankly and bestially immoral by all three. None the less he has his own crooked notions of honour, and his character is fascinating to study. On occasion he will fight without reason given till he is hacked in pieces; on other occasions he will refuse to show fight till he is driven into a corner. Herein he is as unaccountable as the gray wolf, who is his blood-brother.

And these men His Highness rules by the only weapon that they understand—the fear of death, which among some Orientals is the beginning of wisdom. Some say that the Amir's authority reaches no farther than a rifle bullet can range; but as none are quite certain when their king may be in their midst, and as he alone holds every one of the threads of Government, his respect is increased among men. Gholam Hyder, the Commander-in-chief of the Afghan army, is feared reasonably, for he can impale; all Kabul city fears the Governor of Kabul, who has power of life and death through all the wards; but the Amir of Afghanistan, though outlying tribes pretend otherwise when his back is turned, is dreaded beyond chief and governor together. His word is red law; by the gust of his passion falls the leaf of man's life, and his favour is terrible. He has suffered many things, and been a hunted fugitive before he came to the throne, and he understands all the classes of his people. By the custom of the East any man or woman having a complaint to make, or an enemy against whom to be avenged, has the right of speaking face to face with the king at the daily public audience. This is personal government, as it was in the days of Harun al Raschid of blessed memory, whose times exist still and will exist long after the English have passed away.

The privilege of open speech is of course exercised at certain personal risk. The king may be pleased, and raise the speaker to honour for that very bluntness of speech which three minutes later brings a too imitative petitioner to the edge of the ever ready blade. And the people love to have it so, for it is their right.

It happened upon a day in Kabul that the Amir chose to do his day's work in the Baber Gardens, which lie a short distance from the city of Kabul. A light table stood before him, and round the table in the open air were grouped generals and finance ministers according to their degree. The Court and the long tail of feudal chiefs—men of blood, fed and cowed by blood—stood in an irregular semicircle round the table, and the wind from the Kabul orchards blew among them. All day long sweating couriers dashed in with letters from the outlying districts with rumours of rebellion, intrigue, famine, failure of payments, or announcements of treasure on the road; and all day long the Amir would read the dockets, and pass such of these as were less private to the officials whom they directly concerned, or call up a waiting chief for a word of explanation. It is well to speak clearly to the ruler of Afghanistan. Then the grim head, under the black astrachan cap with the diamond star in front, would nod gravely, and that chief would return to his fellows. Once that afternoon a woman clamoured for divorce against her husband, who was bald, and the Amir, hearing both sides of the case, bade her pour curds over the bare scalp, and lick them off, that the hair might grow again, and she be contented. Here the Court laughed, and the woman withdrew, cursing her king under her breath.

But when twilight was falling, and the order of the Court was a little relaxed, there came before the king, in custody, a trembling haggard wretch, sore with much buffeting, but of stout enough build, who had stolen three rupees—of such small matters does His Highness take cognisance.

"Why did you steal?" said he; and when the king asks questions they do themselves service who answer directly.

"I was poor, and no one gave. Hungry, and there was no food."

"Why did you not work?"

"I could find no work, Protector of the Poor, and I was starving."

"You lie. You stole for drink, for lust, for idleness, for anything but hunger, since any man who will may find work and daily bread."

The prisoner dropped his eyes. He had attended the Court before, and he knew the ring of the death-tone.

"Any man may get work. Who knows this so well as I do? for I too have been hungered—not like you, bastard scum, but as any honest man may be, by the turn of Fate and the will of God."

Growing warm, the Amir turned to his nobles

all around and thrust the hilt of his sabre aside with his elbow.

"You have heard this Son of Lies? Hear me tell a true tale. I also was once starved, and tightened my belt on the sharp belly-pinch. Nor was I alone, for with me was another, who did not fail me in my evil days, when I was hunted, before ever I came to this throne. And wandering like a houseless dog by Kandahar, my money melted, melted, melted till—" He flung out a bare palm before the audience. "And day upon day, faint and sick, I went back to that one who waited, and God knows how we lived, till on a day I took our best *lihaf*—silk it was, fine work of Iran, such as no needle now works, warm, and a coverlet for two, and all that we had. I brought it to a money-lender in a by-lane, and I asked for three rupees upon it. He said to me, who am now the King, 'You are a thief. This is worth three hundred.' 'I am no thief,' I answered, 'but a prince of good blood, and I am hungry.'— 'Prince of wandering beggars,' said that money-lender, 'I have no money with me, but go to my house with my clerk and he will give you two rupees eight annas, for that is all I will lend.' So I went with the clerk to the house, and we talked on the way, and he gave me the money. We lived on it till it was spent, and we fared hard. And then that clerk said, being a young man of a good heart, 'Surely the money-lender will lend yet more on that *lihaf*,' and he offered me two rupees. These I refused, saying, 'Nay; but get me some work.' And he got me work, and I, even I, Abdur Rahman, Amir of Afghanistan, wrought day by day as a coolie, bearing burdens, and labouring of my hands, receiving four annas wage a day for my sweat and backache. But he, this bastard son of naught, must steal! For a year and four months I worked, and none dare say that I lie, for I have a witness, even that clerk who is now my friend."

Then there rose in his place among the Sirdars and the nobles one clad in silk, who folded his hands and said, "This is the truth of God, for I, who, by the favour of God and the Amir, am such as you know, was once clerk to that money-lender."

There was a pause, and the Amir cried hoarsely to the prisoner, throwing scorn upon him, till he ended with the dread "*Dar arid*," which clinches justice.

So they led the thief away, and the whole of him was seen no more together; and the Court rustled out of its silence, whispering, "Before God and the Prophet, but this is a man!"

19

The Life of Abdur Rahman, Amir of Afghanistan (1900) and "The Ameer's Memoirs" (1900)

MOHAMMED KHAN, EDITOR, AND THE *SPECTATOR*

In this autobiographical account, which is a translation of the original 1886 *Pandnama-ie-dunya wa din* (Book of advice on the world and religion), Abdur Rahman Khan talks about his early life and his role in directing the key battle of the Second Anglo-Afghan War. Abdur Rahman was emir of Afghanistan from 1880 until his death in 1901 (the exact date of his birth is uncertain). His grandfather was Dost Mohammad, the emir whom the British fought in the first Afghan campaign. Thus Abdur Rahman came from a long line of patrimonial leaders who shaped the fate of central Asia in the Victorian period. He was ushered into power via terms negotiated with the British, who remained eager to prevent Russian alliances in the region. But he soon faced opposition in the person of a local rival, Ayub Khan, whom he ultimately bested, thereby securing his dominion over most if not all of Afghanistan for two decades. Known as the "iron emir," Abdur Rahman was a formidable ruler determined to keep local enemies at bay and to rely on the British not as a supplicant but as the regional sovereign unlike less powerful earlier emirs. The anonymous reviewer of his autobiography in the *Spectator* quotes heavily from the text and works hard to try to redeem the man, who would likely have seemed despotic and alien to fin de siècle readers.

In the year of Hijira, when I was nine years* old, my father sent for me to go to Balkh from Kabul. My father was then King, and Viceroy of Balkh and of its dependencies. At the time of my arrival I found him besieging Shibarghan, and I remained at Balkh for two months, at the end of which period the conquest of Shibarghan was completed; and, on my father's return, I went ten miles south of Balkh to receive him at a place called Dasht-i-Imam (*i.e.*, Desert of the Leader). My eyes were gladdened by the sight of my father, who knelt down and thanked God for my safety. We returned to Balkh together, and a few days after, he ordered me to begin my lessons. I tried to read

*Abdur Rahman was probably born in 1844.

and write all day, but I was very dull. I hated lessons, and my thoughts were too much occupied with riding and shooting. What I learned to-day I forgot to-morrow; but it was compulsory, and there was no getting out of it. My tutor tried hard to teach me with little success. At the end of a year a new school, with a garden attached, was built for me, at a place called Taktapul (Bridge of the Boards) in the suburbs of Balkh. The reason of this was, that Balkh was an old and unhealthy city, also that my father was accustomed to pray at the holy tomb of the King of the Saints, "Ali" Murtza. This blessed tomb was nearer Taktapul than Balkh; and, in time, my father built his Harems, Courts, Cantonments, and workshops there. Gardens were also planted, and in three years a new and beautiful city sprang up.

In the spring of the fourth year my father went to Kabul to pay his respects to his father, the Amir Dost Mahomed Khan, appointing me viceroy in his place. My programme during the next six months was as follows. The hours before 8 o'clock in the morning I employed in studying, and from 8 to 2 P.M. I held my Court. After dismissing my Court, I slept; and, late in the afternoon, I rode my horse for the sake of the fresh air. At the beginning of the winter my father wrote to me from Kabul that my grandfather had graciously bestowed upon me the honour of the Governorship of Tashkurghan, for which place I was to start immediately, accompanied by 1000 sowars, 2000 militia, and six guns. In accordance with these instructions I set out for Tashkurghan, and on my arrival there, Sirdar Mahomed Amin Khan (brother of Wazir Mahomed Akbar Khan) set out for Kabul, first handing over to me the Governorship of the place. My father had appointed an assistant for me, called Haidar Khan. This gentleman, who was a dignified and clever man, was a Kizal Bash chief, who had authority to keep his own flag, a military band, and 200 sowars. His father, Mahomed Khan, was an able man, and had a large number of followers at Kabul. My programme at the time was as follows: From early morning till 9 A.M. study. From 9 A.M. to 2 P.M. holding my Court, hearing cases, and settling the disputes of my subjects. After 2 P.M. I slept, and later practised different kinds of military exercise, big shooting, riding, polo, etc. Friday being a holiday, I generally spent the whole day hunting, returning at night to the fort of Tashkurghan. Five months after my appointment my father and my mother (who had been in Kabul since I left) came to see me, and I was very glad to kiss their hands. My father stayed with me at Tashkurghan until the following spring, when he set out for Balkh, leaving my mother with me, and I continued my studies, and administered the Governorship of the districts. Being kindly disposed towards the army, and the subjects of Tashkurghan, many of whom were my personal attendants, I bestowed certain presents on the people, and reduced the fixed revenues on land when there was any failure in the crops.

At the end of two years my father returned, and requested that the accounts of the province should be submitted to him. On discovering my leniency he at once refused to allow the concessions I had made. I begged him not to insist on the repayment of the money, but he refused, saying he was obliged to do so, as the income of the country was so small, and the army so large. He stayed with us three months, collecting about one lakh of rupees, the amount I had exonerated my subjects from paying, and returned to Balkh. On his departure I resigned the Governorship, stating that I was not invested with full power to govern according to my ideas. I left my assistant governor of Tashkurghan in my place, and took up my residence at Taktapul, again resuming my studies. On Thursday afternoons I always went shooting, returning the evening of the next day, after passing one night and two days out of doors. My shooting party as a rule consisted of nearly 200 dogs, hawks, falcons, and other birds of prey, 100 page-boys, and my mounted suite, numbering in all about 500. We generally chose to shoot and hunt in the jungles near the Oxus, but sometimes we passed our days fishing in the river called Bawina Karā, which is the only river of Hazhdah Nahr of Balkh.

At this time Wazir Yar Mahomed Khan, Governor of Herat, wrote to my father, saying it was his pleasure to bestow on me his daughter's hand in marriage. His request being granted, I was engaged, which strongly cemented the friendship between him and my father. Another great favourite of my father's was Sirdar Abdur Rahim Khan of the family of Sirdar Rahimdād Khan. This man was very treacherous and ill-natured, jealousy being a hereditary disease in his family. He resented my influence at Court, thinking he would lose power if I had the charge of the army, so he made false accusations against me, often causing my father to be angry with me without cause. The head officer in my father's army was an Englishman named General Shir Mahomed Khan, who had changed his religion. This officer, known in Europe by the name of Campbell, was captured by my grandfather's army in 1250 (Hijira) at the battle of Kandahar against Shah Shujāh. He was a very clever military officer, as well as a good doctor. His character was most heroic, and he had a great regard for me. He was one of the ablest men of his day, and occupied the position of Commander-in-Chief over the entire army of Balkh, numbering 30,500, out of which 15,000 were regulars, including cavalry, infantry, and artillery. The remainder consisted of militia soldiers, belonging to three races, Usbeg, Durani, and Kabuli. There were eighty guns, twelve having been sent from Kabul at the time of Sirdar Akram Khan's governorship; the rest being made in Kabul under the superintendence of my father. The army was in very good condition, being drilled regularly every day. One day Shir Mahomed Khan asked my father to place me under his instructions, so that before his death he might impart his knowledge to me. My father consenting to this, instructed me to go to the Governor for two or

three hours daily, as much to train me as to prevent me wasting my time. I said "Ba chishm" (by my eyes), and went willingly. For two or three years I continued to be trained in surgery and military tactics. My father had also sent for a few rifle-makers from Kabul, and opened a workshop near my school. At mid-day, after my lessons and work were finished, I went to this school, and learned to do blacksmith's work with my own hands, also the work of filemen. In this way I acquired the art of rifle-making, and I made three complete double rifles with my own hands. These were considered better than those made by my instructors. The before-mentioned Abdur Rahim Khan showed great jealousy of my progress, and began intriguing against me. One day he told my father I had contracted the habit of drinking wine and smoking Indian hemp. I had never done anything of the kind, but being very young, and very unhappy with these continual scoldings, I made up my mind to run away from Balkh to Herat, where my father-in-law lived. When I was privately making my preparations, my servants reported my intentions to my father, who made enquiries, and finding the report true, put me in prison, taking all my soldiers, slaves, and servants away from me. My foolish mistake had given colour to the accusations Abdur Rahim had been making against me. I was one year in prison, with chains on my ankles, and was very unhappy.

At the end of this time Shir Mahomed Khan died, and Abdur Rahim expected to be made General in his place, but my father suspecting him to be a traitor, appointed instead one of his trusted personal attendants of the Tukhi tribe, named Abdul Rauf Khan, son of Jafr Khan, who had proved himself a very brave soldier in many battles, and who was killed in the battle of Kandahar. This man was also a descendant of Jafr Khan, Wazir of Shah Husam Ghilzai, ruler of Kandahar. When he found himself selected for the post of Commander-in-Chief of the army, he refused to accept it, saying to my father that his own son, who had been one year in prison, and therefore punished sufficiently for his faults, was the proper person to take the place of Shir Mahomed Khan. My father at first refused to listen to such a proposal, saying Abdul Rauf must be mad to think the army could be placed under my care, but being urged to give me a trial, he finally consented to send for me.

I came straight from prison to appear before my father without dressing my hair or washing my face, wearing the same clothes in which he had last seen me, with chains around my ankles.

The moment he saw me his eyes filled with tears, and he said, "Why do you behave like this?" I answered: "I have done no wrong, it is the fault of those who call themselves your well-wishers that I am in this condition." While I was speaking it happened that Abdur Rahim appeared in the Court, and on seeing him I continued: "This is the traitor who has placed me in chains; time will prove which of us is in the wrong." At this Abdur Rahim changed colour with anxiety and anger, but he could do or say nothing. My father addressed himself to all the military officers, saying, "I appoint this my lunatic son to be General over you." To which they replied: "God forbid that your son should be a lunatic: we know well that he is wise and sensible, you also will find this out, and will prove that it is disloyal people who give him a bad character." My father then gave me leave to go and take up my duties. I was overjoyed, and went and refreshed myself with a Turkish bath. My servants meantime gathered round me, congratulating me on my release and good fortune.

The next day I took charge of the army, and inspected the workshops and magazines. I appointed General Amir Ahmad Khan (afterwards my representative in India), who was a commanding officer in the artillery, as a superintendent of the workshops, and Commandant Mahomed Zaman Khan as superintendent of the magazines. Sikander Khan (afterwards killed in a battle between the Russians and the King of Bokhara, and whose

brother, Ghulam Haidar, is now Commander-in-Chief in Kabul*), with another of the same name but of the Barukzai tribe, I appointed as chief officers of battalions. I, myself, inspected all the different departments from morning till night, reporting the progress made daily to my father, who became more pleased every day.

The army was so thoroughly organised that neither before nor since has it been in such good order. One of the reasons of this is that the present officials are over-luxurious. In the reign of Amir Shere Ali they were accustomed to take bribes and neglect their duties. Now they ought to be content with their salaries, doing their work regularly and well. A wise poet says: "Do not consort with thieves; they may make some effect upon your minds." By the grace of God my people may profit by my advice, and will gradually make progress.

My father being satisfied with my military services, gave me full authority over the entire army, keeping to himself the civil affairs of the country, with the accounts of the kingdom. After a short time my father went to Tashkurghan, to which place I accompanied him with my body-guard. On our arrival, Mir Atalik's brother brought a letter with some presents for my father, who received him warmly, and persuaded him to return with a message for his brother, to the effect that as his country lay on the side of the Oxus river, and was in close connection with Afghanistan, he ought to consider himself under the protection of the reigning Amir of Kabul, Dost Mahomed Khan, instead of under the King of Bokhara, and ought to repeat the name of Dost Mahomed in his Khutba, as their present habit was an insult to Afghanistan. On receiving this message Mir Atalik lost his temper with his brother, and tried to imprison him, but he fled towards Tashkurghan. He, however, was pursued and overtaken by Mir Atalik's sowars, at a place called Abdan. Hearing of this, we sent a force to assist him, but he was killed

*He died in 1897.

before they arrived, and all they could do was to defeat Mir Atalik's sowars, and return with the dead body of his brother. Mir Atalik, hearing of the defeat of his sowars, went to complain to the King of Bokhara (Amir Muzaffar). This King had succeeded to the throne that year on the death of his father, and was staying at Hissar to quell a rebellion in that country. The King gave heed to Mir Atalik's complaint, and sent him a flag and a tent, telling him to erect the tent in his country, with the flag in front, to frighten the Afghans. The credulous Mir, believing that this was all he needed, returned to Kataghan, and sent a defiance to us. My father reported his attitude to the Amir, who commanded him to send an army to take possession of Kataghan. My father invited his brother, Sirdar Azim Khan, to leave Kuram Khost (of which country he was Governor), and to come and see him. I was sent as far as Aibak to receive him.

In the spring, before the army was despatched to Kataghan, I took six days' leave to see that everything was thoroughly in order. Being satisfied that this was so, I invited my father to make a personal inspection also. He professed himself satisfied with my arrangements, and gave me a horse with gold harness and saddle, also a jewelled belt and sword, saying: "Go thou, God be with you, I leave you in His protection." I kissed his hands, and two days later being appointed Commander-in-Chief of the army under my uncle Azim Khan, I started. On my arrival in the city of Tashkurghan, the people, with whom I was very popular, received me warmly. I encamped my force in the plain of Namazgah, and to show my gratitude to the people, I invited all the chiefs of the town to a banquet. They afterwards proved faithful to me and my army. In about fifteen days my uncle joined me, and together we started for Aibak, arriving there after a few days' march. We halted three days, arranging provisions and transport animals, and from there marched towards the fort of Ghori, which was fortified by Mir Atalik's infantry and cavalry. We reached this fort after five days' march. On our arrival there, I arranged my troops, 20,000 in number, with 40 guns, in front of the fort, for the enemy's benefit, after which display we encamped in a safe place. Late in the afternoon I inspected the situation of the fort, accompanied by a few officers, pointing out suitable places for guns, etc., also ordering that entrenchments should be made. Under cover of night I gave orders that underground mines should be laid towards the moat of the fort, and these were finished by the following morning.

In the afternoon Mir Atalik showed himself from the top of the hill, with 40,000 sowars, to his soldiers within the fort, to encourage them to make a brave resistance. On seeing him there, I forestalled any attacks he might make on our entrenchments, by an assault on his rear, with 2000 sowars, 12 mule-battery guns, and 4 battalions of infantry. The Mir was unaware of our approach until I ordered the heavy guns to be fired. At this sudden attack, being ignorant of the smallness of my force, he fled with all his army. I returned to my camp and inspected the mines until eleven o'clock that evening when, after seeing the sentries were at their posts, I retired to rest. At sunrise I inspected the troops, and sent 2000 to a distance of 12 miles as an advance guard, to provide for the safety of the transport animals, and against any unexpected attack of the enemy, also to keep me informed of their movements. Three days after, I received the intelligence that 15 miles distant were 8000 sowars, concealed in a place called Chasma-i-Shir (the Spring of Milk). The object of this manœuvre evidently being to attack our transports on their way to and from the camp, I at once appointed 4000 sowars and 2 guns, under the command of Ghulam Mahomed Khan, Populzai, and Mahomed Alam Khan, to attack them. This they did so successfully that after a very slight skirmish the Kataghan sowars were defeated, and 2000 were taken prisoners. The remainder fled to Baghlan, where their Mir was encamped.

When this news reached Kataghan, Mir Atalik being encamped only 18 miles distant lost courage, and retired towards Kunduz. Of the sowars I had sent to Chasma-i-Shir, 1000 remained in possession of Baghlan, while the others returned to my camp in triumph. My uncle bestowed rewards on those who had distinguished themselves in battle, and khilats on others.

In the afternoon of the same day I visited the entrenchments, and spoke from behind to the soldiers in the fort, saying: "You people are Muslims, and I also am a Muslim. You have seen the defeat of your Mir, therefore it is folly to continue killing my Muslims and being yourselves killed by them. Leave the fort to me, and I will make terms to your satisfaction." To this, they made no reply, and in the evening I appointed certain of my officers to attack the fort at daybreak in the following manner: First, they were to attack Sukila, a place outside the moat of the inner fort. This place was also surrounded by a moat. Before the attack was made I directed the heavy guns to be continually fired from sunrise to morning, the object being to alarm the enemy. Directly the guns ceased, a few soldiers were to make several attacks on different aspects of the fort to draw attention from Sukila, the real point of attack. The greater part of my force was to approach this latter place noiselessly, and, having scaled the walls, was to cry out loudly: "Ya chahar yar."* All this was carried out as I instructed, the enemy flying from the outer fort to the inner one. The moat surrounding this fort was ten yards deep, and twenty-three yards in width. Fortunately, the water was exceedingly clear, which enabled my officers to observe a hidden bridge composed of wattled cane which had been constructed about thirty-six inches under the surface of the water. With loud cries of triumph they plunged into the water, and waded to the opposite side. The soldiers immediately followed, and taking possession of the bazaars, they made holes in the walls, through which they fired at the people within the fort.

*"Oh! Four Friends."

While this was happening, I wrote a letter to the Governor in charge of the fort, saying that if he surrendered, I would spare the lives and property of his sowars, and would look upon them as my subjects. I ordered the firing to cease, and sent this letter by one of my prisoners. The Governor and chief officers of the fort came out to answer me personally and discuss the terms of surrender. They agreed to my conditions, and opened the gates, the inhabitants streaming out in large numbers. The majority of these I sent to my uncle, who bestowed khilats on the chiefs, after which he dismissed them to their homes. Their number was fully 10,000, but their Mir having no knowledge of war, had only allowed them provisions for ten days, and had I delayed my attack, they would have been obliged surrender. Their Mir evidently thought the tent and flag bestowed on them by the King of Bokhara was alone sufficient to sustain a large army. God be praised for having created so wise a people!

The followers of Mir Atalik were overjoyed and surprised at our kind treatment, as their chiefs had told them so much of the cruelty of the Afghans. Their fears being now dissipated, they deserted in large numbers, and returned to their homes. The Mir left Kataghan with a few faithful followers, and took refuge in Rustak, under the rule of the Mir of Badakshan. On receiving this news, we immediately marched from Ghori to Baghlan, his capital and from there sent letters to all the chiefs of the country, giving them every promise of our support and on some bestowing khilats. We also appointed governors and magistrates of the religious courts. After this I left Baghlan for Khanabad, encamping on a high ground near the river bank. I sent 2 battalions, 1000 Usbeg militia sowars, 500 Afghan sowars, 500 militia infantry, with 6 mule-guns towards Talikhan. The commanding officer of this force, Mahomed Yamen Khan, son of the great Amir Dost Mahomed Khan, was appointed by my uncle to be Sirdar. The army arrived at Talikhan after crossing the Bargi river, and immediately made entrenchments near the fort, destroying it in a short time. My uncle and I, meantime, were busy in Khanabad, making every alteration necessary in a captured city, one of these being that my grand-father's name was inserted in the prayer-books.

"THE AMEER'S MEMOIRS"

The first volume of this book takes us back four centuries. We seem to be re-reading the famous Memoirs of the Emperor Babar. "when I was nine years old," begins the Ameer, "my father sent for me to go to Balkh from Kabul . . . I found him be-sieging Shibarghan." When Babar was eleven years old, he writes, "I became King of Farghana." Both spent their youth in perpetual fighting in the same country about the Oxus and Jaxartes. Both suffered terrible reverses, endured privations, exile, toils, and adventures almost incredible; both at last attained the kingdom of Kabul, and both loved it better than any other place on earth. The very names of towns and the titles of chiefs and princes are the same; in both stories there are hand-to-hand combats, long fugitive rides over the wild deserts and among treacherous tribes, in-trigues and jealousies among trusted friends and kinsmen; in both we find even the same passion for the water-melons of the Transoxine meadows which Babar used to dwell on with regretful ap-petite when he was mastering Hindustan. The two men are alike in their restless energy, their uncon-querable resolution, their delight in danger and resourcefulness in extremity, in their contempt of fatigue, in their convictions of final success. They are alike too in their superstitions, and both relied on the presage of astrologers; but whilst Babar was highly cultivated, a poet and a philosopher, he had sundry amiable (and unamiable) weaknesses; the Ameer, though extraordinarily unlettered, never seems to have known what weakness means.

The story of his adventures and how he won his throne reads like romance. Indeed, no Prisoner of Zenda or Gentleman of France went through half such tremendous crises in his fate. Yet the narra-tive, written by the Ameer himself in perfectly simple language, reads like truth. There is no ex-planation of how he came to recall the minute de-tails of his early career, whether he kept a journal, or whether he trusted to that marvellous register, an Oriental memory; but however the feat was accomplished, the result has all the appearance of veracity. There is doubtless exaggeration, the numbers engaged in battles are probably guess-work, and the events may be transposed by a trick of memory; but that the facts in general are facts we can hardly dispute. The very vaingloriousness of the hero's account of his exploits is a witness to sincerity. His self-confidence, not to say "brag," and absolute conviction that whatever he did must be right, are too natural and candid to cover rho-domontade. The Ameer is his own hero, and de-scribes himself, as we believe, to the life. He does not shrink from recording his own deeds of blood and fraud. A priest accused him of being an infi-del: the Ameer had the "impure-minded dog" dragged out of [the] sanctuary, and then "I killed him with my bare hands." An example had to be made of the robber-chiefs of Afghanistan; "one of them now hangs in a cage, where I put him, on the peak of the Lataband Mountain," in singular con-trast to the votive rags of superstitious pilgrims at this sacred spot. There is a savage simplicity in all this that reminds us of the wars of the Kings and the Judges of Israel. The Ameer's dealings with the merchants of Badakhshan is typical of his drastic methods. He caught them red-handed in highway robbery, fifty in number, and "ordered them all to be blown from the guns, as they had committed many crimes on my unoffending people. This punishment was carried out on market day, so that their flesh should be eaten by the dogs of the camp, and their bones remain lying about till the festival was over." The capture of the merchants brought a remonstrance and a threat from the Mir of the provinces, though he had not yet learned their fate, but the messenger fared ill in the subse-quent proceedings;—

"I read this letter aloud," says the Ameer, "in the public audience, and asked the man if the Mir was in good health and quite sensible when he wrote it. He replied these words: 'My King, Mir Sahib, has commanded me to bring back your prisoners to him, without loss of time, or he will immediately take steps against you.' To this I answered: 'Do not lose your temper, consider a moment.' But he refused to be warned, and said again rudely, 'Hand over your prisoners. How dare you imprison our people?' Without further conversation I ordered my servants to pull out his beard and moustache, and to dye his eyebrows like a woman. I then took him to the place where the remains of the merchants lay, and put his beard and moustache in a good cloth, advising him to take it to his Mir, both as a caution, and as a reply to his letter. With this man I sent a strong force, consisting of 2 battalions, 2000 cavalry sowars, 100 Usbeg sowars, 2000 infantry, and 12 guns, to Talikan. When they arrived there, the commanders sent this man with his reply to Mir Jahandar Shah, who abused him, and demanded to know why he had returned without the prisoners whom he had sent him to fetch. The man uncovered his face, and threw the gold cloth at the Mir's feet, saying: 'this is what I have suffered by carrying your idiotic messages, and this is what you will suffer if you are not careful.'"

In the result the Mir sent a present and an apology, alleging that "he was always intoxicated and did not know what he was doing. I smiled and told the chiefs that I considered his apology reasonable." Thus the Ameer forgave the Mir whose people he had blown from the guns. When this truculent episode took place, the Ameer was still in his teens, so far as can be ascertained—for he is not certain about the year of his birth. Before this, when a Viceroy and provincial Governor at the age of about fifteen, he had resigned his post because his father would not give him a free hand "to govern according to my ideas." In the same lofty spirit, when a refugee at Bokhara, he refused to make obeisance. He had brought various presents for the King, including a couple of Arab horses and a load of gold tangas, and this is what happened:—

"On our arrival at the palace, the Wazir received me, leading us to the King's rooms. The customs of the Kings of Bokhara is this. The King sits in a big house with two or three favorite page-boys. All his officials sit round the house on small raised terraces around the wall. At the door of the house are two door-keepers, who peep in occasionally to see if the King makes any sign with his eyes. If he gives them a wink, they run to see what he requires, retreating backwards to repeat the message to the Hudachi, or head of the Court. When I arrived near those door-keepers, they ran to the King, then back to the Hudachi, saying their King had been pleased about my presents. I was then told to take the bridles of my two horses in my two hands, also to balance the tangas on my back, and make a bow to the King. I replied that the tangas were one man's load; the two horses required two grooms; and that I would not put my head to the ground for any one in existence. I added: 'I am created by God, and shall kneel to no one but Him.' The door-keeper, who had never heard such a reply from anyone before, was much amazed, so I offered to take my reply to the King himself, or to go to some other country. At last the Wazir said something to the Hudachi, who went to the King, returning to tell me that his Majesty has accepted my salaams. I entered the house, saying in the ordinary way 'Salam alaikum' ('Peace be on you') and I shook hands with the King, who told me to sit beside him."

The Ameer's cool insolence generally succeeded, it would seem, and one cannot but admire his determination to make himself respected, even when his fortune was at its lowest ebb, and his courage against all odds, when everything seemed against him. At the turning-point of his career, when he was making his way back on the bare chance of a possible welcome at Kabul, after eleven years of exile in Russian Samarkand, his ready courage saved him. . . . He was pluck invincible. The only time he gave way to despair was when he was arrested by the Russians, and for a moment he lost hope in his cause. But the arrest was quickly followed by release, and release by escape from Russian territory, and escape by invitation from Sir Lepel Griffin, and the Ameer's succession to his throne. It is a wonderful story from beginning to end, full of hairbreadth escapes and extraordinary vicissitudes. . . .

The use the Ameer has made of his kingship shows that the fine qualities of his days of trial was not exhausted by suffering or enervated by success. He set himself to face the problems of his peculiarly difficult position with seriousness and high-minded devotion. . . . the record of his work since his accession in 1880 is one of which any ruler in any kingdom might well feel proud. . . .

The eleven years in Russia seemed to have opened the eyes of Abdurrahman. He declares boldly that Russia's promises are so much wastepaper, that her advances are treacherous, that her slow approaches are infinitely more dangerous than the impulsive dashes of England. Russia, he says, wishes to see Afghanistan weak and divided, in order to step over her to India, unquestionably the goal of Russian ambition according to the Ameer's knowledge. England, on the other hand, wishes Afghanistan to be strong, in order to hinder the advance of Russia. Hence England is the Afghan's natural ally, and, in the Ameer's opinion, no invasion of India would be possible if Afghanistan joined in opposing it. Therefore his policy and his interest draw him closer to England, and his chief desire is to be permitted to establish an Envoy at the Court of St James. He distrusts the Indian Government, dreads the "forward policy," and whilst admiring Lord Dufferin and Lord Ripon, has nothing good to say of some other Viceroys. . . . the Ameer writes like an honest man—a rare thing, we admit, for an Afghan—and his choice between the devil and the deep sea which encompasses him is obviously the best he can make in his country's interest. Seldom has a powerful ruler—and a King who can muster eight hundred thousand men at Herat in a fortnight is certainly powerful—set forth his political views so squarely, and his frankness seems to merit confidence. At all events, his remarkable book will command the attention of statesmen as well as the interest of all who can appreciate its unique mixture of stirring adventure and wide administration, of blood and thunder, and sweetness and light.

20

The Russians at the Gates of Herat (1885)

CHARLES MARVIN

Even after the conclusion of the Second Anglo-Afghan War, the city of Candahar and its environs remained vulnerable to Russian threat, and India was vulnerable to Russian attack. Charles Marvin's account details the operations of Russian generals and their agents in the wake of the installation of Abdur Rahman Khan as the next emir of Afghanistan and bemoans the comparative lack of concern about Russia's ongoing Asian designs in British territory. Having spent time in Russia as a teenager because his father worked as an engineer there, Marvin was fluent in Russian. He became a correspondent for the *Globe* (London) and a popular expert on the question of Russia and India.

Here Marvin (1854–90) focuses on the Russian general Mikhail Skobeleff's determination to invade India, aided by the completion of the railway between Tiflis (Tbilisi) and Baku, which shortened the journey from Tiflis to the Caspian to just one day. Indeed, railway networks were considered by many British observers, George Nathaniel Curzon included, to be one of the most significant threats to imperial interests in the region, insofar as the railways helped to secure Russia's strategic interests and, via its role in transporting exports like cotton, its commercial interests. Raising the possibility that the Russians would go so far as to incite mutiny in India to achieve their ends, Marvin argues that Russia "has two cards to play: the Afghans and the people of India. If she finds she cannot accomplish her aims with one, she will try to effect them with the other."

"The probability of our having to struggle for Herat, or to defend India, from Candahar, is so remote, that its possibility is hardly worth considering."

These words were penned by Sir Henry Norman, in a memorandum against the retention of Candahar, September, 20, 1880. They illustrate, in a plain and forcible manner, the view of the few, and now utterly discredited experts, who raised their voice in favor of the "scuttle" from Candahar, and invoked the spirit of faction to sanction it.

To-day England is not only morally struggling for Herat, but her Sikhs with Ridgeway at Penjdeh confront the Cossacks with Alikhanoff at Puli-khisti. At any moment shots may be fired, and then the troops that scuttled from Candahar will have to rush back "to defend India from it."

On the 10th of January, 1881, the Duke of Argyll said, in denouncing Lord Salisbury's avowal of alarm at the advance of Skobeleff to Geok Tepé: "We are told by the late Government that the danger they wished to guard against was the danger of a military basis to be formed by Russia on the Caspian. I hold that to be one of the wildest dreams ever entertained."

In four short years the "wildest dream," which, I should point out, was simply the sober military opinion of Valentine Baker, Major Napier, and General Sir Charles MacGregor, who had surveyed the proposed line of advance—in four short years that "wildest dream" has become a practical reality, and the public read, quite as a matter of course, of Russia's preparations for the invasion of India.

Whether the evacuation from Candahar was politic or not in 1881, one thing is certain. Down almost to the very last days of his Viceroyalty, the Marquis of Ripon refused to take serious steps to render the Afghan barrier a real bulwark to our Eastern Empire. The Cabinet in London moved somewhat with the times, but Lord Ripon and Sir Evelyn Baring resisted every change. It is a matter of common notoriety at Simla that the appeals of our greatest generals were pooh-poohed, and that to the very moment of the departure of the Baboo Viceroy from Bombay, the advice of heroes who would have to defend Afghanistan tomorrow, if attacked, was contemptuously rejected for the car-whisperings of two or three insignificant men, of ignominious sentiments.

Why those generals—who, by the way, are now the chief advisers of Lord Ripon's sagacious successor—should have been so uneasy during the last few years, will be apparent in the following pages.

Until the time of the arrival of the Stolietoff Embassy at Cabul, the idea of a Russian attack upon India was generally scouted in this country; and even those who urged the stemming of the Russian advance did not treat an expedition against us as a matter of the immediate present, but as belonging to the future. In Russia, military opinion was more advanced. While war was still undeclared against Turkey in 1876, and England was hoping that the conflict might be averted by peaceful diplomatic means, General Skobeleff, then Governor of Ferghana, the Turkestan district nearest India, forwarded to Kaufmann an elaborate plan for a Central Asian campaign. Even when summoned to Europe to take part in the operations there, he used his utmost influence at Court to put the Turkestan forces in motion, and finally achieved his object in sight of Constantinople, when, after several councils of war, it was decided that if the Congress at Berlin failed, an attack should be made upon India.

Accordingly, Colonels Stolietoff and Grodekoff left the camp for Central Asia, the former charged with a mission to Shere Ali, and the latter—Skobeleff's oldest and most trusted friend—carrying Skobeleff's secret plans, and for himself the special appointment as chief of Kaufmann's staff. One other agent was also sent from the camp—Pashino, an ex-diplomate, who had served as interpreter at Samarcand to the present Ameer, Abdurrahman Khan, and possessed a knowledge of India from a journey he had undertaken through the peninsula a few years earlier. His mission was to proceed to India and secretly ascertain the condition of military and tribal affairs on the frontier, and afterwards push his way through the Khyber and join the Russian mission at Cabul.

The outcome of the enterprise is well known. Kaufmann marched with the invading force to Djam, on the Bokharan frontier, and marched back again when the Treaty of Berlin became known. Stolietoff penetrated to Cabul, and occasioned the Afghan war. Grodekoff returned to

Europe by a famous ride through Herat, and is now Acting-Governor of Turkestan. Finally, Pashino was arrested at Peshawur, and, in spite of his outcry, was sent back to Russia.

Most of these facts are known to the public, but Skobeleff's proposed plan of operations has never received due attention, even at the hands of those commonly supposed to be interested in Central Asian affairs. Briefly, the plan was this: Kaufmann was to have led an army to Cabul, almost denuding Turkestan of its garrison, and was to have there organized the Afghan forces for an attack upon India, while Russian emissaries stirred up the natives to a mutiny. If the people failed to respond to the Russian appeal, Kaufmann was to tie the English army to India by threatening it from Cabul, and, in the event of a rising, he was to push on to the frontier, and attack the English on one side while the mutineers advanced and harried them on the other. Supposing the attempt failed, Kaufmann was to retreat, not upon Turkestan, in case the sight of his shattered forces should cause Bokhara to rise, but upon Herat and the Caspian; being met on the way by a succoring army advancing *via* Askabad and Meshed.

Such was Skobeleff's daring scheme, the revelation of which, since his death, has exercised a remarkable effect upon the imagination of Russian generals, and caused a longing to lead or participate in a campaign offering so many chances of distinction and glory. Had the Congress of Berlin failed, the impression is general among Russian military men that Skobeleff's plan would have been crowned with success. Their belief in the certainty of a mutiny in India is one that Englishmen will not generally share, and hence the probability of an actual irruption into India will be contested; but there is one matter upon which not much difference of opinion can prevail. The Afghans would have doubtless fallen in with the Russian plans, and by their co-operation tied the English troops to the frontier; thereby preventing the reinforcements being sent to Europe. This alone would have been a success of no mean order, for it is no secret that Russia was greatly disturbed by the idea of Sepoys being despatched to Turkey to assist in the defence of Constantinople.

Strangely enough, Skobeleff's plan of invasion has only excited Russia and England since his death. The actual march by Kaufmann toward India provoked little or no attention in this country, and, the details being suppressed in Russia, it was treated as a simple demonstration intended to give weight to Stolietoff's mission. That it was really a serious move, inspired by the deadliest intentions against our rule in India, was only to the most limited degree realized even by the oldest politicians in this country. The military movement was looked upon as subsidiary to the political mission at Cabul, instead of the latter being, as it really was, a pioneering feeler of the former. This indifference to Kaufmann's march was increased by the English disasters in Afghanistan and Lomakin's failure to conquer the Turcomans. It was asserted that while the Afghan and Turcoman barriers existed India was perfectly safe from attack. Then stress was laid upon the Hindoo Koosh, and politicians overlooked the looming advance from the Caspian. Even Skobeleff's decisive success at Geok Tepé did not shake the belief of the Gladstone Cabinet in the sound and permanent character of the barriers beyond, intervening between Askabad and India. The Duke of Argyll said that the new advance was not to be compared with the older ones, and that we had nothing to fear from Skobeleff's triumph. But for the energy displayed by Lord Salisbury, the fall back from Candahar would have been followed by the evacuation of Quetta.

It was while things were in this condition that Mr. Joseph Cowen, M.P., asked me to proceed to St. Petersburg to ascertain the Russian view of the position in Central Asia from the lips of the principal generals and statesmen. Of all the generals I saw, Soboleff was the only one who would agree with the opinion I strongly held at the time, and which was well known to them, that a Russian attack could be made upon India from the Caspian. General Skobeleff was the most incredulous of all. He would not hear of a Russian attack. "The Central Asian difficulty is all humbug," he said. "I do not think a Russian invasion of India would be feasible. I do not understand military men in England writing in the *Army and Navy Gazette*, which I take in and read, of a Russian invasion of India. I should not like to be commander of such an expedition. The difficulties would be enormous. To subjugate Akhal we had only 5,000 men, and needed 20,000 camels. To get that transport we had to send to Orenburg, to Khiva, to Bokhara, and to Mangishlak for animals. The trouble was enormous. To invade India we should need 150,000 troops—60,000 to enter India with and 90,000 to guard the communications. If 5,000 men needed 20,000 camels, what must 150,000 need! And where could we get the transport? We should require vast supplies, for Afghanistan is a poor country, and could not feed 60,000 men; and we should have to fight the Afghans as well as you. If we bribed one Sirdar, you would bribe another; if we offered one rouble, you would offer two; if we offered two, you would offer five—you could beat us in this. No; the Afghans would fight us as readily as they fought you. I believe the new frontier is quite permanent, and that we shall hear no more about Central Asia for many years to come."

"But in regard to the possibility of invading India, General Soboleff expressed to me a clear conviction that Russia could march an army on India if she chose."

"That was diplomacy," replied Skobeleff. "Of course it is possible—all things are possible to a good general—but I should not like to undertake the task, and I do not think Russia would. Of course, if you enraged Russia—if, by your policy, you excited her—if you made her wild—that is the word—we might attempt it, even in spite of all the difficulties. For my part, I would only make a demonstration against India, but I would fight you at Herat." He said this with great animation, but very good-humoredly. "Do you know, I was very much interested during your war whether you would occupy Herat or not. It would have been a mistake if you had done so. It would be difficult to march an army from the Caspian to Herat to fight you there, but we should be tempted to do it in the event of a war."

Whether these were really the sentiments of Skobeleff at the moment, or whether he was purposely minimizing the possibility of attacking India, in order that England might not be terrified into preparing against it in time, is a matter over which much argument might be expended without leading to any satisfactory result. I will not attempt to discuss the point. I will simply point out one or two facts, which are of more importance at the present moment.

After Skobeleff had finished his conversation with me he repeated it to Captain Masloff, one of his favorite officers. Masloff published an account of it in the *Novoe Vremya* which tallied with my own, and he subsequently told me that Skobeleff had spoken of my report as perfectly accurate. The part I have repeated in this book was triumphantly quoted by Madame de Novikoff (otherwise O. K.) two years ago as demonstrating the madness of the Russian scare in this country. But O. K. has never said since that these utterances of Skobeleff fell completely flat in Russia. No Russian newspaper, and no Russian military writer has ever reciprocated those views, or, indeed, ever noticed them at all. On the other hand, Skobeleff's opposite opinions in favor of an expedition to India, which began to appear a few months after his death and have been seeing the light at intervals since, have exercised an enormous influence on the Russian military mind. Many of the documents published were written anterior to his conversation with me, but while the latter is ignored and forgotten, the former are incessantly being cited in proof of what Russia can effect against India.

Several other circumstances have contributed to add to the effect of Skobeleff's aggressive views.

A few months after his death General Soboleff published his "Anglo-Afghan Conflict," a bulky three-volume work, compiled by the Chief of the Asiatic branch of the General Staff before proceeding to Bulgaria as Minister of War. This work was a sort of official history of our Afghan campaign, based on English sources, and was recommended by the General Staff as a standard work for military libraries. His recent utterances in the *Russ* have shown that General Soboleff looks at things through very peculiar spectacles. He is dominated by the bitterest hatred against England, and believes everything said or written to her disadvantage. In this history he sought to make out, or, it would be better to say, did make out, to his own satisfaction, that the Afghan war was too large an enterprise for us, that we were defeated by the Afghans throughout the campaign instead of being mostly victors, and that we were compelled at last to withdraw owing to the damage inflicted on our prestige and the fear of a rising in India.

An English reviewer, noticing Soboleff's work, said it was made up of "lies and nonsense." Upon him, of course, the work make no favorable impression, and he was disposed to minimize its importance. But, as a matter of fact, the book exercised an influence which is displayed pretty clearly to-day. To Russian officers who had not studied the subject, or who had only derived their impressions of the war from the jaundiced statements in the Russian press, the book appeared as worthy of credence as any official work could possibly be. It had been compiled by the Chief of the Asiatic branch of the General Staff, whose express duty it was to watch the war on behalf of the Government and obtain all possible information from England—perhaps India—bearing upon it. If such an official did not know what he was writing about, who in Russia was more competent than he? Thus Soboleff's book was eagerly read and widely read, and strengthened to a remarkable degree the feeling already prevailing that we were a very weak military power, and only maintained our hold on India by a miracle.

Skobeleff's opinion that we could be expelled from the peninsula by means of a hard blow struck in front, simultaneously with a fomented mutiny at the rear of the Indus, has excited more and more attention as Russia has approached nearer our outposts. The belief in its feasibility that has steadily developed in Russia, since his plan of 1876 became known in 1883, has received a considerable impulse from the disappearance of the physical obstacles already existing. Skobeleff's main argument against the feasibility of an invasion, when he discussed the subject with me, was the difficulty of transport, but this is a difficulty that has been daily wearing away ever since. When he proceeded to Geok Tepé in 1880 it took nearly a month for the troops of the Caucasus army to march from Tiflis to the Caspian to join. By the opening of the Tiflis-Baku railway, since his death, the journey can now be done between sunrise and sunset. When he ferried those troops across the Caspian he had to contend with a very limited marine. By the development of the Baku petroleum industry fifty powerful steamers, 150 to 250 feet long, have been added during the last few years to the shipping of the Caspian, and can now convey the largest conceivable army across the sea to Krasnovodsk. The Transcaspian railway, again, was not finished to Kizil Arvat until long after he left Geok Tepé. It is now being pushed on to Askabad, and Lessar has stated that whether there be peace or war, it will be continued to Sarakhs—within six marches of the Key of India. Finally, Skobeleff imagined, or said he imagined, a difficult road to exist between Askabad and Herat. Lessar has since discovered that it is one of the easiest in Asia.

Thus, by Russia's resolute destruction of the Turcoman barrier, and by the rapid disappearance of a series of obstacles, things have come to this pass—that a land march upon India to-day is an enterprise less difficult to the Russian military mind than the march upon Constantinople in 1877.

Such an enterprise might take two forms. Either Russia might adopt Skobeleff's idea of a fomented mutiny, and advance with merely sufficient troops to cleave a passage through the Afghan barrier, or she might ignore for the moment the people of India, and push on with some such army of mammoth proportions as she employed in the last Russo-Turkish war.

Let me deal with the former first.

At the outset I must point out that a wide difference of opinion exists between English politicians and Russians as to the possibility of a mutiny in India, and that this deserves more attention than light-hearted publicists in this country are disposed to give it. English politicians generally assume that India is safe, or sufficiently safe, from the danger of another mutiny. Disturbances, it is admitted, might arise on the Russian approach, but the country generally would stand by us. I do not say that all politicians share this optimist view, but the majority do—or at any rate, they conceal their uneasiness and keep it from the public.

Now Russian Generals, and the entire Russian Press, incline to a totally different opinion. General Skobeleff, General Soboleff, General Tchernayeff, General Kaufmann, General Grodekoff, General Annenkoff, General Petrusevitch, and others less known, may be cited as eminent representative Russian military men who never entertained a doubt on the subject. I have discussed the Anglo-Russian conflict with many Russian officers—some of them personal friends of mine—but have never met one who differed from them in this matter. Yet some have made a special study of India. Skobeleff was always purchasing English books on the country, and I question whether there are half-a-dozen Members of Parliament who have such a good collection of English and foreign books on India as I have pulled out in the library of General Annenkoff.

If we examine more closely the plans of Skobeleff and others, we shall see how important this factor of a general rising really is. Soboleff put the wants of Russia in a neat, compact form the other day when he declared that "Russia does not want

India: she wants the Bosphorus." The Russian invasion of India is commonly ridiculed by certain Radicals on the ground of the hugeness of the enterprise. They assert that the people would never exchange English for Russian masters, and that it would require a larger army than ever Russia could spare to occupy and hold the country. But such assertions are based not upon facts, but illusions. Russia does not propose to occupy and hold India. I have never met a Russian who proposed—at any rate, for the present—such a difficult enterprise as that. Russia does not aim at replacing our administration by her own. None of the Russian generals ever suggested saddling their country with such a burden. What Skobeleff really planned and advocated was, that the 250,000,000 people should be encouraged and helped to throw the 100,000 English off their backs, and that during the universal collapse of our supremacy throughout the world that would ensue (in his opinion), Russia should occupy Constantinople.

Such an enterprise is quite a small affair, compared with the undertaking imagined by those Radicals I have referred to. To secure its success, supposing India to be ready to rise and throw us off, all that is needed is to march to Candahar a force sufficiently strong to overcome the English force holding the frontier; after which the Princes and the mutinous Sepoys themselves could be left to deal with the small garrisons located on the plains and plateaux of India, aided, perhaps, by a few Russian officers. When Skobeleff proposed his plan in 1876, the Russian outposts were too far from the Indian frontier, and the communications connecting them with Russia proper too extended and ill-developed to allow of more than a small force being sent to attack India. He, therefore, had to rely upon Afghan help on the one hand, and an Indian mutiny on the other.

It is well to notice that he provided for two kinds of assistance in his plan. If the Afghan co-operation had been slight, he would have stimulated a general rising in India. If, on the other hand, he had considered himself sufficiently strong with Afghan help, to break through the frontier, he would only have "manipulated the disaffected elements in India to Russia's advantage." The possibility of a general rising in India may be questioned by English politicians; but there is not one who can deny that "disaffected elements" do exist in the country.

The genuine belief of Russia in the probability of a mutiny in India on the approach of a small force against us, is too serious a factor in politics to be brusquely treated as an illusion. The more feasible a Russian attack upon our rule in India appears to the Russian Government, the less disposed will it be to treat us with diplomatic deference in Europe, and refrain from aggressive acts in Asia. Further, the greater the chances seem to it of a successful campaign on the Indian frontier than in Europe, the stronger the impulse to break through the Afghan frontier at any cost and secure Herat. What would Russia care for the Ameer's ill will at seizing Herat if she were sure of an Indian mutiny? The more, therefore, she relies on an Indian revolt the less she may be expected to care for Afghan susceptibilities.

Russia, in a word, has two cards to play—the Afghans and people of India. If she finds she cannot accomplish her aims with the one, she will try to effect them with the other.

"England lays a heavy hand on her dependent peoples," wrote General Soboleff in the *Russ* last January, when he was already aware that Russia had seized the approaches to Herat. "She reduces them to a state of slavery, only that English trade may profit and Englishmen grow rich. The deaths of millions in India from starvation have been caused indirectly by English despotism. And then the press of England disseminates far and wide the idea of Russia being a country of barbarians. Thousands of natives in India only await Russia's crusade of deliverance!

"If Englishmen would only throw aside their misplaced pride, and study a little deeper the foundation of Russia's rule in Central Asia, comparing it with their own, they would soon see plainly why the name of Russia has such *prestige* in Asia, and why the natives of India hate the dominion of England, and set their hopes of freedom upon Russia. Russia gives full liberty to native manners, and not only does not overburden her subjects with fresh taxes, but even allows them exemptions and privileges of a most extensive character. England, on the contrary, is a vampire, sucking the last drop of blood out of India."

21

The Campaign Towards Afghanistan (1885)

ANDREI BOLANDIN

In this excerpt from the translation of his 1885 memoirs, Private Andrei Bolan-din vividly re-creates the world of the Third Turkestan Battalion as it marched to war to protect Russian interests in central Asia. His account is notable for the variety of conversations it reconstructs—between soldiers and officers, and es-pecially between officers and Afghans. The Afghans spar verbally as well as physically, making their case for a religious war and bragging that having beaten the British, they will defeat the Russians too. The passage ends with a spirited rebuttal in the form of an Easter celebration "on a patch of earth won from the enemy" in the name of "Holy Russia."

On 9th March two officers were despatched from Aimak-Dzhar for reconnaissance, to find out where the Afghan troops were located. The outcome of the whole affair would depend on their disposition.

When Merv was annexed to Russia in 1884 it became necessary to delineate the border between the new Russian province and Afghanistan. As is well known, Britain had been interested in Af-ghanistan for a long time. She sent a boundary commission there with a military detachment al-legedly to protect it. Russia sent her commission also with a military detachment under the com-mand of General Komarov. Komarov strung his detachment out from Puli-Khatum to Ak-Tepe. The Afghans, delighted with the arrival of British officers and the small number of our troops, began to infringe the disputed border line more and

more boldly, crossing the River Kushka, and began to construct fortifications here and even fired at Cossacks. It was necessary to scare them off. Therefore Komarov had hurried off to meet Ka-v in order to strengthen his Transcaspian battalion. Having completed their reconnaissance the offi-cers reported that there were between 2,600 and 3,000 men in the Afghan camp.

On 12th March despite a cold downpour and sticky mud Komarov's detachment advanced and spent the night at Urush-Dushana. The tents were erected, but the rain did not let up. Everything was drenched. The bushes were grey. It was al-most completely impossible to light fires. The kind-ling spluttered, smoke filled our eyes, but no fire resulted. Somehow or other fires were lit in a few places and tea was brewed. The soldiers had not a

stitch of dry clothing. It was impossible to get un-
dressed or change one's underwear: even if you
tried the Afghans might attack. It was filth in the
tents, despite the fact that ditches were dug round
them; water crept in under the soldiers. Dampness drifted down from above. If a soldier turned
over the water sloshed around under him. Some
slept nonetheless, exhausted, but others did not
gain a moment's shuteye all night. Towards morning the rain diminished somewhat, but the drip-
ping did not cease. The detachment proceeded
and bivouacked about two versts before the first
Russian post at Kizil-li-Tepe, thus finding themselves about 4–5 versts from the Afghans. Despite
all the Russian officers' negotiations with the
British who were with their troops, as soon as the
Murgab detachment arrived at Kizil-li-Tepe the
Afghans started moving their posts forward on
the Russian flank with militaristic enthusiasm.
They even constructed four redoubts on the left
bank. So, when the thick white mist enveloping
the locality when the Russians arrived there had
dispersed from the ground, flowing upwards and
dissipating, our soldiers found themselves face to
face with the enemy.

On 14th March a general staff captain P-v, who
was with Komarov's retinue, set off to the right
bank of the Murgab with five Dzhigits for reconnaissance. The next day he went to the same place,
but this time with a company of Transcaspian ri-
flemen. Despite the threat from the Afghans who
advanced 800 paces towards him demanding the
immediate surrender of the soldiers, he stood his
ground. Then the Afghans seized a militia constable from the interpreter's section, held him for
above an hour abusing him in every sort of way,
then released him ordering him to communicate
their readiness to meet the Russians with arms in
their hands. But Komarov avoided clashes and the
company sent to the right bank returned to its
bivouac on the evening of the same day. On 15th
March a *sotnia* of the Merv militia under the command of the dashing colonel Alikhanov, a thick

set man with a reddish beard, set off to reconnoitre
the left bank of the Kushka. The head of the Afghan
cavalry, Dzharneil-Gos-Edin-Khan, rode out to intercept him with a large cavalry detachment. But
nevertheless there were no clashes between them.
On the contrary, Lieutenant Alikhanov spoke with
Dzharneil in a friendly fashion and accompanied
him almost to the brick bridge over the Kushka,
or to Tash-Kepra. Dzharneil, for his part, asked
Alikhanov to go away threatening to open fire if
he did not.

It was particularly difficult for the soldiers manning their posts. Here is a soldier from Perm or
Orenburg province, dreaming of his distant northern hamlet with its homely little huts, kind relatives, horses, cows, poultry, meadows and ripening
rye, when suddenly he sees through the mist, almost in front of his nose, wide pantaloon black
Asiatics with high turbans, and hears the long
drawn out shrill blasts of their horns. He thinks it
is dreadful that no orders have been given to fire
at these scum, because at any moment such fuzzy-
wuzzies could shoot him and you couldn't get
anything from them. In a word—Asia!

And the Afghans became more and more bra-
zen. They came up to the post and shouted:

> Beat it! We're not Mervians; we're not Turkmen.
> We're all Afghans. We've beat the British several
> times and we'll smash you if you don't go away.
> What are your troops to us? We'll have our break-
> fast and be in Merv before dinner!

Komarov saw that the situation was not good.
The nervous mood affecting the whole detachment was increasing, and lack of faith in the Russians was already noticeable among the Turkmen:
their former devotion was declining. So he decided to act without further ado. Several times
on the 17th he had demanded that the Afghans
clear the left bank of the Kushka to avoid possible
clashes between the advance posts, but the Afghan
commander, Naib-Salar, refused to accede to his
demands.

At 8 P.M. the same day Komarov assembled all the commanders of the Murgab detachment in his tent for a council of war. He put the situation before them and gave the necessary orders for the following day. The soldiers knew about this gathering of commanders by Komarov and said that a fight was inevitable.

K-v came to our Turkestanis and ordered the distribution of 120 cartridges per man and two days' dry rations. He ordered the men to look to it, change their clothes and be prepared for a fight to the death. Few fires; no tea to be brewed.

"We've got a small detachment," he said, "There's no chance of reinforcements, and if they did come it wouldn't be soon."

The soldiers were about to bawl out that they were "happy to suffer," but the colonel stopped them:

"It's not necessary, lads; it goes without saying!" he said. Then he told each company how and where to go and told them to destroy every crossing over the Kushka except the bridge.

The soldiers began to change their underwear according to the time-honoured Russian tradition. The company commanders asked them only to change their underwear, and to have their cartridges and rifles ready to hand. It was particularly nice to have this clean underwear on bodies which had not seen fresh vests for almost a month and in some cases a month and a half, bodies being subject to constant biting by various insects. But the soldiers did not abstain from vodka. Whoever had money bought some and treated his countrymen.

"Well, comrades in arms, two deaths you don't die, but one is inevitable! It's not death, but how you die" various voices were heard saying.

There were no fires. A cold dampness penetrated the air. Fires in the Afghan camp dimly flickered in the mist. The soldiers involuntarily thought: "Who knows if they'll really become the enemy? Who knows, maybe these high sandy hills will be scattered with corpses in grey coats, irrigating them with their warm blood? How strong the enemy is! Awful dreams, but God is merciful. What's to be will be and it's not known who's going to get it."

Few lay down to sleep. More prepared for the fight and chatted quietly.

At 4 A.M. the order to move was given. It was still completely dark. Impenetrable mud beneath; rain and dampness from above. . . . Irrigation canals, ditches. . . . We stumbled, fell in holes, fished each other out with our bayonets . . . from time to time guffaws were heard from one company or another . . .

"Shut up!" shouted the commander: "Better for us to see the enemy before he sees us!"

But as we went further, so we concentrated more. Our boots simultaneously plopped through the mud. Behind the battalion we occasionally heard the rumble of artillery. That was the guns of the 21st battery. The artillerymen were also silent.

At about 5 A.M. dawn finally began. The ranks of troops could be made out more clearly. We dropped into a sort of gully along which we moved for an hour or more. Before 7 A.M. the Turkestanis came out at some knolls on the enemy's left flank. His ranks were visible on Tash-Keprinsk kurgan, though the mist was still dispersing. There there were about 1,200 cavalry, several companies of infantry and up to eight guns protected by trenches with slits and embrasures. The Turkestanis came out just in front of the cavalry. K-v sent two companies to the bank of the Kushka to the right of the bridge. The soldiers stood boldly. One of the officers, looking at the Afghan advance through his binoculars, asked one of them:

"Are there many of them?"

"Lots, your honour!"

"Are you scared?"

"What is there to be scared of?" the soldier replied jauntily, "It's all one to me."

"Good lad!" praised the officer.

Meanwhile the Afghans had opened fire. Bullets

whistled by. One of them hit the sword of another officer standing on the steppe, but didn't touch him.

The half battery that had come with them began to move forward slightly with the Turkestanis. To the left Cossacks and Lieutenant Alikhanov's Mervian militia could be seen. Contrary to orders it had positioned itself in the centre of the bridge. The soldiers became even more serious: "One, two, three, four. . . . One, two, three, four. . . ." It seemed as if the whole affair was concentrated in this one thing: marching in step.

A platoon of soldiers of the 3rd battalion with its short, light brown haired NCO was detached from the troops to clear the banks of the Afghans who had ensconced themselves under the arches of the bridge. The detail went down the bank and dispatched them all. They reappeared.

"Well, have you shut them up?" asks the company commander.

"Yes, brawled 'em out, your honour. We threw ourselves on the soldiers and bayoneted 'em like worms."

"Great: I'll report to the colonel. No need to take much time with them!"

Colonel Ka-v, riding among the soldiers on his chestnut horse said:

"Well, lads, have you got any cartridges left?"

And suddenly against all expectations the grey people shouted joyfully and loudly:

"Yes sir, your honour!"

In the Afghan tents and marquees set up on thick reed supports they found copper teapots with tea in them, flat cakes in large cups, pistachios, fruits, dried apricots, copper jugs for washing, sheepskin jackets, underwear, turbans and other junk.

In the middle of the camp there was a *barkhan*, a fortified point, though it only contained wounded and an Afghan chained to a British gun. Hooked nosed, bearded and swarthy featured, he was chained by the hands and feet. Anxiously rolling the whites of his eyes he looked at the Russian soldiers surrounding him. They called for an interpreter. It turned out that they had chained him to

the gun because he wouldn't join the line and they forced him to fire on the Russians. Parade was called. The soldiers formed up in the abandoned Afghan camp. The command: "Present arms!" and General Komarov rode along the front line:

"Congratulations on your victory, lads; thank you!"

"Hurrah!" rose from the ranks.

Far off on the steppes incomprehensible cries of joy could also be heard. It appeared that crowds of Saryks and Tekinians who had fled from their huts were also celebrating the victory of the "Urus" over the hated Afghans. Komarov displayed kindness towards them and told the soldiers that the campaign was over, that they would not pursue the Afghans any further and that they could now return home.

And strange to tell a cloud of dissatisfaction appeared fleetingly on all the soldiers' faces.

"Well it's all very well, but we'd rather go to Herat!" many said, apparently dissatisfied that they had escaped death and were no longer going to meet it.

As the troops were returning Komarov ordered the corpses and cartridges to be cleared away, the Afghans to be thrown in the water, but the barley and food stores were to be divided up.

The Saryks were detailed to bury the corpses and a few soldiers were given orders to complete other general commands. About half a dozen of them started fooling about. They got four sacks of powder, placed them side by side and asked one soldier to set fire to them. He took a stick, set fire to it and ignited the powder.

"Boom!" A bright flame suddenly lit everyone up and the soldier toppled over backwards. The other soldiers joked:

"We're not from Viatka but we've made a worse mess than the Viatties!" But when they saw that the soldier was lying there practically motionless and his complete face was singed they rushed up to him, picked him up and took him to the hospital.

"Well," they said later: "He didn't get it in the war, but bought it later, poor devil!"

On 21st March Captain P-v set off with a sotnia of Dzhigits to make a reconnaissance at Kala-i-Mor, and a day later Lieutenant Alikhanov was sent to Meruchak with a hundred Cossacks. On their return they reported that the Afghans had quitted the whole area they had ridden over. Their route was littered with many fresh graves of people who had perished from wounds, cold and hunger and from their desperate flight.

They related that as he was fleeing with the remains of his detachment the Afghan commander Dzharneil had received a letter from Herat's Naib Ul-Gukum in which the latter had urged him to oppose the Russians more forcibly, because strong reinforcements were being sent to his aid. It appeared that on seeing this Dzharneil had exclaimed: "Nothing's needed now, because all is lost!"

The weather became extremely unpleasant: now cold, now rain, now snow, and sometimes all of them together. But the soldiers were not too unhappy: despite the cold they even abandoned the sheepskin jackets they had obtained from the Afghans, because the Afghani lice teeming within them soon made themselves felt by the victors. An orchestra struck up in the camp and the singers sang a song composed by Captain P-v:

> We remember Turkestanis,
> We remember dads and granddads
> Splendid Turkestanis!
> How they taught us
> To fight the enemy without quarter,
> Not to spare the infidel!
> Let's remember, lads, what's past
> How on Kushka's river
> The enemy did a bunk.
> Early morning, hardly dawning
> We swiftly went to flank them,
> And when the dawn arose in glory
> The fusillading thundered.
> The growling of the big guns
> Suddenly began to bark
> And fiercely thundered!
> The Afghans didn't yawn:

> They tried to break our ranks
> But woeful failure
> We're impossible to stop!
> They had to beat it,
> to drag their guns away.
> But we didn't let them
> Even captured all their guns.
> The Afghans did a bunk
> Chucked their rifles and their slippers,
> Now we follow on their tail,
> Send our slugs to help them onward.
> Our music keeps on playing,
> Bravely onwards our detachment
> All across the bridge we march,
> And take their main encampment.
> Our enemy will always think about
> The eighteenth day of March's month.
> Brits and Afghans won't forget,
> And we will never fail to think,
> Of when we bravely beat the foe
> To serve and help our Tsar!

Finally on 25th March it was Easter. Rarely has anyone spent an Easter like the one celebrated by the soldiers who had been at Kushka.

The cold and rain did not stop; little of God's light could be seen. At midnight the early morning Easter service began in the portable church. As the soldiers returned to their tents they were given two eggs apiece which the quartermaster had ridden to Merv to obtain. They gulped their soup down even though it was mixed with earth. Instead of a roast they had fried meat.

"Eh, lads, it was never like this in the Samarkand barracks," some sighed.

"I used to eat far better at home than in the barracks," said one of the recruits.

"What's up, mates, let's just thank God that you're still alive!"

After dinner the music played and for fun the soldiers fired the cannon left by the Afghans.

That's how a little unit thrown into the depths of Asia marked Easter on a patch of earth won from the enemy, whilst far off in Holy Russia all the bells were ringing in every town and village as the Orthodox people celebrated!

22

The Story of the Malakand Field Force (1901)

WINSTON CHURCHILL

In one of his early pieces of frontier journalism, the young Winston Churchill (1874–1965)—later prime minister of Britain—recounts the challenges British soldiers faced on the North-West Frontier as the British imperial century drew to a close. In the excerpt the British hold off the enemy, in this case ethnic Pashtuns unwilling to see their tribal lands controlled by the Western powers (Britain and Russia) most invested in the Great Game. The British Army prevailed, but with difficulty; in large measure because it faced the formidable enemy leader, Saidullah, who declared jihad against the British occupation and led a force of ten thousand strong.

In this selection we get a sense of the grunt work of battle: a small mud-walled enclosure is the site of a particularly intense struggle; keeping the Afghans out "was like caulking a sieve." Here and elsewhere on the North-West Frontier, the British were on the defensive, sustaining significant casualties as well as outright losses. As with many others who memorialized the events surrounding Victorian imperial campaigns, Churchill gave native soldiers their due, recounting as a matter of course how valiantly they fought and how indispensable they were to British success—however halting and fitful it was in this "outpost of our Empire."

AUTHOR'S PREFACE

On general grounds I deprecate prefaces. I have always thought that if an author cannot make friends with the reader, and explain his objects, in two or three hundred pages, he is not likely to do so in fifty lines. And yet the temptation of speaking a few words behind the scenes, as it were, is so strong that few writers are able to resist it. I shall not try.

While I was attached to the Malakand Field Force I wrote a series of letters for the London *Daily Telegraph*. The favourable manner in which these letters were received encouraged me to attempt a more substantial work. This volume is the result.

The original letters have been broken up, and I have freely availed myself of all passages, phrases, and facts that seemed appropriate. The views they contained have not been altered, though several opinions and expressions, which seemed mild in the invigorating atmosphere of a camp, have been modified to suit the more temperate climate of peace.

I have to thank many gallant officers for the assistance they have given me in the collection of material. They have all asked me not to mention their names, but to accede to this request would be to rob the story of the Malakand Field Force, of all its bravest deeds, and finest characters.

The book does not pretend to deal with the complications of the frontier question, nor to present a complete summary of its phases and features. In the opening chapter I have tried to describe the general character of the numerous and powerful tribes of the Indian Frontier. In the last chapter I have attempted to apply the intelligence of a plain man to the vast mass of expert evidence, which on this subject is so great that it baffles memory and exhausts patience. The rest is narrative, and in it I have only desired to show the reader what it looked like.

As I have not been able to describe in the text all the instances of conduct and courage which occurred, I have included in an appendix the official despatches.

The impartial critic will at least admit that I have not insulted the British public by writing a party pamphlet on a great Imperial question. I have recorded the facts as they occurred, and the impressions as they arose, without attempting to make a case against any person or any policy. Indeed, I fear that, assailing none, I may have offended all. Neutrality may degenerate into an ignominious isolation. An honest and unprejudiced attempt to discern the truth is my sole de-fence, as the good opinion of the reader has been throughout my chief aspiration, and can be in the end my only support.

WINSTON S. CHURCHILL
CAVALRY BARRACKS,
BANGALORE, 30TH DECEMBER, 1897

THE ATTACK ON THE MALAKAND

Cry, "Havoc!" and let slip the dogs of war.
—*Julius Cæsar*, Act iii, Sc. i

It has long been recognised by soldiers of every nation that to resist a vigorous onslaught by night is almost the hardest task that troops can be called upon to perform. Panics, against which few brave men are proof, arise in a moment from such situations. Many a gallant soldier has lost his head. Many an experienced officer has been borne down unheeded by a crowd of fugitives. Regiments that have marched unflinchingly to almost certain death on the battlefield become in an instant terrified and useless.

In the attack on the Malakand camp all the elements of danger and disorder were displayed. The surprise, the darkness, the confused and broken nature of the ground; the unknown numbers of the enemy; their merciless ferocity; every appalling circumstance was present. But there were men who were equal to the occasion. As soon as the alarm sounded Lieutenant-Colonel McRae of the 45th Sikhs, a holder of the Gold Medal of the Royal Humane Society and of long experience in Afghanistan and on the Indian frontier, ran to the Quarter Guard, and collecting seven or eight men, sent them under command of Major Taylor, of the same regiment, down the Buddhist road to try and check the enemy's advance. Hurriedly assembling another dozen men, and leaving the Adjutant, Lieutenant Barff, with directions to bring on more, he ran with his little party after Taylor in the direction of the entrance gorge of the Kotal camp. Two roads give access to the Malakand camp, from the plain of Khàr. At one point the Buddhist road, the higher of the two, passes through a narrow defile and turns a sharp corner. Here, if anywhere, the enemy might be held or at least delayed until the troops got under arms. Overtaking Major Taylor, Colonel McRae led the party, which then amounted to perhaps twenty men, swiftly down the road. It was a race on which the lives of hundreds depended. If the enemy could turn the corner, nothing could check their rush, and the few men who tried to oppose them would be cut to pieces. The Sikhs arrived first, but by a very little. As they turned the corner they met the mass of the enemy, nearly a thousand strong, armed chiefly with swords and knives, creeping silently and stealthily up the gorge, in the hope and assurance of rushing the camp and massacring every soul in it. The whole road was crowded with the wild figures. McRae opened fire at once. Volley after volley was poured into the dense mass at deadly range. At length the Sikhs fired independently. This checked the enemy, who shouted and yelled in fury at being thus stopped. The small party of soldiers then fell back, pace by pace, firing incessantly, and took up a position in a cutting about fifty yards behind the corner. Their flanks were protected on the left by high rocks, and on the right by boulders and rough ground, over which in the darkness it was impossible to move. The road was about five yards wide. As fast as the tribesmen turned the corner they were shot down. It was a strong position.

> In that strait path a thousand
> Might well be stopped by three.

Being thus effectively checked in their direct advance, the tribesmen began climbing up the hill to the left and throwing down rocks and stones on those who barred their path. They also fired their rifles round the corner, but as they were unable to see the soldiers without exposing themselves, most of their bullets went to the right.

The band of Sikhs were closely packed in the cutting, the front rank kneeling to fire. Nearly all were struck by stones and rocks. Major Taylor, displaying great gallantry, was mortally wounded. Several of the Sepoys were killed. Colonel McRae himself was accidentally stabbed in the neck by a bayonet and became covered with blood. But he called upon the men to maintain the good name of "Rattray's Sikhs", and to hold their position till death or till the regiment came up. And the soldiers replied by loudly shouting the Sikh war-cry, and defying the enemy to advance.

After twenty minutes of desperate fighting, Lieutenant Barff arrived with thirty more men. He was only just in time. The enemy had already worked round Colonel McRae's right, and the destruction of the few soldiers left alive could not long have been delayed. The reinforcement, climbing up the hillside, drove the enemy back and protected the flank. But the remainder of the regiment was now at hand. Colonel McRae then fell back to a more extended position along a ride about fifty yards further up the road and reinforcing Lieutenant Barff's party, repulsed all attacks during the night. About 2 A.M. the tribesmen, finding they could make no progress, drew off leaving many dead.

The presence of mind, tactical knowledge and bravery displayed in this affair are thus noticed in the official despatches by General Meiklejohn:

"There is no doubt that the gallant resistance made by this small body in the gorge, against vastly superior numbers, till the arrival of the rest of the regiment, saved the camp from being rushed on that side, and I cannot speak too highly of the behaviour of Lieutenant-Colonel McRae and Major Taylor on this occasion."

While these things were passing on the right, the other attacks of the enemy had met with more success. The camp was assaulted simultaneously on the three sides. The glow of the star shells showed that the north camp was also engaged. The enemy had been checked on the Buddhist road by

Colonel McRae and the 45th Sikhs, but another great mass of men forced their way along the graded road in the centre of the position. On the first sound of firing the inlying picquet of the 24th Punjaub Infantry doubled out to reinforce the pickets on the road, and in the water-gorge. They only arrived in time to find these being driven in by overpowering numbers of the enemy. Hundreds of fierce swordsmen swarmed into the bazaar and into the *serai*, a small enclosure which adjoined. Sharpshooters scrambled up the surrounding hills, and particularly from one ragged, rock-strewn peak called Gibraltar, kept up a tremendous fire

The defence of the left and centre of the camp was confided to the 24th Punjaub Infantry. One company of this regiment under Lieutenant Climo, charging across the football ground, cleared the bazaar at the point of the bayonet. The scene at this moment was vivid and terrible. The bazaar was crowded with tribesmen. The soldiers, rushing forward amid loud cheers, plunged their bayonets into their furious adversaries. The sound of the hacking of swords, the screams of the unfortunate shopkeepers, the yells of the Ghazis were plainly heard above the ceaseless roll of musketry. The enemy now tried to force their way back into the bazaar, but the entrance was guarded by the troops and held against all assaults till about 10:45. The left flank of the company was then turned, and the pressure became so severe that they were withdrawn to a more interior line of defence, and took up a position along the edge of the "Sappers' and Miners' enclosure." Another company held the approaches from the north camp. The remainder of the regiment and No. 5 company Sappers and Miners, were kept in readiness to reinforce any part of the line.

It is necessary to record the actual movements of the troops in detail, but I am anxious above all things to give the reader a general idea. The enemy had attacked in tremendous strength along the two roads that gave access on the eastern side

to the great cup of the Malakand. On the right road, they were checked by the brilliant movement of Colonel McRae and the courage of his regiment. Pouring in overwhelming force along the left road, they had burst into the camp itself, bearing down all opposition. The defenders, unable to hold the extended line of the rim, had been driven to take up a central position in the bottom of the cup. This central position comprised the "Sappers' and Miners' enclosure," the commissariat lines and the Field Engineer Park. It was commanded on every side by the fire from the rim. But the defenders stood at bay, determined at all costs to hold their ground, bad though it was.

Meanwhile the enemy rushed to the attack with wild courage and reckless fury. Careless of life, they charged the slender line of defence. Twice they broke through and penetrated the enclosure. They were met by men as bold as they. The fighting became desperate. The general himself hurried from point to point, animating the soldiers and joining in the defence with sword and revolver. As soon as the enemy broke into the commissariat lines they rushed into the huts and sheds eager for plunder and victims.

Lieutenant Manley, the Brigade Commissariat Officer, stuck stubbornly to his post, and with Sergeant Harrington endeavoured to hold the hut in which he lived. The savage tribesmen burst in the door and crowded into the room. What followed reads like a romance.

The officer opened fire at once with his revolver. He was instantly cut down and hacked to pieces. In the struggle the lamp was smashed. The room became pitch dark. The sergeant, knocking down his assailants, got free for a moment and stood against the wall motionless. Having killed Manley, the tribesmen now began to search for the sergeant, feeling with their hands along the wall and groping in the darkness. At last, finding no one, they concluded he had escaped, and hurried out to look for others. Sergeant Harrington remained in the hut till it was retaken some hours later, and so saved his life.

Another vigorous attack was made upon the Quarter Guard. Lieutenant Watling, who met it with his company of sappers, transfixed a Ghazi with his sword, but such was the fury of the fanatic that as he fell dead he cut at the officer and wounded him severely. The company were driven back. The Quarter Guard was captured, and with it the reserve ammunition and the sappers. Lieutenant Watling was carried in by his men, and, as soon as he reached the dressing station, reported the loss of this important post.

Brigadier-General Meiklejohn at once ordered a party of the 24th to retake it from the enemy. Few men could be spared from the line of defence. At length a small but devoted band collected. It consisted of Captain Holland, Lieutenant Climo, Lieutenant Manley, R.E., the general's orderly, a Sepoy of the 45th Sikhs, two or three sappers and three men of the 24th; in all about a dozen.

The general placed himself at their head. The officers drew their revolvers. The men were instructed to use the bayonet only. Then they advanced. The ground is by nature broken and confused to an extraordinary degree. Great rocks, undulations and trees, rendered all movements difficult. Frequent tents, sheds and other buildings increased the intricacies. Amidst such surroundings were the enemy, numerous and well armed. The twelve men charged. The tribesmen advanced to meet them. The officers shot down man after man with their pistols. The soldiers bayoneted others. The enemy drew off discomfited, but half the party were killed or wounded. The orderly was shot dead. A sapper and a havildar of the 24th were severely wounded. The general himself was struck by a sword on the neck. Luckily the weapon turned in his assailant's hand, and only caused a bruise. Captain Holland was shot through the back at close quarters by a man concealed in a tent. The bullet, which caused four wounds, grazed his spine. The party were now too few to effect anything. The survivors halted. Lieutenant Climo took the wounded officer back, and collecting a dozen more men of the 24th, returned to the attack. The second attempt to regain the Quarter Guard was also unsuccessful, and the soldiers recoiled with further loss; but with that undaunted spirit which refuses to admit defeat they continued their efforts, and at the third charge dashed across the open space, bowling over and crushing back the enemy, and the post was recovered. All the ammunition had, however, been carried off by the enemy, and as the expenditure of that night had already been enormous, it was a serious loss. The commissariat lines were at length cleared of the tribesmen, and such of the garrison as could be spared were employed in putting up a hasty defence across the south entrance of the enclosure, and clearing away the cookhouses and other shelters which might be seized by the enemy.

The next morning no fewer than twenty-nine corpses of tribesmen were found round the cookhouse, and in the open space over which the three charges had taken place. This, when it is remembered that perhaps twice as many had been wounded and had crawled away, enables an estimate to be formed of the desperate nature of the fight for the Quarter Guard.

All this time the fire from the rim into the cup had been causing severe and continual losses. The enemy surrounding the enclosure on three sides brought a cross fire to bear on its defenders, and made frequent charges right up to the breastwork. Bullets were flying in all directions, and there was no question of shelter. Major Herbert, D.A.A.G., was hit early in the night. Later on Lieutenant-Colonel Lamb received the dangerous wound in his thigh which caused his death a few days afterwards. Many Sepoys were also killed and wounded. The command of the 24th Punjaub Infantry devolved upon a subaltern officer, Lieutenant Climo. The regiment, however, will never be in better hands.

At about one o'clock, during a lull in the firing,

the company which was lining the east face of the enclosure heard feeble cries for help. A wounded havildar of the 24th was lying near the bazaar. He had fallen in the first attack, shot in the shoulder. The tribesmen, giving him two or three deep sword cuts to finish him, had left him for dead. He now appealed for help. The football ground on which he lay was swept by the fire of the troops, and overrun by the enemy's swordsmen, yet the cry for help did not pass unheeded. Taking two Sepoys with him, Lieutenant E. W. Costello, 24th Punjaub Infantry, ran out into the deadly space, and, in spite of a heavy fire, brought the wounded soldier in safely. For this heroic action he has since received the Victoria Cross.

As the night wore on, the attack of the enemy became so vigorous that the brigadier decided to call for a reinforcement of a hundred men from the garrison of the fort. This work stood high on a hill, and was impregnable to an enemy unprovided with field guns. Lieutenant Rawlins volunteered to try and reach it with the order. Accompanied by three orderlies, he started. He had to make his way through much broken ground infested by the enemy. One man sprang at him and struck him on the wrist with a sword, but the subaltern, firing his revolver, shot him dead, reached the fort in safety, and brought back the sorely-needed reinforcement.

It was thought that the enemy would make a final effort to capture the enclosure before dawn, that being the hour which Afghan tribesmen usually select. But they had lost heavily, and at about 3:30 A.M. began to carry away their dead and wounded. The firing did not, however, lessen until 4:15 A.M., when the sharpshooters withdrew to the heights, and the fusillade dwindled to "sniping" at long range.

The first night of the defence of the Malakand camp was over. The enemy, with all the advantages of surprise, position and great numbers, had failed to overcome the slender garrison. Everywhere they had been repulsed with slaughter. But the British losses had been severe.

British Officers

Killed—
 Hon. Lieutenant L. Manley, Commissariat Department.
Wounded dangerously—
 Major W. W. Taylor, 45th Sikhs.
Wounded severely—
 Lieut.-Colonel J. Lamb, 24th P.I.
 Major L. Herbert, D.A.A.G.
 Captain H. F. Holland, 24th P.I.
 Lieutenant F.W. Watling, Q.O. Sappers and Miners.

Of these Lieut.-Colonel Lamb and Major Taylor died of their wounds.

Native Ranks

 Killed 21
 Wounded 31

The telegraph had carried the news of the events of the night to all parts of the world. In England those returning from Goodwood Races read the first details of the fighting on the posters of the evening papers. At Simla, the Government of India awoke to find themselves confronted with another heavy task. Other messages recalled all officers to their regiments, and summoned reinforcements to the scene by road and rail. In the small hours of the 27th, the officers of the 11th Bengal Lancers at Nowshera were aroused by a frantic telegraph operator, who was astounded by the news his machine was clocking out. This man in his shirt sleeves, with a wild eye, and holding an unloaded revolver by the muzzle, ran round waking every one. The whole country was up. The Malakand garrison was being overwhelmed by thousands of tribesmen. All the troops were to march at once. He brandished copies of the wires he had received. In a few moments official instructions arrived. The 11th Bengal Lancers, the 38th Dogras and the 35th Sikhs started at dawn. No. 1 and No. 7 British Mountain Batteries were also ordered up. The Guides Cavalry had already arrived. Their infantry under Lieutenant Lockhart reached the Kotal at 7:30 P.M. on the 27th, having, in spite of the intense heat and choking dust, covered thirty-two miles in seventeen and a half hours. This wonderful feat was accomplished without impairing the efficiency of the soldiers, who were sent into the picket line and became engaged as soon as they arrived. An officer who commanded the Dargai post told me that as they passed the guard there they shouldered arms with parade precision, as if to show that twenty-six miles under the hottest sun in the world would not take the polish off the Corps of Guides. Then they breasted the long ascent to the top of the pass, encouraged by the sound of firing, which grew louder at every step.

Help in plenty was thus approaching as fast as eager men could march, but meanwhile the garrison had to face the danger as best they could alone. As the 31st Punjaub Infantry, who had been the last to leave the north camp, were arriving at the Kotal, about 1,000 tribesmen descended in broad daylight and with the greatest boldness, and threatened their left flank. They drove in two pickets of the 24th, and pressed forward vigorously. Lieutenant Climo with two companies advanced up the hill to meet them, supported by the fire of two guns of the Mountain Battery. A bayonet charge was completely successful. The officers were close enough to make effective use of their revolvers. Nine bodies of the enemy were left on the ground, and a standard was captured. The tribesmen then drew off, and the garrison prepared for the attack, which they knew would come with the dark.

As the evening drew on the enemy were observed assembling in ever-increasing numbers. Great crowds of them could be seen streaming along the Chakdara road, and thickly dotting the hills with spots of white. They all wore white as yet. The news had not reached Buner, and the sombre-clad warriors of Ambeyla were still absent. The glare of the flames from the north camp was soon to summon them to the attack of their ancient enemies. The spectacle as night fell was strange, ominous, but not unpicturesque. Gay banners of every colour, shape and device, waved from the surrounding hills. The sunset caught the flashing of sword-blades behind the spurs and ridges. The numerous figures of the enemy moved busily about preparing for the attack. A dropping fire from the sharp-shooters added an appropriate accompaniment. In the middle, at the bottom of the cup, was the "crater" camp and the main enclosure with the smoke of the evening meal rising in the air. The troops moved to their stations, and, as the shadows grew, the firing swelled into a loud, incessant roar.

The disposition of the troops on the night of the 27th was as follows:

1. On the right Colonel McRae, with 45th Sikhs and two guns supported by 100 men of the Guides Infantry, held almost the same position astride the Buddhist road as before.
2. In the centre the enclosure and Graded road were defended by—

   31st Punjaub Infantry.
   No. 5 Company Q.O. Sappers and Miners.
   The Guides.
   Two Guns.

3. On the left the 24th Punjaub Infantry, with the two remaining guns under Lieutenant Climo, held the approaches from the abandoned north camp and the fort.

Most of this extended line, which occupied a great part of the rim, was formed by a chain of pickets, detached from one another and fortified by stone breastworks, with supports in rear. But in the centre the old line of the "Sappers' and Miners' enclosure" was adhered to. The bazaar was left to the enemy, but the *serai*, about a hundred yards in front of the main entrenchment, was held by a picket of twenty-four men of the 31st Punjaub Infantry, under Subadar Syed Ahmed Shah. Here it was that the tragedy of the night occurred.

At eight o'clock the tribesmen attacked in tremendous force all along the line. The firing at once became intense and continuous. The expenditure of ammunition by the troops was very great, and many thousands of rounds were discharged. On the right Colonel McRae and his Sikhs were repeatedly charged by the swordsmen, many of whom succeeded in forcing their way into the pickets and perished by the bayonet. Others reached the two guns and were cut down while attacking the gunners. All assaults were, however, beaten off. The tribesmen suffered terrible losses. The casualties among the Sikhs were also severe. In the morning Colonel McRae advanced from his defences, and, covered by the fire of his two guns, cleared the ground in his front of the enemy.

The centre was again the scene of severe fighting. The tribesmen poured into the bazaar and attacked the serai on all sides. The post was a mud-walled enclosure about fifty yards square. It was loop-holed for musketry, but had no flank defences. The enemy made determined efforts to capture the place for several hours. Meanwhile, so tremendous was the fire of the troops in the main enclosure that the attack upon the serai was hardly noticed. For six hours the picket there held out against all assaults, but the absence of flank defences enabled the enemy to come close up to the walls. They then began to make holes through them, and to burrow underneath. The little garrison rushed from place to place repelling these attacks. But it was like caulking a sieve. At length the tribesmen burst in from several quarters, and the sheds inside caught fire. When all the defenders except four were killed or wounded, the Subadar, himself struck by a bullet, ordered the place to be evacuated, and the survivors escaped by a ladder over the back wall, carrying their wounded with them. The bodies of the killed were found next morning, extraordinarily mutilated.

The defence of this post to the bitter end must be regarded as a fine feat of arms. Subadar Syed

Ahmed Shah was originally promoted to a commission for an act of conspicuous bravery, and his gallant conduct on this occasion is the subject of a special paragraph in despatches.*

On the left, the 24th Punjaub Infantry were also hotly engaged, and Lieutenant Costello received his first severe wound from a bullet, which passed through his back and arm. Towards morning the enemy began to press severely. Whereupon Lieutenant Climo, always inclined to bold and vigorous action, advanced from the breastworks to meet them with two companies. The tribesmen held their ground and maintained a continual fire from Martini-Henry rifles. They also rolled down great stones upon the companies. The 24th continued to advance, and drove the enemy from point to point, and position to position, pursuing them for a distance of two miles. "Gallows Tree" hill, against which the first charge of the counter attack was delivered, was held by nearly 1,000 tribesmen. On such crowded masses, the fire of the troops was deadly. The enemy left forty dead in the path of Lieutenant Climo's counter attack, and were observed carrying off many wounded. As they retreated, many took refuge in the village of Jalàlkòt. The guns were hurried up, and ten shells were thrown into their midst causing great slaughter. The result of this bold stroke was that the enemy during the rest of the fighting invariably evacuated the hills before daylight enabled the troops to assume the offensive.

Thus the onslaught of the tribesmen had again been successfully repelled by the Malakand garrison. Many had been killed and wounded, but all the tribes for a hundred miles around were hurrying to the attack, and their numbers momentarily increased. The following casualties occurred on the night of the 27th:

---

*The Subadar and the surviving Sepoys have since received the Order of Merit.

British Officer

Wounded—
Lieutenant E. W. Costello

Native Ranks

Killed 12
Wounded 29

During the day the enemy retired to the plain of Khàr to refresh themselves. Great numbers of Bunerwals now joined the gathering. The garrison were able to distinguish these new-comers from the Swatis, Utman Khels, Mamunds, Salarzais and others, by the black or dark-blue clothes they wore. The troops were employed in strengthening the defences, and improving the shelters. The tribesmen kept up a harassing and annoying long-range fire, killing several horses of the Guides Cavalry. Towards evening they advanced to renew the attack, carrying hundreds of standards.

As darkness fell, heavy firing recommenced along the whole front. The enemy had apparently plenty of ammunition, and replied with effect to the heavy fire of the troops. The arrangement of the regiments was the same as on the previous night. On the right, Colonel McRae once more held his own against all attacks. In the centre, severe fighting ensued. The enemy charged again and again up to the breastwork of the enclosure. They did not succeed in penetrating. Three officers and several men were however wounded by the fire. Lieutenant Maclean, of the Guides Cavalry, who was attached temporarily to the 31st Punjaub Infantry, had a wonderful escape. A bullet entered his mouth and passed through his cheek without injuring the bone in any way. He continued on duty, and these pages will record his tragic but glorious death a few weeks later at Landakai.

Lieutenant Ford was dangerously wounded in the shoulder. The bullet cut the artery, and he was bleeding to death when Surgeon-Lieutenant J. H. Hugo came to his aid. The fire was too hot to allow of lights being used. There was no cover of any sort. It was at the bottom of the cup. Nevertheless the surgeon struck a match at the peril of his life and examined the wound. The match went out amid a splutter of bullets which kicked up the dust all around, but by its uncertain light he saw the nature of the injury. The officer had already fainted from the loss of blood. The doctor seized the artery and, as no other ligature was forthcoming, he remained under fire for three hours holding a man's life between his finger and thumb. When at length it seemed that the enemy had broken into the camp he picked up the still unconscious officer in his arms and, without relaxing his hold, bore him to a place of safety. His arm was for many hours paralysed with cramp from the effects of the exertion of compressing the artery.

I think there are few, whatever may be their views or interests, who will not applaud this splendid act of devotion. The profession of medicine, and surgery, must always rank as the most noble that men can adopt. The spectacle of a doctor in action among soldiers, in equal danger and with equal courage, saving life where all others are taking it, allaying pain where all others are causing it, is one which must always seem glorious, whether to God or man. It is impossible to imagine any situation from which a human being might better leave this world and embark on the hazards of the Unknown.

All through the night the enemy continued their attacks. They often succeeded in reaching the breastworks—only to die on the bayonets of the defenders. The guns fired case shot, with terrible effect, and when morning dawned the position was still held by the Imperial Forces. The casualties of the night were as follows:

British Officers

Wounded severely—
Lieutenant H. B. Ford, 31st Punjaub Infantry.
H. L. S. Maclean, the Guides.
Wounded slightly—
Lieutenant G. Swinley, 31st Punjaub Infantry.

Native Ranks

Killed 2
Wounded 13

On the morning of the 29th signalling communication with Chakdara was for a few moments re-established. The garrison of that post announced their safety, and that all attacks had been repulsed with heavy loss, but they reported that ammunition and food were both running short. During the day the enemy again retired to the plain to rest, and prepare for the great attack, which they intended making that night. The hour would be propitious. It was Jumarat, on which day the prophet watches with especial care over the interests of those who die for the faith. Besides, the moon was full, and had not the Great Fakir declared that this should be the moment of victory? The Mullah exhorted them all to the greatest efforts, and declared that he would himself lead the assault. Tonight the infidels would be utterly destroyed.

Meanwhile the troops were busily employed, in spite of their terrible fatigues, in strengthening the defences. The bazaar and the serai were levelled. Trees were blown up, and a clear field of fire was obtained in front of the central enclosure. Great bonfires were also prepared on the approaches, to enable the soldiers to take good aim at their assailants while they were silhouetted against the light. In such occupations the day passed.

The tribesmen continued to fire at long range and shot several horses and mules. These sharp-shooters enjoyed themselves immensely. After the relief of Chakdara, it was found that many of them had made most comfortable and effective shelters among the rocks. One man, in particular, had ensconced himself behind an enormous boulder, and had built a little wall of stone, conveniently loopholed, to protect himself when firing. The overhanging rock sheltered him from the heat of the sun. By his side was his food and a large box of cartridges. Here for the whole week he had lived,

steadily dropping bullets into the camp and firing at what an officer described as all "objects of interest." What could be more attractive?

At four o'clock in the afternoon Major Stuart Beatson, commanding the 11th Bengal Lancers, arrived with his leading squadron. He brought a small supply of ammunition, which the garrison was in sore need of, the expenditure each night being tremendous, some regiments firing as much as 30,000 rounds. The 35th Sikhs and 38th Dogras under Colonel Reid arrived at Dargai, at the foot of the pass, in the evening. They had marched all day in the most intense heat. How terrible that march must have been may be judged from the fact that in the 35th Sikhs twenty-one men actually died on the road of heat apoplexy. The fact that these men marched till they dropped dead is another proof of the soldierly eagerness displayed by all ranks to get to the front. Brigadier-General Meiklejohn, feeling confidence in his ability to hold his own with the troops he had, ordered them to remain halted at Dargai, and rest the next day.

The attack came with the night, but the defences in the centre had been much improved, and the tribesmen were utterly unable to cross the cleared glacis which now stretched in front of the enclosure. They, however, assailed both flanks with determination, and the firing everywhere became heavy. At 2 A.M. the great attack was delivered. Along the whole front and from every side enormous numbers swarmed to the assault. On the right and left, hand-to-hand fighting took place. Colonel McRae again held his position, but many of the tribesmen died under the very muzzles of the rifles. The 24th Punjaub Infantry on the left were the most severely engaged. The enemy succeeded in breaking into the breastworks, and close fighting ensued, in which Lieutenant Costello was again severely wounded. But the fire of the troops was too hot for anything to live in their front. At 2:30 the Mad Mullah being wounded, another Mullah killed and several hundreds of tribesmen slain, the whole attack collapsed. Nor was it renewed again with vigour. The enemy recognised that their chance of taking the Malakand had passed.

The casualties were as follows on the night of the 29th:

British Officers

Wounded severely—
Lieutenant E. W. Costello, 24th P.I., who had already been severely wounded, but continued to do duty.
Lieutenant F. A. Wynter, R.A.

Native Ranks

Killed 1
Wounded 17

All the next day the enemy could be seen dragging the dead away, and carrying the wounded over the hills to their villages. Reinforcements, however, joined them, and they renewed their at-tack, but without much spirit, at 9:30 P.M. They were again repulsed with loss. Once, during a thunderstorm that broke over the camp, they charged the 45th Sikhs' position, and were driven off with the bayonet. Only two men were wounded during the night.

In the morning the 38th Dogras and 35th Sikhs marched into the camp. The enemy continued firing into the entrenchments at long range, but without effect. They had evidently realised that the Malakand was too strong to be taken. The troops had a quiet night, and the weary, worn-out men got a little needed sleep. Thus the long and persistent attack on the British frontier station of Malakand languished and ceased. The tribesmen, sick of the slaughter at this point, concentrated their energies on Chakdara, which they believed must fall into their hands. To relieve this hard-pressed post now became the duty of the garrison of Malakand.

23 /
"The Indian Frontier Troubles,"
The Graphic (1897)

Saidullah—also known by the pejorative British nickname the "mad Fakir" or "mad mullah of Swat"—was a religious mendicant who raised the cry of jihad against the British on the North-West Frontier in 1897. His holy war against British imperialism and his mobilization of Pashtun tribes were given attention by Winston Churchill in the *Daily Telegraph* (London) dispatches that he wrote while embedded with the Malakand Field Force and later in his book on the subject. Churchill wrote of Saidullah: "Civilization is face to face with militant Mahommedanism. What Peter the Hermit was to the regular bishops and cardinals of the Church, the Mad Mullah has been to the ordinary priesthood of the Afghan border."[1] In this London-based *Graphic* image, Saidullah appears as a charismatic figure "haranguing" tribal warriors and embodying British "troubles" on the Indian frontier.

"The Indian Frontier Troubles," *The Graphic*, September 18, 1897.

1. Victoria Schofield, *Afghan Frontier: Feuding and Fighting in Central Asia* (London: I.B. Tauris, 2003), 107.

24

The Judgment of the Sword (1913)

MAUD DIVER

As late as 1913, "the Kabul tragedy" of the First Anglo-Afghan War—and with it, the fate of British prestige in the region—was still being rehearsed in fictional form. For the novelist Maud Diver (1867–1945), the real hero of the story was Major Eldred Pottinger, who succeeded the ill-fated Sir William Macnaghten as envoy to the Afghan court. In this passage the drama of Macnaghten's murder is reenacted, in all its horror and treachery. Diver had firsthand experience of the Raj: born in North India, she was the daughter of an officer in the Indian Army, and she married one, Thomas Diver, as well. Though she concedes that "judgment is for historians," Diver makes it clear that she views Macnaghten's assassination as just one in a series of "disastrous mistakes" of the kind that led to Britain's inglorious defeat in 1842.

Macnaghten had promised that Elphinstone's army should march in three days; but the 16th found him still sitting in his familiar *dufter*, still awaiting provisions and transport, without which no move could be made. Yet the Bala Hissar had been evacuated—the Bala Hissar where all might have held out to the last. Major Ewart with the 54th, and gallant Captain Nicholl, with his half troop of Horse Artillery, had marched into cantonments that morning, ruefully enough, hard pressed by Ghazis, whom the chiefs declared themselves unable to control, and who now infested the gates, beating back friendly folk with grain to sell. On these sacred uncontrollables not a shot might now be fired without the most urgent necessity, lest Afghan good feeling be checked!

A lakh of rupees sent to Akbar had produced neither camels nor provisions; and there now lay before Macnaghten a letter from Elphinstone, pointing out that the cattle would soon be too weak to march unless forage were immediately supplied. Thus pressed, Macnaghten sent a line of remonstrance to the chiefs; and their reply betrayed the measure of sincerity that was in them: "So long as your people occupy such strong positions as the Magazine, the Musjid, and the Forts of Rikab Bashi and Zulfikar, our people do not believe you are intending to depart. Let these forts be made over to us and grain in plenty shall be sent."

Insolence heaped on injury! Even Elphinstone denounced the demand as unwarrantable: even Shelton was strongly opposed to such wholesale and injudicious surrender. Macnaghten grew hopeful. "Then, for God's sake," cried he, "let us have done with treaties and march out in order of battle. Now that fresh troops have come in, why not enter the city or fight under its walls?"

Such wild talk restored them to their senses. Battles had no place in their scheme of things.

"In that case," replied Macnaghten, "the forts must be given up. Refusal would only exasperate the chiefs; and we are completely in their hands as regards provisions."

The forts were given up accordingly, on the understanding that they should be garrisoned by men well under control.

That afternoon Lawrence and Macnaghten, with tears of shame and indignation in their eyes, stood together on a mound near the Masjid, while those four strongholds—the last props of British power in Kabul—which had cost so much blood to secure, were made over to their exulting enemies.

Before sunset, those enemies—converted by a stroke of the pen into "allies"—were in full possession. Crowds of them gathered on the ramparts of the Magazine Fort, in view of the whole cantonment, and there sat exchanging sallies over the discomfited garrison within.

That night Lady Sale sat down to write up her journal with bitterness in her heart. "To prove our good faith and our belief in the chiefs," she wrote, "we are to-day placed entirely in their power. They know we are starving; that our horses and cattle have pretty well eaten up the twigs and bark of the trees. The horses gnaw tentpegs. I was even gravely told they had eaten the trunion of a gun! *Nothing is satisfied* except the pariah dogs who are gorged with eating dead camels and horses. . . ."

On the 19th they woke to find snow falling quietly, relentlessly. The earlier slight fall had vanished and given place to prolonged frost. But the chance of departure before the worst came had either not been taken or given; and to-day from dawn to dark the air was thick with feathery flakes that whirled and fell, till all the valley was white with them; till they gleamed, near a foot deep, on the walls of forts and the flat roofs of Kabul city. Difficult to realize that this marvel of softness and brilliance, which in a few hours had translated their world into fairyland, was to prove an enemy more pitiless than the steel of Afghan knives or the stone of Afghan hearts.

Whatever the reason of that week's delay— whether the bad faith of the chiefs, the Shah's irresolution, or the Envoy's reluctance to face enforced withdrawal from the scene of his former triumphs—it had cut away from under their feet all hope of an orderly retreat on Jalálabad, and on the 19th Macnaghten's last straw broke in his hand. He learnt now for certain that Macfarlane, finding snow in the Ghazni highlands, and hampered by loss of cattle, had returned to Kandahar— the more readily, perhaps, because Nott was sure to approve his decision. News of the latter, and of Sale, had arrived two days earlier. Both were faring well. All was reported quiet again round Kandahar; and the reason is not far to seek. Nott's measures had been miles removed from those of Elphinstone. He had not scrupled to discourage Afghan attentions by ordering a captured chief to be blown away from a gun. Thereafter, alert and ready, to the last least buckle on the uniform of the last least recruit, he sat waiting for the rest to "come on."

"*I* am not to be caught sleeping like my Kabul friends," he wrote to his elder daughter at this very time. "I have made every preparation . . . and when the day arrives, I think I shall give a satisfactory account of the enemy—that is, if I am not interfered with by men in power. . . . I have hitherto turned a deaf ear to those around. I dare say they think themselves right; but I am not going to sit quiet and see the throats of my officers and men cut, owing to the folly of others. . . . It is cold and frosty. We go to parade at ten and remain at exercise till twelve. I have concentrated my troops here, and have nine thousand of all kinds. . . . At present we have only the ground we stand on; but when weather will permit of field operations, I hope to make these people here *know our power* . . ."

Pure refreshment to turn from the tale of Kabul to an atmosphere so vigorous and manly as these words suggest. With Nott at his elbow, Macnaghten had never been degraded to such pitiful shifts; to that last most fatal error of trying to beat Orientals at their own game. Yet he owed it to his own prejudice, his own amazing ignorance of men, that this indomitable General had not long since reigned supreme at Kabul.

Sale's position, though better than Elphinstone's, was worse than Nott's; for Jalálabad—the Abode of Splendour—was even more miserably ruinous and indefensible than the "folly on the plain." But Sale, though an indifferent General, was happy in possessing exceptionally fine officers; unhappy only by reason of increasing anxiety as to the outcome of the deadlock at Kabul. All dreaded the "insanity" of premature capitulation, though they had Macnaghten's assurance that he would postpone it to the last.

And by the 20th Macnaghten knew that the "last" had come indeed. More snow had fallen; the "uncontrollable" Ghazis grew daily more insolent in their bearing towards troops forbidden by their own commandant to retaliate with grape. Supplies of grain sent in were far from sufficient; and Shelton, it transpired, had been privately arranging with Akbar to send in forage for his own use, which transaction earned him a severe reprimand.

Táj Mahomed—the faithful Barakzai who would have saved Burnes—had been to see Sturt, and assured him privately that Akbar meant treachery. Sturt, fully convinced of that same, went straight to the General, and pleaded that a treaty, already broken by both parties, should no longer be held binding; that the garrison should immediately and openly fall back on Jalálabad, there to await reinforcements now coming up through the Punjab. If all private property were abandoned he would undertake to find transport for ineffectives, ammunition, and stores. But the thing must be done *at once*. He might have spared himself the pains. Elphinstone, with his unfailing courtesy, assured him Macnaghten had just gone out to "settle matters in a friendly conference with the chiefs," and the superfluous subaltern returned home in disgust.

So also did Macnaghten from his "friendly conference," whereat Akbar Khan, grown arrogant and overbearing, had demanded immediate surrender of the nine-pounder guns and four hostages, naming Shelton, Grant, Conolly, and Airey as men of some standing. Macnaghten had conceded the hostages, but refused the guns. Trevor—by reason of his wife's urgency—was to be sent back next day, and the departure of the troops had been fixed for Thursday the 22nd. More money was given for baggage animals, but none had been sent, and there were those who believed that Akbar was using these funds to further his own ends. Hasan Khan, the faithful and devoted, was of this mind. Urgently, respectfully, he entreated the Envoy to hold no more personal meetings with the Sirdar, unless he and his Jezailchis were allowed to be present. He, who best knew his own countrymen, bade the Sahib remember that for them treachery was no dishonour, but common tactics of war. Macnaghten, impressed by the man's loyalty and courage, could do no less than echo Sturt's appeal of the morning to "break off all negotiations as futile and vain, and take our chance in the field." But for all such vigorous counsels Elphinstone had one answer—too few troops could be spared, and even those could not now be depended on for discipline and courage against heavy odds. Macnaghten knew that it was so; yet he laid small blame on the men, demoralized by such leadership as they had been cursed withal.

For himself, wedged between imbecility on one hand and systematic treachery on the other, worn out with plotting, counter-plotting, and sleepless nights, he was driven to his wits' end. Treachery or no, insanity or no, there seemed never a loophole through which he might escape the disgrace and peril of capitulation. In this last resort, neither men, money-bags nor bayonets availed him anything. Distracted by doubt as to whom he could trust—even were a treaty signed and sealed—he had latterly been turning his attentions from one to another, snatching at any fresh-combination that seemed to promise the best results. By advertising his friendship with the Barakzai, he had hoped to make the Duranis and Kazzil-bashes rally round the Shah—not altogether in vain. To-night, therefore, haunted by Hasan Khan's warning, he wrote to Mohun Lal: "You can tell the Ghilzais and Khan Shereen [Kazzilbash] that after they have declared for His Majesty and us, and sent in a hundred *kurwars* of grain, I shall be glad to give them a bond for five lakhs. . . ."

That afternoon—in pursuance of Barakzai arrangements—Connolly and Airey were sent over to the city as hostages, while Lawrence was persuaded to part with a pair of double-barrelled pistols, so pointedly admired by Akbar, that Macnaghten wished to send them by Connolly as a gift. Lawrence frankly owned his reluctance but Macnaghten pressed the point as a personal favour—and he gave in. So the two hostages, *plus* the pistols, went forth to the city; Drummond and Trevor being graciously permitted to return.

Of the two other hostages demanded, Shelton flatly refused; and Grant either did the same, or Elphinstone did it for him. It was a dangerous and distasteful duty, this of acting hostage to an enemy as treacherous as he was cruel. Shelton had more than once declared that nothing would induce him to undertake it; but happily for Macnaghten there were others in cantonments ready to go, if need be, though they disliked it no less. Pottinger— still suffering from his inflamed wound—and War- burton, of the Shah's Gunners, offered themselves

instead; and Macnaghten sent word that they should be handed over on the departure of the troops.

The 22nd brought no friendly declaration from the Kazzilbash folk, so the final ignominy of departure seemed fixed without hope of change. In this, his hour of extremity, all things and all men conspired against William Macnaghten. Every staff he leant on proved a broken reed. Elphinstone and Shelton had failed him utterly; Sale and Nott scarcely less. Now the Kazzilbashes failed him like the rest. Yet even so, he could not tamely accept the inevitable as the General and his Council appeared to do. Still he ransacked his distraught brain for fresh possibilities, still clung desperately to the hope of a reprieve. These last weeks of perilous uncertainty had told upon him cruelly. To those who knew him best he seemed a changed man, restless, irritable, and distrait, swayed violently between the extremes of hope and despair.

To-night the last prevailed; to-night he was in the mood to catch at any straw; and to-night—as if by some fiendish intuition—it pleased Akbar to set before him a gilded snare that should test his sincerity once for all.

The Sirdar's suspicions—wakeful always—had been roused by his evident reluctance to depart. Ignorant of the apathetic spirit that baulked him, Akbar found Macnaghten's conduct inexplicable, save on the ground that he cherished some deep design, such as that which had led to the deaths of Mir Musjidi and Abdullah Khan. Wherefore—late on the 22nd, when dinner was half over at the Residency—there entered the Rajput Jemadar of Chuprassies, announcing visitors from Kabul city, Captain Skinner Sahib, with Afghan friends.

Macnaghten rose from his seat. "*Salaam do— salaam do!*" he said hurriedly; and "Gentleman Jim" appeared on the words—very handsome and distinguished-looking in his *choga* and turban. None had seen him since the 1st of November, and he was a man beloved of all.

The first glad greeting over, Macnaghten asked him anxiously of his errand. Skinner laughed.

"I feel like a man loaded with combustibles," said he. "I am charged with a message from Akbar of the most portentous nature! But dinner first, business afterwards; and for details I am to refer you to my companions, Mahomed Sadík, and our Lohani friend, Surwar Khan."

Dinner, as may be imagined, was swiftly disposed of; and thereafter the four disappeared into Macnaghten's office, leaving Mackenzie puzzled and more than a little anxious for the man whom he loved, less blindly, yet no less loyally than did George Lawrence, who chanced to be dining out that night.

Within the study came revelations—so superbly daring that they fairly upset the balance of Macnaghten's harassed mind.

Akbar's proposal, in plain terms, was on this wise. Let Sir William come out next morning to meet himself and a few immediate friends, that a final arrangement might be made. Let the General have a large body of troops in readiness; and let these, on a given signal, join with the followers of Akbar, assault Mahmud Khan's fort and secure the person of Aminullah, now in command there with several thousand men. "For a certain sum," added Mahomed Sadík with an insinuating leer, "the Lord Sahib should be presented with Aminullah's head."

But Macnaghten indignantly waved the proposal aside. "It was not his custom," said he, "nor the custom of his country, to pay a price for blood."

Mahomed Sadík raised polite eyebrows, possibly sceptical. The distinction between paying for a man's death or for his capture by treachery was too nice to be appreciated by an Afghan, who, moreover, believed that the Envoy had indirectly compassed the earlier "removal" of rebel chiefs. But let that pass, and let the Lord Sahib hear the rest, which was greatly to his advantage. Aminullah being captured, and all others subdued by the combined strength of British and Ghilzai arms, the former would be permitted to "save their purdah" by remaining in the country six months longer, and then departing as if of their own free-will. Shah Shuja, if he chose, might continue King, with Mahomed Akbar for his Wazir; and—here came the crowning item—the said Akbar was to receive, as reward from the British Government, a bonus of three hundred thousand pounds, plus forty thousand a year for life!

"To this wild proposal," says Mackenzie, "Sir William gave ear with an eagerness which nothing can account for but the supposition that his strong mind had been harassed till it in some degree lost its equipose, for he not only assented to these terms, but actually gave Mahomed Sadík a Persian paper to that effect written in his own hand."

And so an end of that fatal conference, from which Macnaghten emerged with eyes unnaturally bright, a nervous, hurried manner, and lips that breathed no word of the transaction even to Trevor, Lawrence, or Mackenzie. Distracted though he was, the man must have known in his secret heart that he had set his hand to a compact as impracticable as it was dishonest; and he could not bear—yet—to see the reflection of that knowledge in the eyes of his friends.

Wherefore Lawrence and Mackenzie had to sleep on their anxiety, while Skinner and his companions carried back to Kabul proofs that may well have astounded Akbar Khan. Unable to gauge the full measure of Macnaghten's desperate plight, he saw only the Envoy's readiness to snatch at an offer which involved the perfidious sacrifice of an "ally"; saw himself justified, his worst suspicions confirmed. After such clear proof, he argued, no reliance could be placed even on the most solemn engagement; no blame cast on him or his friends if they resolved "to ensnare Macnaghten in the net he was spreading for another; to take vengeance on him and his starving troops for the insults and injuries which a selfish ambitious policy had heaped upon Afghanistan."

Whether William Macnaghten slept soundly that night, as a man reprieved, or lay awake tormented with doubts, none knew—nor ever will know. But with morning came the call for action that implied, first, the call for speech. Lawrence and Mackenzie must know. Elphinstone must know. What would they all think? What did he think himself? The probability is, he did not allow himself to think at all. Wedged helplessly between a perfidious enemy, a paralyzed General and a starving army, he saw only the gleam of daylight ahead—the lives of thousands saved; British "purdah" saved; the old King saved also from the ignominy of deposition; and, dazzled by the delusive brilliancy of that gleam, he could not or would not haggle over the means to so great an end.

But with Mackenzie and Lawrence it would be otherwise; hence his reluctance to speak. Nerving himself for the ordeal, he sent word bidding them accompany him to a conference at noon. Mackenzie came first, and to him Macnaghten unburdened his soul.

Mackenzie was silent a moment, scarcely daring to speak his honest thought. Then he said gravely: "I beg of you, sir, be very careful. I feel convinced it is a plot against you."

"A plot!" Macnaghten started, then added hastily, testily: "Let me alone for that—trust me for that. I must see the General and give the needful directions."

Mackenzie said no more. The time for argument was passed; but his eyes were eloquent, and Macnaghten must have been glad to escape their mute appeal.

Elphinstone proved no less encouraging. Dreading fresh complications, and all unused to the shifts and trickery of Eastern diplomacy, he shook a dubious head over Macnaghten's tale. The whole thing sounded to him extravagant, and very dangerous. But for seven weeks the word had been so persistently on his lips, that now, when he spoke common prudence, it fell unheeded on Macnaghten's ears.

The prominence of Akbar alarmed him. "And

what," he asked, "have our good friends Osman Khan and Zeman Khan to say to all this?"

Macnaghten hurriedly waved them aside. "Nothing at all. Nothing at all. They are not in the plot."

"Plot? I don't like that word, Macnaghten. It has an ominous sound. Are you quite sure there is no fear of treachery?"

Macnaghten was by no means sure; and the very uncertainty made him irritable. "My dear sir, pray don't disturb yourself," he retorted with a touch of heat. "Leave it all to me. I understand these things—"

"I'm hanged if *I* do!" Elphinstone answered with a wry smile. "And there is really nothing more I can do for you?"

"Nothing at all, except to have those two regiments with two guns under arms just outside, without making any fuss, ready to march on Mahmud's fort; and have the garrison thoroughly on the alert."

"I will do my best," the old man answered; and did not see the Envoy again till near noon, when he met him riding with his three brave companions and sixteen sowars towards the Siah Sung gate.

"You are actually off?" he asked with an anxious glance at Macnaghten, whose manner was unusually hurried and perturbed. "I don't half like this business. I have no faith in it."

At that the Envoy drew rein, and anger flashed in his eyes. "If *that's* the case, sir, why not order out the troops and meet the enemy in open fight? I'll go with you gladly. I am certain we should beat them—and all would be well."

The General's sigh was almost a groan. "Macnaghten, I *can't*. The troops are not to be depended on—you know that."

It was the old unanswerable lament, and Macnaghten with a gesture of acquiescence rode on, sick at heart. Dependable or no, he would have given the troops another chance that day and risked the result.

Their way out lay through the Siah Sung gate,

the spot chosen being close to Mahmud Khan's fort; and around the gateway hovered a rabble of Ghazis, fully armed. Lawrence requested the officer on guard to disperse them, and thereafter to tell the field officer that, as the Envoy was holding a conference, he wanted the reserve guard drawn up outside, to be ready for any emergency; an order that was either not given or flatly ignored. Hurrying on to join Macnaghten, Lawrence found him in a state of nervous tension, heightened by the fact that no troops or guns were yet to be seen.

"Isn't it disgraceful, Lawrence?" he said bitterly. "Elphinstone and Shelton are both aware that this is a most critical business. Yet nothing is ready. Not even the ramparts fully manned. But it's all of a piece with the rest. Come now, we must get on." He glanced nervously over his shoulder. "Surely the escort is smaller than usual?"

"You said ten men, sir," Lawrence answered, "I've brought sixteen. Shall I ride back and tell Le Geyt to bring on the rest? He wanted very much to come."

"Do so; and tell Shelton I have started."

It was a day of still, keen frost; a day of blue and gold and unsullied whiteness. Shadows had shrunk to vanishing-point; all angles were hidden, all roughness made smooth by myriads of snowflakes woven into a glittering mantle that left no crevice gaping, no hilltop uncrowned. By contrast, the faces and forms of the approaching Afghans looked sinister as the shadow of death in the sunlit eyes of youth.

When Lawrence, with Mackenzie, rejoined the party, they found the bodyguard had been ordered to halt near the fort, while Macnaghten and Trevor rode forward alone to meet Akbar's cavalcade. Truly if Macnaghten's game was a desperate one, and his nerves overwrought, his courage was more than equal to the occasion. For there were signs abroad sufficient to excite alarm. The advancing party far outnumbered their own. Crowds of armed Afghans hung about the fort, and a large body of horsemen hovered expectant, on the Siah Sung heights. Yet Macnaghten spoke hopefully, as he rode, of the possibility of binding Akbar's interests firmly to their own.

"You, Lawrence," he said, "must be ready to ride on to the Bala Hissar and tell the Shah of our coming."

Lawrence assented. "And I hope to Heaven, sir," he added fervently, "that matters will turn out as you expect. But I am afraid there is great danger of treachery."

"Danger? Treachery? Of course there is!" Macnaghten interposed with sudden passion. "But what can *I* do? The General won't fight. No aid can reach us from any quarter. The Afghans are only playing with us. Not one item of their treaty have they fulfilled. But the chance of saving our honour is worth any risk. *You* know well enough the life I've led these last six weeks. Before God, I'd rather die a hundred deaths than live them over again."

And in that spirit he went forward to meet the handsome young Afghan, who—in his close-fitting steel helmet and cloak—looked more than ever like a Paladin of the Crusades, his romantic figure and haughty bearing contrasting notably with that of his ally—or victim, as events should prove.

With him came his father-in-law, Mahomed Shah Khan; his half-brother Sultan Ján, handsome, and vain as himself; the Chief of Kabul police, and others of the Ghilzai clan, including a brother of Aminullah Khan. This fact alone might have disturbed Macnaghten had he noted it—which he probably did not. His mind, set upon a desperate errand, saw nothing but the end in view and to Akbar's formal greeting, "*Salaam Aleikum,*" he answered cordially: "Sirdar Sahib, here is Grant Sahib's Arab that you so admired."

Akbar smiled suavely, as the fowler might smile upon a netted bird, not yet aware of the toils. "Many thanks," said he. "Also for the pistols of Lawrence Sahib which you see I am wearing! Shall we dismount?"

"By all means."

They had halted some three hundred and fifty yards from cantonments, near a group of hillocks; and now, on the farther side of these, rugs were laid upon the snow. The whole party dismounting, Macnaghten reclined on a slope, Trevor sat by him, and Lawrence, keenly watchful of the dark faces round, stood, as it were on guard, close behind his beloved Chief.

Mackenzie—his spirit strangely shadowed by presentiment of evil—could scarcely bring himself to dismount. But any sign of hesitation would have been fatal: and as he alighted, he heard Akbar ask the Envoy with pointed significance if he were prepared to carry out the whole proposition sent in the night before.

"Why not?" asked Macnaghten, a hint of challenge in his tone. Then the two lowered their voices, while Mackenzie's attention was drawn off by his old friend, Moyanud-din, Chief of the Kabul police. He rose; and they stood apart, the Afghan larding his talk with extravagant compliment. For all that, Mackenzie noted how Akbar's armed followers closed in and in upon the group, till Lawrence quietly suggested that they should be kept farther off since the meeting was confidential. A few of the chiefs affected to discourage them with whips; but Akbar cried out jovially: "Let them alone. Lawrence Sahib need not be alarmed! They are all in the secret."

And Mackenzie went on with his talk; but not for long.

Suddenly he saw Akbar rise to his feet; heard him call out hurriedly: "*Bigeer! Bigeer!*"* and at the same time grasp the Envoy's left wrist, his jovial face distorted with diabolical passion. Sultan Ján seized the right wrist; and between them they dragged him stooping and resisting down the slope.

Straightway the crowd closed in upon them. A shout went up: "The troops are coming!" And Mackenzie, starting forward, realized that his own right arm was imprisoned, the muzzle of a pistol at his temple, and all about him a thicket of drawn swords and cocked jezails.

One glimpse he had of Macnaghten's face, blanched with horror and amazement: one cry he heard from him—a vain cry: "*Az baráe Khudá!*"[†] He saw a scarlet figure flash past,—and fall; and knew it for the devoted Rajput Jemadar. He saw Lawrence, surrounded and dragged towards the horse of Mahomed Shah Khan: saw how the escort turned about and fled;—the rest was a confused struggle of horses and men, of shouts and shots and trampled snow—but never a sign of the supposed troops from cantonments.

Mackenzie, relieved of his sword, was hurried through the snow by the Chief of police, whose exhortations were enforced by the whistle of bullets over their heads.

At last they found a horse. "Mount, Mackenzie Sahib, mount behind me," cried his captor, now his zealous defender, and they set off at a canter over the frozen snow towards the fort.

Around and behind them surged an infuriated crowd, shouting: "Kill the Kafir! Let him be *kurbán!*"[‡]

Blows rained right and left; but the men dared not fire, lest they harm Moyan-ud-din or those of his party, who defended Mackenzie more than once at the risk of their own lives.

At length, scrambling up a frosty slope, the over burdened horse slipped and fell. Mackenzie's cap had been snatched off; and now, stunned by a blow on the head, he fell forward—happily clear of the animal's hoofs. With a rush, Moyan-ud-din's people closed round him. Seizing him in their arms and warding off other blows that fell, they hurried on toward the fort.

By the time Mackenzie's brain had cleared, they were under its walls, where he spied the mounted figure of Akbar Khan—proudly exultant, sitting at

---

*Seize! seize!

†For God's sake.
‡Sacrifice.

the receipt of congratulation. Relief was momentary. An infuriate Ghazi pounced on him, and a dozen others rushed forward. But Akbar laid about among them manfully; and again Moyan-uddin's people surrounded their charge, pressed him up against the wall and covered him up with their bodies, crying out that none should touch him.

Safe for the moment, his eyes sought anxiously for some trace of his friends. Trevor he had seen once, riding behind him with another chief. No sign of him now, or of the other two, and Mackenzie's brave heart failed him.

Then did Akbar, who had shielded him from blows, turn in the saddle and jeer at his helplessness. "*You'll* seize my country, will you?" he cried in triumphant derision. "*Bismillah!* You'll seize my country!" And shaking his sword at his prisoner, he galloped off towards the city.

Being gone, the wolves made another rush upon their prey. But Akbar's father-in-law, coming out of the fort with a strong guard, baulked them again; and Mackenzie, feeling very much like a football in a close scrimmage, found himself half shoved, half carried, into the shelter of the very stronghold they had come out to attack.

Here, in a low, dark room, lit only by a grated window in the outer wall, he recognized with a leap of the heart George Lawrence—disarmed, bruised, and exhausted, like himself, but otherwise unhurt.

"Mackenzie!" "Lawrence!" The cries were simultaneous. Then, as Mackenzie sank back against the wall, his friend whispered hoarsely: "Sir William—Trevor—where *are* they?"

"God knows!"

Lawrence groaned; and for a long while they sat silent, each thankful at least for the other's presence. Impossible to talk much, even had they any heart for speech. The clamour without grew deafening; and the Ghazis, discovering them, thronged round the window, blocking it up with murderous faces, cursing and spitting at them through the bars. Once the faces dispersed, and the snout of a blunderbuss appeared, only to be knocked up by one of the guard. It exploded harmlessly; and in its place a severed hand, stuck on a spike, was jerked up and down to the accompaniment of jeering cries: "*Yulli—Yulli!* Your own hands will soon be as this one. Look well!"

Instead, they covered their eyes and shuddered at the hideous implication that might or might not be true. Soon came chiefs to reassure them, all so friendly in their bearing that Lawrence ventured the one question that ached for utterance.

"The Lord Sahib, Trevor Sahib—are they also safe? And why not here?"

"Let not your heart be disturbed, Lawrence Sahib," answered Mahomed Shah, his own defender. "They are unharmed like yourselves, but have been taken on to the city, whither we shall take you also to-night when these clamourers have departed."

Lawrence thanked him, and prayed God his words were true. Certainly his own and Mackenzie's treatment seemed to justify such a hope.

All the afternoon their friends remained in that lower room, not merely to entertain, but to protect them; for the crowd made more than one violent attempt to force the door. Toward evening came Aminullah himself, their destined prisoner. Whether or no he realized this fact, there was here no show of friendship, but frank and even bloodthirsty hate.

Nodding a palsied head, he showed his teeth in a vulpine snarl. "Wait only a little and you shall be blown away from guns. Any death is too merciful for such dogs!" Certain of his followers pushed forward officiously, as if to make good the threat, but were at once thrust back by Ghilzai chiefs, who roundly abused Aminullah for using such language to his guests.

Throughout the day, parties of retainers had dropped in to join in the general congratulations; among them all was only one noble-looking old Mullah who took another view of the matter. Strong in the courage of disapproval, he stood up in the midst of them, like some old Jewish prophet come to life, and denounced the seizure of men who trusted them as foul treachery, a disgrace to Islam, that would surely bring down the wrath of God upon their heads.

But the wrath of God, though a high-sounding calamity, was vague and far off, while the capture of four high-caste political officers was an immediate and tangible good. So they paid no heed to his words. Instead—being practical men, with practical work on hand—they gave their prisoners food, and poshteens to sleep on till midnight; then, with the true meanness of your well-born Afghan, despoiled them, sleeping, of watches, silk handkerchiefs, and rings.

At midnight they were roused, set upon horses, and escorted through the ghostly valley, through dark and soundless streets, with their snow-capped houses, till they came to that of Mahomed Akbar Khan. He rose from his bed and gave them courteous greeting, lamented the sad events of the day, and supposed they would be glad to see Skinner Sahib.

Glad? They would be overjoyed; and were led at once to his room. They found him awake, sitting on his charpoy in Afghan undress. On their entrance he rose, without a word, and the flickering light of two *chirágs* showed his face unnaturally grave, even constrained.

Lawrence ran forward impulsively and grasped his hands. "Here we are, all safe, Jim. And *here's* a pretty mess!"

Still Skinner's face did not relax. His lips moved, but no sound came; Lawrence—startled and bewildered—loosed his hands.

"My dear fellow, what's the matter?" he asked blankly.

"Matter? Don't you *know?*"

"We only know we've escaped with our lives, like the others, and we're prisoners—what else?"

"Only this,"—Skinner spoke slowly, solemnly—"they have lied to you. The Envoy—is *dead*. I myself saw his head brought into this courtyard. And

poor Trevor was killed too. The horse fell, and before he could be saved he was set upon by Mullah Momin, who hated him—and cut to pieces."

The two men listened in a stunned silence, hearing the words, yet scarcely able to grasp the hideous fact. Lawrence—who had loved Macnaghten as his own father—stepped backward blindly, uncertainly, sat down on Skinner's truckle bed, and hid his face in his hands. Sitting thus, he heard other details; heard them with a kind of numb detachment, as though the familiar voices were talking in another world.

Akbar, it seemed, had not publicly admitted the murder. It was assumed to be the work of Ghazis—always conveniently beyond control. No killing had been included in the original design. Each officer was to be carried off by a chief, and the four were to be held as hostages for the restoration of Dōst Mahomed. But when Akbar announced that he must take Macnaghten to see Newab Zemán Khan, the Envoy had remonstrated and risen up to go. It was then that Akbar had caught hold of him. Angered by still further resistance, he had lost his temper, and upon the cry that troops were coming to foil his plan, he had whipped out Lawrence's pistol and fired twice—

The rest was left to the Ghazis—certain to be thorough in their work. Both bodies had been dragged with indignity through the streets of Kabul and hung up in the bazaar; while Macnaghten's head gruesomely adorned the Char Chowk—the most public part of the city. Such was the account of Mahomed Sadík, who saw all, and who had now confessed to Skinner that Akbar's proposition was a trap to test the sincerity of Macnaghten in his dealings with the chiefs.

The three spent a miserable night, Mackenzie sharing Skinner's charpoy, Lawrence rolled in a sheepskin on the ground, his unsleeping brain tormented with visions called up by Skinner's tale.

Morning brought no sign from cantonments; only more friendly amenities from Akbar. They were his honoured guests, like Skinner Sahib; but he advised the precautionary adoption of Afghan dress.

Thus transformed, they accompanied him later to the house of Nawab Zemán Khan, where they found Conolly and Airey with the principal chiefs sitting in council on the next move. All, including Akbar Khan, were loud in lamentation of Macnaghten's death, while they frankly blamed him for having brought it on himself by non-fulfilment of the original treaty, ignoring—Afghan-like—the fact that this had been promptly annulled by their own bad faith. Followed a lively consideration of new concessions to be wrested from a garrison shorn of its Lord Sahib.

Drafted and signed by the four principals—Akbar, Zemán Khan, Aminullah, and Osman Khan—their amended treaty was despatched by special messenger to the General; and with it went a note from Lawrence to Lady Sale, enclosing one to Lady Macnaghten from Conolly and one for poor Mrs. Trevor, whose very natural anxiety for her husband's return to cantonments had proved fatal both for herself and him.

The council ended, back they fared to Akbar's house; and there they were closely confined in an inner room, not of discourtesy, but of necessity, as their double journey gave proof. And now Lawrence—who had born up stoically so far—broke down altogether. It was as if the actual fact of his loss had reached his ears without reaching his heart until he saw it set down by his own hand in those notes to Mrs. Trevor and Lady Sale. Now, as he lay prone upon his charpoy, choking back the tears that pricked like knives, the words he had written echoed with maddening iteration through the chambers of his brain.

"Sir William has been murdered—murdered—murdered," repeated the devils within, as though seeking to familiarize him with the hideous word, the still more hideous fact. The man on whom he had lavished a blindly chivalrous devotion—gone before his time; his reward unreaped, his policy and labour in Afghanistan brought utterly to naught. In the eyes of Lawrence, Macnaghten could do no wrong. Even in respect of accepting Akbar's proposals his supreme champion found him "perfectly justified" on the plea that the chiefs had broken their treaty, and that no reliance could be placed on them *as a body*. Yet were there others, unbiassed by personal contact, like Durand, who saw him as "the victim of his own truthless, unscrupulous policy," a victim whose "high courage almost atoned for his moral and political errors." Easy for men far removed, in time and space, from the harassing misery of those six weeks to sit in judgment on one tempted beyond the common limit, distracted by a fiendish tangle of events that seemed deliberately hounding him to his doom.

Judgment is for historians. Here, in the plain tale of his ambition, triumph, and undoing, he stands revealed as a man of many lovable and even noble qualities; high principled in theory, yet hampered in action by a strain of mental and moral obliquity; hampered above all by an abnormal development of that metaphorical blind spot in the eye, which, however convenient individually, is fatal to administrative work of the first quality. Even the best of his friends—Lawrence always excepted—saw that in spite of his brilliant attainments he was woefully out of place in his self-chosen post of honour. "Poor Macnaghten," wrote Broadfoot afterwards, "ought never to have left the Secretary's office. He was ignorant of men even to simplicity, and utterly incapable of forming or guiding *administrative* measures."

But like many another man of ability, the one thing he could not do was the one thing he would do—to the dire disadvantage of others besides himself. Taken all in all, his Afghan service figures as a series of disastrous mistakes followed by heroic and equally disastrous efforts to atone for them—too late.

25

"Our Relations with Afghanistan" (1919)

DEMETRIUS C. BOULGER

Demetrius C. Boulger (1853–1928) wrote on numerous empire-related topics, from the history of Belgium to the Battle of the Boyne to reflections on the Congo, but his specialty was the Indian empire and its various frontiers. In his contribution to the *Contemporary Review* on the eve of the third Afghan war in 1919, he resists looking backward to the previous two wars in the region and notes that nearly every forty years the British find themselves locked in struggle in the region. The Russians are now Bolsheviks and Soviets; the emir has been assassinated; and the context is the unfinished business of the aftermath of global war. Yet the specter of an invasion of India is never far from the surface. Boulger is confident that Indians will prefer the British Raj to an Afghan one, though he is not sanguine that this will be enough to deter the Afghans if they decide on an invasion plan. Far more unnerving is the "armed rabble" of "enemy races" roaming, untethered, across the postwar East. With that realization comes an acknowledgment that the "nominal friendship" of the emirs of Afghanistan may be, once again, an unstable basis for imperial security on the North-West Frontier.

The recent assassination of the Amir Habibulla will probably come to be regarded as a turning point in our relations with Afghanistan. Thirty-nine years had almost expired since British troops last quitted that country, and it is a little curious to note that nearly the same interval separated the close of our first intervention in the time of Lord Ellenborough and that of our last incursion under Lord Lytton. There is one marked difference between those two intervals. In the first, from 1842 to 1878, we did nothing: we kept the Afghans in every sense of the term at arm's length; in the second, we took the Amir into our service (from 1883, to be exact), by paying a fixed annual subsidy without any conditions except a general one to the effect that his foreign policy was to be under our control. Both Abdurrahman and his son and successor, Habibulla, kept faith with us. The experiment of paying an annual subsidy without any corresponding advantages or any adequate supervision was a very risky proceeding. It answered for a certain period; its defects have now been revealed, and the force of Lord Lawrence's old formula, "If we give you money and material, we must send officers to see that they are property applied," is revived. There can be little doubt, then, that whatever development there may be in the military position, we shall have to modify the policy we have followed towards Afghanistan for considerably more than a generation.

Our very slight and imperfect acquaintance with the true facts of the situation in Afghanistan and along the borders that march with Russian territory must be attributed to our own shortsightedness in not requiring the Amirs to give us the right to station agents and consuls at special places in return for our financial support. Had we possessed this, the only sure means of obtaining reliable information, we should have been able to nip the Bolshevist danger in the bud, and at least we should have known what was coming. As things have been happening during the last six months behind a dark and impenetrable veil, and under influences of which we had no ken, a grave peril has been sprung upon us at the most important door into India. Had the supporting insurrectionary movement in Peshawur not been crushed before it fully developed, we might have had cause to remember the warning of the Sikh sirdar, who declared during the worst days of the Mutiny, "If Peshawur goes, the whole Punjab will be rolled up in rebellion."

But if we did not know much about facts, and currents of feeling and opinion in Afghanistan, we knew a good deal about what was happening in Russian Turkestan and Bokhara. We knew of the massacres at Tashkent and elsewhere. We knew that the Reds had released and armed the German and Austrian prisoners of war who had been practically starving. These desperate men were told to feed themselves and to spread the doctrines of Lenin and Trotsky. They have become the masters rather than the servants of Bolshevism, and with

them are associated the remnants of the old Russian garrison. There is consequently a very considerable trained military force in the part of Central Asia that touches Afghanistan. It has given proof of its vigour by the recapture of Merv from the mixed forces which had, under our patronage, conquered it. The name may convey little meaning to the present generation, but Merv is, and always has been, the commanding position between the Oxus and the Caspian, and it lost nothing of its importance in the hands of the Russians, who made it one of their chief railway centres. The capture of Merv is only the first step towards the recovery of the whole of the trans-Caspian railway, and it must be perfectly clear that in numbers, at least, the forces we have near the scene are quite inadequate to withstand a serious movement by 50,000 or 60,000 Bolshevist troops, and this is a very modest estimate of the forces that are available in Turkestan.

It is quite possible, however, that the seizure of Merv is intended as part of a plan of campaign to induce the Afghans to participate in an invasion of India with the co-operation of the hybrid Bolshevist army which is moving south in probably other directions than Merv. No explanation has yet been offered as to the source whence the Afghans obtained the Krupp field pieces we captured near Dakka. There is hardly any doubt that they were received from the Russians. It seems safe to assume that other military supplies have reached the Amir, and probably also sums of money to replace the Indian subsidy that was to be forfeited. Even these inducements might have failed to induce the Afghans—ruler and army—to embark upon a hazardous adventure if they had not received some encouragement from India itself to lead them to believe that they would have the support of Indian sympathisers with that mysterious Bolshevist cause which, so far as it is based on plunder, commands the sympathy of all the cut-throats and ruffians of Afghanistan. But they forgot one thing, and that was the general knowledge among the peoples of India of the true character of the Afghan tribes. The Indian may conceive that he has injuries and wrongs under the present dispensation of power, but at least he is in no doubt that they would sink into insignificance beside those that must follow an Afghan invasion. Outside alien agitators, and Islamic extremists at Peshawur and Lahore, India would stand united in the resolve to keep the Afghans out of the peninsula at all costs.

At the moment of writing it is impossible to say whether the military operations will continue, or come to an end without our having to send armies once more to Cabul and Candahar. The issue depends on the extent of the support that the Amir will receive from the Russians. If they send larger forces to Herat and Cabul, then the old lure of the invasion of India will prove irresistible, and we must be prepared for a serious struggle. If, on the other hand, no Bolshevist forces come south of the Oxus and the Paropamisus, then it may be assumed that the Afghans will remember the wise words of the late Amir, when he was assured by Turkish emissaries that a Turko-German army would be on the Indian frontier before the war was over, and that he ought to throw in his lot with Islam and its friends: "I will decide when it arrives." It must be pretty plain to them that their young ruler, in rushing impetuously into action without waiting, has committed an act of folly for which they have had to pay the price.

If the Afghans were the only persons to be taken into account we should know pretty well how we stand, and the collapse of their adventure, now that their fingers have been burnt, might be counted upon with some confidence. But everything becomes uncertain if the desperate and well-armed men of enemy races, who have been long prisoners of the Russians, have decided to recoup themselves for all their sufferings and losses by the invasion of India, gathering round them as they advance the predatory Afghan tribes, as was done in old days by Timur, Baber, and Nadir Shah.

That possibility forms the only real danger, and the seizure of Merv is a warning to us to be well prepared for it. But it may be said that these German-Austrian prisoners represent only an armed rabble without leaders. We do not know who is leading them, but at least there is a suspicion of higher direction, so far as the matter has already gone, in the way in which the Afghans have been testing our defences at so many different points from Chitral to Chaman. I cannot hide the thought that if a plan has been drawn up by some superior intellect from Potsdam the main attack will be delivered on our positions in the South round Quetta and the railway to Seistan; but at all events we shall have the means of measuring this possibility by the movements of the force at Merv. If it comes up the Murghab and Heri Rud—the two parallel lines of advance on Herat—their purpose will be no longer obscure. They will be on the old historic road of Indian invaders by Herat and Candahar.

Enough has been written to show that if the menace is solely one from the Afghans it is not very serious. We have already countered the blow by a prompt offensive which has kept them off our own territory. But if the danger is one of an enemy origin in which the Afghans are only playing a minor part, then we must be cautious and patient until we know something more about the forces with which we shall have to cope. It may well be that all our possible adversaries are playing a waiting game. The Bolshevists may have hurried on the Afghans to make an advance with the view of finding out what they were worth in the military sense, and also how far we were ready. On the other hand, the Afghans, baulked in their first attempt to raid the Indian borders, may only be asking for a cessation of hostilities in the hope of gaining time to allow of their Russian and other allies to reach the scene of action. In short, the military peril, if it exists in any acute degree, lies not in the Afghan army, but with the Bolshevist levies of all kinds—thousands of starving and desperate men well accustomed to the use of arms—that necessity or some hostile influence may set moving for the Indus. We know by the Merv incident that they have begun to move; we do not know whither they will go, or where they will stop. That is the cloud on the Indian frontier. It will long remain there, nor is it easy to see how it can be quickly dispersed.

In the face of what amounts to a complete change in the position of affairs in Central Asia, seeing that we are confronted with the old Russian menace in a new form that wise men like Sir Henry Rawlinson and General John Jacob could not possibly have imagined, but one that makes their warnings all the more pregnant, we are bound to modify our casual treatment of the Afghan question, and to define some new line of policy for our own guidance and for the security of India. The military phase of the present complications will, sooner or later, pass away, only, however, to leave us with a permanent political problem of deep interest, and possibly sinister portent.

When, after our defeat at Maiwand, we recognised Abdurrahman in a hurry as the best way of getting out of the country, we left behind us a State torn by civil strife and without a generally recognised central government. Moreover, there can be no doubt that, if Lord Roberts had not defeated Ayoob, the victor of Maiwand, and scattered his army, Abdurrahman's reign south of the Hindu Kush at least would have been brief. We secured for him a breathing space of which he made good use, and, assisted by us with money, arms, and stores, he established his power at Cabul. In 1883, after one critical period, he got possession of Herat, and drove his cousin Ayoob into exile. Then he came cap in hand to the Indian Government for money. He wanted something more definite than the gifts he had received in August, 1880, something on which he could depend—in fact, a regular subsidy. Mr. Gladstone was in office, Lord Ripon was Viceroy, and they were opposed in principle and by tradition to the grant of "a fixed annual subsidy." They were opposed to it because Lord Lawrence had declared that no subsidy should be given because it must entail the despatch of British officers into Afghanistan to superintend its application. They decided to give the subsidy without the supervision, and they gave it because Abdurrahman left them in no doubt that if they did not comply with his request he would apply to Russia.

Then came the Penjdeh crisis, and Abdurrahman visited India. He received some arms, a considerable extra present of money, and the assurance of support of all kinds in the event of war. The matter between England and Russia was composed, and then it became necessary to define more clearly the limits of British and Afghan influence in the No Man's Land between Cabul and the Punjab. This was accomplished by Sir Mortimer Durand, who went to Cabul to negotiate the new Convention known by his name. The Amir was a good man of business. He obtained the increase of his subsidy from twelve to eighteen lakhs a year, and it has remained at that figure ever since.

What have we obtained in return for this subsidy? The nominal friendship of the Amirs, the avoidance of any open quarrel, and the shelving of the problem how India and Afghanistan were to live together on good terms as neighbours. But we had got absolutely the same results from 1842 to 1878 without paying a penny, and as for good neighbourship, there never has been anything else than the isolation of Afghanistan and our exclusion from it. We have been so rigidly excluded that we know nothing about the course of events beyond what rumours, varying from day to day, bring to our ears. We do not know, for instance, why and by whom Habibulla was murdered, what has been the fate of his eldest son, Inayatulla, what influences are behind Amanulla, whether Turk and German agents are in the capital, or Bolshevist forces on Afghan soil. All we can conclude is that Afghanistan has not changed. It is still the

vilify leaders
like in 19ment
China during opium
wars

"Our Relations with Afghanistan" / 249

same land of palace plots, followed by assassinations, that it was in the time of Dost Mahomed and Shere Ali. The millions of our money that have gone into the Amir's treasury have not altered things one jot. Abdurrahman spent some part of them on machinery and electric light for his palace; Habibulla spent more on motor-cars and laying out golf courses, which are the excrescences and not the essentials of civilisation.

In other words, our money, or rather the money of India, given blindly and without system to a family of despots, has been simply thrown away. We are confronted with the treachery of the Afghan ruler upon whose family we have showered favours, just as we were in 1878 by that of Shere Ali, whom, to tell the truth, we had treated rather badly. Nor can the view be accepted that the sudden and unprovoked attack on the Indian frontier was due solely to the impulse or dynastic necessities of the young ruler who has seized the reins of power from his elder brother. He could not have struck his blow if he had not possessed the sympathy and support of his army and the Afghans themselves. They all believed that the Indian Government was unprepared and beset with internal difficulties, and there was some reason for the latter opinion. The regular subsidy, the long list of special gifts, the scrupulous observance of our promise to leave them alone, did not count at a hair's weight when they thought that the moment had come to enrich themselves with the plunder of Indian cities and bazaars, as their ancestors had done so often in the past. The only new point about their programme was that they had persuaded themselves that the Indian peoples would welcome and assist them in carrying out their plans. How they arrived at this conclusion, and on whose assurance, certainly calls for a little elucidation.

There is clear need, then, for us to reconsider the policy that we have followed towards Afghanistan since the installation of Abdurrahman in August, 1880, and more especially since the intro-

duction of the fixed subsidy in the autumn of 1883. The first question that has to be answered is, Is it worth our while to continue the fixed subsidy on the old conditions, or on any? The answer does not depend on the personality or the fate of the offending Amir, Amanulla. He may promise to reform, or he may share his father's end. The question at issue should be considered on its merits and answered by the light of the needs and interests of India. Amanulla's lapse is only a fresh proof, where none was required, that the Afghan does not change, and that without control and supervision of some kind the payment of a fixed annual subsidy is a one-sided arrangement from which we derive no solid advantage. It is no advantage to have a fair-weather friend as a neighbour, and then to discover that for a mere whim, or in the belief that we are embarrassed, he can suddenly and without warning turn himself into an active and bitter enemy. The example has been set by Amanulla, but the object lesson with which he has provided us stands good for all time. There does not seem any sound reason for not replying in the negative to the first question. The fixed annual subsidy cannot be continued on the old conditions, which were, practically speaking, none at all. Shall it be continued on some new ones when the present storm clouds have blown away? That is the real matter to be examined.

We return, then, to Lord Lawrence's oft-repeated formula: "If we give you money and material we must send officers to see that they are properly applied." The world has not stood still since those words were first used fifty-five years ago. India has changed, Asia is changing, and Afghanistan can no longer be left as a derelict of barbarism and brutal force among the nations. Amanulla has shown us, even if we were not already aware of it, that his towns and villages would not be safe places of residence for British officers. Lord Lawrence knew this, and his formula meant "As I cannot send officers you cannot have a subsidy," and the principle underlying his aphorism remains sound. But there are ways, which did not exist in Lord Lawrence's time, by which we could, without risking lives unnecessarily, or offering up fresh victims like William Macnaghten, Alexander Burnes, and Louis Cavagnari to Afghan treachery, secure guarantees and an equivalent for the fixed annual subsidy.

They are quite simple. Without particularising the exact positions, any Amir, in order to be entitled to receive our pay, must accord us the right to extend our railways into his country, to fix wireless telegraph stations, and to organise a courier service at regular intervals. These concessions would not merely give us an equivalent for our money, but they would provide some guarantees of reform in Afghanistan. It is quite possible that the most sincere of Afghan rulers would reply in the negative. His refusal need not be regarded as proof of hostility, but it would leave us free to refuse the subsidy. When he became ready to discuss the matter in accordance with our pronouncement, then we could fix the fair and reasonable details on which we should be willing to disburse. But the moment has arrived when we ought to decline firmly, once and for all, to pay over large sums of money for which we get nothing in return, and over which we have no control.

This decision should be quite independent of what is happening, or may still happen, in Afghanistan. Amanulla has thrown off the mask of feigned friendship and come into the open as a foe; and by so doing he has furnished us with the opportunity of ending a one-sided arrangement, concluded, moreover, at a time when the international position was widely different from what it is to-day. If circumstances allow of some fresh convention with whatever friend may sit on the Cabul *musnud*, then it must be drafted on the principle of reciprocity. Even if a period of uncertainty intervenes all we shall have to do is to wait patiently till the needs of the Afghans themselves bring them round to our views. Nothing will tend to promote the dictates of reason and common sense among the Afghans more than the firm withholding of the subsidy, so that they may learn that the days of free-giving without any return on their side are gone for ever.

Even if we have to deal with the Afghans alone this will be the wise course. But we cannot eliminate from our survey the far darker cloud outside the Afghan borders caused by the advance of Bolshevist forces towards the Indian frontier. We cannot explain how it happens that Bolshevism has gained a footing not only in the Khanates, but in Afghanistan and even in India. It would seem incredible that its subversive doctrines could make way among Mahomedan peoples if the fact were not there to prove it. The conservative State of Bokhara, after resisting and even defeating Bolshevist forces, seems now to have joined in and gone with the others. Bolshevism must have been invested with some special significance in their minds different from the reality for Pan-Islamism to rally round its Red flag. Is it possible that it can have been accepted as an anti-English movement, and that the bait held before all the tribes is the spoil of India? More unlikely movements have in the past devastated the fairest regions of Asia and destroyed the most famous dynasties, and we should certainly not forget at the present juncture what Lord Lawrence affirmed, in agreement with many other of our Frontier authorities, that "the Afghans have always joined, and will always in the future join, any army which, with reasonable prospect of success, advances on the Indus with the intention of invading India."

DEMETRIUS C. BOULGER.

The New Statesman was in its infancy in 1919, having been founded by the English socialists Sydney and Beatrice Webb in 1913 with the support of a variety of Fabian Society members, George Bernard Shaw included. The Webbs had paid a "flying visit" to the North-West Frontier during their Asian tour of 1911–12, and they reflected only in passing on contemporary politics there.[1] Contemplating the advent of a third Afghan war in late summer, this *New Statesman* contributor recognizes that traditional models for stabilizing the region can no longer hold—in part because of the Bolshevik threat and in part because the age of the Victorian emir is over. The author maintains that "the old system of subsidy and control is obsolete," and, as significantly, that India can profit from allying with a new "more enlightened" Afghan nation. Though it was by no means to serve as a permanent solution, the call for recognition of Afghanistan as the site of an independent frontier region at this moment anticipated the struggle over that very outcome in the century that has followed.

So little has appeared in the newspapers about the Third Afghan War that probably most respectable citizens do not know there has been one. Yet, at any other time than this, it would have been the subject of the keenest debate; and though the war concluded this week and only began in May, it has been one of the biggest and least creditable of our small wars, and it has caused the maximum of anxiety and annoyance to those who have had relatives engaged in it, for it has been fought, in part at least, by Territorial troops who have felt their detention in India after the German war was over as a great personal injustice. It has even been said that there has been trouble with them, and their indignation has contributed not a little to the strong feeling at home against our military policy.

The reasons that led the new Ameer of Afghanistan to begin war in India are obscure, and the version of his motives given by the Indian Government make him out to be little better than a fool. One feels that there must be another and more reasonable side to the whole business. The old principles of our Afghan policy, which worked on the whole remarkably well for nearly forty years, when Abdurrahman and Habibullah were Ameers, were simple enough. We gave Afghanistan a stiff subsidy, and in return claimed the right to the control of its foreign relations. The country was independent and enjoyed the right to import arms and munitions from India, but the condition was that it should have no windows looking on the outside world, except towards India. Abdurrahman, a ruler of quite remarkable ability, did not like the arrangement, but he accepted it, because he distrusted Russia as much as or more than he distrusted India. He compared himself to a swan swimming on a lake, with a tiger watching him from one bank and a bear from the other. But he was quite successful in keeping his feathers intact. When Russia, however, turned Bolshevist, the situation changed. The bear seemed to have lost its claws, while the tiger was seen to be devouring Turkey—no doubt from humanitarian motives. Bolshevist ideas produced a ferment in Bokhara, and the murder of Habibullah was a distant imitation of the murder of the Czar. When Amanullah, the new Ameer, seized the throne, he posed as a man of democratic ideas. In his proclamation, in the beginning of April, he promised reforms in the system of government (which it certainly needed); that there should be no forced labor, no tyranny or oppression, and that Afghanistan should be free and independent, by which he apparently meant that it should no longer be bound by existing treaties with India.

A month later, in May, Afghan regulars crossed their borders into the No-Man's-Land between it and the frontier of India and threatened Landi Kotal, in the Khyber. The British, under General Barrett, rushed troops up the Khyber and occupied Dakka, just over the Afghan border; and there they stuck, unable to move forward. The new macadam roads are said to be unfit to carry the weight of military traffic; at any rate, our transport completely broke down. Thereupon the Afghans turned our flank to the south, penetrated the Kuram, and the Tochi Valleys, and attacked the

important frontier position of Thai. We retaliated by aeroplane raids on Kabul and by the more legitimate use of our air power to bomb and disperse gatherings of Afghan troops. In June, an armistice was concluded, which has just been converted into a Treaty of Peace. By this Treaty, we withdraw from the Ameer the privilege of importing arms and cancel the subsidy, arrears and all, but about the future control of Afghan foreign policy nothing is said in the Treaty. The Ameer will say that as we have withdrawn the consideration on which he agreed to abstain from relations with foreign powers, he is free to conduct his foreign policy as he sees fit. The Indian Government, on the other hand, will maintain that our old rights to control the foreign policy of Afghanistan not having been expressly abrogated still persist. There are all the makings in the Treaty of a fourth Afghan war, unless a discussion in this country can put our policy towards Afghanistan on a new and better footing.

There are two questions raised by this little war, to which the country must insist on getting an answer. What ails the Indian Army that it should have made such a mess of the operations? If there is one subject that the Indian Army ought to have studied, it is the defense of this frontier. Yet the Afghans, cut off as they are from communication with the outside world, showed themselves much more mobile troops than our own army. They penetrated the Khyber before we were ready to meet them; they outmaneuvered us by their attack on the Kuram, and, in addition, it would appear that some of the hospital scandals of the Mesopotamian campaign were repeated in this war. There was the same breakdown of transport, with far less excuse; the same shortage of hospital equipment; and the same (in kind if not in amount) preventable disease and suffering. A Commission of Enquiry into the Indian Army has been appointed, and the facts, so far as they are known, point to something radically wrong in its administration. If our Indian Frontier policy in the future is to rely mainly on the tactics of defense, and to avoid military adventures, it is necessary that our frontier organization should be as nearly perfect as we can make it. It is evident that it is in need of drastic reforms, and until these are made the Government of India should be given no rest.

As for our Frontier policy, it is quite evident that Afghanistan has outgrown the old restrictions. The Afghan is no longer the man who lives on quarrels and fighting. He is anxious to become civilized; he has strong domestic instincts, and he has the makings of a progressive country. There are 25,000 Afghans in Bombay alone, all behaving like decent members of society, and some of them making a good deal of money. . . . there is no fear of Afghanistan turning Bolshevist, and if we wish to fight the Bolshevist intrigue in Afghanistan— there is plenty of evidence of that—we shall best do it by abandoning India's claims to stand between Afghanistan and the outside world. The old system of subsidy and control is obsolete; the new alternatives are, either to assume responsibility ourselves for the government of Afghanistan or to encourage Afghanistan to develop on her own lines, and to let India take her chance with other powers of influence in Afghanistan. If India appears as a friend, not of the old despotism at Kabul, but of the new and enlightened Afghanistan that is beginning to emerge, she will stand to gain. The first alternative of assuming responsibility for the internal affairs of Afghanistan is, under present conditions, clearly out of the question, for it would lead to an enormous increase in India's military burdens just at the time when we need all the assistance she can give elsewhere, and perhaps to serious revolution.

It is a corollary of this new policy of leaving Afghanistan perfect freedom in her foreign relations that the Indian Frontier system should be put in a perfect condition of defence. It is the finest natural frontier in the world, and if we cannot defend it we are certainly not capable of conducting field operations in Central Asia. The German theory of waging defensive war beyond one's own borders may have good military reasons in country like Europe, but they do not apply to the barren hills of Afghanistan. The sound policy of defence for India is to avoid entanglement in Afghanistan. Between the administrative frontier of India and the Durand line, which is the frontier of Afghanistan, there is a zone sufficiently wide to serve as a buffer to India against foreign attack. It is to our interest to keep this zone independent, alike of Afghanistan and of our own administration. More than that, we need not do, except to convince Afghanistan that we are her friend and have no wish to stand between her and a place in the sun.

NOTE

1. George Feaver, ed., *The Webbs in Asia: The 1911–12 Travel Diary* (Basingstoke, UK: Macmillan, 1992), 285–93.

SELECTED BIBLIOGRAPHY
OF SECONDARY SOURCES

Aslami, Zarema. *The Dream Life of Citizens: Late Victorian Novels and the Fantasy of the State*. New York: Fordham University Press, 2012.

Barfield, Thomas. *Afghanistan: A Cultural and Political History*. Princeton, NJ: Princeton University Press, 2012.

Barthorp, Michael. *The North-West Frontier: British India and Afghanistan; A Pictorial History, 1839–1947*. Dorset, UK: Blandford Press, 1982.

Bean, Richard, et al. *The Great Game: Afghanistan*. London: Oberon Books, 2010.

Chahryar, Adle, Madhavan K. Palat, and Anara Tabyshalieva, eds. *History of Civilizations of Central Asia*. Vol. 6, *Towards the Contemporary Period: From the Mid-Nineteenth to the End of the Twentieth Century*. Paris: UNESCO, 2005.

Clements, Frank A. *Conflict in Afghanistan: A Historical Encyclopedia*. Santa Barbara, CA: ABC-CLIO, 2003.

Dani, A. H., and V. M. Masson, eds. *History of Civilizations of Central Asia*. Vol. 1, *The Dawn of Civilization: Earliest Times to 700 B.C.* Paris: UNESCO, 1992.

D'Encausse, Hélène Carrière. *Islam and the Russian Empire: Reform and Revolution in Central Asia*. Berkeley: University of California Press, 1988.

Durand, Henry Marion. *The First Afghan War and Its Causes*. London: Longman's Green, 1879.

Edwards, David B. *Heroes of the Age: Moral Fault Lines on the Afghan Frontier*. Berkeley: University of California Press, 1996.

Ewans, Martin. *Conflict in Afghanistan: Studies in Asymmetric Warfare*. New York: Routledge, 2005.

Featherstone, Donald. *Colonial Small Wars: 45 Victorian Campaigns Described and Illustrated with 79 Maps*. Newton Abbott, UK: David and Charles, 1973.

Feaver, George, ed. *The Webbs in Asia: The 1911–12 Travel Diary*. Basingstoke, UK: Macmillan, 1992.

Fremont-Barnes, Gregory. *The Anglo-Afghan Wars, 1839–1919*. Oxford: Osprey Publishing, 2009.

Herlihy, Patricia. "Ab Oriente ad Ulteriorem Orientem: Eugene Schuyler, Russia, and Central Asia." In *Space, Place, and Power in Modern Russia: Essays in the New Spatial History*, edited by Mark Bassin, Christopher Ely, and Melissa K. Stockdale, 119–41. DeKalb: Northern Illinois University Press, 2011.

Hopkins, Benjamin D., and Magnus Marsden. *Fragments of the Afghan Frontier*. New York: Columbia University Press, 2011.

Ingram, Edward. *The Beginning of the Great Game in Asia, 1828–1834*. Oxford: Clarendon Press, 1979.

Jalal, Ayesha. *Partisans of Allah: Jihad in South Asia*. Cambridge, MA: Harvard University Press, 2008.

Kakar, M. Hassan. *A Political and Diplomatic History of Afghanistan, 1863–1901*. Leiden, Netherlands: Brill, 2006.

Loewen, Arley, and Josette McMichael, eds. *Images of Afghanistan: Exploring Afghan Culture through Art and Literature*. Oxford: Oxford University Press, 2010.

Macrory, Patrick, ed. *Lady Sale: The First Afghan War*. Hamden, CT: Archon Books, 1969.

Malleson, G. B. *A History of Afghanistan, from the Earliest Period to the Outbreak of the War of 1878*. Peshawar, Pakistan: Saeed Book Bank, 1984 [1878].

Marshall, Alex. *The Russian General Staff and Asia, 1800–1917*. New York: Routledge, 2006.

Misdaq, Nabi. *Afghanistan: Political Frailty and Foreign Interference*. London: Routledge, 2006.

Noelle, Christine. *State and Tribe in Early Afghanistan: The Reign of Amir Dost Muhammad Khan (1826–1863)*. Surrey, UK: Curzon, 1997.

Norris, J. A. *The First Afghan War, 1838–1842*. Cambridge: Cambridge University Press, 1967.

Schofield, Victoria. *Afghan Frontier: Feuding and Fighting in Central Asia*. London: I.B. Tauris, 2003.

Siegel, Jennifer. *Endgame: Britain, Russia, and the Final Struggle for Central Asia*. London: I.B. Taurus, 2002.

REPRINT ACKNOWLEDGMENTS

PART I

Wilson, Robert. *A Sketch of the Military and Political Power of Russia*. New York: Kirk and Mercein, 1817, 134–58.

Conolly, Arthur. *Journey to the North of India*. Vol. 1. London: R. Bentley, 1838, 1–8 and 310–46.

Osborne, W. G. *The Court and Camp of Runjeet Sing*. London: Henry Colburn, 1840, 98–121.

A Narrative of the Russian Military Expedition to Khiva, under General Perofski. 1839. Translated from the Russian for the Foreign Department of the Government of India. Calcutta: Office of Superintendent of Government Printing, 1867, 46–55.

PART II

Havelock, Henry. *Narrative of the War in Affghanistan in 1838–39*. Vol. 2. London: Henry Colburn Publishers, 1840, 1–38.

Henty, G. A. *To Herat and Cabul: A Story of the First Afghan War*. London: Blackie and Sons, 1902, v–vi, 243–94.

Sale, Florentia. *A Journal of Disasters in Affghanistan, 1841–42*. London: John Murray, 1843, 1–38.

"English Captives at Cabul: A Personal Narrative by one of the Female Prisoners." *Bentley's Miscellany* 15 (1843), 140–62.

Mohan Lal. *The Life of the Amir Dost Mohammed Khan, with His Political Proceedings Towards the English, Russian and Persian Governments*. London: Longman, Brown, Green and Longmans, 1846, 1–70.

Forbes, Archibald. *The Afghan Wars*. London: Seeley and Co., 1896, 1–13, 60–121.

PART III

"Gorchakov Circular." 1864. In Alexis Krausse, *Russia in Asia: A Record and a Study, 1558–1899*. New York: Henry Holt and Company, 1899, 224–25.

Schuyler, Eugene. *Turkistan: Notes of a Journey in Russian Turkistan, Khokand, Bukhara, and Kuldja*. New York: Scribners, 1877, 258–301.

Cossham, Handel. "The Afghan War: A Lecture." Pamphlet. Bath, UK: J. B. Keene and Co., 1878, 3–20.

"Afghanistan and Its Peoples." *Newcastle Courant*, November 22, 1878.

"Afghan Women and Children." *Hampshire Telegraph and Sussex Chronicle*, March 24, 1880.

Osborn, R. D. "India and Afghanistan." *Contemporary Review* 36 (1879): 193–211.

"The Magnitude of the Afghan War." *Spectator*, January 17, 1880, 68–69.

"The Disaster in Candahar." *Spectator*, July 31, 1880, 964–65.

"Abdurrahman Khan." *Spectator*, July 24, 1880, 932.

"The First Lesson of Candahar." *Spectator*, August 7, 1880, 996–97.

"The Rumour from Cabul." *Spectator*, October 30, 1880, 1370–71.

"The Death of Abdurrahman Khan." *Spectator*, October 12, 1901, 505–6.

PART IV

Curzon, George Nathaniel. *Russia in Central Asia in 1889 and the Anglo-Russian Question*. London: Longman's Green, 1889, 383–414.

Kipling, Rudyard. "The Amir's Homily." In *Life's Handicap: Being Stories of Mine Own People*. London: Macmillan and Co., 1891, 27–31.

Khan, Mohammed, ed. *The Life of Abdur Rahman, Amir of Afghanistan*. Vol. 1. London: John Murray, 1900, 1–14 and 210–19.

Anonymous. "The Ameer's Memoirs." *Spectator*, December 8, 1900, 842–43.

Marvin, Charles. *The Russians at the Gates of Herat*. New York: Charles Scribner's and Sons, 1885, 126–48.

Bolandin, Private Andrei. *The Campaign Towards Afghanistan*. 1885. In *Britain and Russia in Central Asia, 1880–1907*, vol. 1, edited by Martin Ewans. London: Routledge, 2008, 174–203. Reprinted with permission from the publisher.

Churchill, Winston. *The Story of the Malakand Field Force*. London: Longmans Green and Co., 1901, 33–50.

"The Indian Frontier Troubles." *The Graphic*, September 18, 1897, cover image.

Diver, Maud. *The Judgment of the Sword: The Tale of the Kabul Tragedy, and of the Part Played Therein by Major Eldred Pottinger, the Hero of Herat*. London: Constable and Co., 1913, 226–65.

Boulger, Demetrius C. "Our Relations with Afghanistan." *Contemporary Review* 116 (1919): 52–58.

"Third Afghan War." *The New Statesman*, August 16, 1919, 484–86.

INDEX